W9-BLF-363

# THE NEW TESTAMENT

## An Historical and Analytic Survey

# THE NEW TESTAMENT

## *An Historical and Analytic Survey*

BY

Merrill C. Tenney, ph.d.

Dean of the Graduate School,
Wheaton College, Wheaton, Illinois

WM. B. EERDMANS PUBLISHING COMPANY
Grand Rapids          1955          Michigan

THE NEW TESTAMENT
An Historical and Analytic Survey
*by* MERRILL C. TENNEY

*Copyright,* 1953, *by*
*Wm. B. Eerdmans Publishing Company*
All rights in this book are reserved.  No part may be reproduced
in any manner without permission in writing from the publisher,
except brief quotations used in connection with a review in a
magazine or newspaper.

## Library of Congress Number 53-9742

*Third printing, September,* 1955

TO BETH AND WALLACE PADDON

Whose Fraternal Interest

Has Been a Constant Delight

# PREFACE

Among evangelical believers there has always been the profound conviction that a broad knowledge of the Bible is an integral part of basic education. The material which is learned in the home or in the Sunday school needs to be reinforced by academic study if the young believer is to become settled in his faith. To accomplish this end many Christian educational institutions have established required courses in Bible for all their students.

Bible survey is fundamental to all Bible study. If a student expects to comprehend any part or doctrine of the Scriptures, he must know what they teach as a whole. Each book is a part of that whole, and can be fully understood only when it is seen in relation to the entire stream of divine revelation that begins with Genesis and that ends with the Apocalypse.

The message of the New Testament can be apprehended best when one has some comprehension of the world into which it first came. The literary, political, social, economic, and religious backgrounds of the first century are the context for the revelation of God in Christ. The terms which the apostles and their associates used for teaching were taken from the common life of their day and were familiar to the average man in the streets of Alexandria, of Antioch, or of Rome. As these terms become plain to the modern reader, their message will become increasingly clear.

The interpretation of the New Testament, nevertheless, does not depend solely upon antiquarian knowledge. Its precepts are binding not because modern civilization accidentally duplicates the culture of the Graeco-Roman world, but because man's relation to God is ever the same, and because the eternal God is unchanging in His attitude to man. The vitality of the word of God is not dependent upon the chance similarity of two eras. Its eternal quality transcends local conditions of space, time, and society. Once the meaning of the words of Scripture is correctly understood, the words are as true today as they ever were, and they cannot be discarded as the obsolete sentiments of a vanished civilization. They still convey the living gospel of the eternal God to the thirsty souls of sinning men.

*The New Testament: A Survey*

In this book each writing of the New Testament has been placed in its setting and has been outlined for the reader in order that he may readily discern its main line of thought. The aim of the textbook is not to substitute the opinions of the author for the discoveries of the student, but rather to place at his disposal a compact guide to the essential facts that will help him to interpret the Bible for himself. Like the Ethiopian eunuch who asked that someone should direct him in his initial study of the written word, the modern student needs a helper through the perplexities that confront him.

Technical problems of introduction and of theology are not treated here at any length because they do not belong properly in a survey course. For investigation of these fields the student may have recourse to adequate works which are mentioned in the bibliography. Minute points of interpretation are omitted, since this book does not pretend to be a commentary. Footnotes have been generally restricted to references to primary sources of information. They have been kept at a minimum to avoid confusing the reader who is not a professional scholar. Secondary sources have been included in the final bibliography. The sole aim is to offer a general integrated approach which will increase understanding of the New Testament and a love for it. As the devout believer sees how the revelation of God was pertinent to the world of the first century, he will discover how it is applicable also to the surroundings of his own life.

In the use of this book in class, the teacher should supplement it with his own lectures, developing in detail the phases of thought which are only suggested here. The classified list of books at the end will provide ample material for collateral reading and for research. Outlines are intended chiefly as models by the aid of which the teacher or the student may construct others that are original. Biblical references will facilitate the independent study of the text to verify or to enlarge the themes which it presents.

The author acknowledges gratefully the kindness of the trustees and administration of Wheaton College who released him from all teaching duties in the summer of 1952 in order that this manuscript might be completed. Without this concession early publication would have been impossible.

Permission to quote from George Foot Moore's *Judaism* has been generously granted by the Harvard University Press of Cambridge,

Massachusetts, and the quotation has been identified by a footnote reference.

Special thanks are due the author's wife, Helen J. Tenney, for her stimulating encouragement and keen criticism during the process of writing and of revision; to Dr. A. Berkeley Mickelsen and to Professor Stefania Evans of the Wheaton College faculty for reading the manuscript and for offering helpful suggestions; to Miss Edna M. Smallwood for her professional assistance in preparing the manuscript for publication; and to the many students of former years whose needs have become the directions in shaping this book.

M. C. T.

Wheaton College
Wheaton, Illinois

# List of Charts and Maps

10

# Table of Contents

## Contents

**PART III: The Records of the Early Church**

**The Period of Expansion: A.D. 29 to 60**

**PART IV: The Problems of the Early Church**
**The Period of Consolidation: A.D. 60 to 100**

# Contents

# INTRODUCTION

## The New Testament: Its Meaning and Content

# INTRODUCTION

## The New Testament: Its Meaning and Content

### The Name

### The Content
### Literary Character
### Authors
### Periods

# CHAPTER I

## The New Testament: Its Meaning and Content

### The Name

The name, *New Testament*, which is given to the second half of the English Bible, comes from the Latin *Novum Testamentum* which is itself a translation of the Greek H KAINH ΔIAΘHKH (*He Kaine Diatheke*, anglicized). The Greek term was generally used to mean "a last will, or testament," as the Latin translation indicated, but this translation did not exhaust its meaning. The word really meant an arrangement made by one party which may be accepted or rejected by another party, but which he cannot alter; and which, when accepted, binds both parties by its terms. Since a will is the best example of such an instrument, the Latin *Testamentum*, preserved in the English *Testament*, was used.

The term *covenant* used in the Revised Version is derived from the Old French *covenir*, to agree, which in turn is derived from the Latin *convenire*, to come together. It means an agreement, stipulation, or contract which involves both parties in the agreement. It implies more than a promise; for a promise obligates only the person making it, whereas a covenant obligates both parties concerned in it. In this respect it approximates the modern term "contract." Such is the meaning of the word *covenant* as used in Exodus 24:1-8 which describes the acceptance of the law by the people of Israel at Mt. Sinai. The fact that the Greek translator of the Old Testament uses *diatheke* in this passage to render the Hebrew word for covenant indicates that *diatheke* may on occasion have this meaning; and this usage is confirmed by the language of Luke 22:14-20, where the old covenant (*diatheke*) of Exodus 24:1-8 is contrasted with the new covenant (*diatheke*) which Jesus made with His disciples at the last supper. The general meaning of the Greek term must be the same in both instances as the contrast of *old* and *new* implies. The New Testament, then, is the record of the character and establishment of a new dealing

21

of God with men through Christ. God sets the terms which man can accept or reject but cannot alter; and when man accepts them, both he and God are obligated to fulfil their requirements. The Old Covenant involved a revelation of the holiness of God in a righteous standard of law which those who received it were solemnly enjoined to keep. The New Covenant embodied a revelation of the holiness of God in an utterly righteous Son, who empowered those who receive the revelation to become sons of God by making them righteous (John 1:12).

## The Content

The contents of the New Testament consist of the revelation of this new covenant through the recorded words of Jesus Christ and of His followers. It comprises twenty-seven distinct pieces of writing by nine different authors, unless Paul is regarded as the author of Hebrews, in which case the number is reduced to eight. These documents were written over a span of a little more than half a century, probably from A.D. 45 at the earliest to about A.D. 100. The historical allusions in them cover the entire first century, and their background of cultural thought reaches back into the fourth or fifth century B.C.

The contents of the New Testament may be classified in three ways: by literary character, by authors, and by periods.

### *Literary Character*

The first five books of the New Testament, Matthew, Mark, Luke, John, Acts, are *historical* in character. All of them narrate a story. The first four sketch from different viewpoints the life and work of Jesus. Acts is a companion volume to Luke and carries on the story of Jesus' followers after the close of His earthly life, with special emphasis on the career of Paul, the missionary.

The following books are largely *doctrinal*: Romans, I and II Corinthians, Galatians, Ephesians, Philippians, Colossians, I and II Thessalonians, Hebrews, James, I and II Peter, Jude, I John. Most of these were written in the form of letters to churches for the purpose of instructing them in the elements of Christian belief and in the practice of Christian ethics. None of them, with the possible exception of Romans, was written as a formal argument. They were largely informal in approach and dealt with the current emergencies in the groups to which they were directed.

Still another group can be called *personal*: I and II Timothy, Titus, Philemon, II and III John. These were written as personal letters to individuals, not to groups, and were intended to be used for private

22

instruction and counsel. Because their recipients were engaged in the leadership of the churches, however, the books took on a significance wider than that of private epistles and came to be regarded as public documents.

Revelation, the last book of the New Testament, is *prophetic*. It purports to deal with the future as well as with the present. Because of its highly symbolic style, involving visions and supernatural disclosures, it is also classed with *apocalyptic* literature.

This classification is not final or exclusive. There is much doctrine in the historical books and some prophecy in the doctrinal epistles. The classification holds only for general content.

## *Authors*

These books may also be grouped by authors. All of the writers were Jews, except Luke. Three, presumably Matthew, Peter, and John, were members of the apostolic band. Mark, Jude, and James had been active in the early church, or had been in contact with the apostolic group even before the death of Jesus. Luke and Paul, while not eyewitnesses of the life of Christ, were well known to those who were, and were certainly able to compare notes with them if necessary. Of the author of Hebrews nothing is known by external evidence; hence his name does not appear in the summary.

| AUTHOR | BOOK | AUTHOR | BOOK |
|--------|------|--------|------|
| Matthew | Matthew | | Romans |
| Mark | Mark | | I Corinthians |
| | | | II Corinthians |
| Luke | Luke | | Galatians |
| | Acts | | Ephesians |
| | | | Philippians |
| | | Paul | Colossians |
| | | | I Thessalonians |
| | John | | II Thessalonians |
| | I John | | I Timothy |
| John | II John | | II Timothy |
| | III John | | Titus |
| | Revelation | | Philemon |
| James | James | ? | Hebrews |
| Jude | Jude | Peter | I Peter |
| | | | II Peter |

23

## Periods

The books of the New Testament were not written in the order in which they appear in the Bible. One must not assume that because the Gospels precede the Pauline epistles in literary order that they are necessarily older. Furthermore, there may be a considerable difference between the date at which a writing was composed and the period with which it deals. Mark, for instance, describes the events in Jesus' life which took place within the last of the third decade of the first century; but the Gospel may not have been circulated publicly until between A.D. 65 and A.D. 70.

In order to facilitate the study of the history of the first century, it may be divided into three periods of unequal length, each of which marks a definite stage in its development.

The first is the period of INCEPTION, which covers the lifetime of Christ from 6 B.C. to A.D. 29. This period is described by the four Gospels, which narrate with differing degrees of fulness the significant facts in the career of Jesus, and which give casual references to other historical events.

The second period of EXPANSION, A.D. 29 to A.D. 60, witnessed the development of the missionary enterprise. Groups of preachers traveled the Roman roads in all directions, evangelizing and founding new churches in various important centers. The narrative of Acts affords chiefly a view of the Pauline mission to the Gentiles, with only occasional glimpses of the activities of other apostles and preachers. During this time the gospel progressed from Jerusalem to Rome, and doubtless into many other localities not noted by the author of Acts. Within this period fall also the majority of the Pauline epistles which were written during Paul's missionary career. Considerable knowledge of the growth of the Gentile church can be gleaned from them.

The third period from A.D. 60 to A.D. 100 may be called CONSOLI-DATION. In some respects it is the period of mystery, for little is told of the history of the church at this time. There is no consecutive account of it as the book of Acts affords for the preceding epoch, and what little history can be reconstructed must be pieced together from hints provided in various writings. To the early part of this period belong the Pastoral Epistles of Paul and the Petrine writings. Luke-Acts and Matthew were probably published between A.D. 60 and A.D. 70. Mark may have been composed at an earlier date, but if tradition be correct it may not have been widely published until this era. Hebrews and Jude probably precede A.D. 70. The Johannine writings, the Fourth Gospel and the Epistles, may have appeared as

## CHART OF NEW TESTAMENT CHRONOLOGY

| PERIOD | DATE | EVENT | HISTORY | PUBLICATION |
|---|---|---|---|---|
| **INCEPTION**<br><br>B.C. 6<br>to A.D. 29 | B.C. 6<br>B.C. 4 | BIRTH OF JESUS<br>DEATH OF HEROD | | |
| | | | MATTHEW<br>LUKE | |
| | A.D. 26<br>A.D. 29 | BAPTISM<br>CRUCIFIXION | MARK<br>JOHN | |
| **EXPANSION**<br><br>A.D. 29<br>to A.D. 60 | A.D. 31-33 | PAUL'S<br>CONVERSION | | *Learn Order of Publication* |
| | A.D. 45 | | ACTS | JAMES |
| | A.D. 49<br>A.D. 52 | COUNCIL OF<br>JERUSALEM | | GALATIANS                    (MARK) |
| | A.D. 54<br>A.D. 55<br>A.D. 56<br><br>A.D. 60 | <br><br>PAUL'S FIRST<br>IMPRISONMENT | PAULINE<br>EPISTLES | I & II THESSALONIANS<br>I CORINTHIANS    MATTHEW (?)<br>II CORINTHIANS<br>ROMANS<br>COL., EPHESIANS<br>PHILEMON<br>PHILIPPIANS         LUKE-ACTS |
| **CONSOLID-ATION**<br><br>A.D. 60<br>to A.D. 100 | <br>A.D. 68<br>A.D. 70 | PAUL'S SECOND<br>IMPRISONMENT<br>DESTRUCTION OF<br>JERUSALEM | | I TIMOTHY<br>TITUS<br>I PETER<br>II TIMOTHY<br>II PETER<br>HEBREWS              MARK<br>JUDE |
| | | | GENERAL<br>EPISTLES | *written to group of people "at large" rather than specific person.* |
| | A.D. 85 | | | I, II, III JOHN          JOHN |
| | A.D. 95 | | REVELATION | REVELATION |

late as A.D. 85 to A.D. 90. The Apocalypse should probably be assigned to the reign of Domitian in A.D. 96, or thereabouts.

A survey of this literature will show that in the last third of the first century the church was rapidly consolidating into a recognized institution. From being a scattered collection of isolated bands of believers, each with its own problems and with its own standards, it was beginning to acquire social and doctrinal solidarity and to be regarded as a potent factor in society.

The Gospels show that the narrative preaching about the life of the Lord Jesus had become an accepted type of evangelism and had crystallized into a pattern which was used for instruction of believers. Acts, the first history of the Christian church, is a conscious attempt to explain the fusion of Jew and Gentile into one body through Christian experience. The epistles of the period deal with heresies which in themselves imply the existence of some orthodox framework of belief. The book of Hebrews and the Johannine writings show that the church had already been compelled to face the claims of the law and the inroads of a "progressive" faith which "progressed" by abandoning a sound Christology. The threat of persecution, too, is reflected in Hebrews, I Peter, and Revelation. The Pastorals indicate that even at the close of Paul's career many of these issues were current and that a decline of spiritual life had already affected some of the churches.

Exact chronological placement of the books of the New Testament is impossible. No one of them is dated by figure, and only a few contain such unmistakable allusions to the time of their writing that they can be assigned to a given year of the Christian era. Opinions of scholars vary greatly on some of these books. John, for instance, has been dated from the fifth decade of the first century to the middle years of the second century. Most conservative scholars would locate it about A.D. 85, though it may be earlier. One can only approximate a correct order for these books; exactitude is impossible in consideration of present lack of knowledge.

The accompanying diagram is intended to show approximately how the books are related to the time which they describe and in which they were written. Further discussion on the chronological problems will be offered in connection with each individual writing.

In dealing with the Gospels, three chronological relations must be considered: The first is the time of which the Gospels speak and to which their narrative mainly relates. The second is the period in which their material was composed and in which it was shaped to the needs and usage of the church. The composition may have been wholly written or wholly oral, or it may have been partly both. The third is the actual date of publication, when the written copy of each Gospel first saw the light and began to be used as an authoritative document by some church or churches. The epistles were apparently written for some specific occasion and were "published" at some definite date without having been previously connected with the general body of preaching except where noted in the individual treatment of each book.

*Part I*

# THE WORLD OF THE NEW TESTAMENT

# THE WORLD OF THE NEW TESTAMENT

The Political World
The Social World
The Economic World
The Religious World
Judaism

# THE POLITICAL WORLD

# THE POLITICAL WORLD

The Empire of Rome
The Provincial Government
The Hellenistic Kingdoms
The Jewish State

# CHAPTER II

# The Political World

## The Empire of Rome

At the time when the New Testament was written the entire civilized world, with the exception of the little known kingdoms of the Far East, was under the domination of Rome. From the Atlantic Ocean on the west to the Euphrates river and the Red Sea on the east, and from the Rhone, the Danube, the Black Sea and the Caucasus mountains on the north to the Sahara on the south there stretched one vast empire under the headship and virtual dictatorship of the emperor, called in the New Testament both "king" (I Pet. 2:17) and "Augustus" (Luke 2:1).

Rome took its name from the capital city in Italy, the original settlement from which the Roman state grew. Founded in 753 B.C., it was at first a community comprising a union of small villages in its vicinity and ruled by a king. About the beginning of the fifth century B.C. it had achieved a degree of solid political organization under a republican form of government. By alliances with surrounding communities and through a long succession of wars against the Etruscans in the north and against other tribes in the south, Rome became mistress of the Italian peninsula by 265 B.C. The conquered peoples were bound by treaty to keep the peace and were absorbed gradually into the Roman domain.

During the next two centuries Rome was engaged in a great struggle with Carthage, the chief maritime power of the western Mediterranean. Carthage was originally a colony of Phoenicia; but with the overthrow of the mother country by Alexander, the colony had been compelled to act independently. By following the pattern of the Phoenicians, it had become a wealthy and powerful nation. Its ships carried the commerce of the Mediterranean. Its civilization was oriental in character, its society was an oligarchy maintained by a mercenary army, and it was governed by autocratic rule. As Rome expanded it came into conflict with the outposts of the Carthaginian empire. Aside from the fact that the two civilizations were alien to each other in racial

THE ROMAN WORLD

origin and in political theory, there was not enough room for both of them in the same territory; one had to succumb. The wars between them ended in 146 B.C. when the Roman general Scipio Aemilianus captured the city of Carthage and razed it to the ground. Rome thus established dominion over Spain and over North Africa. At the same time Macedonia was made a Roman province, and with the sack of Corinth in the same year (146 B.C.) Achaia came under Roman control. In 133 B.C. Attalus III, king of Pergamum, died, and bequeathed his realm to the Romans. Out of it they organized the province of Asia. Wars in the eastern part of Asia Minor continued until Pompey completed the conquest of Pontus and the Caucasus. In 63 B.C. he organized Syria into a province and annexed Judea. In 58 to 57 B.C. Caesar conducted his famous campaigns in Gaul and made it a Roman country. Thus through five hundred years of almost uninterrupted war Rome grew from an obscure village on the banks of the Tiber to become the ruling empire of the world.

The rapid territorial expansion, however, brought great changes in the life of the Roman people. As the military leaders gained a taste of power, they began to use their armies not only for foreign conquest, but also for enforcing their supremacy at home. The century between the conquest of Carthage and of Greece and the death of Julius Caesar was marked by a constant succession of civil wars. Marius, Sulla, Caesar, Antony, and Octavian — one after the other strove to make himself master of the Roman state, until finally Octavian, or Augustus as he was called by the Senate, succeeded in exterminating his opponents in 30 B.C., and became the first emperor.

## *Augustus* 27 B.C. to A.D. 14

Under his rule the Roman *imperium,* or power of the imperial state, was thoroughly established. The people, tired of war, longed for peace. Augustus became the *princeps,* or first citizen of the land. He ruled wisely and well. Politically, the new principate was a compromise between the old republicanism and the dictatorship which Julius Caesar had advocated. The Senate was retained as the theoretical ruling body. In 27 B.C. it conferred on Augustus the office of commander-in-chief of the armed forces of the empire. In 23 B.C. he was given the tribunician power for life, which meant that he had control over the popular assemblies, and was appointed the permanent representative of the people. He was given the prerogative of introducing the first topic of discussion in the Senate and the right to call

35

its meetings. All of his rights were founded upon a constitutional basis rather than upon any arbitrary seizure of power.

During the reign of Augustus many reforms were effected. The Senate was purged of unworthy members. A large part of the army was demobilized, and the discharged veterans were settled in colonies or on land supplied by purchase. A regular professional army was created which became a school for citizens. Upon retirement from the ranks the veterans were given a bonus and were settled in colonies in the provinces, where they could make a good living and at the same time be community leaders loyal to Rome.

Augustus sought also to improve the morale of the people. He revived the state religion and rebuilt many temples. The imperial cult, a worship of Rome as a state, was introduced to the provinces. In many places the emperor himself was worshiped as *Dominus et Deus* (Lord and God), although he did not demand such worship. The Julian laws of 19 and 18 B.C. attempted to restore family life by encouraging marriage and the establishment of homes.

To consolidate the empire at large, he took a census of the population and of all property as a basis for recruiting the army and for taxation. Spain, Gaul, and the Alpine districts were subjugated. He strengthened the defense of the frontiers, though his armies suffered a crushing defeat at the hands of the Germans in the Teutoberg forest. Augustus organized the police and fire departments of Rome and appointed a supervisor for the grain supply.

Augustus' boast was that he had found Rome brick and had left it marble. During the forty-one years of his administration he brought order out of chaos. He restored confidence in the government, replenished the treasury, introduced an efficient public works department, and promoted peace and prosperity.

### *Tiberius* A.D. 14 to 37

At the death of Augustus his adopted son Tiberius was chosen to succeed him. The *imperium* or power which Augustus had received under constitutional regulations and for a limited period was conferred on Tiberius for life. He was fifty-six years old at the time of his succession and had been engaged during most of his life in the service of the state, so that he was no novice in politics. Unfortunately, Augustus insisted that he divorce the wife whom he loved and that he marry Julia, Augustus' daughter, a woman of openly profligate life. The bitterness of this experience soured his temper permanently. He was distant, haughty, suspicious, and irascible. Although he was impartial and wise in his policies, he was never popular and was generally feared and disliked. During his reign the Roman armies suffered reverses in Germany, with the result that he withdrew the frontier to the Rhine. Domestic troubles clouded his later years. In A.D. 26 he retired to Capri, leaving the government in the hands of the city prefect. The absence of Tiberius gave opportunity to Aelius Sejanus, the captain of the pretorian guard, to carry out a conspiracy to seize the principate. By A.D. 31 he had almost perfected his plans when Tiberius discovered them. Sejanus was executed and the plot was overthrown, but its effect on Tiberius was disastrous. He became even more suspicious and cruel, so that the merest whisper against a man would bring calamity down upon him. When he died in A.D. 37, the Senate could once more breathe freely.

### *Caligula* A.D. 37 to 41

Gaius Caligula, or "Little Boots," as he was affectionately called by the soldiery, was made Tiberius' successor by the Senate. He was at the outset of his career as popular as Tiberius had been unpopular. He pardoned political prisoners, reduced taxes, gave public entertainments, and endeared himself generally to the populace. Before long, however, he began to show signs of mental weakness. He demanded to be worshiped as a god, which alienated the Jews in his realm. When Herod Agrippa visited Alexandria the citizens insulted him publicly by lampooning him and his followers, and then tried to compel the Jews to worship the images of Gaius. The Jews appealed to the emperor, who not only paid no heed to them, but ordered his Syrian legate to erect his statue in the temple at Jerusalem. The legate was wise enough to delay action rather than to risk an armed rebellion, and the death of Caligula in A.D. 41 prevented the issue from coming to a crisis. Some think that Mark's reference to the "abomination of desolation" (Mark 13:14) reflects the threatened erection of the emperor's statue in the temple at Jerusalem.

Caligula's reckless expenditure of the funds that Augustus and Tiberius had so carefully gathered quickly exhausted the public treasury. In order to replenish it he resorted to violent means: confiscation of private property, compulsory legacies, and extortion of every kind. His tyranny finally became so unbearable that he was assassinated by a tribune of the imperial guards.

## *Claudius* A.D. 41 to 54

At the death of Caligula the Senate debated the idea of restoring the republic; but the question was quickly decided for them when the pretorian guard saluted Tiberius Claudius Germanicus as emperor. He was already in middle life, of less than mediocre mental ability, and more interested in literary pursuits than in government. He was completely dominated by his freedmen who served as his secretaries and by his wives. Under his rule Rome became a bureaucracy, governed by committees and secretaries. He extended the privilege of citizenship to provincials. His generals succeeded in gaining a foothold in Britain and conquered it as far north as the Thames river. At this time Thrace, upon the death of its prince, who had been an ally of Rome, was made a province.

Under the rule of Claudius the Jews were expelled from Rome because of some riots that had taken place, according to Suetonius[1] "at the instigation of one Chrestus." It is uncertain whether Suetonius misunderstood Chrestus for Christus, and was referring to a disturbance among the Jews occasioned by the preaching of Jesus as the Christ, or whether Chrestus was the actual name of some insurgent. In any case, the order of expulsion is probably the one that caused the removal of Aquila and Priscilla from Rome (Acts 18:2).

Through the influence of one of his freedmen, Pallas, Claudius was persuaded to take his niece, Agrippina, as his fourth wife. She was determined to obtain the succession for Domitius, her son by a previous husband. Domitius was formally adopted by Claudius under the name of Nero Claudius Caesar. In A.D. 53 Nero married Octavia, Claudius' daughter. A year later Claudius died, leaving to Nero the succession of the imperial throne.

## *Nero* A.D. 54 to 68

The first five years of Nero's reign were peaceful and successful. With Afranius Burrus, the prefect of the pretorian guard, and L. Annaeus Seneca, the philosopher and writer, as his advisors, Nero managed his realm very well. Agrippina, however, sought to maintain an ascendancy over him which both he and his advisors resented. In A.D. 59 he had his mother murdered and took full charge of the government himself.

Nero was by temperament an artist rather than an executive. He was more eager to enter upon a stage career than to excel in political

---

1. Suetonius, *Claudius*, 25, 4.

administration. His carelessness and extravagance emptied the public treasury, and he, like Caligula, resorted to oppression and violence in order to replenish it. By so doing he incurred the hatred of the Senate, whose members feared that at any time he might give orders for their death and for confiscation of their property.

In A.D. 64 a great fire broke out in Rome which destroyed a large part of the city. Nero was suspected of having deliberately set it in order to make room for his new Golden House, a splendid palace which he built on the Esquiline hill. In order to divert the blame from himself, the Christians were accused of having caused the disaster. Their attitude of aloofness from the heathen and their talk of the ultimate destruction of the world by fire lent plausibility to the charge. Many of them were brought to trial and were tortured to death. Tradition says that Peter and Paul perished in this persecution, the first one conducted by the state.

There is little evidence to show how extensive this persecution was. Probably it did not affect any territory outside of Rome and its immediate environs, although the provinces may have been threatened with it. (Cf. I Pet. 4:12-19.)

In the meantime the excesses of Nero had rendered him increasingly unpopular. Several conspiracies against him had failed and were suppressed by the execution of his enemies. Finally a revolt of the troops and provincials in Gaul and Spain proved successful. Nero fled from Rome and was killed by one of his own freedmen at his command in order to avoid capture.

## *Galba* A.D. 68

The revolt of the legions had shown that the empire was really commanded by the army, since it could nominate and enthrone its candidate without reference to the Senate. Galba, Nero's successor, was not the unanimous choice of the legions. When he adopted as his successor Lucius Calpurnius Piso, Otho, who had once supported him in hope of being emperor himself, persuaded the pretorian guards to kill Galba and to make him emperor.

## *Otho* A.D. 69

Otho's rule was short-lived. The Senate concurred in his appointment, but Vitellius, the legate of Germany, marched on Rome with his troops. Otho was killed in battle and Vitellius took his place.

## *Vitellius* A.D. 69

Vitellius was recognized by the Senate, but he was unable to control the soldiery, nor could he establish any stable government. The army of the east intervened in the affairs of state and made its general, Vespasian, emperor. At that time Vespasian was engaged in the siege of Jerusalem. Leaving it in charge of his son, Titus, he proceeded to Egypt, where he gained control of the country and cut off the food supply of Rome. His lieutenant, Mucianus, set out for Italy. In spite of the spirited resistance of the troops of Vitellius, Vespasian's partisans captured and sacked Rome. Vitellius was killed, and Vespasian was proclaimed ruler.

## *Vespasian* A.D. 69 to 79

Vespasian was a plain old soldier, who was frugal in his habits and vigorous in his administration. He suppressed revolts among the Bataviae and among the Gauls, while Titus completed the reduction of Jerusalem. The city was completely destroyed and the province was put under a military legate. He strengthened the frontiers by reducing dependent principalities to the status of provinces. The treasury was made solvent by strict economy and by the imposition of new taxes. He built the now famous Coliseum. He died in A.D. 79, leaving his office to Titus, whom he had made his co-regent. He was the first of the Flavian dynasty, which included his sons, Titus and Domitian.

## *Titus* A.D. 79 to 81

The brevity of Titus' reign did not allow much time for the accomplishment of any remarkable deeds. In spite of the handicap, however, he was one of the most popular emperors that Rome ever had. The magnificence of the public entertainments that he sponsored and his personal generosity disarmed the potential antagonism of the Senate, who feared that he would be a dictator like his father.

During his reign occurred the catastrophic overthrow of Pompeii and Herculaneum, villages on the bay of Naples, in the eruption of Vesuvius. Titus appointed a commission and did his utmost to rescue as many of the victims as possible. A few months later Rome suffered a severe fire which destroyed the new Capitol, the Pantheon, and Agrippa's Baths. Titus even sold some of his private furniture to contribute to the general need. He erected new buildings, including a large amphitheater.

## Domitian A.D. 81 to 96

Titus died in A.D. 81, leaving no son, and the Senate conferred the imperial power upon his younger brother Domitian. Domitian was a thorough autocrat. He tried to raise the moral level of Roman society by restraining the corruptions of the Roman stage and by checking public prostitution. The temples of the older gods were rebuilt and foreign religions were suppressed, especially those which sought to make converts. A persecution of Christians was attributed to him, though evidence for any extensive legislation or action against them in his reign is lacking. He demanded worship for himself and insisted on being hailed as *Dominus et Deus*. As an economist, he was a good manager. The business affairs of the empire were conducted efficiently by his subordinates.

Domitian was hard by nature and suspicious of rivals. Lacking the geniality of his brother Titus, he made numerous enemies. When their plots were discovered he was pitiless in his vengeance. The last years of his reign were a nightmare to the senatorial order, who were kept in constant terror of spies and informers. Even his own family did not feel safe, and finally in self-defense, they procured his assassination.

## Nerva A.D. 96 to 98

Nerva, Domitian's successor, was selected by the Senate. He was a man of advanced years and of mild demeanor, who was probably regarded by the senatorial order as a "safe" candidate. His general administration was kindly and was relatively free from internal tensions. The army had resented Domitian's assassination, for the Flavians were popular in military circles. Nerva, however, was astute enough to provide as his successor Trajan, who was capable of holding the troops in subjection and of administering government with a strong hand.

## Trajan A.D. 98 to 117

Nerva died in A.D. 98, and Trajan succeeded him. He was a Spaniard by birth, a soldier by profession, energetic and aggressive in temperament. He annexed Dacia, north of the Danube, and began the enlargement of the eastern frontiers by the conquest of Armenia, Assyria, and Mesopotamia. A revolt of the Jews in the Near East was suppressed in A.D. 115; but new insurrections in Africa, Britain, and on the Danubian border occasioned his recall to Rome. He died enroute to the capital in Cilicia in A.D. 117.

In this environment of imperial expansion Christianity grew from an obscure Jewish sect to become a world religion. Jesus was born in the reign of Augustus (Luke 2:1); His public ministry and death occurred in the time of Tiberius (Luke 3:1); the great period of missionary expansion came in the reigns of Claudius (Acts 18:2) and of Nero (Acts 25:11, 12). According to tradition, the Apocalypse was written in the reign of Domitian,[2] and its allusion to imperial power and to governmental tyranny may have been reflections of conditions prevalent at that time.

The relative scarcity of allusions in the New Testament to contemporary events in the Roman world is not surprising. The national interest of the Gospels and of much of the Acts, which are the principal historical works, lies in Judaism rather than in Rome. Furthermore, the message of the New Testament was directed to the inner lives of its readers rather than to their outward circumstances. The spiritual rather than the political and the eternal rather than the temporal were stressed. Nevertheless, at numerous points the New Testament does connect with the political surroundings of the first century and its historical importance must be interpreted in that connection.

## The Provincial Government

Unlike the United States of America, in which the federal authority presides over forty-eight states that are generally uniform in government and in organization, the Roman empire was a miscellany of independent cities, states, and territories — all of which were subject to the central government. Some of them had become part of the empire by voluntary alliance; others had been annexed by conquest. As Rome extended its sovereignty over these allied or subject peoples, its governmental machinery grew also into the Roman provincial system.

The word *provincia,* from which "province" is derived, meant originally the office of carrying on war, or a post of command. As applied to the authority of a general it was extended to the sphere of his authority, and hence to the territory that he conquered, which became his *provincia*. When Rome conquered new domains, they were organized into provinces which became part of the general imperial system.

Rome's acquisition of provinces began with Sicily, which was taken from Carthage in the first Punic War, 264-241 B.C. In succession

---

2. Irenaeus, *Against Heresies,* V, xxx, 3.

she added Sardinia (237 B.C.), two provinces in Spain (197 B.C.), Macedonia (146 B.C.), and Africa (146 B.C.). Asia was not taken by force of arms, but was bequeathed to the Roman people by its king in 133 B.C., and was organized as a province in 129 B.C. Transalpine and Cisalpine Gaul were added about 118 B.C. Cyrene was bequeathed to Rome in 96 B.C., and Bithynia was also presented to Rome in 75 B.C. In 67 B.C. Pompey annexed Cilicia and Crete and in 63 B.C. he took over Palestine and made it into the province of Syria. (Except for Italy itself, the bulk of the Roman world consisted of territory under provincial government. )

This government was of two kinds. The provinces that were relatively peaceful and loyal to Rome were under proconsuls (Acts 13:7) who were responsible to the Roman senate. The more turbulent provinces were under the authority of the emperor, who often stationed armies in them, and they were governed by prefects, procurators, or propraetors who were appointed by the emperor and who were answerable directly to him. To the former class belonged Achaia, of which Gallio was proconsul at the time of Paul's visit (Acts 18:12). Palestine in the time of Christ was under the supervision of the emperor, whose agent was the procurator Pontius Pilate (Matt. 27:11, translated "governor"). Proconsuls held their office by annual appointment and were generally changed every year. Procurators and propraetors held office as long as the emperor wanted them at a given post.

Under the administration of these officers the provinces enjoyed considerable liberty. The individual city states were permitted to retain their own local sovereignty and even to mint coins. The Romans never interfered with the religious freedom of the subject peoples, so that the indigenous worship was customarily retained in each place. The Roman rulers usually took the advice of the provincial councils in their administration. Officials who plundered their subjects were subject to prosecution and recall. Although it is true that some of the proconsuls and procurators indulged in the time-honored pastime of graft, the majority probably gave more to the provinces in administrative wisdom than they took out in money. Roads were constructed; public edifices were erected; and commerce was developed rapidly.

In order to unite the provinces more closely with the mother city of Rome, little settlements of Romans were begun at strategic centers in the provinces. Gradually the Roman civilization spread, so that in time the provinces became more Roman than Rome. In the second century when Rome still used Greek as its predominant language, Gaul, Spain, and Africa were predominantly Latin.

The imperial cult had its widest following in the provinces. The worship of the Roman state and of the reigning emperor began with Augustus. He ordered that temples be erected to the honor of Julius Caesar at Ephesus and at Nicaea by the citizens of Rome who resided there and he permitted the nationals of the country to establish shrines in his own honor. The worship of the state was fostered by the local councils, who assumed the responsibility of directing the provincial worship.

A good illustration of a provincial council appears in Acts 19:31, where the "Asiarchs" are mentioned. They were magistrates who were regarded as the responsible leaders of the province and who may have served as high priests of the state worship. In Acts they were represented as friendly to Paul, since they warned him against exposing himself to the violence of the multitude in the theater.

The Roman provinces which appear in the New Testament are: Spain (Rom. 15:24), Gaul (II Tim. 4:10, variant reading), Illyricum (Rom. 15:19), Macedonia (Acts 16:9), Achaia (Rom. 15:26), Asia (Acts 20:4), Pontus (I Pet. 1:1), Bithynia (Acts 16:7), Galatia (Gal. 1:2), Cappadocia (I Pet. 1:1), Cilicia (Gal. 1:21, Acts 6:9), Syria (Gal. 1:21), Judea (Gal. 1:22), Cyprus (Acts 13:4), Pamphylia (Acts 13:13), and Lycia (Acts 27:5). Some of these are mentioned more than once; and in the case of Illyricum its later name, Dalmatia, appears in the Pastoral Epistles (II Tim. 4:10). Paul usually employed provincial names in alluding to divisions of the empire, while Luke used also national divisions. Provinces often included more than one ethnic group, such as the Lycaonians of Lystra and Derbe (Acts 14:6, 11), who were under the province of Galatia.

Governorship of the provinces was sought by public officials because they found it a fruitful source of income. So rapacious were some of these rulers that the provinces were rapidly impoverished by heavy taxation. Others who were more public-spirited made wise use of the taxes by building roads and harbors, so that commerce throve and the general economic level of life improved. Rome regarded the provinces as her rightful field of exploitation. Until the time of Constantine they were tributary to the central government and never were treated as equal states within a common federation.

## The Hellenistic Kingdoms

The cultural atmosphere of the first century owed its origin not only to the political organization of Rome but also to the diffusion of the

INDIA

Indus

INDIAN OCEAN

PERSIAN GULF

CASPIAN SEA

Tigris

Euphrates

Antioch

ARABIAN GULF

SYRIA
(Seleucids)

CILICIA

Sidon
Tyre

BLACK SEA

Byzantium

CYPRUS

Nile

THRACE

MACEDON

Alexandria
EGYPT
(Ptolemies)

CRETE

Cyrene

MEDITERRANEAN SEA

**THE HELLENISTIC KINGDOMS**
**At the Division of Alexander's Empire**

Hellenic spirit which had permeated both the West and the East. Rome's conquests had absorbed the Greek colonies which had been established along the seacoasts of Gaul and Spain, in the island of Sicily, and on the mainland of the lower Italian peninsula. The conquest of Achaia, ending in the sack of Corinth, 146 B.C., had made available to the Romans vast treasures of art which they deported to grace their own villas. Greek slaves, many of whom were more learned than their masters, became part of Roman households. Often they were not only employed in the more menial tasks of the house, but were teachers, physicians, accountants, and overseers of farms or of businesses. Furthermore, the Greek universities of Athens, Rhodes, Tarsus, and other cities were attended by aristocratic young Romans who learned to speak Greek in much the same way that the nineteenth century Englishman learned French as the language of diplomacy and culture. So thoroughly did the vanquished Greeks conquer their victors culturally that Rome itself became a Greek-speaking city. Juvenal, one of the famous satirists of his day, complained: "I cannot, fellow Romans, bear a city wholly Greek."[3]

## The Conquests of Alexander

In the eastern half of the Roman world where most of the action of the New Testament took place, the spread of Greek civilization began with the Greek traders who carried the commerce of the Peloponnesus far and wide. As early as 600 B.C. Greek musical instruments and weapons were known in Babylonia, and Greek mercenaries fought in the armies of Cyrus, as Xenophon's well-known *Anabasis, The March of the Ten Thousand,* attests. The Hellenizing of the East was greatly accelerated by the campaigns of Alexander the Great. Philip, his father, the king of Macedonia, had forged the Macedonians into a unified military state. From the sturdy peasants and shepherds of his mountainous country he had organized an army of unusual mobility and endurance. In twenty years' time Philip succeeded in making the Greek city states subservient to Macedonia. When Philip died in 337 B.C. he had completed an alliance with the Greeks by which he hoped to undertake the conquest of Asia.

Alexander possessed his father's aggressiveness and military genius overlaid with a thicker veneer of Greek culture. He had been brought up on Homer's *Iliad* under the tutelage of Aristotle, so that he had profound admiration for Hellenic traditions and ideals. In 334 B.C. he crossed the Hellespont into Asia Minor and defeated the Persian

---

3. Juvenal, *Satire III,* 60, 61.

forces at the battle of the Granicus river. He liberated the Hellenic cities of the coast and then penetrated the hinterland. He routed the Persians again at the battle of Issus, which gave him command of all Asia Minor, and then he turned southward down the Syrian coast into Egypt, where he founded the city of Alexandria.

Having subdued Syria and Egypt, he moved eastward and inflicted a final defeat upon the Persian army at Arbela. In rapid succession he occupied Babylon and the capitals of Persia, Susa, and Persepolis.

The next three years were spent in consolidating the new empire. Alexander encouraged the marriage of his soldiers to oriental women. He began the education of thirty thousand of the Persians in the Greek language. Through further campaigns in India he extended the borders of his domain to the Indus river. He established numerous colonies and he explored country which had not up to that time been seen by Europeans.

Upon his return to Babylon Alexander began preparations for the invasion of Arabia, but he was not destined to complete them. If he had succeeded in partially Hellenizing the East, the East had also partly orientalized him. He took on more and more of the attitude of the oriental despot and became increasingly arbitrary and suspicious. The luxury and the revels of Babylon weakened his constitution so that he contracted fever and died in 324 B.C. at the age of thirty-two.

Alexander's empire did not long survive his death. He left no heirs who were capable of managing it and finally it was partitioned among his generals. Ptolemy took Egypt and southern Syria; Seleucus claimed most of the territory in northern Syria and west through Asia Minor, including Phrygia; Lysimachus held Thrace and western Asia Minor; and Cassander ruled Macedonia and Greece. The kingdom of Lysimachus did not endure long and was absorbed into the realm of the Seleucidae.

The constant hostility between the Seleucidae of Syria and the Ptolemies of Egypt kept Palestine between the hammer and the anvil. The coastal plain of Sharon was the corridor along which the armies of these two powers marched to war. The varying fortunes of conflict put Palestine sometimes under the dominion of one and sometimes under the dominion of the other.

### The Seleucidae in Syria

The Seleucid dominion in Asia Minor gradually diminished as the local people asserted their independence and founded kingdoms of their own. In Syria, however, the rule of the Seleucidae was maintained and their influence was potent in the political affairs of Palestine. In the year 201-200 B.C. Antiochus III of Syria, called the Great, defeated the Egyptian army under a general named Scopas at the battle of Panias, near the springs of the Jordan in northern Palestine. In two years Antiochus III gained control of all of Palestine and became the new overlord of the Jews. Their attempt to Hellenize the Jews provoked the Maccabean revolt which resulted in the revival of the Jewish commonwealth. Their rule ended when Pompey made Syria a Roman province in 63 B.C.

The effect of the Seleucid dominion was tremendous. Antioch, the capital of their country, became the third largest city of the Roman empire and was the meeting place of the East and West. Greek language and literature were widely disseminated through the Near East and afforded a common medium of culture for oriental and western peoples. Many of the cities of Palestine, especially in Galilee, were bilingual and their religions savored both of eastern and western deities.

### The Ptolemies of Egypt

Similar to the career of the Seleucidae was the reign of the Ptolemies in Egypt. The rivalry between the two kingdoms was bitter and caused numerous wars of varying fortunes. With the death of Cleopatra in 30 B.C. the last of the Ptolemies perished, and Rome annexed Egypt to serve as her granary. The city of Alexandria grew in importance and became an outstanding mart of commerce and a center of education. Under the patronage of the Ptolemies a great library was founded in which the chief literary treasures of antiquity were preserved. Its librarians were noted scholars and initiated the study of Greek grammar and of textual criticism.

The Jewish influence in Alexandria was strong from the founding of the city. Alexander himself assigned a place to Jewish colonists and admitted them to full citizenship. Under Ptolemy Philadelphus (285 to 247 B.C.) the Jewish scriptures were translated into Greek. This version, known as the Septuagint, became the popular Bible of the Jews of the Dispersion and was generally used by the writers of the New Testament. When they used the Old Testament they took most of their quotations from the Septuagint. Its Greek varies in quality from book to book. Some of the translation is polished and some is baldly literal. It is nevertheless a valuable aid for present Bible study because it shows how the translators interpreted the Hebrew scriptures, and sometimes its renderings reveal that underneath them is a Hebrew text differing markedly from the one which is extant now.

The constant wars of the Seleucidae and the Ptolemies brought radical increase in taxation of their lands. So severe was the drain upon the public treasury that the peasants, on whom the burden rested most heavily, were reduced to abject poverty. The Punic wars of Rome destroyed Egypt's western markets and consequently trade languished. Popular unrest culminated in revolt against the government, or in the abandonment of property which could no longer be utilized profitably because of the excessive taxation. There was a marked decline in the fortunes of both kingdoms in the first century before Christ which, perhaps, accounts for the ease with which Rome overcame them.

## Cultural Effects

The political effects of the Hellenistic conquest of the East were not lasting. The Seleucidae and the Ptolemies were regarded as foreign dynasties who did not belong to the people; and while they were supported by the ruling class, they never succeeded in making their realms wholly Greek in character. On the contrary, these kings assumed the absolutism of the oriental monarch who demanded obeisance from his courtiers. The free camaraderie of the Greek democracy. or even the more formal organization of the Macedonian court was eclipsed by the capricious despotism of the kings who claimed to be deity. Jesus alluded to the Seleucidae and the Ptolemies when He said that the kings of the Gentiles call themselves "benefactors" (Luke 22:25), for the Greek word *euergetes* (benefactor) was one of their titles. The masses over which they ruled paid taxes to them and prostrated themselves before them, but they would have done the same for any other master.

Culturally, the Seleucidae and the Ptolemies introduced Greek customs and manners in the East. Greek architecture prevailed in the urban centers where they lived. Greek was the language of the court and became the common speech of the people as the papyri show. Love letters, bills, receipts, amulets, essays, poetry, biographies, business communications were all written in Greek. In Egypt the titles of the popular officials were Greek, even into the time of the Roman occupation. The rulers sought to unite the Hellenistic culture with the life of the people. Greek names were given to the local gods, and gymnasiums and amphitheatres were built in the major cities. The veneer of western civilization was spread over the Near East.

Through the medium of this culture the gospel of Christ was disseminated in the earliest of its missionary endeavors. With a Greek Bible from which to preach and with the Greek language as its universal medium of communication, it soon reached the outposts of civilization.

## The Jewish State

### *The Exile* 597-322 B.C.

When Nebuchadnezzar, king of Babylon, overran Judea and captured Jerusalem in 597 B.C., the independence of the Jewish state came to an end. Jehoiachin, the king, was taken prisoner to Babylon, together with all the court. The ruling classes of the people, including the skilled artisans, were also deported. Jehoiachin's uncle, Mattaniah, was renamed Zedekiah, and was placed on the throne as a puppet king (II Kings 24:10-17).

From 597 to 586 B.C. Judea enjoyed a twilight existence as a tributary kingdom. Zedekiah was obligated by oath to serve the king of Babylon; but the temptation to intrigue with Egypt was strong, especially when the stake was independence. There was a division of opinion even in the prophetic circles. Hananiah, the son of Azzur, declared repeatedly that God would break the yoke of Babylon and that in two years' time from his prediction the golden vessels that Nebuchadnezzar had taken away from the temple would be restored (Jer. 28:1-4). Jeremiah, on the other hand, charged Hananiah with lying, and predicted that Babylon's grip would not be relaxed. The radical party expected that Egypt would come to their aid; the conservative group, represented by Jeremiah, cherished no such illusions (Jer. 28:12-17).

In 590 B.C. Zedekiah thought that his opportunity to rebel had come. Psammetichus II of Egypt was pushing northward along the Palestinian coast and was steadily encroaching upon the domains of Babylon. Feeling that at last he had a champion, Zedekiah cast in his lot with Egypt.

Nebuchadnezzar did not overlook the challenge. He marched to the defense of Tyre and in 588 B.C. laid siege to Jerusalem. The siege was lifted temporarily at the advance of the Egyptian army, but the latter soon beat a retreat into Egypt and the Babylonian army resumed operations. In 586 B.C. the walls were breached and the Babylonians took the city. Zedekiah was captured in an attempted escape, and after being blinded, was taken in chains to Babylon. The sacred vessels of the temple were plundered; the building itself, together with the royal palace and the mansions of the nobles, was burned. The walls of the city were leveled and the population was deported to Babylon (Jer. 39:4-10).

In order to preserve a semblance of organization, Nebuzaradan, the Babylonian general in charge of the campaign, appointed Gedaliah as governor. The dissident factions within the land still persisted, however. Baalis, the king of the Ammonites, instigated a rebellion in which Gedaliah was assassinated. General civil strife followed in which the insurgent party was finally beaten. The remnant of them escaped to Egypt, taking the prophet Jeremiah with them into involuntary exile (Jer. 41 to 43).

The end of the Jewish state did not mean the end of Judaism; in fact, the practice of "orthodox Judaism" had its beginning in these events. Many of those who went into captivity took with them the Law and the Prophets, which they cherished as their Scriptures. Although the sacrifices of the temple had ceased, the worship of God continued. Some of the most devout and best educated of the Jews had been taken to Babylon, and with their settlement in that land there sprang up a community that took the place of Jerusalem in religious leadership.

In no small measure the religious development of this community was promoted by Ezekiel who had been carried away in the first deportation under Jehoiachin. He was a combination of visionary and Puritan. The imagery of his preaching is grotesque, but his ethics were stern and his spiritual standards were lofty. He predicted the restoration of the people to their own land and expected revival that would purify them from the abominations that they had committed during the years of their captivity (Ezek. 36:22-31).

The seventy years of the Babylonian captivity witnessed the rise of the synagogue worship among the Jews. Though the sacrifices and ritual of the temple had ceased, worship did not die. Groups of the faithful banded themselves together in the name of Jehovah and formed congregations in which the law was taught and revered. Teachers were appointed who took the place of the temple priesthood as religious leaders of the people. The study of the law became a substitute for animal sacrifices and ethical observances took the place of ritual.

The fall of Babylon occurred in 538 B.C. Cyrus, king of Persia, captured Babylon by the strategem of diverting the waters of the Euphrates from their usual channel, so that they no longer flowed through the city. His armies marched through the dry bed of the river under the gates into the city and so captured it almost without a battle. The sovereignty of the Middle East passed to the Medo-Persians.

Cyrus proved to be a benevolent despot. From the very first he treated the conquered peoples with consideration. In the initial year of his reign he issued a decree that the Jews should be permitted to return home and that the spoils of their temple should be restored to them. The rebuilding of the temple was to be financed by the royal treasury (Ezra 1:1-5).

Not all of the Jews in Babylonia returned to Palestine under the decree of Cyrus. The majority preferred to remain with their businesses and with their homes. About forty-two thousand, mostly from the tribes of Judah, Benjamin, and Levi, set out for Jerusalem. Under the leadership of Sheshbazzar, a prince of royal blood whom Cyrus appointed governor, they reached the city about 537 B.C. (Ezra 1:3, 5-11). They commenced to rebuild the temple (Ezra 3:1-13), but the construction was not completed at that time. There was opposition to the project from the people who had stayed in the land (Ezra 4:1-5). For seventeen years nothing further was done, though the returning exiles prospered and built homes for themselves (Haggai 1:4). Under the urgent preaching of the prophets Haggai and Zechariah the work was resumed about 520 B.C. (Ezra 5:1, 2). The provincial officials, apparently ignorant of the original decree of Cyrus, ordered the Jews to desist. The Jews appealed to Darius, who searched the records, and reaffirmed by special decree the privileges which Cyrus had granted. The work then went forward rapidly and the building was completed in 516 B.C. (Ezra 6:1-15). Worship was resumed at the time of the Passover and the priestly ministry was re-established.

For another period of about sixty years between 516 B.C. and 458 B.C. the records are silent concerning the state of the Jews in Palestine. In 458 B.C., "the seventh year of Artaxerxes the king" (Ezra 7:7), another migration set out from Babylon under the leadership of Ezra the scribe, a descendant of Hilkiah, who had been high priest in the reign of Josiah. He was accompanied by a number of priests and singers and possessed a letter from Artaxerxes which gave him authority to renew the temple services, and which provided for financial aid by the magistrates for such worship under penalty of punishment.

The new settlement was absorbed into the population of the land and seemingly effected no change in general conditions. "In the twentieth year of Artaxerxes the king" (Neh. 2:1) (446 B.C.) a messenger from Jerusalem approached Nehemiah the Jewish cupbearer of the Persian king, and informed him that the wall of Jerusalem had been broken down and that its gates had been burned with fire. In all probability the devastation of the city was fairly recent at the time of Nehemiah, for there would have been no point in taking a long journey to announce to him the results of the siege occurring nearly a century and a half previously. From the hints given in the book of Nehemiah one may conclude that the revival of Jewish political activities provoked hostility from the other inhabitants of Palestine, especially the Samaritans. Perhaps the calamity which Hanani announced was the result of some guerrilla raid on Jerusalem which the Jews were not well organized enough to resist.

The appeal of Hanani brought direct results. Nehemiah obtained leave of absence from his royal master, who also gave him a requisition on Asaph, the keeper of the royal forest, for lumber with which to rebuild the gates. Nehemiah promptly proceeded to Jerusalem. On the third night after his arrival, he inspected the fortifications of the city and resolved to rebuild immediately. Various sections of the wall were assigned to different men, making the work proceed rapidly. So bitter was the enmity of Sanballat, the governor of Samaria, that he threatened violence, and the construction had to be done under an armed guard. Under Nehemiah's energetic administration the repairs were completed in less than two months (Neh. 6:15, 16) and the ramparts of the city were again intact.

Nehemiah promoted economic and social reforms also. In the time of destitution the people had mortgaged their lands and chattels for money with which to buy food. The ruinous interest exacted by the money-lenders had made recovery impossible. Nehemiah abolished interest on loans between brethren and required restitution of property.

He brought the public records up to date (Neh. 7:5) so that the descendants of those who had returned from captivity might be known.

The knowledge of the law was renewed under Ezra the scribe, who read and interpreted it. Apparently he read in Hebrew, which was translated into Aramaic by his assistants (Neh. 8:2, 7, 8). The law had doubtless been forgotten in the strenuous years of conflict and of rebuilding and its reading produced a profound effect upon the Jews. "All the people wept, when they heard the words of the law" (Neh. 8:9). The feast of tabernacles was celebrated (Neh. 8:13-18) and a moral reform was effected.

Nehemiah's application of the principles of the law was strict. The temple worship was renewed and contributions were exacted for its support. Mixed marriages with the people of the land were forbidden

(Neh. 10:30); sabbath-breaking was proscribed (Neh. 10:31); and regular administration of tithes was established (Neh. 12:44). By the close of Nehemiah's administration twelve years later the chief elements of Jewish orthodoxy had been well planted among the remnant in Jerusalem.

During Nehemiah's regime Manasseh, a grandson of the high priest, who had married the daughter of Sanballat the governor, was expelled from the country. According to Josephus he fled to Samaria where he built a temple on Mt. Gerizim, and established a rival cult which became the center for the worship of the Samaritans.

The reforms of Nehemiah left a permanent effect. Throughout the rest of the Persian period down to the times of the Maccabees a stalwart group remained who were tenaciously loyal to the law of God, in spite of the strong influences of paganism to which many of the people and even of the priesthood succumbed.

Jewish history from the time of Nehemiah until the second century B.C. is almost a complete blank. The priesthood persisted as the central political power in the land. Josephus says that Alexander the Great, pushing through Palestine on his way to Egypt from the conquest of Tyre, was greeted by Jaddua, the high priest, and offered worship to the true God.[4] Most modern historians reject the story as pure fiction.[5] Whether it be fiction or legend, it reflects the concept that the priesthood was dominant in Judaism during these comparatively silent centuries. The royal house of David had disappeared, and the reference to it in the New Testament shows that it was represented by commonplace artisans, such as Joseph of Nazareth.

Two aspects of Jewish life disappeared during the Persian and Greek periods: the monarchy, and the prophetic office. All pretensions to independence seem to have centered in the priesthood. Prophecy, after Malachi, vanished completely. There is no trace of the reforming and predictive message of the prophets in the Dispersion of this time.

The priesthood retained some of its ancient power and became much more political in its influence than it had been under the monarchy. One or two new religious emphases appeared. The intensive study of the law which began in the exile produced a new class of leaders, the scribes. The wide dispersion of the people into congregations created a demand for copies of the law, since each congregation wanted to own one. The professional copyists had to make a study of the text in

---

4. Josephus, *Antiquities,* XI, vii, 4, 5.
5. See Pfeiffer, R. H., *History of New Testament Times,* (New York, Harper and Brothers, Publishers) 1949, p. 9. fn. 2.

order to transcribe it correctly, and consequently became expert at it. When Herod wished to learn about the prophecies of the Messiah, he called together the chief priests and the scribes of the people (Matt. 2:4). The scribes were regarded as on a plane of equality with the priesthood in religious matters.

Another development which perhaps began in Ezra's time was the rise of the "Great Synagogue," a council of one hundred and twenty members which was formed for the purpose of administering the law and which was the forerunner of the Sanhedrin of Jesus' day. Simon the Just, who is probably to be identified with the high priest Simon I, living at the beginning of the third century B.C., is reputed to have been the last surviving member of the body. Since the references to this Great Synagogue all come from late Talmudic literature, which is notoriously inexact in historical allusions, the very existence of this body has been challenged. Some sort of government by eldership may very well have existed, but the formal establishment of this particular organization seems unlikely.[6]

## *Under the Ptolemies* 322-198 B.C.

With the death of Alexander the Great came the collapse and the inevitable partition of his empire. He left no heirs old enough or strong enough to be his successors, and his four generals divided the realm among themselves. Ptolemy took Egypt, and Antigonus became ruler of Syria. Palestine became the battleground and the prey of both. In 320 B.C. Ptolemy invaded the land and captured Jerusalem. In 315 B.C. Antigonus recovered it, but lost it again three years later at the battle of Gaza. In 301 B.C. Antigonus was killed at the Battle of Ipsus and so Ptolemy reasserted his claim. Antigonus was succeeded by Seleucus II in the rule of Syria.

Comparatively little is known of the state of the Jews in Palestine during this period. Palestine lay between the two hostile powers of Syria and Egypt and suffered equally from both. One aspect of this strife was favorable for the Jews. Both the Egyptian and Syrian rulers desired their favor, since they held the balance of power in the land. The result was that whenever one king came into possession of Palestine the Jews who had favored the other migrated to his domain. Under the first Ptolemy a group of Jews were deported to Egypt and were settled in Alexandria. Commercial opportunities and working

---

6. See H. L. Strack, "Synagogue, the Great," in *The New Schaff-Herzog Encyclopedia of Religious Knowledge*, XI, 217.

conditions there were so good that others followed them so that within a few years a large colony had become established. Apparently Jews were quite acceptable as colonists in the new Hellenistic cities that were being founded in this era for they were sober, energetic, and industrious.

Under the Ptolemies the Jews in Palestine enjoyed many of the privileges of a free community. The high priest was the governing officer by whom the law was administered. He was aided by the council of priests and elders. The temple was the center of national life. The Feasts of the Passover, of Weeks, and of Tabernacles were regularly observed and were attended by devout pilgrims from the whole world. The study of the law was zealously maintained, and during this period its interpretation was developed in detail.

The economic status of the people under the Ptolemaic regime seems to have been poor. They paid a very low tax, which, in consideration of the prevalent avarice of the kings and of the tax collectors of that day, probably means that they were unable to pay much. Constant warfare and emigration had impoverished the land. In the latter part of the Ptolemaic rule Joseph, a nephew of the high priest Onias, persuaded Ptolemy III Euergetes to delegate to him the commission of collecting the taxes. So successful was his diplomacy that Ptolemy gave him also two thousand troops to assist in enforcing the collections. Those who refused to pay suffered confiscation of their entire property. Ptolemy was satisfied and Joseph grew wealthy, but the land was drained of its few remaining resources.[7] Perhaps the financial oppression of the last few years of the third century caused the people to turn their allegiance more readily from Ptolemy V to Antiochus III of Syria.

The Ptolemies, for the most part, treated the Jews very well. Under Ptolemy Philadelphus (293-244 B.C.), the successor of Ptolemy Lagus, thousands of the Jewish slaves were liberated at royal expense. Some of these were given posts of responsibility to fill. The younger generation took on Greek customs and spoke the Greek language so that they began to lose their distinctively Semitic habits of thought.

During the reign of Ptolemy Philadelphus the Greek version of the Old Testament, known as the Septuagint, was created. According to the story current in Josephus' time, Ptolemy's librarian, Demetrius, was collecting copies of all known books for the great library which he was assembling in Alexandria. Hearing that the Jews had written records of their nation, Demetrius petitioned Ptolemy to secure them

---

7. Josephus, *Antiquities*, XII, iv, 2-6, 10.

for him in accurate translation. Ptolemy sent to Eleazar, the Jewish high priest, asking that he send delegates, six elders from each tribe, who should be able to perform the work of translation. Eleazar reciprocated by sending the men and a copy of the law. The legend says that the seventy-two elders completed their work in seventy-two days and that when the resulting translation was read to the Jews, they all approved it.[8] The accuracy of some of the details in the story is questionable; but there can be no doubt that the Septuagint arose in Alexandria, and that it was translated to meet the demand for the Scriptures by a Greek-speaking Jewish population. By the time of Christ it was widely circulated throughout the Dispersion in the Mediterranean world and became the Bible of the early Christian church.

## *Under the Seleucidae* 198-168 B.C.

Parallel with the development of the Ptolemaic empire in Egypt there grew up the dominion of the Seleucidae in Syria, whose capital was Antioch on the Orontes river. The rivalry between the two kingdoms involved them in constant strife. Antiochus I of Syria (280-261 B.C.) attempted to conquer Palestine, but failed to do so. His son, Antiochus II, agreed to marry Berenice, the daughter of Ptolemy (249 B.C.), if he could secure with her the rights to the land. Upon the death of Ptolemy he divorced Berenice to take back his former wife, Laodice. She, however, had him poisoned and had Berenice and her child murdered. Ptolemy III Euergetes (247-222 B.C.), thirsting for revenge, invaded Syria, and plundered it. The war went on with varying fortunes until Antiochus III was defeated at Raphia by Ptolemy IV in 217 B.C. The Syrians were driven from Jerusalem and the country was claimed by Egypt. In 198 B.C. the tide of war turned again. The Egyptian army was severely beaten and Palestine came again under the rule of the Seleucidae.

As might be expected, the advent of the Syrians was not unanimously welcomed. A large party of the Jews, led by the priesthood under Onias III, persisted in their allegiance to Egypt. Their opponents, the house of Tobias, were more liberal in their interpretation of the law and favored Syria. In a conflict which arose between them, the house of Onias prevailed and expelled the followers of Tobias. The disgruntled Tobiads promptly reported their woes to Seleucus IV with the hint that he might be able to replenish his empty treasury with

---

8. Josephus, *Antiquities*, XII, ii, 4-7, 13.

funds from the temple. Legend says that he sent his treasurer, Heliodorus, to Jerusalem for the purpose of confiscating the temple treasure, and that he was prevented from doing so by a vision which terrified him.

Seleucus died in 175 B.C., and was succeeded by his brother, Antiochus IV, who was a thorough Hellenist. He was a vigorous ruler, but was so erratic that many called him Epimanes, "the madman," rather than Epiphanes, "the manifest god," which was his official title. Antiochus interfered in the affairs of Palestine by replacing Onias III by his brother Jason, who promised to pay large sums into the royal treasury and to introduce Greek customs into Jerusalem if the Jews could be registered as citizens of Antioch. The appointment of Jason was followed by the establishment of a gymnasium in Jerusalem almost under the shadow of the temple. The priests left the service of the temple for the games. Jason actually stooped to sharing in the games in honor of the Tyrian god Melkarth and sent gifts for offerings. Even his messengers refused to participate in this sacrilege, and so the gifts were applied to the building of the Syrian navy.

Antiochus became embroiled in a contest with Egypt. Fearing that Jason would not be loyal to him, he replaced him by Menelaus, another Hellenizing Jew, who favored Syria's program. Antiochus' invasion of Egypt was a failure, for the Roman envoy compelled him to withdraw. Enraged by this defeat, he returned to Jerusalem in a bad mood and proceeded to vent his anger on the Jews. A large number of the inhabitants of the city were sold as slaves. The walls of the city were destroyed. The temple was plundered of its treasures and was converted into a shrine of Olympian Zeus. On December 15, 168 B.C., an image of the god was set up on its altar, and ten days later a sow was sacrificed in its honor. Heathen altars were erected everywhere throughout the country, and the observance of heathen festivals was made compulsory. Judaism was proscribed completely. The death penalty was inflicted upon those who possessed or read the Torah. Sabbath observance and circumcision were forbidden.[9]

The situation became intolerable for all devout adherents of the law and conflict was inevitable. The spark that touched off the conflagration of war was the revolt of Mattathias, an old priest in the village of Modin. When the royal agent came to Modin to compel heathen sacrifices, he offered rewards to Mattathias if he, as the oldest and most respected citizen of the village, would be the first to comply.

---

9. I Maccabees 1:21-50.

Mattathias protested vehemently against the request, and when some less conscientious Jew approached to offer his sacrifice, Mattathias killed him at the altar. Aroused by the profanation of God's law, he killed the king's agent also and demolished the altar.

Mattathias and his sons fled into the wilderness with their families, where they were joined by others. In the war that followed, the Jews were worsted at first. Mattathias died shortly after and was buried at Modin. The contest was carried on by his son Judas, nicknamed Maccabeus, "The Hammer." The Syrians regarded the Maccabees as guerrilla fighters of negligible importance, but after a strong Syrian detachment was routed at Beth-horon, Antiochus began to take the revolt more seriously. He raised a large army, paid it for a year in advance, and left it in charge of his general Lysias while he himself went on an eastern expedition. In a short but decisive campaign Judas twice defeated the Syrians and expelled them from Jerusalem. The temple was cleansed and a new altar was erected. A rededication service was held, and a new feast was established to commemorate the occasion. He completed his success by the conquest of the lands east of the Jordan and had Palestine within his grasp.

When the news of his army's defeat reached Antiochus IV he was so shocked that he died soon thereafter. The contest was maintained by his successor. Judas Maccabeus appealed to Rome for help, but though the reply was friendly, he received no material aid. He was killed in battle and was succeeded by his brother Jonathan. The war dragged on until 143 B.C., when Simon, another brother, was recognized as an ally by Demetrius II, contestant for the crown of Syria. In 142 B.C. Demetrius gave Simon political freedom and release from all taxes present and future. The independence of Judea was won and the struggles of the Maccabees had ended.

The victory of the Maccabees really terminated the influence of the Seleucidae in Palestine and gave virtual autonomy to the Jewish state until the advent of the Romans. Nevertheless, the effect of the Seleucid dominion was tremendous. Its Hellenizing pressure consolidated the Jews into a resistance group jealous of its national life and practically indissoluble among the nations through whom it was scattered.

## Under the Hasmoneans 142 B.C. to 37 B.C.

With the attainment of Jewish freedom, Simon was made high priest for life. His reign, though brief, was prosperous. A treaty was negotiated with Rome which was confirmed in 139 B.C., recognizing the independence of the Jewish state and commending it to the friendship of Rome's subjects and allies. Economic conditions improved; justice was ably administered in the courts; and Jewish religious life was revived.

The happy interval, however, was all too short. Demetrius II of Syria was dethroned and captured by the Parthians (139 B.C.). His brother who succeeded him, Antiochus VII, broke the pact of friendship with Simon and demanded heavy tribute in the place of free aid. Under Simon's sons, Judah and Jonathan, the Syrians were defeated, and so the external danger was averted.

The real peril to Judea was internal strife. Simon and two of his sons were treacherously murdered by Ptolemy, his son-in-law, in 135 B.C. His surviving son, John Hyrcanus (135 B.C. to 104 B.C.) took possession of Jerusalem before Ptolemy could capture it and then besieged Ptolemy in his castle. Ptolomy finally fled to Egypt.

In the meantime Antiochus VII of Syria had besieged Jerusalem. The Jews were forced to capitulate and to pay tribute to the king of Syria. At his death the claimants for the throne plunged Syria into civil war. Hyrcanus immediately made the most of his opportunity by conquering Idumea on the south and the Samaritans on the north, as well as Medeba and the neighboring cities on the east of the Jordan. Hyrcanus became high priest and head of the state and the founder of the Hasmonean dynasty.

When he died he committed the government of the state to his wife and to his oldest son, Judah Aristobulus. Aristobulus imprisoned his mother and his brothers and seized the government for himself. In a year's time he died, and his widow, Salome Alexandra, married the next surviving brother, Alexander Jannaeus, who was king from 103 B.C. to 76 B.C. Alexander continued the conquest of Palestine. His reign was filled with civil turmoil, in which he nearly lost his throne.

Aristobulus II, son of Salome Alexandra, became king after her death. He removed his older brother, Hyrcanus II, from the priesthood. By this time the general chaos in the affairs of Palestine and of Syria had attracted the attention of Rome. Pompey detached his lieutenant, Securus, to investigate and to settle the political fracas. Securus decided for Aristobulus, who suddenly revolted. The Romans attacked Jerusalem, and the following of Aristobulus would have fought to the death, had not Hyrcanus surrendered the city. The Romans reappointed him as king and took Aristobulus with his family and many other captives to Rome to grace the triumphal procession.

Alexander, Aristobulus' son, escaped while enroute to Rome, and attempted a revolt against Hyrcanus. He was overcome by the Roman proconsul of Syria, who placed all of Palestine under the governor of Syria.

In the civil war between Pompey and Caesar in 49 B.C., Hyrcanus aided Caesar, who rewarded him by recognizing him as the responsible head of the Jewish nation, and by restoring the coastal cities to his rule. His minister Antipater was granted Roman citizenship. Antipater was the real power behind the throne. He appointed his own son Phasael prefect of Jerusalem, and his other son, Herod, as prefect of Galilee.

Through the changing fortunes of the civil wars of Rome, Herod succeeded in keeping himself in favor with the ruling party. Hyrcanus gave Herod his support. Antony appointed Herod and Phasael co-rulers of Judea. While Antony was in Egypt, the Parthians attacked Jerusalem and captured Hyrcanus and Phasael. Herod escaped from the city in time to save his life. Antigonus (40 B.C. to 37 B.C.), who had been appointed ruler by the Parthians, marched against Herod. The latter, with the aid of the Roman legions, finally defeated Antigonus and had him beheaded. With Antigonus ended the Hasmonean dynasty.

## Under the Herods 37 B.C. to A.D. 6

The Herodian dynasty began with Antipater. His son Herod, called the Great, inherited all of his father's ability in diplomacy and government, in addition to the throne of Judea, which had been vacated by the death of Hyrcanus. Farrar says that "Antipater built the superstructure; Herod put on it the coping-stone; and turned the tent of his Idumean ancestors into a royal palace, which was regarded during his lifetime as one of the most splendid of all the world."[10]

### Herod the Great 37 B.C. to 4 B.C.

Herod began his reign in 37 B.C. at the age of twenty-two. Driven from Palestine by the invasion of the Parthians who supported Antigonus as the successor of Hyrcanus, he succeeded in making his escape. In his company were his mother Kypros, his sister Salome, and Mariamne, the daughter of Hyrcanus, who was engaged to him. Leaving them under the care of his brother Joseph at the fortress of Masada on the Dead Sea, he fought his way to Alexandria and thence sailed to Rome.

---

10. F. W. Farrar, *The Herods* (London: Service & Paton, 1898) p. 61.

By persuasive speech or by secret intrigue he obtained the favor of Antony and Octavia and was duly inaugurated as king of the Jews. He returned to Palestine, rescued his family from the siege, and proceeded to make himself master of the country. He exterminated the brigands who infested Galilee. He contested with Antigonus for the possession of Jerusalem and finally captured it with the aid of Roman forces. Antigonus was sent in chains to Antioch, where he was executed by the Romans.

Among Herod's first acts was the appointment of a high priest. Inasmuch as he could not hold the office himself because of his Idumean blood, and because he did not want to take a member of the Hasmonean family who might cherish political ambitions, he selected Hananiel of Babylon, probably identifiable with Annas who is mentioned in the Gospels. Alexandra, the mother of Mariamne, sought the post for her son Aristobulus III, and by her intrigues with Antony through Cleopatra of Egypt forced Herod to appoint him, though he was under age. Hananiel was deposed and Aristobulus took his place. So great was the esteem in which the populace held Aristobulus that Herod was jealous. At a banquet given in Aristobulus' honor at Jericho Herod's servants did away with him by drowning him while bathing.

Herod was summoned to Egypt to answer for his crime. He entrusted Mariamne to her uncle Joseph, giving orders that if he were condemned, Joseph should slay both Mariamne and her mother. Herod returned safely, having made peace with Antony, only to find that Mariamne had discovered his order. He interpreted Joseph's failure to keep his secret as proof that Mariamne had been unfaithful, and so he executed Joseph at once.

In 29 B.C. the Roman Senate declared war on Antony and Cleopatra. Herod was forced to make the choice of deserting his friend or of fighting a hopeless battle with Rome. This disastrous dilemma was resolved by Cleopatra, who, fearing Herod as an enemy, persuaded Antony to send him on a minor campaign in Arabia. Herod won the campaign. When Antony and Cleopatra lost the naval battle of Actium, Herod realized that he could no longer support them, and so he withdrew from his embarrassing alliance.

Herod made peace with Octavian, the victor of Actium, and was confirmed in his position as king of Judea and ally of the Roman people. The death of Cleopatra removed one of his chief dangers, for her constant plots to acquire the kingdom of Judea had been the source of many of his troubles.

The victorious return from the conference with Octavian was
poiled for Herod by the coldness of Mariamne, the one woman whom
e really loved.  She had learned that when he left for Rhodes to
neet Octavian, he had repeated the instructions of the former occasion
hat she should be killed if he failed to return.  She accused him of
he murder of her grandfather, Hyrcanus, who had been executed for
omplicity in a plot of her uncle and of her brother.  The tension
etween them was made more acute by the lies of Herod's sister and
nother, who were intensely jealous of her.  Mariamne was imprisoned
nd was ultimately executed.

Remorse so gripped Herod that he became physically and mentally
1.  Alexandra, thinking that his end had come, plotted to put his sons
nd her grandsons, Alexander and Aristobulus, on the throne.  Enraged
y this conspiracy, Herod ordered that she should be destroyed.

Herod conferred many benefits upon the people through subsidies
1 time of famine and by erecting public works.  The military installa-
ons and fortifications which he built made Palestine free from foreign
ivasion.  Because of the greatly stimulated building program the
rades flourished and economic conditions improved greatly.  Peace
rought prosperity, and in spite of the incessant intrigues which went
n in his court, Herod's reign was in some measure successful.

Herod did not succeed in winning the friendship of the Jews.  His
dumean blood made him a foreigner in their eyes, and his willingness
› support heathen cults by his gifts aroused suspicion concerning his
yalty to Judaism.  In spite of the fact that he built a new temple
f great magnificence at which he gave occasional perfunctory attend-
nce, he was never a truly godly Jew.  His cynical use of the priesthood
; a political tool and the looseness of his personal life made him
enerally hated by the devout men of Judaism.

In 23 B.C. Herod married another wife named Mariamne, the
aughter of Simon, son of Boethus, a priest.  In order to please her
e removed the high priest and gave his office to Simon.  The new
riest soon became the target of universal hatred.  Four years later
hen the two sons of Mariamne I were recalled from Rome, where
Ierod had sent them to be educated, the populace acclaimed them with
ndisguised enthusiasm.  The people recognized them as scions of the
asmoneans through their mother, and evidently hoped that they might
›me day relieve the miseries which the oppressive policies of their
ther had created.  The young princes, who had learned at Rome to
›eak their minds, were a little too free with their sentiments.  They
curred the enmity of their half-brother, Antipater, who accused them

to Herod; and after a long and tortuous series of accusations an
reconciliations, they too met death.

The last days of Herod were filled with violence and hatre
Antipater, who had tried to accelerate his father's death in order tha
he might succeed to the throne, suffered the same fate as his brother
Augustus, to whom Herod appealed for permission to execu
Antipater, remarked in a biting witticism that he would rather k
Herod's hog than his son.[11] Smitten with cancer of the intestines an
dropsy and haunted by the memory of his murders, Herod died c
April 1, 4 B.C.

The jealous and unscrupulous character of this man explains tl
duplicity of his dealing with the Magi from the East and his brutali
in ordering the massacre of the children in Bethlehem (Matt. 2:1-18
The silence of history concerning the massacre at Bethlehem can k
explained easily, for the slaughter of a dozen infants in an obscu
Judean village would not arouse much comment in comparison wit
the enormity of Herod's greater crimes.

## Herod's Successors

By Herod's last will the kingdom was bequeathed to Archelau
In order to secure confirmation of the appointment, Archelaus resolv
to go to Rome as speedily as possible. The resentment against tl
cruelties of the Herodian family was so strong in Judea that he fe
the necessity of pacifying the country before he left. A rebellion bro
out at the Passover that was quelled only by the use of troops.

Archelaus went to Rome, leaving his brother Philip in charg
Antipas, a third brother, who had been appointed as Herod's success
in his second will, also went thither to press his claims. August
did not render an immediate decision at the first hearing, because
the conflicting parties that were represented.

Before the case was continued, a second revolt broke out in Jud
Sabinus, the procurator whom Augustus had sent out to administ
affairs after Herod's death until some settlement could be made wi
the heirs, seized Jerusalem and plundered the temple. He was besieg
in turn by the rebels and was only rescued by the arrival of Varus, t
governor of Syria, and his legions. The Jews sent an embassy
Rome asking that none of the Herods be appointed king, but that th
should be given autonomy. Philip also appeared at the tribunal
support the claims of Archelaus.

---

11. Greek: *hus*-hog; *huios*-son.

At the second hearing, Augustus confirmed Herod's will. Archelaus obtained Judea, Samaria, and Idumea, with the title of ethnarch. Antipas became tetrarch of Galilee and Perea. Philip was made tetrarch of Batanea, Trachonitis, and Auranitis, north of the Sea of Galilee on the east side of the Jordan.

## *Archelaus* 4 B.C. to A.D. 6

Archelaus married Glaphyra, daughter of the Cappadocian king Archelaus, who had been the wife of his half-brother Alexander, and, after his death, the wife of Juba of Mauretania. This marriage brought Archelaus into further disfavor with the Jews, because he had divorced his own wife to marry her, and because she already had children by Alexander.

Like his father, Archelaus promoted the building of public works. His rule was so distasteful to his people that after nine years a delegation of the Jewish and Samaritan leaders went to Rome to file complaint against him. Augustus, after listening to their petition, deposed Archelaus from his office and banished him to Vienne in Gaul in A.D. 6.

The character of Archelaus' reign receives a curious confirmation in an incidental reference in the Gospels. Matthew, in telling of the return of Joseph and Mary from Egypt, says:

> *But when he [Joseph] heard that Archelaus was reigning over Judea in the room of his father Herod, he was afraid to go thither; and being warned of God in a dream, he withdrew into the parts of Galilee.* (Matthew 2:22)

Evidently Archelaus' reputation for jealousy of possible rivals and for general vindictiveness was equal to his father's.

## *Philip, the Tetrarch* 4 B.C. to A.D. 34

The territory assigned to Philip included the northeast corner of Palestine bounded on the west by the Sea of Galilee, the upper Jordan river, the lake of Merom, and the southern Lebanon range. On the north it extended to the borders of Abilene near Damascus. On the east and southeast it projected into the desert, and on the south it bordered on the Decapolis. Its population was largely Syrian and Greek, with a much smaller Jewish element than lived in Archelaus' domain.

Philip was a happy exception to the Herods in general. He followed their precedent as a builder; but in his dealings with his people he was just and fair. Caesarea Philippi, mentioned in the Gospels (Matt. 16:13, Mark 8:27), was built on the site of the ancient Panias, at the springs of the Jordan, and was named for the emperor and for him. Bethsaida Julias, on the northwest side of the Lake of Galilee, was also one of his cities.

He married Salome, the daughter of Herodias. Josephus had only good to say of him.[12] He died peacefully in A.D. 34. His tetrarchy was placed under the Roman administration of Syria until, in A.D. 37, it was given by Caligula to his nephew, Agrippa I.

Philip is mentioned by Luke as being tetrarch of Iturea and Trachonitis (Luke 3:1). He is not mentioned elsewhere in the narrative of the New Testament.

### *Herod Antipas* 4 B.C. to A.D. 39

The Herod who is most prominent in the Gospels is Herod Antipas, the tetrarch of Galilee and Perea. Jesus alluded to him as "that fox" (Luke 13:32), or, more exactly, "that vixen." The epithet was a characterization not only of his slyness, but of his craftiness and of his vindictiveness as well.

During his reign of forty-three years he built a new capital on the shores of the Lake of Galilee named Tiberias. Because the city was erected on the site of an ancient graveyard, the strict Jews would not live in it, and so he had to colonize it by force. Its government was modeled on the Greek system.

By religion, Herod Antipas was a Jew. He took the side of the Jewish populace in protesting against Pilate's setting up a pagan votive shield in Jerusalem, and he attended the feast of the Passover when it was held in that city (Luke 23:7).

Herod Antipas appears in the Gospels as the murderer of John the Baptist, and as the one before whom Jesus was tried (Luke 23:7-12). His wife, Herodias, was the daughter of his half-brother, Aristobulus and had been originally the wife of another half-brother, Herod Philip I (Matt. 14:3, Mark 6:17, Luke 3:19), mentioned only in the Gospels and not to be confused with Philip the Tetrarch. When Antipas went to Rome he stayed with Herod Philip who was living there as a private citizen, and became enamored of Herodias. Antipas promptly divorced his own wife, who was a daughter of the Arabian king Aretas. Aretas

---

12. Josephus: *Antiquities XVIII*, V, 4.

daughter, learning of Antipas' intentions, fled to her father, who made war on Herod.

Herod carried through his marriage with Herodias, who, with her daughter Salome, joined him at Tiberias. Perhaps at this time Herod went down to the fortress of Machaerus in Perea in order that he might watch more closely the ministry of John the Baptist. Although Herod seems to have respected the blunt honesty of the prophet who rebuked him boldly for his misdeeds, Herodias was infuriated and finally succeeded in securing his death. Antipas was too weak or too indifferent to justice to save the life of the man who had told him the truth (Matt. 14:1-12; Mark 6:14-29; Luke 3:19).

The marriage with Herodias finally cost Antipas his kingdom. When Caligula became emperor at Rome after the death of Tiberius in A.D. 37, one of his first acts was to make Agrippa I, brother of Herodias and son of Aristobulus, king of the territory that had formerly been the tetrarchy of Philip. Agrippa's good fortune incited Herodias to urge her husband to petition Caligula for a royal title. When he arrived at Rome and presented himself to Caligula, Fortunatus, the representative of Agrippa, accused him of treasonable negotiations against Rome. Caligula promptly deposed Antipas and banished him to Lyons in Gaul, where he died. Agrippa succeeded to his rival's tetrarchy.

### Herod Agrippa I A.D. 37 to A.D. 44

Herod Agrippa I was the son of Aristobulus and his cousin Berenice, daughter of Salome, sister of Herod the Great. After completing his education at Rome, he returned to Palestine in A.D. 23 and secured an appointment from Herod Antipas, his brother-in-law, as overseer of markets in Tiberias. He quarreled with Herod and later with the Roman governor in Antioch to whom he had fled for refuge. Upon returning to Italy, he became tutor of Tiberius' grandson and was an intimate friend of Caligula, to whom, on one occasion, Agrippa suggested that he should be the next emperor. When Tiberius learned of this remark, he threw Agrippa into prison, but the death of Tiberius occurred soon afterward, and Agrippa was released.

Caligula immediately upon his accession gave Agrippa his appointment. Agrippa had enough sympathy for the Jews and enough influence with Caligula to keep the latter from erecting an image of himself in the temple at Jerusalem. By so doing he averted what would have been a violent uprising of the Jews.

When Caligula was murdered in A.D. 41 Agrippa was still in Rome. He supported Claudius' succession, and Claudius in return confirmed not only the realm which Caligula had given to him, but also Judea and Samaria. Agrippa I, then, held under his own power the reunited domain of Herod the Great.

Upon his return to Palestine he took up his residence in Jerusalem and worshiped regularly at the temple. He lived in accord with the strict Jewish law and suppressed all attempts to bring pagan ceremonies or images into the synagogues. Agrippa's devotion to Judaism made him one of the first persecutors of Christianity. During his rule the tension between the Pharisaic party and the new sect of believers in Jesus had been mounting until finally the king intervened. He arrested and executed James the Son of Zebedee and imprisoned Peter also. The latter was released by divine interposition. Agrippa ordered that the guards should be punished by death, and he went down to Caesarea (Acts 12:11-19).

Herod's death occurred suddenly in A.D. 44. Josephus and Luke agree[13] in the general details of the account. The former says that he attended games in honor of the emperor at Caesarea, dressed in a silver robe. The resplendent appearance of his garments as they glistened in the sun caused his flatterers to avow that he was a god. Shortly afterward he was stricken with severe intestinal distress and died within five days.

## *Herod Agrippa II* A.D. 50 to A.D. 100

Herod Agrippa I left four children, three daughters and a son. Drusilla, one of the daughters, married Felix, the Roman procurator of Judea. Agrippa II, the son, was in Rome at the time of his father's death. In A.D. 50, after the death of his uncle, Herod of Chalcis, he was given the kingdom, which included the right to appoint the high priest of the temple in Jerusalem. In A.D. 53 he relinquished the kingdom of Chalcis and was given the former tetrarchies of Philip and Lysanias. After the death of Claudius in A.D. 54, Nero added to his realm some parts of Galilee and Perea.

When Festus became procurator of Judea, Agrippa, in company with his sister Bernice who had become his consort, went down to Caesarea to welcome him to his new office. At this time he acted as the religious adviser for Festus in the case of Paul, whose status was a puzzle to the pagan Roman (Acts 25:13-26:32). Though Agrippa

---

13. Cf. Acts 12:20-23 with Josephus, *Antiquities*, XVIII, vi, 7.

had a good knowledge of Judaism, he was indifferent to its deeper claims; and while he observed its ceremonial requirements, he never exhibited any sincere convictions of its truth.

In the revolution of A.D. 66 he openly sided with the Romans. He gave his allegiance to Vespasian, and joined with Titus in the triumph over his own people. His kingdom was enlarged by the new emperor. In A.D. 75 he and Bernice moved to Rome, where Bernice and Titus became involved in a scandal. Titus had planned to marry her, but he desisted when he realized the intensity of the popular feeling against them. Agrippa died in A.D. 100.

## Under the Priests to the Fall of Jerusalem A.D. 70

The varying succession of foreign rulers that dominated Palestine — the Ptolemies, the Seleucidae, the Herods, and later the Romans — were generally regarded by the Jewish people as usurpers whose rule had to be tolerated but who were never the rightful sovereigns. The people may have had to submit to their political yoke, but they never gave to them hearty allegiance. The real controlling power of the Jewish mind was the priesthood.

During the history of Israel various types of civil government had prevailed at different times. Under Moses elders represented the tribes and counseled with the leader concerning his action. In the period of the Judges there was no central government, but as need arose from time to time aggressive leaders appeared who gained a popular following but who established no permanent order. In the eras of the united and divided kingdoms the king was the head of the state. In all of these regimes, however, the word of the priest was final because he was a spokesman for God and in the Jewish state religious authority was regarded as supreme. If the priesthood was corrupt, political life was also debased; and if there was a revival, the worship of Jehovah was restored and the civil authority was strengthened.

During the exile the functioning of the priesthood as a class was temporarily suspended by the destruction of the temple. The priests, however, did not disappear; for when the captives returned in 536 B.C. a large company of priests and Levites were among them (Ezra 2:36-54). When the temple was rebuilt these resumed their duties, and with some few interruptions the worship continued until the final destruction of Jerusalem by the Romans.

Throughout this long period the priesthood served as the central control in Judaism. The high priest took office by hereditary right and retained it for life. He exercised supreme authority in the state under the overlord who happened to possess the country at the time. To what extent the conquerors of Judea gave a free hand to the high priest cannot be ascertained positively. Probably he was independent as long as he did not interfere with tribute or with foreign policies. Both the Greeks and the Romans gave considerable latitude to the subject peoples in administering their national affairs.

Associated with the high priest was a council of elders comprised of the wisest and most experienced men of the nation. Some of them were priests; some, like Ezra, were scribes and professional students of the law; others were drawn from the wealthy and better educated landholders and business men. The government was really in the hands of a religious aristocracy, of which the Sanhedrin, as this body was later called, was representative.

The succession of the priesthood through the Persian period is given without comment in Nehemiah 12:1-11. Josephus adds that John, the high priest (evidently identical with Jonathan in Nehemiah 12:11), had a brother, Jesus, whose friend Bagosus, a general of the Persian army, had promised to procure him the priesthood. The two brothers quarreled in the temple, and so John killed Jesus, to the general scandal of the people and of the Persian authorities.[14]

The place of the high priest as the leader of that nation was clearly demonstrated in the negotiations with Alexander as reported by Josephus. When Alexander invaded Palestine and laid siege to Tyre, he demanded of the high priest that all support which the Jews had formerly given to Persia should be transferred to him. The high priest refused, because he had given his oath to Darius and would not go back on it. Alexander replied with a threat that when he had finished his conquest, he would teach the priest to whom he should give his oaths.

Josephus' account states that when Alexander approached Jerusalem, Jaddua, the high priest, went out to meet him with a procession. Alexander was deeply impressed and gave reverence to the priest, who showed him predictions of his conquest in the Jewish scriptures. The negotiations proceeded peacefully and the Greek army departed from Palestine, leaving the Jews to govern themselves.[15]

---

14. Josephus, *Antiquities* XI, vii, 1.
15. *Op. cit.* XI, viii, 4, 5; XII, 11, 5.

In the Ptolemaic period the priesthood remained powerful and provided good government. Onias I, son of Jaddua, and his son, Simon I, the Just, received favorable mention in Josephus. With the passing of time, however, the high priesthood became a political prize that was generally sold to the highest bidder. The successful candidate had to comply with the wishes of his political lord if he wished to hold his position. Consequently the high priesthood lost much of its independent influence and was, until the time of the Maccabees, largely subservient to the state.

With the Maccabean revolt came a change in the priesthood. The older line of priests who had held office under the Seleucidae was displaced by the Hasmonean dynasty whose progenitor was John Hyrcanus, himself a descendant of the Maccabees. Under the last of the Seleucidae and under the Herods the priesthood maintained its ascendancy in Judaism, except for some few lapses when Herod changed the priestly appointment.

From the death of Herod the Great until the fall of Jerusalem the priesthood was again the chief political power of Judea. The high priest acted as adviser to the Roman procurator and not infrequently his political pressure caused the governor to change his policy. Through his influence over the populace the high priest was able to mold public opinion and thus he could bend stubborn officials to his will or else compel them to risk the emperor's displeasure for failing to keep on good terms with their subjects. The cry of the populace at Jesus' hearing before Pilate, "If thou release this man, thou art not Caesar's friend" (John 19:12), was a good example of such machinations; for Mark says that "the chief priests stirred up the multitude" (Mark 15:11).

The rule of the priests was concurrent with the three periods previously mentioned and it continued until the fall of Jerusalem, at which time the temple was destroyed and the priesthood was dispersed.

### Under the Romans until Bar-Cochba A.D. 135

Clear-cut chronological divisions between the successive national sovereignties over Judea are impossible to establish. Just as the priesthood was concomitant with the sovereignty of the Ptolemies, of the Seleucidae, and of the Herods, so the Herods and the priesthood held sway simultaneously with Rome. From the conquest of Pompey in 63 B.C. Rome had assumed a protectorate over Judea, and had regarded both Herod and the priesthood as vassal kings. When upon the death of Herod the Great his less capable son Archelaus followed him as king, he proved to be so unpopular a ruler that Rome deposed him, and appointed Coponius as procurator of Judea. From that time, with some local exceptions, Rome ruled the country directly until the last futile revolt in A.D. 135.

The procurators were not generally popular, and many of them did not remain in office longer than three years. Valerius Gratus (A.D. 15-26) was disliked because he had interfered with the succession of the priesthood by appointing one of his own candidates. His successor, Pontius Pilate, (A.D. 26-36) is perhaps the best known of the procurators because of his connection with the trial and death of Jesus. At the very beginning of his term he offended the Jews needlessly by insisting that his troops should carry into Jerusalem banners bearing on them the image of the emperor. The Jews protested violently against such a profanation of the city. Pilate yielded only when he saw that nothing but useless bloodshed could follow his course of action. Later he became embroiled in a dispute with the Samaritans and was replaced in A.D. 36 by Marcellus.

The accession of the emperor Caligula in A.D. 37 brought a new crisis. Under the delusion that he was a god, Caligula issued orders that his statue should be set up in the temple at Jerusalem. Petronius, the legate of Syria, was delegated to carry out the command. He was thus faced with the dilemma of disobeying the emperor's command by refusing to erect the image or of plunging the whole country into a religious war. He succeeded in postponing action, and fortunately for him the dilemma was solved by the death of Caligula in A.D. 41.

Throughout the entire period up to the opening of the Jewish War in A.D. 66 there was constant tension between the Roman officials and the people. Local outbursts of armed resistance were not infrequent. The party of the Zealots, who were stronger in the rural sections and in the highlands of Galilee, openly advocated a holy war on Rome. The procurators had to maintain vigilance to the point of oppressiveness to maintain order. The popular hatred of Rome was only increased by the occasional skirmishes between the Jewish outlaws and the Roman legionaries, and the appearance of a leader with Messianic ambitions was enough to draw after him a numerous and fanatical crowd of followers.

Among the later procurators M. Antonius Felix and Porcius Festus are mentioned in Acts in connection with Paul (Acts 23:24-24:27,

25:1-26:32). Under Felix' regime the latent hostility of Jews against Romans began to crystallize into a definite attempt to break the Roman yoke. Josephus records an incident of an Egyptian Jew who gathered a group of supporters by promising to make the walls of Jerusalem fall at his word, but Felix' soldiers dispersed them and compelled their leader to flee.[16] Evidently the centurion who took Paul into protective custody had this episode in mind when he asked him if he were not "the Egyptian, who before these days stirred up to sedition and led out into the wilderness the four thousand men of the Assassins" (Acts 21:38).

Whether because of malice or of mismanagement Felix' procuratorship was characterized by constant turmoil. The contrast between the opening words of Tertullus and of Paul at the latter's hearing before Felix is significant. Whereas Tertullus flattered Felix by saying,

> *Seeing that by thee we enjoy much peace, and that by thy providence evils are corrected for this nation . . .* (Acts 24:2),

Paul introduced his defense by stating that Felix had "been of many years a judge unto this nation" (Acts 24:10), a statement that was strictly true. The stern measures that Felix took to repress the riots that recurred in Caesarea and the general miseries that Judea suffered under his rule prompted his recall to Rome, where he would certainly have been punished for malfeasance had not his brother Pallas, a favorite of Nero, interceded for him.

Porcius Festus, his successor, seems to have been an honest man and a conscientious administrator. He died in office after two years, but his successors undid whatever small good he had been able to accomplish.

Between the death of Festus and the opening of the Jewish war the political conditions in Judea deteriorated rapidly. The high priests were avaricious and cruel and the Roman governors were rapacious and oppressive. The Gentile inhabitants of Caesarea went out of their way to provoke the ire of the Jewish population, and Florus plundered the temple treasury. Finally the Jews, infuriated by constant abuse, rebelled.

The conflict began in A.D. 66 with a series of local uprisings in various cities, in which the Roman garrisons were massacred by the Jewish rebels; or, if the Gentiles proved the stronger, the Jewish population suffered frightfully. Cestius Gallus, the legate of Syria,

---

16. Josephus, *Antiquities,* XX, viii, 6. Cf. Acts 21:38.

marched on Jerusalem and laid siege to the city, but for some unaccountable reason he lifted the siege suddenly and retreated in disorder. This unexpected good fortune convinced the Jews that divine aid was on their side and they united their forces for war.

Nero appointed Vespasian as commander of the Roman forces in Judea. Early in A.D. 67 he mustered an army of 60,000 men and proceeded to Jerusalem. In the meantime John of Gischala, a leader of the Zealots, had entered Jerusalem and had plunged the city into civil war. Vespasian, realizing that Jerusalem was torn by internal strife, used the opportunity to conquer Perea, Judea, and Idumea, and was about to resume the siege of the city when he received news of Nero's death. In July of A.D. 69 the legions of the East proclaimed him emperor. Leaving his son Titus in charge of the operations in Judea, he went to Alexandria and thence to Rome, where he arrived in A.D. 70.

Within Jerusalem John of Gischala had been joined by another Zealot, Simon Bar-Giora, and by Eleazer, son of Simon. The three leaders quarreled among themselves, and so their followers fought each other with utter savagery. In the spring of A.D. 70 Titus tightened the siege. Weakened by famine and by the internecine strife, the city fell to the Romans in August, when the walls were breached and the gates were burned. Contrary to Titus' orders, the temple was set on fire; the population was either massacred or sold into slavery; and the city was razed to the ground.

Three more years were required to complete the conquest of the remaining fortresses of Herodium, Machaerus, and Masada. The contest was hopeless, however. For all practical purposes it may be said that the Jewish commonwealth ended with the destruction of the temple.

During the reign of Trajan there were insurrections of the Jews in Egypt and in Cyrene which were crushed relentlessly. The last spark of Jewish independence was extinguished with the revolt of Bar-Cochba in A.D. 135 under Hadrian. Bar-Cochba, "son of the star," was so named because he was regarded by the rabbinate as the "star out of Jacob" (Num. 24:17) prophesied by Balaam. The revolt was caused by Hadrian's law which forbade circumcision and by his order to build a temple of Jupiter on the site of the former temple in Jerusalem. Bar-Cochba was driven from the city and was captured; Jerusalem was made a Roman city which no Jew could enter under pain of death; and the temple of Jupiter was built where formerly sacrifices to Jehovah were offered by His worshipers.

The nation perished politically, but Judaism had not died. In A.D. 90, Jonathan Ben Zakkai, a Jewish teacher, opened at Jamnia a school for the study of the law. With him were associated other teachers, Pharisean by creed, who kept alive the observances of their faith. Although the priesthood disappeared and although the sacrifices were ended, the teachers of the law persisted, substituting good works and study for the offerings that no longer had an altar.

# THE SOCIAL WORLD

## AND

# THE ECONOMIC WORLD

# THE SOCIAL WORLD

Jewish Society

Pagan Society
    The Aristocracy
    The Middle Class
    The Plebs
    The Slaves and the Criminals

Cultural Attainments
    Literature
    Art and Architecture
    Music and Drama
    The Arena
    Languages
    Science
    Schools

Moral Standards

# THE ECONOMIC WORLD

Agriculture
Industry
Finances
Transportation and Travel

# CHAPTER III

# The Social World and
# the Economic World

## THE SOCIAL WORLD

The world of the first century was not unlike the modern world of
the twentieth century. Rich and poor, virtuous men and criminals,
freemen and slaves lived side by side, and the social and economic
conditions that prevailed were similar to those of the present day in
many respects.

### Jewish Society

Both in Judaism and in the pagan world there was a wealthy
aristocracy. In Judaism it was a religious group, consisting chiefly
of the families of the priesthood and of the leading rabbis. The clan
of the Hasmoneans had dominated Palestinian society from the days
of the Maccabees until the time of Herod the Great. During his reign
and during the reigns of his sons the Hasmonean priesthood was in
control, and the glimpses of the hierarchy which appear in the
Gospels show that they were the virtual rulers of Judea. They controlled the business traffic that was connected with the temple, and
they participated in the revenues that were derived from the sale of
animals for sacrifice and from the exchange of money involved in the
temple taxes.

Among the members of the Sanhedrin, which was the high council
of Judaism, were well-to-do men like Nicodemus and Joseph of Arimathea. Probably they were landowners who rented out their farms
and profited by a share of the crops.

The majority of the Palestinian people were poor. Some were
farmers; some were artisans; a few were business men. Slavery was
not widely practiced in Judaism, and probably the vast majority of
the Palestinian Jews were freemen. Some, like the fishermen who

79

became disciples, owned small independent enterprises that supported them fairly well.

Social divisions among the Jews were somewhat restrained by the common obligation which the law imposed upon its followers. If they were all equally responsible to God for obedience to it, they were consequently morally equal in His sight. Although the Jew regarded the wealthy man as blessed especially by God's favor, and as therefore righteous, there was no reason why any man should not by good works merit equal favor. While an aristocracy tends to be self-perpetuating, there was at least the inherent moral equality which kept the Jewish oligarchy from becoming too oppressive.

## Pagan Society

### *The Aristocracy*

In the pagan world of the first century the strata of society were more sharply contrasted. The civil wars of Rome, which had preceded the rise of the principate, had disrupted the entire social life of the empire. The old free landholding populace of Italy had disappeared. Many of the earlier senatorial families had perished in the party struggles, though some had survived. In their places had risen a new aristocracy, the landholders, who controlled public lands by their influence and who bought cheaply the private lands of those whose families were impoverished by war or by the impossibility of making a living from a small farm. The exploitation of the newly conquered provinces opened another avenue of profit, and the businessmen who acted as government contractors and as speculators reaped an enormous harvest. The consequent luxury enervated the aristocracy and discouraged the lower classes, who found that for all their toil they seemed to prosper less as the years rolled along.

### *The Middle Class*

Largely because of the rise of slavery, which was built upon the use of military captives, the middle class was almost crushed out of the empire. Many had been killed in the wars and proscriptions. Many others had been unable to meet the competition of slave labor and had slowly been starved out of their small farms and estates. Gradually they swelled the homeless and foodless mobs which filled the great cities, especially Rome, and they became dependent for their sustenance upon the state. The hungry, idle crowds, who would vote for any candidate whose promises sounded better than those of his competitor, were a dangerous and unpredictable factor in the social life of the empire.

## The Plebs

The plebs, or poor people, were numerous and their condition was pitiful. Many lacked steady employment and were worse off than slaves, who had at least assurance of food and of clothing. The unemployed proletariat were ready to follow any man who would give them a dole to feed their stomachs and amusements to while away their idle hours. They were easy prey for demagoguery of every description.

## The Slaves and the Criminals - *condition was bad.*

Slaves made up a large proportion of the population of the Roman empire. No exact figures are obtainable; but probably less than half of the inhabitants of the Roman world were free men, and only relatively few of them were citizens with full rights. War, debt, and birth recruited the ranks of the slave population at a rapid rate. Not all of them were ignorant. Many, in fact, were physicians, accountants, teachers, and skilled artisans of every kind. Epictetus, the renowned Stoic philosopher, was one of them. They performed most of the work in the great agricultural estates; they acted as household servants and as clerks in business houses, and publishers employed them as copyists. Where modern enterprises operate by machinery, the ancients used cheap labor.

The effect of slavery was debasing. The ownership of slaves made the masters dependent upon the labor and skill of their servitors to the extent that they lost their own ingenuity and ambition. Morality and self-respect were impossible among those whose only law was the will of an arbitrary master. Trickery, flattery, fraud, and fawning obedience were the slave's best tools to obtain what he wanted from his superiors. In many households the children were intrusted to the care of these menials who taught them all of the vices and sly tricks that they knew. Thus the corruption that prevailed among the oppressed classes spread to their overlords.

Undoubtedly there were many instances of masters and mistresses who treated their servitors kindly, as there were many slaves who labored in the bond of friendship rather than in the bond of fear. Some of them were able to amass a bit of property from tips and gifts, with which they purchased their freedom, and some were manumitted by their masters either during the lifetime of the latter or at death. Consequently a steady stream of freedmen poured into the life of the empire, filling with trained workers the ranks of the lower and middle classes which had been depleted by the wars. Many of these freedmen, like Pallas under Claudius, became prominent in the government, and were important in the growth of the bureaucracy.

The institution of slavery is reflected in the New Testament by the frequent use of the term "slave," and by occasional references to the ownership of them. Nowhere in its pages is the institution attacked, nor is it defended. According to Paul's letters to the Asian churches, there were both slaves and slaveholders who were Christians. The slaves were enjoined to obey their masters and the masters were commanded not to be cruel to them. Such was the power of Christian fellowship, however, that the institution of slavery gradually weakened under its impact and finally disappeared.

The restless hordes of the unemployed, the sharpers who made their way to the great cities for the purpose of preying on society, the despairing and the disinherited — all made a fertile ground for the breeding of criminals. To say that crime prevailed in the empire might be unfair, for there were a large number of decent citizens; but in consideration of the unscrupulous and immoral character of so many of the emperors and higher officials, it is not surprising that society at large was permeated with all kinds of evils. The ghastly picture of the heathen world that appears in Romans 1:18 to 32 was not overdrawn. There was no inherent standard in paganism to check the downward moral drift.

## Cultural Attainments

### Literature

Under Augustus came a literary revival in Rome. Vergil, the poet, became the prophet of the new era. His *Aeneid* was an attempt to glorify the Rome of Augustus by showing through the epic adventure of his hero the divine origin and destiny of the empire. In his writings the hope of a golden age to come was also reflected, and at least one of the Eclogues (the Fourth) seems to show that he had some knowledge of the Old Testament. The Augustan age was the golden period of Roman poetry, graced by Horace, who cast Latin poetry in Greek molds, and by Ovid, whose stories of Greek and Roman mythology reveal the contemporary moral attitudes of the Roman people.

Nothing of note was produced between the periods of Augustus and of Nero. Seneca, the Stoic moralist and Nero's tutor, wrote philosophic essays and dramatic tragedy. Petronius, the wealthy social arbiter of Nero's court, composed a novel which is still one of the best sources for understanding the common life of his day.

In the latter third of the first century Pliny the Elder wrote his *Natural History,* one of the first attempts at a scientific account of the natural world. It was encyclopedic in scope and showed a vast amount of research, although it was quite uncritical and inadequate when judged by modern standards. Grammar and rhetoric were treated extensively by Quintilian. Martial, whose spicy epigrams still make pungent reading, was the newspaper columnist of his day.

Under the governments of Nero, of Trajan, and of Hadrian, literature took the turn of self-criticism. Tacitus and Suetonius, the historians, narrated the history of the Caesars in unvarnished language. Tacitus in particular, since he was connected with the old republican aristocracy, was not very friendly toward the emperors. The content of his *Annals* and of his *Histories* shows the feeling against the principate that smoldered under the surface of public opinion. The satirist Juvenal also wrote in the early second century. Like Martial, he was a bitter critic of the manners and morals of his day. Even if it be granted that some of his caricatures are overdrawn, they reveal the prevalent corruption of high Roman society and generally confirm the impression left by his predecessor, Martial.

## Art and Architecture — *good, not actually original* —

Under the emperors of the first century, Rome expanded materially, and new construction was continually going on. Although the Romans were not singularly original in their decorative art, they excelled in producing enduring monuments of utilitarian character. Many of their bridges, aqueducts, theaters, and baths still remain as a witness to the Roman thoroughness in construction. They knew how to use the principle of the arch to good effect and were skilled in building with brick and cement.

In ornamental and memorial art they created a great deal of statuary which generally represented persons rather than abstract ideas. Funerary carvings on tombs and sarcophagi, busts and equestrian statues of the reigning emperors, and historical sculpture such as the Arch of Titus in Rome were common.

## Music and Drama - *rather*

Music and the stage were committed to entertainment of the mob rather than to stimulating the thought of intellectuals. The Roman stage degenerated rapidly and contributed directly to the moral degradation of the people. The farces and mimes of the early empire were coarse and cheap; their plots dealt with the lowest kind of life and their presentation was shameless. The theatrical representations of the first century A.D. were far different from those of the great Greek tragedians such as Aeschylus and Euripides, who were almost as much philosophers and theologians as they were playwrights.

Music of all kinds was familiar in the empire. Stringed instruments and flutes were used chiefly, but brass, wind instruments, and drums and cymbals were employed occasionally. The lyre and the harp were the most popular instruments. Religious rites and processions were generally accompanied by music and the aristocracy entertained guests by dinner music which their slaves provided.

## The Arena

The amphitheater was a more pernicious influence on the Roman public than the stage. The bloody contests between men and beasts or between men and men were promoted by the emperor, or occasionally by aspirants for political office who wished to gain the favor of the crowds. The participants were usually trained gladiators who were slaves, captives of war, condemned criminals, or volunteers who sought fame in the arena as a modern pugilist does. Some of them succeeded in winning favor and fortune for themselves so that they were able to retire to peaceful private life. The majority probably died in the arena. The gladiatorial shows accustomed the audience to the sight of bloodshed, and even whetted their appetite for it. In order to please their patrons, the spectacles became increasingly elaborate and increasingly shocking. If the stage with its coarse mimes and farces schooled the populace in obscenity and lust, the gladiatorial shows glorified brutality.

## Languages

The chief languages of the Roman world were four: Latin, Greek, Aramaic, and Hebrew. Latin was the language of the law courts and of the literature of Rome. As a popular tongue it was spoken mostly in the western Roman world, particularly in North Africa, Spain, Gaul, and Britain, as well as in Italy itself. It was the language of the conquerors and was learned by the subject peoples, who quickly adapted its pronunciation and vocabulary to their own dialects. Greek was the cultural language of the empire, familiar to all educated persons, and was the *lingua franca* of the majority of the populace from Rome eastward. Even in Palestine Greek was currently spoken and was probably used by Jesus and by His disciples whenever they had to deal with Gentiles. Aramaic was the predominant tongue of the Near East. Paul addressed the people of Jerusalem in Aramaic (Acts 22:2) when he made his impromptu defense from the steps of the Castle of Antonia, and some recorded quotations of Jesus indicate that He used it customarily (John 1:42, Mark 7:34, Matt. 27:46). It appears also in the religious phraseology of the early church, such as *Abba* (Rom. 8:15), *Maranatha* (I Cor. 16:22), showing that the earliest believers spoke Aramaic. Classical Hebrew, to which Aramaic was closely related, had been a dead language since the times of Ezra, except among the learned rabbis who made it a medium for theological thought. It was not understood by the rank and file of the people.

The wide use of the first three of these languages is shown by the statement that the inscription on the cross over the head of Jesus was written "in Hebrew [Aramaic], *and* in Latin, *and* in Greek" (John 19:20). Even in Palestine all three were current and were recognized.

Such interchange of language in the center where Christianity originated brought to bear on it the influence of the civilization and literature which these languages represented and gave to Christianity a means for universal expression. Neither Latin nor Hebrew played a large part in the history of the church during the first century, but Aramaic and Greek did. Tradition says that some of the earliest accounts of the words of Jesus were composed in Aramaic, and the fact that the New Testament as a whole was circulated in Greek almost from the time of its origin is too patent to need comment. All of the epistles were composed in Greek, and the Gospels and Acts have survived only in Greek form, even if it should be granted that some Aramaic accounts of the words of Jesus were extant in the middle of the first century.

## Science

The Romans, who dominated the world of the first century, were not interested primarily in mathematical and in scientific pursuits. They were largely content to confine themselves to such elementary processes as were necessary in the measurement of land or in the calculation of

finance. The appliances that they possessed, such as ships for naviga
tion and engines of war, had all been invented by the Greeks, from
whom they borrowed.

Certain fields of learning had already been explored by the time
of Christ. Geometry, literally the science of measuring land, had begun
with the Babylonians and with the Egyptians, and was brought to the
Greek world by Thales of Miletus, if tradition be correct. Euclid of
Alexandria (c. 300 B.C.) developed plane geometry so completely that
his propositions have been studied with little change to the modern
day.

Mechanics and physics had been investigated by Archimedes of
Syracuse (287 to 212 B.C.), who developed the theory of the lever and
discovered the principle of estimating the composition of bodies by the
relation of their weight to the weight of the volume of water that they
displaced. He found the formula for the ratio of the circumference of
a circle to its diameter, and in doing so he discovered the basic approach
to calculus. Several of his numerous mechanical devices were used in
the wars of Syracuse against Rome.

Astronomy made great advances in the pre-Christian world. The
sphericity of the earth and its revolution on its own axis were known
to some Greek scientists in the fourth century B.C. Hipparchus
(c. 160 B.C.) invented both plane and spherical trigonometry and cal
culated the size of the moon and its distance from the earth. The pre
dominant theory of the motion of the earth and of the planets was not
that all revolved about the sun, but that the planets revolved around
the earth. Eratosthenes of Alexandria (273 to 192 B.C.) calculated
the circumference of the earth to a surprising degree of accuracy in
spite of his crude instruments.

The science which owed its greatest advance to the period including
the first century was geography. Ptolemy of Alexandria (A.D. 127 to
151) wrote a work on astronomy which remained the standard until
the rise of the Copernican theory in modern times. He created maps
of the world which included all regions known at that time.

Medicine flourished in various centers of the world. The university
of Tarsus had an affiliated hospital in the temple of Aesculapius, where
the sick went to be healed. A school of Greek medicine was begun
in Rome during the reign of Augustus. Celsus, a physician, who lived
in the reign of Tiberius, wrote a treatise on surgery which showed
extensive knowledge of the technique of operating. Another doctor,
Dioscorides, wrote a description of some six hundred plants and their
medical uses. Galen (A.D. 129 to 200) reduced Greek medical knowl-

dge to a system. He carried on biological experiments and made otes of his discoveries. Although many of his conclusions were rroneous, he exercised a powerful influence on medical science down ɔ the close of the Middle Ages.

Such scientific knowledge as the Romans did possess showed little riginality or intellectual curiosity. Pliny's *Naturalis Historia* was an ncyclopedia of the learning of his day in thirty-seven volumes. It overed every subject from agriculture to zoology. Pliny drew heavily n other writers as well as on his own observations. He may be re-arded as an honest witness to the culture of his times, but he failed ɔ distinguish between fact and fable, so that his conclusions were not lways reliable.

The Hebrews were not particularly interested in speculative science. n the first century none of them were renowned for proficiency in 1athematics or in the natural sciences. The church, which sprang from he matrix of Judaism, did not concern itself with science as such, for ts main interests were in the ethical and religious fields. On the other 1and, the revelation on which the church based its teaching was not nherently opposed to science. Paul, speaking of God, says that "the nvisible things of him since the creation of the world are clearly seen, •eing perceived through the things that are made, *even* his everlasting •ower and divinity . . ." (Rom. 1:20). There is no conflict between he theological investigation of God's revelation through His Spirit nd the scientific investigation of His revelation through creation. The Jew Testament is not primarily a book of science, nor was it written •y men whose training could be called scientific in the full modern ense of the term, but it is not anti-scientific either in its statements or n its spirit.

## *chools*

The modern system of free compulsory education for all children in he state under the age of sixteen was unknown in the Roman empire. Jot until the time of Vespasian did the rulers take any active interest n supporting public education. The training of the child in the average Roman household began with the *paidagogos,* a slave who was charged vith the responsibility of teaching the child his first lessons and of onducting him to and from one of the private schools in the city where ιe lived. Up to the time of his acknowledgment as a young man with .dult responsibilities, the Roman boy was under the superintendence ɔf his tutor.

The schools themselves were rather dreary affairs, held in the public alcoves or halls where the markets and the shops were located. School masters knew and practiced little of educational psychology, but taught by endless repetition, punctuated with corporal punishment. With rare exceptions these schoolrooms were bare, chilly, unattractive halls devoid of the blackboards, charts, decorations, and other equipment regarded as essential to the modern school.

The curriculum was essentially practical. Reading, writing, and arithmetic were the basic subjects of the elementary curriculum. As the pupil progressed, he studied the Greek and Latin poets, and memorized long passages which he had to recite with the proper expression. Later he might learn the elements of oratory: how to compose a speech and how to deliver it convincingly. Sometimes the wealthier youth went abroad to study in the Greek universities of Athens, Rhodes, Tarsus, or Alexandria, or they might attend the lectures of traveling philosophers.

The education of the Jewish boy followed somewhat the same pattern except that his curriculum was more restricted. He learned to read and to write from the Old Testament. Among the Jews of the Dispersion the synagogue schools doubtless used both Greek and Hebrew. He learned also the traditions of the fathers and was schooled in the ritual of Judaism. In some instances he was permitted to read Gentile literature. If he aspired to become a scholar, he usually went to study with some great rabbi, as Paul received instruction at the feet of Gamaliel according to the strict manner of the law of his fathers (Act 22:3).

No adequate data exists for drawing conclusions concerning the state of education in every corner of the empire. Apparently each municipality of people within its bounds was responsible for its own educational program. The prevalence of writing, however, even in the poorest parts of Egypt as attested by the papyri, shows that a fair degree of literacy was attained by the people of the first century and that reading and writing were practiced by the lower classes. Probably the average attainment of the early empire would compare very favorably with that of the Middle Ages, or even with some parts of Europe in the eighteenth century of the present era.

## Moral Standards

The moral condition of the Roman empire as a whole may not have been as black as some historians have painted it. As usual the virtuous people went unnoticed because of their virtue and the criminals were singled out for attention. Only crime was "news." Nevertheless, all indications in the history, literature, drama, and art that have survived point to a standard of morality generally lower than our own. The tremendous indictment of mankind in Romans 1:18 to 3:20 was originally directed against the empire, and all available witness supports its accuracy.

Moral declension does not mean that no comparatively decent people existed, or that virtue was completely stifled. It does mean that the prevailing trend in society verged downward to indulgence and to lawlessness. Human life was cheap and murder was frequent. Divorce was easy to obtain and was generally accepted in "society." The exposure of unwanted infants was a common practice, as illustrated in the well-known letter of Hilarion to his wife, Alis: "Should you bear a child, if it is a boy, let it live; if it is a girl, expose it."[1] Superstition and trickery of every kind flourished.

There were moralists like Seneca, Nero's tutor, who in their writings advocated lofty ideals and spoke words of wisdom; but their protestations made little impact upon the entrenched evils of their day. They imparted to their readers no spiritual dynamic that could make their precepts effective, and, as in the case of Seneca, they did not exemplify their own counsel. Paganism was devoid of any power to lift it above itself, and the growing consciousness of its own impotence brought upon it a pessimism and a depression that it could not escape. Corruption in politics, debauchery in pleasure, fraud in business, deceit and superstition in religion made life in Rome depressing for the many and unendurable for the few.

## THE ECONOMIC WORLD

The Christians of the first century, like the Christians of today, had to earn their living in a workaday world. The propagation and practice of their faith was affected by prevailing economic conditions much as Christianity is affected today. Agriculture, industry, finance, transportation and travel — all had a bearing upon the spread of the gospel.

### Agriculture

During the time of Christ and the early church the Roman empire occupied the lands surrounding the Mediterranean basin. Judging by the ruins of towns that are still extant, the coastal territories were more

---

1. *P. Oxy.* 744, dated B.C. 1. "Expose" meant to abandon the child to die.

fertile than they are today. North Africa, which is now semi-arid or else largely desert, contained immense farms on which cattle grazed or which grew fruits and vegetables. In Italy were large estates which the owners rented out to tenant farmers and sharecroppers, where almost all kinds of fruits and grains could be grown. In the western provinces of Britain, Gaul, and Germany, agriculture flourished, and some of the farms were irrigated by government projects established by Augustus.

## Industry — *mainly domestified*

Manufacturing never was so important in ancient times as it is today, for machine tools were practically unknown, and goods had to be produced by human labor. In many cases the factories were private enterprises employing slaves. Small shops were the rule rather than the exception. Certain types of goods were produced in particular localities: copper vessels were manufactured in Campania; linens and paper came from Egypt; the best quality of earthenware originated in north Italy. Small wares, furniture, and household goods were generally produced locally, in the same way that similar commodities were supplied in the early American colonies by the skill and ingenuity of the town craftsmen such as the blacksmith and the carpenter. Probably every small village in the empire had its workmen who provided for the needs of their fellow-townsmen. Jesus Himself was a carpenter (Mark 6:3), and Saul of Tarsus worked occasionally at the tentmaker's trade (Acts 18:3).

Luxury goods were imported. Gold, ivory, and rare woods came from Africa and from the East; pearls and jewels were found in India; furs came from central Asia and Russia, and amber came from the far north. Caravans were cumbersome and were subject to attack by robbers. Although the empire had a large number of good roads, vehicular transportation was dependent upon animals for motive power, so that traffic was costly and slow. Shipping was carried on only by navigable rivers and on the ocean during the summer months. Mass production of cheap goods was practically impossible, for neither machinery nor transportation was available.

## Finance

The standard coins in the empire were the *denarius* and the gold *aureus*, or pound. One pound was worth forty *denarii*. The *denarius* is mentioned several times in the New Testament, where it is variously translated "penny" or "shilling." Its actual monetary value was about seventeen cents of United States money, although its purchasing power was considerably greater. It was the ordinary day's wage for a laboring man in the East (Matt. 20:2). Many of the cities of the empire had the right to mint their own coinage, and the coins of the conquered nations were not retired from circulation, so that many various kinds of money were used concurrently within the realm. Money-changers did a thriving business in dealing with travelers, as the episode of Jesus' cleansing of the temple showed (Matt. 21:12).

Banking was generally practiced, although there was not the intricate system of finance that is known to the modern world. The banks were not subsidized by the state, but consisted usually of private companies. Sometimes mercantile firms with foreign connections carried on negotiations for their customers. Borrowing, lending, discounting of notes, and foreign exchange were undertaken, and letters of credit were issued. Funds were often supplied to the banks by private individuals, whereas the bank acted only as agent. The normal rate of interest varied from four to twelve per cent, though individual brokers often charged more. Brutus on one occasion paid as high as forty-eight per cent on a loan. The parables of the talents (Matt. 25:15) and of the pounds (Luke 19:13) show that money lending was a common means of enlarging one's fortune.

## Transportation and Travel

The rule of Rome over the provinces was greatly facilitated by its excellent system of roads, which, until the recent era of the automobile, were the best that the world had ever seen. The Romans built their roads as straight as possible, making cuts through hills and using viaducts to bridge valleys and streams. In building their highways they excavated the top soil and filled the roadbed with three different layers of road material, crowning the center to throw off water, and then paving the top with stone. The roads were seldom more than fifteen feet wide, but they were smooth and durable. Some of them are in use to the present day.

Along these roads which stretched in every direction from Rome to the frontiers moved the armies and the caravans of commerce. The imperial post carried the government dispatches, whereas private businesses had their own couriers.

Several of these roads were famous in antiquity. The Appian Way was the main line of communication between Rome and the south of

THE ROMAN ROADS

Italy. It ran from Rome through Capua to Brundisium. From Brundisium a traveler could sail eastward to Dyrrhachium on the western side of Illyricum, from which the Egnatian highway crossed Illyricum and Macedonia to Thessalonica, and thence to Byzantium, now Constantinople. Another route led from Troas down to Ephesus on the western coast of Asia Minor, and then eastward through Laodicea and Colosse to Antioch of Pisidia, and thence southward through Iconium and Derbe to the pass of the Cilician Gates, through which it went on to Tarsus and to Syrian Antioch. From Antioch roads led eastward to the Euphrates, where they tapped the trade routes to India.

The Via Flaminia ran northward from Rome to Ariminum and thence to Mediolanum. From Mediolanum several roads branched out westward to Gaul, Germany, Rhaetia, and Noricum. The Via Claudia Augusta, begun in 15 B.C. and completed by Claudius, connected Verona with the Danube. Roads along the Danube connected Verona with Byzantium.

To the west, the Via Aurelia ran from Rome to Genoa, from which the Via Domitia communicated with Massilia (Marseilles). From Massilia the Via Augusta crossed the Pyrenees to Tarraco, and thence southward to the Sucro River, and through Corduba and Hispalis to Gades in Spain.

In Gaul and in Britain there were numerous shorter roads that connected the chief towns with each other.

The vehicles on these roads varied according to the wealth of their owners. Some people trudged the weary miles on foot. Some rode on donkeys. The more well-to-do afforded horses or mules, and officials or magnates might travel in light carriages. Inns were located at convenient intervals, so that the travelers could stop for meals and shelter. Few of the inns were luxurious, and probably still fewer were really clean. Middle and upper class travelers usually counted on the hospitality of their friends, so that they were not at the mercy of avaricious landlords and their conscienceless servants.

Most of the commercial transportation was by water rather than by land. The Mediterranean Sea abounded in good ports which were busy all through the season for navigation. Alexandria was the chief port, since it was the outlet for the grain crop of Egypt.

The Alexandrian merchant ships were the largest and finest of the day. Some of them were more than two hundred feet in length. They were propelled by sails and carried enough oars so that the crew could maneuver the ship in an emergency. One of the largest ships of which there is any record carried twelve hundred passengers in addition to its cargo. Most of the Alexandrian ships were engaged in the corn trade which supplied Rome with grain. Under Claudius, their upkeep was subsidized by the government in order to insure a regular delivery of grain for the needs of the populace. St. Paul, at the time of his shipwreck, was aboard an Alexandrian ship (Acts 27:6), and after his rescue at Malta sailed for Italy in another (Acts 28:11) named "The Two Brothers."

Warships were lighter and faster than merchantmen, and were generally propelled by oars pulled by galley slaves. Ships with two, three, and five banks of oars were not at all uncommon, while some had even ten banks. Sails were sometimes used in cruising. In battle, where the outcome depended on the action of the ships, propulsion by hand became necessary for safe and accurate control.

On the inland rivers and canals barges were used, chiefly for carrying cargoes of freight. Apparently they were not greatly patronized by passenger trade. No mention of such travel appears in the New Testament.

# THE RELIGIOUS WORLD

# THE RELIGIOUS WORLD

The Graeco-Roman Pantheon

Emperor Worship

The Mystery Religions

The Worship of the Occult

The Philosophies
  Platonism
  Gnosticism
  Neo-Platonism
  Epicureanism
  Stoicism
  Cynicism
  Scepticism
  Evaluation of Philosophies

# CHAPTER IV

# The Religious World

Christianity did not begin its growth in a religious vacuum in which it found men blankly waiting for something to believe. On the contrary, the new faith in Christ had to fight its way against entrenched religious beliefs that had been in existence for centuries. Many had degenerated into feeble superstitions and meaningless rituals; others were relatively new and vigorous. In general there were five distinct types.

## The Graeco-Roman Pantheon

The primitive religion of Rome in the early days of the republic was animism. Each small farmer worshiped the gods of his own farm and fireside, which personified for him the forces with which he had to deal in living his daily life. Gods of the forest and field, gods of the sky and stream, gods of the sowing and of the harvest — all received his worship in their proper places and at their proper seasons. Some vestiges of local feasts and rites survive to this present day among the peasants of Italy and of Greece. It is possible that the festivities of the Roman Saturnalia which celebrated the turning of the year at the winter solstice are still echoed in the Christian observance of Christmas.

With the growth of the military state and the consequent contacts with Greek civilization came a fusion of deities under the dominating influence of the Greek pantheon. Jupiter, the god of the sky, was identified with the Greek Zeus; Juno, his wife, with Hera; Neptune, the god of the sea, with Poseidon; Pluto, the god of the underworld, with Hades, and so on. The entire list of Homeric deities was assimilated to their Roman counterparts. Under Augustus new temples were erected and new priesthoods were founded. There were many worshipers who followed the old gods, whether Roman or Greek, and who paid them homage.

The worship of the Greek pantheon, however, had begun to decline by the time of Christ. The gross immoralities and the petty squabbles of these deities, who were only magnified men and women, exposed them to the ridicule of the satirists and to the scorn of the philosophers. Plato, more than three centuries before Christ, had said that the tales of the gods should be excluded from the ideal state, since they would tend to corrupt youth by their evil example.[1] The philosophic cults had no place for the gods in their scheme of things and openly made fun of them. Undoubtedly there were many devout worshipers of the gods, but their numbers were diminishing rather than increasing.

Another factor tended to destroy the older attitude of reverence toward the gods. Up to this time they had not been uniformly worshiped in all cities, but each city or city-state had one of them as a patron. Worship was semi-political; a man was a worshiper of Zeus or of Hera or of Artemis because he happened to live in a town over which that particular deity presided. When the city-states capitulated to the military might of Rome, the question would naturally be asked, "Why did not the local deity protect his people?" The vanquished peoples tended to abandon faith in gods who were either too weak or too fickle to aid them.

The public observance of religious rites survived well beyond the first century. An outstanding example in the New Testament of such a cult is the worship of Artemis of Ephesus, the image which reputedly had fallen from heaven (Acts 19:27, 35). The fanatical devotion which was given to a local goddess is well illustrated by the shrieking mob who crowded the amphitheater and shouted aloud, "Great *is* Diana [Artemis] of the Ephesians" (Acts 19:34). *blasphemy!*

## Emperor Worship

Although the worship of local deities persisted, the growing cosmopolitan consciousness in the empire prepared the way for a new type of religion, the worship of the state. For many years the Hellenistic kingdoms of the Seleucidae and the Ptolemies had exalted their kings to the position of deity and had applied to them such titles as Lord (*Kyrios*), Savior (*Soter*), or Manifest Deity (*Epiphanes*). The concentration of the executive functions of the Roman state in the person of one man had vested him with powers unprecedented in the history of the world. The fact that he was able to utilize those powers for the good of the empire created the feeling that there must be something divine in him.

---

1. Plato: *Republic* II, 376; III, 390.

The imperial cult was not established arbitrarily. It grew gradually out of the increasing ascription of superhuman honors to the emperor and out of the desire to centralize the allegiance of the people in him. Julius Caesar was after his death called *Divus Julius*. From Augustus' time each of the emperors was deified at his death by vote of the Senate, although some of them did not take the honor very seriously. Caligula ordered that his statue should be set up in the temple at Jerusalem, but since he was generally considered to be insane, his action cannot be regarded as representative of the general imperial policy. Not until the time of Domitian at the close of the first century did a reigning emperor attempt to compel his subjects to worship him.

The refusal of all Christians to participate in such worship precipitated violent persecution, for the Christians consistently objected to worshiping a human being. The polytheistic Romans, who could always add one more god to their list of deities, looked upon their refusal as a lack of proper recognition for the emperor and as a distinctly unpatriotic attitude. Between these two viewpoints there could be no reconciliation. The Christian attitude on this question of the worship of the state, or of its head, is reflected in the Apocalypse, which reveals unmistakably the hostility between the claims of Christ and the claims of the emperor.

There can be no doubt, however, that emperor worship had great value for the state. It unified patriotism and worship and made the support of the state a religious duty. It was the totalitarianism of the first century.

## The Mystery Religions

Neither the state religion nor the emperor worship proved completely satisfying. Both were observed by ritual sacrifices; both were maintained collectively rather than individually; both sought protection by deity rather than fellowship with deity; and neither offered any personal solace or strength for times of stress and trouble. Men were seeking a more personal faith that would bring them into immediate contact with deity, and they were ready for any sort of experience that would promise them that contact.

The mystery religions fulfilled that desire. They were mostly of eastern origin, though the Eleusinian mysteries had been celebrated in Greece for a long time. The cult of Cybele, the Great Mother, came from Asia; that of Isis and Osiris or Serapis, from Egypt; Mithraism originated in Persia. While all of them differed from each other in origin and in detail, all were alike in certain broad characteristics. Each was centered about a god who had died and who was resuscitated. Each had a ritual of formulas and lustrations, of symbol and of secret dramatic representations of the experience of the god, by which the initiate was inducted into that experience, and so was presumably rendered a candidate for immortality. The procedure of these initiations was somewhat similar to that of modern secret societies. Each religion maintained a brotherhood in which slave and master, rich and poor, high and low met on the same footing.

The mystery religions satisfied the desire for personal immortality and for social equality. They offered an outlet for emotion in religion as the state religion seldom did and they made religious experience emphatically personal. Nothing is said of them directly in the New Testament, but it is thought that Paul may have used their vocabulary on occasion, and that the "worship of angels" mentioned in Colossians (2:18, 19) is a reflection of an attempted fusion of some eclectic philosophic cult with Christianity at Colosse.

## The Worship of the Occult

Akin in many ways to the mystery religions was the occultism of the day, the superstitious observances and regard of the masses for the powers of the universe which they could not understand but which they could vaguely feel. For them the entire world was peopled with spirits and demons who could be invoked or commanded to do one's bidding if only one knew the correct rite or formula to use. Allusions in contemporary literature and fragments from the papyri bear witness to the widespread belief in magic that prevailed throughout the Roman domain. Jew and Gentile alike shared these superstitious beliefs; in fact, the Jews were often more interested in magic than were the Gentiles.

Reliance on magic began in early times. Augury or foretelling the future by the examination of the entrails of slaughtered animals or by observing the flight of birds had been practiced by the Romans since the founding of Rome. The Greeks were familiar with the oracles where the gods were supposed to communicate their will to men through priests or priestesses whom they possessed. The Babylonian captivity brought many Jews into contact with the mystic lore of the East, and they became professional exorcists and necromancers. The conquests of Alexander established contacts with the Persians, from whom the mysticism of the East flowed back into the West. Under

Tiberius the mania for horoscopes reached its peak, but magic was popular down through the succeeding centuries, as the papyri show.

Jewish interest in magic appears in the New Testament. The Pharisees cast out demons, and sorcerers are mentioned in Acts as rivals of the preachers of the Gospel (Acts 8:9-24, 13:6-11). The pagan magic was recognized as hostile to Christianity by the Ephesian Christians, who burned their books of spells in a bonfire that cost fifty thousand pieces of silver (Acts 19:19). The biblical attitude toward occult worship, however, was invariably hostile. Although the reality of demonic forces was recognized, commerce with them was strictly forbidden both in the Old and in the New Testaments (Deut. 18:10-12, 20; Micah 5:12; I Cor. 10:20, 21).

Specimens of magical formulas that were used to control the spirits or to bring good luck appear in the papyri. One of these, an excerpt from the great Paris magical papyrus of the third century, will show the curious combination of pagan, Jewish, and Christian phraseology which was used as a charm for exorcising a demon:

> A notable spell for driving out demons. Invocation to be uttered over the head [of the possessed one]. Place before him branches of olive, and standing behind him say: Hail, spirit of Abraham; hail, spirit of Isaac; hail, spirit of Jacob. Jesus the Christ, the holy one, the spirit [here follow a series of apparently meaningless words] drive forth the demon from the man, until the unclean demon of Satan shall flee before thee. I adjure thee, O demon, whoever thou art, by the God Sabarbarbathioth Sabarbarbathiuth Sabarbarbathoneth Sabarbarbaphai. Come forth, O demon, whoever thou art, and depart from so and so at once, at once, now! Come forth, O demon, for I shall chain thee with adamantine chains not to be loosed, and I shall give you over to black chaos in utter destruction.[2]

The foregoing formula illustrates both the respect of the pagan world for the power of the gospel of Christ and also its misconception of that gospel. Had there been no real power in Christianity against the demonic influences of paganism, the names of Abraham, Isaac, Jacob, and Jesus would never have been used at all. This misconception lay in taking for granted that these terms made just one more magical charm to be used at the convenience of the exorcist. The user of this formula was repeating the error of Simon Magus, who thought that the power of God could be bought with money. Such a mixture of

---

2. George Milligan: *Selections from the Greek Papyri* (Cambridge: The University Press, 1910), pp. 112-114.

faith and superstition was by no means uncommon among a people who were intensely religious in nature, but who had no access to regular teaching or to a written copy of the Scriptures.

Astrology was also popular in the empire during the first century. It had originated in Babylonia, where the clear night skies afforded full opportunity for unobstructed vision of the stars and of the planets. Because the Babylonian priests had regarded the planets as emblematic of their gods, they had kept a careful record of their movements. The order of the universe impressed them and they sought to connect it with the course of human life. Through the conquests of Alexander which made contacts between the Eastern and Western worlds, astrological lore became known to the Greeks. Through them and through the Eastern soothsayers who went westward to seek their fortunes, astrology was introduced into the Roman empire.

The theory of astrology was based upon the assumption that the sovereign powers of the world who controlled the planets and human life worked simultaneously in both, and so often presaged the careers of men by the courses of the planets under which they were born. In order to find what the celestial bodies had to say, the path of the sun and of the planets through the heavens was divided into the twelve signs of the zodiac, each of which was marked by a special constellation. By knowing the exact time of the birth of a person, one could ascertain under which sign he was born, and one could calculate the positions of the various planets at that moment. From their positions, their potential influence on his career could be determined, and his future could be predicted, or he could be warned what to expect and what to avoid. The tabulation of these data was called a horoscope.

With the rise of the Copernican system of astronomy which made the sun the center of the solar system rather than the earth, astrology waned in importance. In the time of Christ, however, it commanded considerable attention not only from the lower classes, but also from the aristocracy. Augustus employed it on occasion and Tiberius resorted to it regularly. Never did it penetrate Christianity, for the Christians repudiated it utterly.

## The Philosophies

When religion degenerates into empty ritualism or into ignorant superstition, thoughtful men may abandon it altogether because they feel that it has no real satisfaction to offer them. They cannot, however, ignore the necessity of finding some rational answer to the problems which the world poses for them. The mysteries of the universe call for explanation unless one is content to be such a dolt that he never is disturbed by them.

Philosophy is the attempt to correlate all existing knowledge about the universe into systematic form and to integrate human experience with it. Philosophies have been crude, or naive, or subtle, or profound. Some of them have acknowledged the existence of a supreme power or a personal deity. Others have been frankly materialistic and have dismissed the concept of gods as either ridiculous or as unnecessary. In any case, philosophy never depended upon a revelation from God. It has always assumed the potential adequacy of man to understand his own world and to decide his own fate. The knowledge by which decisions are to be determined will be derived from individual or communal experience. The formulation of knowledge into a coherent system should be governed by the rules of logic which man has devised. Through the increasing scope of his observation and through the advancing perfection of his logic man should be able at last to attain full comprehension of the mysteries of which he is a part.

To achieve this end various systems of philosophy were created. Insofar as they reflect basic attitudes toward life, they still persist to the present day, though perhaps not under their original titles. All of these were founded on premises different from basic Christian principles. Although many of them possessed features which resembled those of Christianity, and although the vocabulary and even some usages of these competing faiths later were absorbed into the thought of the church, they can generally be regarded as opposing forces rather than as the material out of which Christianity was formed. An elementary understanding of them is essential to a clear comprehension of the intellectual and religious environment of the first century.

## Platonism — *The realistic in the World of idea.*

Platonism derived its name from Plato, the great Athenian philosopher and founder of the Academy, who lived in the fourth century before Christ. He was the friend and pupil of Socrates. From his master he inherited an inquiring mind and a habit of thinking in abstract concepts. The world, he taught, consisted of an infinite number of particular things, each of which is a more or less imperfect copy of a real idea. For instance, there are many kinds of chairs, but no one of them could be the chair from which all other chairs are derived. The real chair, then, is not the one that is made of wood, but is the ideal chair of which the wooden one is a copy.

The real world, then, is the world of ideas of which the material world is only a shadow. These ideas are organized into a system, at the head of which is the idea of the Good. Plato never seemed to personalize the idea of the Good, nor did he identify it with the Demiurge, or Creator, who produced the material world. He did regard the ideas as having objective existence; in fact, they were the only real existence, of which the present world is a feeble and garbled reflection.

Such a concept of the world led inevitably to dualism. If the real world is the unseen realm of ideas, and if the changing cosmos in which man lives is only transitory, his quest will be to escape from the unreal to the real. Reflection, meditation, and even asceticism will open the way to deliverance. Knowledge is salvation; sin is ignorance. By seeking the Highest Good, the End, the Supreme Idea, man may liberate himself from the enslaving material world and may rise to a comprehension of the real world.

Platonism was too abstract to gain the attention and thought of the common man. It is not mentioned directly in the New Testament as one of the philosophies that Christianity encountered. Its dualism, however, was reflected by Gnosticism, which may have taken its rise in the first century, and by Neo-Platonism, which was sponsored by Plotinus in the third century.

### Gnosticism — *Salvation by Knowledge*

Gnosticism, as its name implies, (derived from the Greek *gnosis,* knowledge) was a system which promised salvation by knowledge. God, said the Gnostics, was too great and too holy to have created the material world with all of its baseness and corruption. The Gnostics held that from the supreme Deity had proceeded a series of successive emanations, each one a little inferior to the one from which it sprang, until finally the last of these emanations, or "aeons," as they were called, created the world. Matter was thus equated with evil. If man wished to obtain salvation, he could do so by renouncing the material world and by seeking the invisible world. Two contradictory ethical conclusions arose from the argument. The first was asceticism, which contended that since the body was material, it was evil, and should therefore be kept under strict control. Its appetites should be curbed and its impulses should be disregarded and suppressed. The other conclusion was drawn from the assumption that the spirit was real and that the body was unreal. If the body were only temporary, its acts were inconsequential. Full gratification of its desires would thus have no effect on the ultimate salvation of the spirit, which alone would survive.

There is a possibility that this teaching promoted the heresy to which Paul alludes in Colossians, where he warns his readers to "take heed lest there shall be any one that maketh spoil of you through his philosophy and vain deceit, after the tradition of men, after the rudiments of the world, and not after Christ" (Col. 2:8). Apparently this heresy denied the fulness of the Godhead in Christ and perhaps made Him one of the lesser emanations or manifestations of God. Furthermore, the asceticism which certain forms of Gnosticism promoted may be echoed in the attitude of "Handle not, nor taste, nor touch" (Col. 2:21) which Paul so roundly condemned. Absolute identification of this error with Gnosticism is not possible, but there are similarities.

## Neo-Platonism

The principles of Plato were adopted by Plotinus (A.D. 204 to 269) of Lycopolis in Egypt, who taught philosophy in Rome for twenty-five years. Plotinus was indebted for his training to Ammonius Saccas of Alexandria who had been a Christian but who had returned to heathenism. He was also strongly influenced by Persian ideas of dualism which he had encountered while serving in a Roman military expedition.

Neo-Platonism was distinctly a religious philosophy based on the Platonic dualism of the universal ideal and the particular thing, and on the Persian dualism of light and darkness. In Neo-Platonism the spirit was considered to be inevitably good and the body was inherently evil. Salvation consisted in eliminating completely all bodily desires as one gradually retreated from the life dependent on sensation and moved toward the life of the spirit, which would finally be achieved at death. Then the body's evil influence would cease and the true spiritual life would blossom forth.

Neo-Platonism went beyond Platonism by teaching that the attainment of spiritual life would not be reached by intellectual effort but by a mystical absorption into the Infinite. Since no reasoning can compass God, only feeling can establish communication with Him.

In the dualistic thinking of Gnosticism and of Neo-Platonism there is a great gulf fixed between reality and matter, not only in the metaphysical sense that the two are irreconcilable in essence, but also in the ethical sense that the one is good and that the other is evil. There is consequently no room in either for the Christian doctrine of the incarnation. Consistent Neo-Platonists would regard the union of God and man, deity and flesh, as simply unthinkable. The atonement would be unnecessary, since no act which took place in the material world could leave any effect upon the real world of spirit. The resurrection of the body would be a hideous mistake, since it would only perpetuate the evil of material existence. Julian, "the Apostate," Christianity's last imperial opponent, was a Neo-Platonist.

### Epicureanism

Epicureanism was named for Epicurus, the son of an Athenian, who studied at Athens and who founded his own school about 306 B.C. His teaching was best represented in the works of his pupil, Lucretius, the materialistic Roman philosopher and poet of the pre-Christian century. The world, he taught, began in a shower of atoms, some of which, by pure chance, moved a trifle obliquely and collided with others. These collisions produced other collisions, until finally the ensuing movement brought into being the present universe. The cosmology of Epicureanism is similar to that of modern materialistic evolution.

In such a world of chance there could be neither purpose nor design. There could not be, therefore, any final or absolute good. The highest possible good, Epicurus said, was pleasure, which he defined as the absence of pain. Contrary to the popular conception of Epicureanism, both then and now, it did not advocate sensuality, but rather it urged the choice of those enjoyments which would give the longest and fullest satisfaction to the individual. If abstinence from some indulgences would bring greater ultimate satisfaction than the indulgences themselves, abstinence was recommended. Epicureanism did not advocate dissipation, but it offered no check to selfishness.

Epicureanism was essentially anti-religious. If the world originated with matter and chance, no creative power was necessary. If chance dominates the outcome of cosmic affairs, there is no room for a directive, purposeful Mind. The Epicureans, to be sure, did speak of the gods, and did not categorically deny their existence; but the gods as they pictured them were confined to a distant haven of bliss where they enjoyed their own society and had no interest in the trivial affairs of men. Epicureanism at best was deistic and in effect was atheistic, for a god who is inaccessible or uninterested in human affairs might as well not exist at all.

As a philosophy Epicureanism was quite popular because it did not indulge in much abstract reasoning. It appealed to emotional considerations, for it supplied a philosophic justification for doing what most people do anyway — make pleasure the chief goal of life. It brushed aside all thought of sin or of accountability at a final judgment, because it predicated neither purpose nor terminus for the present world-process. There was no recognition of immortality, for a body composed only of atoms did not survive the present life. In consideration of the main tenets of Epicureanism, it is small wonder that the Athenians laughed at Paul's address at Areopagus when he preached "Jesus and the resurrection" (Acts 17:18, 32).

## Stoicism

Coupled with Epicureanism in the foregoing New Testament passage was Stoicism. Stoicism was founded by Zeno (340 to 265 B.C.), a native of Cyprus, and possibly of Semitic descent. Zeno did not recognize a personal God, but he taught that the universe is controlled by an Absolute Reason, or divine will immanent in it and pervading it thoroughly. The world-process is thus governed not by chance but by a progressive purpose.

Conformity to reason, then, becomes the highest good. Personal feeling is immaterial or even harmful since it tends to unbalance the rational solution of human problems. Perfect self-control, unmoved by sentimental considerations, was the goal of the Stoic. The resulting attitude has given the chief meaning to the modern use of the term.

Because the Stoics believed that nature was as it should be and that whatever came to pass was regulated by Providence, there was no room for altering the process or for staying its inexorable course. The universe was to be accepted, not to be changed. This fatalistic attitude inculcated self-restraint and consequently fostered a fairly high type of morality. It appealed to the rigid, legal Roman mind, and many of the better Roman statesmen, such as Cicero, adhered to its tenets.

The Stoic creed, however virtuous, was not Christianity. In it was no allowance for free will or for the real existence of evil. All apparent evils were for the Stoic only parts of a larger good. Such an attitude would exclude any idea of reform or of change in the existing order of things. The individual was obligated to act virtuously himself and to conform to the highest reason that he knew, but he was under no obligation to seek to change the common lot of men nor to shield them from adversities.

No personal dealing with God was possible to the Stoic. If nature dealt impartially with all men, it would not play favorites with any.

Furthermore, the idea of personal relation with universal reason or with the cosmic process would seem about as incongruous as showing affection for the law of gravitation. God, according to the Stoic, took no personal interest in the affairs of men because He was not personal. The entire concept of the Christian gospel, in which God had countered evil by sending His Son into the world to die for men, would be utterly ridiculous to the Stoic. Although much of the Stoic ethic was commendable, and although in some points it resembled the highest standards of Christian ethics, the two systems in their presuppositions and in their practice were leagues apart.

One or two other systems deserve notice, although they were less popular and influential than those heretofore mentioned.

### Cynicism

Cynicism, like Platonism, grew out of Socratic teaching. Since Socrates taught that the man with simple needs can usually survive under conditions which would frustrate completely one who had elaborate wants, the Cynics contended that the height of virtue would be to have no wants at all. In order to be independent of all desire they sought to abolish desire. They abandoned all standards and conventions and became complete individualists. Often the Cynics were purposely scurrilous and indecent in language and in behavior simply for the purpose of demonstrating that they were "different." Socrates' criticism of Antisthenes, the founder of the Cynic sect, was probably the most penetrating analysis of the whole movement that has ever been given. "I can see your pride," he said, "through the holes in your cloak."

### Scepticism

Pyrrho of Elis (365 to 295 B.C.) was the first of the Sceptics. Briefly, their argument was as follows: If knowledge rests upon experience, there can be no final standard, since the experience of each man differs from that of all his fellows. Customs acceptable in one country are regarded as reprehensible in another. Impressions of the same objects will vary with the time and with the conditions where they are observed. All terms of judgment are relative: a weight that is light to one man may be heavy for the next man. Unless some one final starting-point for reasoning can be found, no criterion of judgment is valid, and no such thing as truth can exist. The Sceptics, if they proceeded by their own logic, would be unable to make any statement whatsoever, since they could prove nothing by any acceptable premises.  Scepticism would logically end in complete intellectual paralysis.

Cynicism and Scepticism arose from the abandonment of standards. The former dealt with ethics; the latter, with intellect.  Christianity differed from both by its assertion that God is the ultimate standard for man.  It insisted that man is necessarily dependent on God, which fact set a limit to Cynic independence; and that God is the beginning of all thinking, so that His personal revelation serves as the regulating factor in the acquisition of knowledge by experience.

## Evaluation of Philosophies

However popular these and other variant philosophies may have been, they were unsatisfactory because they were too abstract for the ordinary man to grasp in their entirety, and because they lacked finality. Their reasonings always ended in a peradventure.  Plato expressed this failure exactly when he put into the mouth of Simmias the following statement:

> For I dare say that you, Socrates, feel as I do, how very hard or almost impossible is the attainment of any certainty about questions such as these [immortality] in the present life.  And yet I should deem him a coward who did not prove what is said about them to the uttermost, or whose heart failed before he had examined them on every side.  For he should persevere until he has attained one of two things: either he should discover or learn the truth about them; or, if this is impossible, I would have him take the best and most irrefragable of human notions, and let this be the raft upon which he sails through life — not without risk, as I admit, if he cannot find some word of God which will more surely and safely carry him.[3]

Thus philosophy, according to its own acknowledgment, had not been successful in the quest of truth.  To Simmias' dilemma Christianity has the answer: "The Word became flesh, and dwelt among us (and we beheld his glory, glory as of the only begotten from the Father), full of grace and truth" (John 1:14).

---

3. Plato: *Phaedo* 85.  See Benjamin Jowett, *The Dialogues of Plato* (New York: Scribner, Armstrong, & Co., 1873), Vol. I, p. 414.

# JUDAISM

# JUDAISM

Its Origin

Its Theology

The Temple

The Synagogue

The Sacred Year
  The Passover
  Pentecost, or The Feast of Weeks
  The Feast of Trumpets
  The Day of Atonement
  The Feast of Tabernacles
  The Feast of Lights
  The Feast of Purim

The Educational System

The Literature

The Sects of Judaism
  The Pharisees
  The Sadducees
  The Essenes
  The Zealots

The Diaspora
  The Hebraists
  The Hellenists

# CHAPTER V

# Judaism

Among the religions of the Roman empire in the first century, Judaism held a unique place. It was national, having originated with the Jewish people, and yet it was not confined to them, for its proselytes were numbered by the hundreds. It was not the only cult that emphasized the worship of one God, but unlike the others it was exclusively monotheistic in the sense that its adherents were not allowed to worship or even to admit the existence of any other god or gods. Other religions had temples and sacrificial worship, but in no other faith did the temple with its imageless sanctuary play so great a part or hold the single allegiance of so large a company of people. Many of the philosophies had well articulated ethical systems, but the ethics of Judaism were inherent in the nature of its worship and were rigidly enforced upon all of its adherents. Most of the ethnic religions of the day were founded on tradition or on mystic intuition. Judaism was based on a revelation from God recounted in the sacred Scriptures of the law and the prophets, which claimed to be the reproduction of the words of God Himself as He spoke to His chosen servants.

Some understanding of Judaism is indispensable to the student of the New Testament, for Christianity is the child of Judaism. The books of the New Testament, with two exceptions, were written by Jews. The teachings of the New Testament concerning God, man, sin, salvation, law, grace, prayer, and many other subjects fundamental to the Christian life, strike their roots back into Old Testament soil. Even the arguments of the New Testament against legalism are drawn from statements in the Old Testament, and the text of the writings of the apostolic age is filled with Old Testament quotations. Christians were first known as "the sect of the Nazarenes" (Acts 24:5, 14), which was regarded as a rivulet from the main stream of Judaism. Jesus Himself was a Jew who was born of a Jewish family (Matt. 1:16), and was circumcised as all Jewish male infants were (Luke 2:21). He was taken to Jerusalem as a boy that He might participate in the Passover feast (Luke 2:41) and throughout His life He observed Jewish customs and moved in Jewish society. The present rift between Christianity and Judaism is not the result of a wide difference in historical and theological origins. It is the outcome of the repudiation of the Lord Jesus by the Jewish people, as John said: "He came unto his own [home], and they that were his own [people] received him not" (John 1:11).

## Its Origin

Judaism as it existed in the first century was largely the product of the exile. Prior to the captivity the people of Israel and Judah had given only spasmodic loyalty to the law. The worship of Jehovah had been their rightful and official faith, but it had frequently been "more honored in the breach than in the observance." In the ninth century B.C. the entire northern kingdom had been alienated to the worship of Baal under the influence of Jezebel, Ahab's Phoenician queen, and had been brought back to the worship of Jehovah only by the heroic ministry of Elijah. Similarly the temple worship of the southern kingdom fell into neglect and disuse during the reigns of Manasseh and of Amon in the eighth century, who sponsored the introduction of foreign deities. Under Josiah's vigorous administration, the temple was cleansed, the worship of Jehovah was restored, and the book of the law which was brought to light during the reconstruction of the temple was put back in its rightful place of authority (II Chron. 34:1-33). As long as the people lived in Palestine, surrounded by prosperous and powerful heathen neighbors and subjected to their influence, they were tempted to experiment with alien worship and to desert the God of their fathers. The prophets protested in vain against this tendency which had appeared during the wilderness wanderings of the people (Num. 25:1-3), and which had persisted even to the period of the captivity and exile (Ezek. 14:1-5, Jer. 7:16-20).

The captivity confronted the Jewish people with a stern alternative. Either they must commit themselves utterly to the worship of Jehovah, the one true God, by which allegiance they would retain the genius and purpose of their national existence, or they would be absorbed both religiously and politically by the nations among whom they were driven into exile. If they were to choose the former alternative, they would have to pay closer attention to the requirements of the law, and they would have to devise some means of worship to take the place of the temple ritual which had ceased with the destruction of the central building and with the subsequent dispersion of the priesthood. The book of the law could be carried with them to their new resting place, but the cult of the temple, as far as they could see, was gone forever.

While the captives of the southern kingdom were in Babylonia in the sixth century B.C. the new Judaism began to take form. Idolatry was first banned. Whereas the worship of Baal and of other Canaanite deities had been madly espoused prior to the capture of Jerusalem, the bitter discipline of the captivity schooled the survivors to look toward Jehovah. The whole spirit of the book of Daniel, in which all participation in heathen worship is scorned and in which Daniel and his friends avowed their will to worship Jehovah alone at any cost, is a witness to the salutary change in spiritual temper which came over the exiles.

With the enforced cessation of sacrifice, the study of the law, or Torah, began to take its place. In the kingdoms, the individual worshiper may have relied largely upon participation in public worship as an expression of his faith. That expression may have been sincere, but it could hardly have been as vital as the personal study of God's precepts could become. In the reform of Josiah the law was read to the people (II Chron. 34:29, 30) as a special feature of a reforming movement, but in the exile there was an increasing tendency for each man to study the law for himself. The scribe like Ezra who studied and interpreted the law became as important a personage among the people as the priest had been while the temple was standing (Ezra 7:1-6). In the days of Jesus the scribes were potent figures in the religion of Judaism.

A new center of worship was established by the rise of the synagogue. The wide dispersion of the people in the captivity and their wanderings in the years that followed made some local form of gathering necessary. Even when the temple was re-established, there were many who could not attend its ceremonies. In order to hold them together around the study of the law, wherever ten men could be found to form a regular congregation, synagogues were created in the various communities where they lived. In these the people gathered for prayer and for worship on the seventh day of the week. So firmly established was the synagogue as an institution that it continued even after the rebuilding of the temple, and in the first century in Jerusalem there were synagogues which carried on their activities concurrently with those of the temple (Acts 6:9). Although no mention of the synagogue as such occurs in the Old Testament, there can be little doubt that it grew up in the years between the captivity and the advent of Christ, for in His lifetime it was flourishing in Palestine.

The religious life that grew up around the synagogue was an adaptation of the older rites and observances of Judaism to the new conditions under which the people had to live. Many of them had been moved from the pastoral and agricultural life of Palestine to the busy commercial activity of great cities. Feasts could not be observed with all the features that might be utilized in village worship. Problems and queries prompted by the new life called for new answers. New influences from the Gentile world surrounding them pressed in upon them with great force. Some changes were inevitable, but in the main Judaism retained the essential principles of the older worship prescribed by the law and preached by the prophets.

## Its Theology

Central to the whole faith of Judaism was its tenacious belief in the unity and transcendence of Jehovah. In contrast to the multiplicity of deities which the heathen world acknowledged, the Jew guarded jealously his short, sharp creed of Deuteronomy 6:4: "Hear, O Israel: Jehovah our God is one Jehovah." Jewish exclusivism in worship is amply attested by the attitude which the Gentiles took toward them. They were generally accused of atheism, not because they denied the existence of any god at all, but because they consistently refused to recognize the reality of any deity except their own.

Among the rabbinic teachers considerable emphasis was placed upon the fatherhood of God. The introductory phrase of the Lord's Prayer, "Our Father who art in heaven," was no novelty. Isaiah had addressed God with this title:

> For thou art our Father, though Abraham knoweth us not, and Israel doth not acknowledge us: thou, O Jehovah, art our Father; our Redeemer from everlasting is thy name.
>
> (Isa. 63:16)

Rabbi Akiba taught that the Israelites were sons of God:

> Beloved (of God) are the Israelites, in that they shall be called sons of God; still more beloved in that it is made known to them that they are called sons of God.[4]      (cf. Deut. 14:1)

This personal relation of God to Israel as expressed by the figure of fatherhood was emphasized chiefly by Palestinian teachers.

Philo, who belonged to the Hellenistic wing of Judaism, had a more philosophic conception of God. God is eternal, unchangeable, holy,

---

4. See G. F. Moore, *Judaism* (Cambridge: Harvard University Press, 1927), Vol. II, p. 203, fn. 2.

ιree, and perfect. Because He is superior to all other beings, He is not definable by comparison with them, since definition would thus be equivalent to limitation. This concept illustrates a trend toward depersonalizing God which is still extant in modern Judaism. God thus becomes an actual but a vague and shadowy being concerning whose character and attitudes no definite assertions can be made. Perhaps this uncertainty about the nature of God which sprang originally from a hesitation to limit Him was the reason for the indefiniteness expressed in John 1:18: "No man hath seen God at any time . . ." At this point Christianity went beyond Judaism by presenting a God who was not only sole God and real, but who was also personal and knowable.

Man, according to Jewish theology, was the creation of God, endowed with the ability to choose between obedience and disobedience to God's revealed law, and by so doing to choose the consequences of life and of death (Deut. 30:11-20). Man's chief end in life was to keep the commandments of God and to maintain all of the forms that were prescribed for the people as a whole: namely, circumcision, the observance of the sabbath, the various annual feasts, and the worship of the synagogue. The law summarized the whole duty of man and established his relation to God.

Sin for the Jew consisted chiefly in a wrong relationship to the revealed law of God. The failure to obey one of its prescriptions, whether "weighty," such as the command, "Thou shalt not kill," or "light," such as the prohibition of taking a bird from the nest with her fledglings or with the eggs (Deut. 22:6, 7), was regarded as a sin. This Jewish attitude is reflected in the New Testament in James 2:10: "For whosoever shall keep the whole law, and yet stumble in one *point,* he is become guilty of all." Judaism drew no distinction between the moral and ceremonial law, for both were inextricably connected with the life of the people as a whole. Severance from the elect people, which was the penalty for sin, was meted out to all offenders, not only upon those who had committed some outrageous crime or who neglected some fundamental ordinance such as circumcision, but also upon those who ate flesh with blood remaining in it (Lev. 17:14).

In the period before the exile, rewards and punishments were connected with the fate of the nation as a whole. If the nation observed God's law and worshiped Him alone, it prospered. If the nation lapsed into idolatry and into neglect of the law, it suffered political and economic reverses. Sin was thus evaluated and judged on a communal scale rather than individually. There was, of course, per-

117

sonal consciousness of sin, as Psalm 51 shows, but the social and national implications of the individual's conduct were more marked in Judaism than they are in modern Protestant Christianity.

The uprooting of the nation in the captivity tended to destroy the connection of reward and punishment with ebb and flow of national prosperity in the land. The captivity itself was a discipline which the nation must endure until such time as God should see fit to restore them, but in the interim the generations that should be born and die must face the issues of life and death for themselves. This was the problem that confronted Ezekiel. When he was told by the fatalists of his day that "the fathers have eaten sour grapes, and the children's teeth are set on edge." he replied that one's relation to God is not determined by the sins or by the virtues of one's ancestors but by his own.

> *As I live, saith the Lord Jehovah, ye shall not have* occasion *any more to use this proverb in Israel. Behold, all souls are mine; as the soul of the father, so also the soul of the son is mine: the soul that sinneth, it shall die.* (Ezek. 18:3, 4)

This reaffirmation of individual responsibility accords with the position of Judaism as it is reflected in the New Testament. The rich young ruler showed deep concern for his individual relation to God, in spite of the fact that he felt that he had kept completely all the precepts of the moral law (Matt. 19:16-22). Communal responsibility was transferred from the people as inhabitants of a land to the people as the elect of God, whose manifestation of that election lay in their social solidarity rather than in their location.

The theology of punishment and of reward, when applied to the individual life, opened the question of immortality and of the life hereafter. Little is given in the Old Testament concerning these subjects. Jacob and David both alluded to Sheol, a dim and shadowy region of the dead, where they might be reunited with their children who had suffered an untimely death (Gen. 37:35, II Sam. 12:23). Nowhere in the earlier records is there any direct statement concerning the resurrection of the body, although Jesus interpreted God's declaration to Moses, "I am the God of Abraham, the God of Isaac, and the God of Jacob" (Exod. 3:6) to mean that He was not the God of the dead but of the living (Matt. 22:32). The suggestion of resurrection emerges first in the poetical books and later in the prophets. The sixteenth Psalm, attributed to David, says:

*poetical*

*For thou wilt not leave my soul to Sheol;*
*Neither wilt thou suffer thy holy one to see corruption.*
*Thou wilt show me the path of life:*
*In thy presence is fulness of joy;*
*In thy right hand there are pleasures for evermore.*

(Ps. 16:10, 11)

Isaiah, in predicting the future judgments of God and the salvation of Israel, says:

*Thy dead shall live; my dead bodies shall arise.*
*Awake and sing, ye that dwell in the dust; for*
*thy dew is as the dew of herbs, and the earth*
*shall cast forth the dead.*

(Isa. 26:19)

In Daniel also occurs a prediction of resurrection:

*And many of them that sleep in the dust of the earth shall*
*awake, some to everlasting life, and some to shame and ever-*
*lasting contempt.*

(Dan. 12:2)

*prophetic*

The relative scarcity of references to the life hereafter or to a resurrection may seem strange when one contemplates the fact that Judaism was a part of the divine revelation to men. The revelation, however, carried with it an educative process which was closely connected with Israel's development in the land of Palestine. Their tenure of the land was conditioned upon their behavior in this life, and their reward as a group was confined to this world, for common reward and common punishment would scarcely be meted out in another life where individual destiny was the determining factor. The emphasis under law for the Jewish nation was upon collective salvation here, rather than upon individual salvation hereafter.

The apocryphal and apocalyptic writings are more explicit. The unknown author of the Wisdom of Solomon, who wrote probably at Alexandria in the middle of the second century B.C., says: "The souls of the righteous are in the hands of God, and no torment shall touch them . . . and although they are chastened for a little time, they shall receive great blessings, for God tested them and found them worthy of Himself" (Wisdom of Solomon, 3:1, 5). In Second Maccabees, a work drawn from the original of Jason of Cyrene, the concept of a resurrection emerged clearly. Judas Maccabaeus, according to the account given in II Maccabees 12:42-44, had, by a surprise attack upon Gorgias, governor of Idumea, retrieved the bodies

**119**

of some Jews who had been killed in a previous skirmish with the Idumeans. When the bodies were removed for burial, under the coats of the dead were found things consecrated to idols. Judas, to expiate the sin that the deceased had committed, acted as follows:

> *And when he had made a gathering throughout the company to the sum of two thousand drachmas of silver, he sent it to Jerusalem to offer a sin-offering, doing therein very well and honestly in that he was mindful of the resurrection: for if he had not hoped that they that were slain should have risen again, it had been superfluous and vain to pray for the dead.*
>
> (II Maccabees 12:43-44)

Sheol was regarded as an intermediate state preceding the resurrection and the final rewards and punishments. In II Maccabees 6:23 Eleazar, a martyr, speaks of going to Hades; and since he as a righteous man must be destined for the resurrection mentioned above, his stay in Hades would be only temporary.

A day of judgment in which the wicked should be sent to well-deserved doom and in which the righteous would be vindicated also appears in the apocryphal writings. The just "having been a little chastised . . . shall be greatly rewarded" (Wisdom 3:5), while the wicked "have no hope, neither comfort in the day of trial" (Wisdom 3:18). In II Esdras and in Enoch there are numerous allusions to a future day of doom, although the statements are not always coherent.

The Messianic expectation of the advent of a political deliverer for Israel was strong in the inter-testamental period. In the Apocrypha, II Esdras is outstanding as a Messianic apocalypse. Oesterley thinks that it is the compilation of the work of several authors who wrote between A.D. 100 and 270.[5] The book, even at this late date, may still be independent of Christian influence, since it is unmistakably Jewish and contains no allusion to the person of Christ. It bears some traces of being a translation from a Hebrew original. It predicts that the divine kingdom shall succeed the rule of Rome; that the Messiah shall rule by law; and that after He has completed his work, He shall die and the judgment will follow. The Psalms of Solomon, written in the first century before Christ, depict the coming of a righteous ruler for Israel who shall be sinless and who shall rule over the Gentiles (Psalm 17). In all of this literature the Messiah is nowhere represented as suffering for men or as redeeming them by his personal sacrifice. The Messianic hope and the apocalyptic concept of it which

---

5. W. O. Oesterley, *An Introduction to the Books of the Apocrypha* (New York: The Macmillan Company, n.d.), pp. 147, 155, 156.

is apparent in Daniel and which is treated at length in later books formed the background for the apostles' questioning of Jesus that evoked His well-known Olivet discourse (Matt. 24, 25).

## The Temple

The original temple of Solomon was destroyed when Jerusalem was sacked and burned by the troops of Nebuchadnezzar in 586 B.C. The second temple, built in the restoration and mentioned by Haggai and by Zechariah, prophets of that period, was begun about 537 B.C., and was completed after many delays in 516 B.C. (Ezra 6:13-15).

Little is known of the history of this temple. In 168 B.C. Antiochus Epiphanes plundered it and desecrated it by introducing into it an altar to Olympian Zeus on which he offered sacrifice. Three years later Judas Maccabaeus cleansed and repaired it. It was standing in 63 B.C. when Pompey conquered Jerusalem, and was robbed of its treasures by Crassus in 54 B.C. When Herod the Great took the city in 37 B.C. some of the temple structures were burned, but the main building was probably not greatly damaged.

Herod, however, in the eighteenth year of his reign (20-19 B.C.) undertook the rebuilding of the temple. He collected the material before he began the actual process of demolition and reconstruction and proceeded slowly in order that the worship might be disturbed as little as possible. The work was done by the priests. The sanctuary itself was completed in a year and a half, but the outer buildings and porticoes were not finished until A.D. 62 or 64. When Jesus' enemies said that the temple had been forty-six years in building, they implied that the work was still going on (John 2:20).

The building itself was made of white marble, a large part of which was covered with gold, which reflected the sunlight and made it an object of dazzling splendor. The temple court occupied a rectangular space about 585 feet east to west and about 610 feet north to south. Inside the wall of this court was a set of cloisters with a double row of columns on the south side. The eastern cloister was known as Solomon's porch (John 10:23, Acts 3:11, 5:12) because it was traditionally a survival from Solomon's temple. Offices were located along the walls or between the porticoes.

The outer court was known as the court of the Gentiles. No restrictions were placed upon access to it, and it was at times used as a market place. At the northern end of the court and transverse to it was the temple proper, consisting of the inner court with its buildings.

121

At the eastern end was the women's court, and at the western end was the court of the Israelites from which women were excluded. Centered within the court of the Israelites was the court of the priests, in the middle of which was the sanctuary. The inner court stood on higher ground than the outer court. Between the two, on the edge of the inner court, was a stone parapet, on which were inscriptions warning all Gentiles to stay out of the second enclosure under penalty of death. The wall was pierced by nine gates, four on the north, four on the south, and one on the end which may have been the Beautiful Gate, mentioned in Acts 3.

The sanctuary itself was elevated above the inner court and was reached by a flight of twelve steps. Its divisions were similar to those of the Tabernacle: the Holy Place, on the east, which was about 60 feet long, and the Most Holy Place, which was about 30 feet long. The former contained the table of shewbread on the north, the seven branched lampstand on the south, and the altar of incense between them. Only the priests were allowed to enter the Holy Place. The Most Holy Place was empty, for the ark of the covenant had been lost when the temple of Solomon was destroyed. The high priest entered the Most Holy Place once a year on the Day of Atonement, when he made propitiation with blood for the sins of the people. The division between the Holy Place and the Most Holy Place was a thick double veil, which shut off the inner sanctuary from prying eyes. On the outside of the sanctuary were built small rooms, arranged in three stories and accessible by a staircase, in which priests lived, or which could be used for storage.

Within the court of the priests, east of the sanctuary, was the great altar of burnt-offering, about 18 feet square and 15 feet high. On this altar perpetual fire burned and the animal sacrifices were consumed in the daily ritual. Just north of the altar was a space for slaughtering the victims and for preparing them for sacrifice.

Only the priests could remain within the court of the priests, except for those who brought animals to be offered as sacrifices, since they had to lay their hands on the victim before it was slaughtered.

The Jews were allowed by the Romans to maintain a police corps to keep order within the temple precincts. Its chief officer was called a *strategos,* or "captain of the temple" (Acts 4:1, 5:24-26). It is possible that a detachment from these men took Jesus at the betrayal, rather than a cohort of Roman soldiers. They were charged with the apprehension and safe-keeping of Peter and John when the latter were arrested for preaching, probably within the temple enclosure. The guard watched the temple day by day to see that no unauthorized person entered forbidden enclosures. At night the gates were shut and a watch was stationed to prevent the entrance of marauders.

The temple was the main center of worship in Jerusalem. Jesus Himself and later His apostles taught and preached within its courts. As late as A.D. 56 the church in Jerusalem still had in its ranks men who made vows in the temple (Acts 21:23-26) and who adhered closely to its legal observance. Only with the development of the Gentile church did its connection with Christianity cease.

## The Synagogue

The synagogue played a large part in the growth and persistence of Judaism, as previously noted.[6] The Jews of the Dispersion founded synagogues in every city of the empire where there were enough Jews to maintain one, and foreign synagogues flourished in Jerusalem. Galilee, which in the days of the Maccabees was largely Gentile (I Maccabees 5:21-23), was filled with synagogues in the time of Christ. The synagogue was the social center where the Jewish inhabitants of a city gathered weekly to meet each other. It was the educational medium for keeping the law before the people and for providing instruction for their children in the ancestral faith. It was the substitute for temple worship, which was precluded by distance or by poverty. In the synagogue the study of the law took the place of ritual sacrifice, the rabbi supplanted the priest, and the communal faith was applied to individual life.

Each synagogue had as its leader the "head of synagogue," (Mark 5:22) who was probably selected from among the elders by vote. The leader presided over the services in the synagogue, acted as instructor in case of any dispute (Luke 13:14), and introduced visitors to the assembly (Acts 13:15). The synagogue attendant, or Hazzan, acted as custodian of the property and had the responsibility of caring for the building and its contents. His duties included warning the village people of the beginning of the Sabbath on Friday afternoon and notifying them also of its close. Probably he was the official mentioned in Luke 4:20 who brought forth the roll of Scripture from which Jesus preached in the synagogue at Nazareth and who replaced the roll in its proper niche when He had finished reading from it. On occasion the Hazzan served as the master of the local synagogue school.

The synagogue buildings were usually substantial structures of stone, sometimes richly furnished if the congregation or sponsor were

---

6. Cf. *Supra* p. 115.

wealthy. Every synagogue had a chest in which the roll of the law was kept, a platform with a reading desk from which the Scripture of the day was read, lamps for lighting the building, and benches or seats for the congregation. Most of the equipment in use in the ancient synagogues still appears in their modern counterparts.

The synagogue service consisted of recitation of the Jewish creed or Shema, "Hear, O Israel: Jehovah our God is one Jehovah: and thou shalt love Jehovah thy God with all thy heart, and with all thy soul, and with all thy might" (Deut. 6:4, 5), accompanied by sentences of praise to God called *Berakot* because they began with the word "Blessed." Following the Shema was a ritual prayer, concluding with an opportunity for individual silent prayer on the part of the members of the congregation. The reading of the Scriptures, which came next, began with special sections of the law which were assigned to holy days; but as time went on the entire Pentateuch was divided into sections which gave a fixed cycle of one hundred fifty-four lessons to be read in a definite period of time. The Palestinian Jews read through the Pentateuch every three years, whereas the Babylonian Jews completed the reading in one year. The Prophets were also used, as Jesus reading in the synagogue shows (Luke 4:16 ff.) Probably on that occasion Jesus Himself selected the reading. A sermon followed the reading of the Scripture, explaining the portion which had been read. The sermon in the synagogue at Nazareth was in full keeping with the regular procedure of the day. The service was closed with a blessing, pronounced by some priestly member of the congregation. If no person with priestly qualifications was present, a prayer was substituted for the blessing.

The influence of the nature and order of synagogue worship upon the procedure followed by the church of the first century is fairly obvious. Jesus Himself attended regularly the service of the synagogue and took part in it. His disciples also had been accustomed to its ritual. Paul in his travels made the synagogues of the Dispersion his first points of contact whenever he entered strange cities, and he preached and debated with the Jews and proselytes who gathered to hear him (Acts 13:5, 15-43; 14:1; 17:1-3, 10, 17; 18:4, 8; 19:8). The many close resemblances between the usages of the synagogue and those of the church may doubtless be accounted for by the fact that the latter absorbed or followed to some degree the procedure of the former. As a matter of fact, some early Christian worship may have been carried on within the synagogue; for the Epistle of James implies that the Christian community to whom it was written was still worshiping there (Jas. 2:1, 2). Because of the summary and persistent rejection of the gospel of Christ by the Jewish people, the church and the synagogue parted company. Today they are far apart and are in many respects antithetical. Nevertheless, in the prominence given to the written Scriptures and in the use of homily and sermon, the synagogue and the church still show a close relationship.

## The Sacred Year

The Jewish year consisted of twelve lunar months, with an intercalary month which was added to the calendar whenever it was needed to equate the lunar year with the solar year. The civil year commenced with the seventh month, corresponding roughly to October on the modern calendar. The religious year began with the first month, in which occurred the Passover, the first great feast of the Jewish cycle. The sequence of the months is as follows, using the religious year as the standard:

| Month | | Special Days |
|---|---|---|
| Nisan | (April) | 14 — Passover |
| | | 15 — Unleavened Bread |
| | | 21 — Close of Passover |
| Iyar | (May) | |
| Sivan | (June) | 6 — Feast of Pentecost — seven weeks from the Passover (Anniversary of the giving of the law on Mt. Sinai) |
| Tammuz | (July) | |
| Ab | (August) | |
| Elul | (September) | |
| Tishri | (October) | 1 & 2 — The Feast of Trumpets *Rosh Hashanah,* the beginning of the civil year |
| | | 10 — Day of Atonement |
| | | 15-21 — Feast of Tabernacles |
| Marchesvan | (November) | |
| Kislev | (December) | 25 — Feast of Lights, or Dedication *Hanukkah* |
| Tebeth | (January) | |
| Shebet | (February) | |
| Adar | (March) | 14 — The Feast of Purim |

The festivals, or feasts, were seven in number, as follows: Passover, the Feast of Unleavened Bread, the Feast of Pentecost, the New Year and Day of Atonement, the Feast of Tabernacles, the Feast of Dedi-

cation, and the Feast of Purim. Of these, the first five were prescribed
by the Mosaic law; the last two were post-exilic in origin.

## The Passover

The Passover was the most important of all, historically and religiously. It marked the anniversary of the deliverance of the Jews from
Egypt and their establishment as an independent people by the
redemptive act of God. Jewish usage distinguished between the
"Egyptian Passover" and the "permanent Passover." The former was
to be observed on the tenth of Nisan, when the blood was sprinkled
on the doorposts and when the lamb was eaten in haste. The permanent Passover was observed for seven days with the use of unleavened
bread. Both were closely connected in time and constituted one festal
season.

The public celebrations of the Passover were intended to be annual
but the Old Testament mentions only a few of them during the span of
its recorded history (II Chron. 8:13, II Chron. 30:15, II Kings 23:21,
Ezra 6:19). Doubtless it was kept more or less regularly, although
there were probably occasional lapses during periods of religious
declension. The feast seems to have been held regularly during the
New Testament period, for Mary and Joseph took the boy Jesus up to
Jerusalem at the time of the Passover (Luke 2:41) as their regular
custom, and He Himself kept the feast during His ministry.

On the day of the feast every male Jew who was physically fit for
travel and who was not disqualified by ceremonial uncleanness was
requested to appear in Jerusalem if he lived within fifteen miles of
the city. Women participated also in the worship though they were
not obligated to do so. Pilgrims came from the outlying sections of
Palestine and even from foreign provinces to bring their offerings and
to join in the festive worship. Josephus states that at the Passover
season the total population of Jerusalem may have reached three
million.[7] Many of these people camped outside the city at night, since
all accommodations within the walls were filled.

During the Feast of Unleavened Bread sacrifices of two bullocks,
one ram, and seven lambs of the first year were offered daily together
with a goat as a sin-offering (Num. 28:19-25). On the second day
a sheaf of new grain was offered as a wave-offering with a lamb of the
first year for a burnt-offering (Lev. 23:10-14).

---

7. Josephus, *Jewish Wars* II, ix, 3; II, xiv, 3.

## Pentecost, or The Feast of Weeks

The Feast of Weeks, or the Day of the Firstfruits, was celebrated in the month Sivan, seven weeks after the offering of the wave-sheaf after the Passover. The name *Pentecost* originated from the interval of fifty days which separated the two. According to Jewish tradition, it took place on the anniversary of the giving of the law at Mt. Sinai. The special feature of the day was the offering of two wave-loaves of leavened bread, made from the ripe grain which had been harvested. Although the feast is not mentioned in the history of the Old Testament, it is of great importance in the New Testament as the time at which the Holy Spirit was poured out upon the disciples of the Lord Jesus, who, in obedience to His command, were waiting in Jerusalem. It became the birthday of the church.

## The Feast of Trumpets, or the New Year (Rosh Hashanah)

The civil year of the Jews began on the first day of Tishri. During the entire New Year's Day horns and trumpets were blown in the temple from morning to evening. Unlike the Passover and Pentecost, the feast did not attract many pilgrims to Jerusalem, for it was celebrated in the synagogue as well as in the temple. The book of Nehemiah states (Neh. 8:2-12) that the feast was observed by those who returned from the exile by the public reading of the law and by general rejoicing.

## The Day of Atonement

The Day of Atonement was more properly a fast than a feast and is so called in the New Testament (Acts 27:9). The special feature of the day, apart from the ordinary daily sacrifices, was the presentation of the annual atonement by the high priest. Laying aside his ceremonial robes and dressed in plain white linen, he entered into the Holy of Holies with a censer full of coals taken from the altar and with a basin full of blood from the bullock that had been killed as a sin-offering. As the incense rose like a veil between the priest and the mercy-seat, the priest sprinkled the mercy-seat with the blood. The same process was repeated with the blood of the goat that had been made a sin-offering. The altar of incense and the brazen altar outside of the sanctuary were also sprinkled with blood. A live goat was presented by the priest, who placed his hands upon its head and confessed the sins of the people. The live goat was then taken out into the wilderness and released, apparently as a sign that the people's sins had been carried away forever (Lev. 16:23, 27-32; Num. 29:7-11).

When these ceremonies were completed, the high priest took off his linen clothes, bathed, and resumed his official robes, after which the usual routine sacrifices were offered. Much of the symbolism of the Day of Atonement is applied to Christ by the book of Hebrews. Many of the functions of His priesthood are described in terms of the ritual of the Old Testament.

In modern Judaism the New Year and the Day of Atonement are united in the days of penitence, during which the devout worshiper searches his heart and seeks forgiveness for the sins of the past year in order that he may enter forgiven into the year to come.

### The Feast of Tabernacles

Five days after the Day of Atonement was the Feast of Tabernacles (Lev. 23:34; Deut. 16:13). The feast included the fifteenth to the twenty-second days of the month. It commemorated the wandering in the wilderness and was a thanksgiving at the close of the harvest. It was celebrated by the construction of booths or huts made of branches, in which the people lived temporarily as a reminder of the sojourning of their forefathers in the wilderness. Many sacrifices were offered on the successive days of the feast, and at the close there was one great day of convocation, called in John "the last day, the great *day* of the feast" (John 7:37), which marked the conclusion of the ecclesiastical year. Among the observances of this day which came into existence later than the giving of the law were the pouring out of water at the altar from a golden pitcher, the singing of the Hallel (Psalms 113-118), the lighting of the four great candelabra in the court of the women, and the singing of selected Psalms. The Feast of Tabernacles was popular and joyous in nature.

Two other feasts were added later in post-exilic times: the Feast of Lights and the Feast of Purim.

### The Feast of Lights

The Feast of Lights or the Feast of Dedication was observed for eight days beginning with the twenty-fifth of Kislev. It is mentioned in John 10:22. It was first established in 164 B.C. when Judas Maccabaeus cleansed the temple which had been profaned by Antiochus Epiphanes, and rededicated it to the service of God. Every Jewish home was brilliantly lighted in its honor and the stories of the Mac-

128

cabees were repeated for the benefit of the children. It corresponds almost exactly in time to the Christian Christmas.

## The Feast of Purim

Purim, or "lots," as the word signifies, was kept on the fourteenth and fifteenth days of Adar. On the evening of the thirteenth day the whole of the book of Esther was read publicly in the synagogue. It contained a minimum of religious observances and was rather a national holiday, corresponding somewhat to the Fourth of July as Americans used to celebrate it. It is not mentioned in the New Testament, unless John 5:1 is an allusion to it.

There were a few other minor fasts and feasts that were current in the Judaism of the first century, but they were of no great importance and do not appear in the records of the New Testament.

## The Educational System

Among the Jews of the Dispersion, education must have taken on an important place at an early date, for they were dependent solely upon the perpetuation of their national convictions for their survival. Uprooted from their land, with no military defence of their own, they could keep their national identity only as they maintained themselves as a separate group with their own culture and spiritual life. As far back as the time of Ezra, there was public reading of the law and instruction in its meaning — a kind of adult education that was consistently maintained by the synagogue.

Along with the synagogue developed the school. There never was in Judaism the general compulsory education that prevails in America at the present day; but the Jewish community usually provided some sort of instruction for children that they might learn to read the Torah, to write, and to do some simple arithmetic.

The schools of Palestine in the time of Christ were traditionally the result of the influence of a famous Pharisee and scribe, Simon ben Shatach, who lived about 75 B.C. According to the Talmud, he decreed that all children should attend an elementary school. His words as quoted are ambiguous. They may imply that all children should be put in schools already established, or they may mean that schools should be organized for them. In either case, Simon is credited with a reform by which the state provided teachers for boys from the provinces, and by which it also founded schools in the country towns. Joshua ben Gamla instituted public schools for boys of six or seven years of age in all the cities of Palestine. One teacher was provided for every twenty-five boys. If there were forty in the school the teacher was given an assistant.

The instruction was limited but it was thorough. Before the child went to school at all he would have learned at home the *Shema,* or the Jewish creed (Deut. 6:4), to which Jesus referred when He was asked what was the great commandment of the law (Matt. 22:35-38). He would also have memorized passages from the Torah, certain common proverbs, and some selected Psalms. In the school itself he would repeat the words of the Torah as he was drilled by the teacher. Usually the teacher sat on a low platform with his pupils seated in a semicircle on the ground before him, as Paul sat "at the feet of Gamaliel" (Acts 22:3). As the pupil advanced he would be instructed in the Mishna and in the Talmud, and if he proved to be bright and alert he might ultimately be sent to one of the training schools for scribes.

Jewish education was narrow but precise. The student was trained to make fine distinctions of definition and to remember exactly what he had learned. What he studied he mastered, and he could interpret the law from every possible approach. Original thinking and scientific research were not encouraged, however. The rabbis of Jesus' time were astute in interpreting minute points of the law and in unraveling casuistic questions, but they laid little emphasis upon the knowledge of the natural world that has so large a place in the curricula of modern schools.

Jewish education was thoroughly integrated, for every branch of Jewish knowledge merged with theology. The law was the core of the curriculum. Some knowledge of Greek and perhaps a little Latin were permitted in the most advanced schools, but many of the rabbis frowned upon Gentile learning, and would not permit their pupils to indulge in it.

Vocational education was favored by the Jews. The rabbis had a saying, "Whosoever does not teach his son a trade makes him a thief." Usually every Jewish boy learned how to work with his hands and thus to support himself. The Lord Jesus was a carpenter (Mark 6:3), and Paul made tents (Acts 18:3). This healthy emphasis on manual training made the Jewish male citizen independent. It balanced his intellectual pursuits with physical skills and it enabled him to find gainful employment.

Girls were not generally educated in the synagogue schools. They were trained at home in household arts in preparation for marriage.

With the fall of the Jewish state, Judaism succumbed to Hellenism in the Diaspora. In Palestine the Jewish schools expelled the Greek learning and laid the foundation for the strict system which has characterized Jewish orthodoxy to the present day.

Enthusiasm for education was a marked characteristic of Jewish life. The study of the Torah was a sign of piety and the devout Jew spent much time with the law. Since educational culture was regarded as an aspect of religion, the Jewish people preserved an intellectual standard that many Gentiles did not have. As Moore says:[8]

> . . . the endeavor to educate the whole people in its religion created a unique system of universal education, whose very elements comprised not only reading and writing, but an ancient language and its classic literature. The high intellectual and religious value thus set on education was indelibly impressed on the mind, and one may say on the character of the Jew, and the institutions created for it have perpetuated themselves to the present day.

## The Literature

More than any other nation of antiquity the Jews were the people of a book. Others may have possessed a larger and more varied literature or even a more ancient one; but none, not even the Greeks in the heyday of the Periclean Age, showed such an absorbing interest in their national writings as the Jew showed in his law. For him the Torah was not simply representative of a cherished national culture, it was the voice of God. Its precepts were to be obeyed unquestioningly, and its most remote implications were to be regarded as sacred mandates. The ordinances were woven into the very fabric of his life and the underlying theism of the law colored all his thinking.

The influence of the canonical Jewish Scriptures upon the New Testament is so obvious that it scarcely needs comment. The Lord Jesus Christ and His disciples were familiar with them from their earliest years. Jesus quoted with equal readiness from the Law, from the Psalms, and from the Prophets (Luke 24:44), the three divisions of the Hebrew Bible, and argued from them as the basis of revelational authority (John 10:34-36) concerning His own person. Throughout the Acts and Epistles the apostolic writers show by their frequent quotations their familiarity with the Old Testament, whether they used the Hebrew text or the Greek Septuagint. Paul asserted that the Old Testament was "God-breathed" (inspired of God, II Tim. 3:16)

8. George Foot Moore, *Judaism* (Cambridge: Harvard University Press, 1927), Vol. I, p. 322. Quoted by permission.

and declared to Timothy that the scriptures of the Old Testament were "able to make . . . wise unto salvation through faith which is in Christ Jesus" (II Tim. 3:15). So thoroughly did the early church take over the Jewish Scriptures that a new Jewish version of the Old Testament in Greek was made, because the Septuagint had become to all intents and purposes a Christian book. At least one new translation was made in the early centuries to furnish a more literal rendering of the Hebrew text that would be less amenable to Christian uses.

Following the era of the Old Testament, which closed with Malachi, the last of the prophets, at 450 B.C. or thereabouts, there grew up in Palestinian Judaism a body of works later called the *Apocrypha*. The term *Apocrypha*, which is of Greek derivation, means "hidden," "recondite," or "secret," as applied to matters which are not to be disclosed to common people, but which are to be revealed only to the initiated few. As time went on the name was applied to those works which had biblical or religious flavor, but which were not generally accepted as authoritative. They might be read for educational and moral purposes, but would not be regarded as on a par with the authoritative text. The Old Testament Apocrypha appear as an integral part of the Septuagint, being distributed throughout its text rather than being grouped in one place, as they appear in the Latin Vulgate and later in certain of the English versions, such as the Great Bible of 1539 and the original King James Version of 1611.

The apocryphal books are given as follows in their usual order: I Esdras, II Esdras, Tobit, Judith, The Rest of Esther, The Wisdom of Solomon, Ecclesiasticus, Baruch, The Song of the Three Holy Children, The History of Susanna, Bel and the Dragon, The Prayer of Manasses, I Maccabees, II Maccabees. This order is not chronological. Exact dating is impossible, but an approximate location of these books with respect to their time of writing is given here, after the sequences proposed by Oesterley:[9]

### Pre-Maccabean

| | |
|---|---|
| I Esdras | c. 300 B.C. |
| Tobit | c. 250 B.C. |
| The Hymn in the Song of the Three Holy Children | c. 200 B.C. |
| Ecclesiasticus | c. 200 B.C. |

---

9. W.O.E. Oesterley, *An Introduction to the Books of the Apocrypha* (New York: The Macmillan Company, n.d.), pp. 24, 25.

## Maccabean

| | |
|---|---|
| The Prayer in the Song of the Three Holy Children | c. 160 B.C. |
| Judith | c. 150 B.C. |
| The Rest of Esther | c. 140-130 B.C. |
| Bel and the Dragon | c. 150 B.C. |

## Post-Maccabean

| | |
|---|---|
| I Maccabees | 90-70 B.C. |
| II Maccabees | 50 B.C. |
| Susanna | ? |
| Wisdom | A.D. 40 |
| Baruch | A.D. 70 or after |
| II Esdras | A.D. 100 |
| Prayer of Manasses | ? |

Most of these books were written in the period of unsettled national life and struggle between the return from the exile and the destruction of Jerusalem. They reflect the restlessness and the dissatisfied spirit of the Jews, who were still dreaming of an independent commonwealth. Their themes indicate the Jewish reaction to the oppression, uncertainty, and hope that characterized the entire period.

Of the list given above, three are historical: I Esdras, which corresponds in content somewhat to Ezra and Nehemiah; I Maccabees, which is a simple and straightforward narrative of the revolt of Mattathias and his sons in 168 B.C. that terminated in the defeat of the Syrians and the establishment of the Hasmonean state; and II Maccabees, an inferior digest of the work of Jason of Cyrene, which supplements in some degree the content of I Maccabees. Tobit, Judith, The Rest of Esther, and The Story of Susanna are romantic tales illustrating God's justice in vindicating His people. Bel and the Dragon, a spurious addition to the book of Daniel, belongs in the same category. The Wisdom of Solomon and Ecclesiasticus are philosophical treatises in the form of epigrams, somewhat like the book of Proverbs. The Song of the Three Holy Children and The Prayer of Manasses are expressions of devotion to God and of hope in His promises.

The language and style of all these books resembles that of the canonical Old Testament; but with the exception of the book of I Maccabees their historical allusions are not accurate and they have no solid connection with identifiable characters as authors. Their effect on the writers of the New Testament was slight, although occasionally there seem to be references to them in the text. Ecclesiasticus

44:16, "Enoch pleased the Lord, and was translated," may be echoed in Hebrews 11:5:

> *By faith Enoch was translated that he should not see death; and he was not found, because God translated him: for he hath had witness borne to him that before his translation he had been well-pleasing unto God.*

These two passages do not correspond so exactly that one can be called a quotation of the other. Both could originate from independent comments on the account given in Genesis.

A second list of works which have never been included in the scriptures, whether Jewish or Christian, is given below. These consist of writings which were either never of canonical status, or which were considered as representative of individual or group viewpoint.

| | |
|---|---|
| The Book of Jubilees | 150-200 B.C. |
| The Testimony of the Twelve Patriarchs | |
| The Psalms of Solomon | 100-50  B.C. |
| III Maccabees | |
| IV Maccabees | |
| The Assumption of Moses | A.D. 1-50 |
| Adam and Eve | |
| The Martyrdom of Isaiah | |
| The Book of Enoch | |
| II Baruch | |
| The Sibylline Oracles | |

In this list several of the books can be dated approximately, whereas others cannot be. The Book of Enoch, for instance, is apparently composed of sections written at different times, all of which were finally combined not long before the Christian era. Some of its phraseology is paralleled in the New Testament, especially the well-known passage in Jude 14, 15, which is an exact replica of Enoch 1:9:

> *And to these also Enoch, the seventh from Adam, prophesied saying, Behold, the Lord came with ten thousands of his holy ones, to execute judgment upon all, and to convict all the ungodly of all their works of ungodliness which they have ungodly wrought, and of all the hard things which ungodly sinners have spoken against him.*

The Book of Enoch, the Assumption of Moses, II Baruch, II Esdras, and parts of the Sibylline Oracles belong to the class of apocalyptic literature. Apocalyptic literature is predictive, generally using symbolism which seems grotesque and often inconsistent with itself. Uniformly it prophesies dire physical judgments on the wicked, from which the righteous shall be delivered by the supernatural intervention of God. Angels are frequently actors in the drama of apocalypse. Many apocalyptic works are pseudonymous, or are ascribed falsely to eminent men who never could have written them. For example, the Book of Enoch was not written by Enoch, but it was attributed to him because he had a reputation for piety and for wisdom.

In style and in imagery the Old Testament books of Ezekiel and Daniel have been classed as apocalyptic, although they could not rightly be called pseudonymous. Revelation, in the New Testament, is also of the same literary type.

Apocalyptic literature was usually produced in a period of persecution, when men's hopes turned to future deliverance. It was intended to encourage the believers to persist in their allegiance to God, and its imagery discouraged hostile readers from attempting to fathom its meaning. The fact that certain of the canonical books are apocalyptic does not disqualify them as inspired writings, since the inspiration of the Spirit appears in all kinds of literature within the covers of the Bible.

With the overthrow of Jerusalem in A.D. 70 Judaism lost its independent political expression and began to be only a religion. With the cessation of the temple sacrifices came the decline of the priesthood and the rise of the rabbinate. The study of the law took the place of offerings, and the teacher supplanted the priest. As the teachers sought to interpret the law, they codified the traditions which had grown up around it and ultimately reduced them to writing. The Pharisees looked upon these traditions as contemporaneous with the written law and equally as binding, while the Sadducees repudiated them entirely.

Undoubtedly there were ethical standards observed among the Hebrew people prior to the giving of the law at Sinai. Certain regulations and observances were connected with the lives of Noah and of Abraham as recorded in Genesis, and there could scarcely have been the perpetuation of unity during the bondage in Egypt had there not been some stable form of morals and of worship to hold the people together. Whether these traditions were actually transmitted through the many vicissitudes of Israel's history to the first and second centuries A.D. is uncertain. One thing is certain — the mass of tradition contained in the Talmud includes much that is older than the writing of the book itself. The existence of the oral law is attested by the

135

references which Christ made to "the tradition of the elders" (Mark 7:3).

The collection of these traditions with the comments upon them by early rabbis constitute the Talmud. The name is derived from the verb *lammid,* which means "to teach." The Talmud comprises two elements, the Mishna and the Gemara. The Mishna is the oral law as it was known up to the end of the second century A.D. The Gemara is the interpretation of the oral law which the scholars of Babylon and of Jerusalem produced between the beginning of the third century A.D. and the end of the fifth century. These interpretations or discussions were of two kinds: the Halakah, which dealt with the code of law, and the Haggadah, which was general preaching, or everything that was not Halakah.

The Halakah stated the rule or statute by which one is guided, the definite religious usage of the day. Strack says that "anything becomes Halakah (1) when it is held in acceptance for a long period; (2) when it is vouched for by recognized authority; (3) when it is supported by accepted proof from Scripture; (4) when it is established by majority vote. Any one or all of these reasons could establish a principle of the oral law."[10] Since no new principle of law could be established by invention, but rather by relation to an already existing principle, the rabbis became expert in manipulating the inferences from the existing law, oral and written, in order to cover all possible cases that might be brought before them. The records of these cases and the reasonings concerning them made the Halakoth.

The Haggadah included all scriptural interpretation which is non-halakic in character. It was an attempt to develop the meaning of the implication of the law rather than to enlarge upon its explicit statements. The argument of Jesus for the resurrection from Exodus 3:6 follows somewhat the pattern of Haggadic procedure (Matt. 22:31-33). Together, the Halakah and Haggadah are called the Midrash, a word derived from the Hebrew verb *darash,* meaning "to search," or "to conduct research." The research into the meaning of the law, oral and written, was thus made a part of the Talmud.

The Talmud contains sixty-three sections or tractates, each of which deals with some aspect of the law. Two Talmuds, representing the Palestinian and Babylonian schools of the Amoraim, or doctors, are in existence. The Palestinian Talmud, the shorter of the two, written

---

10. Hermann L. Strack, *Introduction to the Talmud and Midrash* (Authorized Translation from the Fifth German Edition. Philadelphia: The Jewish Publication Society of America, 1945), pp. 5-7.

in Eastern Aramaic, dates from the close of the fourth century. The Babylonian Talmud was written about the end of the fifth century in Western Aramaic dialect. Both are incomplete, lacking whole sections or parts of sections. In the thirteenth century the Talmud came under the ban of the church, and so many copies were destroyed or damaged that its survival was threatened. The marvel is that it exists at all.

To this day the Talmud is the standard of orthodox Judaism, regulative of faith and of ritual practice. It sets the interpretation of the law and is often more directly influential on beliefs and on life than is the Old Testament itself.

## The Sects of Judaism

Judaism was no exception to the human trend toward sectarianism in religion, even though its solidarity was greater than that of the other religions of the Roman world. Although all of the sects gave allegiance to the law, their emphases ranged from liberalism to rationalism and from mysticism to political opportunism.

### The Pharisees

The largest and most influential sect in the New Testament times was that of the Pharisees. Their name is derived from the verb *parash*, "to separate." They were the separatists, or Puritans of Judaism, who withdrew from all evil associations and who sought to give complete obedience to every precept of the oral and written law. They originated as a separate group shortly after the times of the Maccabees, and by 135 B.C. they were well established in Judaism.

Their theology was founded upon the entire canon of the Old Testament which included the law of Moses, or Torah, the Prophets, and the Writings. In interpretation they used the allegorical method in order to allow for elasticity in applying the principles of the law to new questions that might be raised. They attached great value to the oral law or tradition which they observed scrupulously. They believed in the existence of angels and spirits, in the immortality of the soul, and in the resurrection of the body. They practiced ritual prayer and fasting, and tithed their property meticulously (Matt. 23:23, Luke 11:42). They kept the Sabbath very strictly, allowing not even for healing the sick nor for the casual plucking of grain for eating by the wayside (Matt. 12:1, 2).

Kohler lists seven types of Pharisees who were extremists:[11]

---

11. Kaufmann Kohler, "Pharisees," in *Jewish Encyclopedia,* IX, 661-666.

1. The "shoulder" Pharisee, who paraded his good deeds before men like a badge on the shoulder.
2. The "wait-a-little" Pharisee, who would ask someone to wait for him while he performed a good deed.
3. The "blind" Pharisee, who bruised himself by walking into a wall because he shut his eyes to avoid seeing a woman.
4. The "pestle" Pharisee, who walked with hanging head rather than observe alluring temptations.
5. The "ever-reckoning" Pharisee, who was always counting his good deeds to see if they offset his failures.
6. The "God-fearing" Pharisee, who, like Job, was truly righteous.
7. The "God-loving" Pharisee, like Abraham.

Although many of the Pharisees were so introspectively intent on obedience to the law that they often became fussily self-righteous, there were many among them who were truly virtuous and good men. Not all of them were hypocrites. Nicodemus, who earnestly sought out Christ during His earthly ministry, and who ultimately shared with Joseph of Arimathea the responsibility of burying Jesus' body, was a Pharisee. Saul of Tarsus, vehement persecutor of the church though he was, avowed that he was a Pharisee and the son of a Pharisee (Acts 23:6), and that "touching the righteousness which is in the law, [he was] found blameless" (Phil. 3:6). The moral and the spiritual standards of Pharisaism may have tended toward self-righteousness and consequently toward hypocrisy, but they were high in comparison with the average of their day, notwithstanding.

Of all the sects of Judaism, Pharisaism alone has survived. It became the foundation of modern orthodox Judaism, which follows the pattern of Pharisaic morality, ceremonialism, and legalism.

### The Sadducees

The Sadducees, according to tradition, derived their name from the sons of Zadok, who was high priest in the days of David and of Solomon. The sons of Zadok were the priestly hierarchy in the time of the captivity (II Chron. 31:10; Ezek. 40:46, 44:15, 48:11), and apparently the name persisted as the title of the priestly party in the days of Christ. Less numerous than the Pharisees, they possessed political power and were the governing group in the civil life of Judaism under the Herods.

As a party in Judaism, the Sadducees adhered to the strictly literal interpretation of the Torah, which alone they held to be canonical, having a higher authority than the Prophets and the Writings. There was consequently no room in their thinking for the oral tradition which the Pharisees studied with delight. As rationalists and anti-super-naturalists, they denied the existence of angels and spirits (Acts 23:8) and did not believe in personal immortality. Their religion was coldly ethical and literal and was much more open to Hellenizing influences than was Pharisaism. Politically the Sadducees were opportunists and were quite ready to ally themselves with the dominant power if by so doing they could maintain their own prestige and influence.

Unlike the Pharisees, they did not survive the destruction of Jerusalem. The cessation of the priesthood, to which most of the Sadducees belonged, and the hostility with Rome, which had formerly protected the Saducean clan, ended their existence as a group.

## The Essenes

Little is known of this sect which Josephus described in detail in his *Wars of the Jews.*[12] The meaning of their name is uncertain, but it was connected by some with the Greek word *hosios,* meaning "holy."

The Essenes, unlike the Pharisees and the Sadducees, were a definite ascetic brotherhood which could be entered only by those who were willing to submit to the regulations of the group and to undergo ceremonies of initiation. They abstained from marriage and recruited their ranks by adoption or by receiving converts. Their communities held all property in common, so that none were rich and none were poor. Self-support was maintained by manual labor. They ate the plainest of food and dressed habitually in white garments when they were not working.

In behavior the Essenes were sober and restrained, not giving way to anger nor using oaths. They observed the Sabbath with utmost strictness and were exceptionally attentive to personal cleanliness. Any digression from the rules of their order was punished by expulsion from the community.

Theologically the Essenes were akin to the Pharisees in their close observance of the law and in their supernaturalism. They taught that the soul of man is intangible and immortal, imprisoned in a perishable body. At death, the good pass to a region of sunshine and cool breezes,

---

12. Josephus, *Wars of the Jews,* II, viii, 2-13.

while the wicked are relegated to a dark and stormy place of continual torment.

The ascetic tendencies of the Essenes are comparable in many ways to the monasticism which grew up in early Christianity. Some of their doctrines seem to have sprung from a contact with Gentile thought, for in their attitudes they resembled the Stoics. Curiously enough, they are never mentioned in the Gospels. Some writers have suggested that John the Baptist and Jesus were Essenes, so that Christianity was an outgrowth of Essenism. In spite of some superficial likenesses, the strict legalism of Essenism in contrast to the Christian emphasis on grace makes such a connection extremely improbable.

There may be a connection between the Essenes and the sect whose "Discipline" appears among the recently discovered Dead Sea Scrolls. Full proof for this connection is not yet available, but evidence for this conclusion seems to be increasing.[13]

## The Zealots

The Zealots were not a religious sect in the same class with the Pharisees or the Essenes. They were a group of fanatical nationalists who advocated violence as a means of liberation from Rome. At the time of the siege of Jerusalem under Titus they formed one of the factions within the city, and the dissension which they caused contributed heavily to its downfall. Perhaps they were connected with the "Assassins" mentioned in Acts 21:38. One of Jesus' disciples, Simon, had belonged to them, as his name indicates (Luke 6:15, Acts 1:13).

## The Diaspora

Although Palestine was the traditional homeland of the Jewish race, by far the largest number of Jews in the Roman empire lived outside the borders of the Holy Land. Known as the Diaspora, or the Dispersion, they were found in almost all of the large cities from Babylon to Rome and in many of the smaller settlements also, wherever commerce or colonization had taken them. The scattering of the Jewish people began with the captivity of the northern kingdom in 721 B.C.

---

13. See A. Dupont-Sommer, *Observations sur le Manuel de Discipline etc.*, (Paris, 1951), Wm. H. Brownlee, "The Historical Allusions of the Dead Sea Habakkuk Midrash," *Bulletin of the Society of Oriental Research* CXXVI (April, 1952), 10-20, and Ralph Marcus, "Philo, Josephus, and the Dead Sea *Yahad*," *Journal of Biblical Literature* LXXI (1952), 207-209.

when Sargon of Assyria deported the inhabitants of Israel and settled them in new colonies in Assyria. The southern kingdom of Judah was conquered by Babylon in 597 B.C., and many of the upper class were carried away to Babylon. A second and third deportation followed, leaving only the poorest people of the land unmolested. Although several thousand returned from captivity in the restoration under Ezra and Nehemiah, a large number chose to remain in the land of their captivity where they had established themselves and had begun to prosper.

The conquests of Alexander in the fourth century B.C. opened new opportunities for migration and settlement. The domination of the Near East by one great military power removed temporarily the petty hostilities between kingdoms that had made free travel almost impossible. As business opportunities increased and as the Seleucid and Ptolemaic successors of Alexander encouraged colonization by offering citizenship and exemption from taxation to those who would migrate to their own domains, many Jews took advantage of these offers and established new homes in the growing Hellenistic settlements. Some of them became temporary residents of the Greek cities, while others were granted citizenship and settled down in new homes and in new occupations. In Alexandria one entire section of the city was Jewish, with its own governor and officials who were practically autonomous. Its population has been estimated at two million and it represented the largest single concentration of Jews in any one city of the world of that time.

In the Roman empire the Jewish settlements increased rapidly. The slaves that Pompey brought back from Palestine to Rome were ultimately freed and settled on the right bank of the Tiber near the docks. In 4 B.C. there were about eight thousand in the city. Under Julius Caesar and Augustus they were given legal standing, and in some cities such as Corinth they were freed from military service and from the jurisdiction of the heathen courts.

Unquestionably the Greek influence affected the Jews of the Dispersion, and many of them lost the distinctive characteristics and faith that marked them off from other peoples. The majority of them, however, remained Jews. They clung tenaciously to their monotheistic faith based on the law of Moses. They kept contact with the temple at Jerusalem by pilgrimages to the annual feasts and paid the yearly tax of half a shekel. They observed the Sabbath and maintained synagogue services wherever there were enough of them to constitute a worshiping group.

Within the Diaspora were two distinct groups — the Hebraists and the Hellenists.

## The Hebraists

The Hebraists, or "Hebrews," were mentioned by Paul, who was one of them. He said that he was "circumcised the eighth day, of the stock of Israel, of the tribe of Benjamin, a Hebrew of Hebrews; as touching the law, a Pharisee . . ." (Phil. 3:5). The Hebrews were those Jews who retained not only the religious faith of Judaism but also the use of the Hebrew or Aramaic language and the Hebrew customs. Paul said that he was brought up "according to the strict manner of the law of our fathers" (Acts 22:3). His quotations from the Old Testament show that he was familiar with the Hebrew Bible as well as with its Greek version. Although he was born in Tarsus, a Greek city, and although he proudly claimed Roman citizenship (Acts 21:39, 22:25-29), he was still a thoroughgoing Jew, uncorrupted by the Gentile heathenism that surrounded him from youth. Doubtless there were many others like him. Probably the bulk of the Hebraists, however, lived in Palestine itself, where their worship centered in the temple. Acts pictures some of these Hebraists of the Diaspora in the Jews of Asia who accused Paul of desecrating the temple by bringing a Gentile into its sacred precincts (Acts 21:22-29).

## The Hellenists

A far larger number of Jews, however, had absorbed the Graeco-Roman culture and had ceased to be Jewish except in matters of faith. They spoke Greek or whatever happened to be the language of the country where they dwelt; they adopted the customs of their neighbors; and in many cases were virtually indistinguishable as Jews. Syncretistic elements appeared in their worship, as in a synagogue at Dura-Europos on the Euphrates which had heathen mythology depicted in the mosaics and paintings on its walls.

Both classes of Jews are mentioned in Acts 6, where the division between them began to endanger the unity of the church. Apparently the Hellenists were somewhat broader in their sympathies than the Hebraists and were perhaps a bit more ready to see the wider implications of the Old Testament Scriptures. Stephen was probably one of them.

Counting both classes, the Jews in the Roman empire numbered about four and one half million. They were not generally popular

142

because of their clannishness and because they would not join in the public worship of heathen gods. Frequently they were dubbed atheists by those who did not understand how anybody could worship an invisible God. On the other hand, their sobriety, industry, and upright morality commended them to their neighbors, who were compelled to acknowledge their ability and their integrity.

On occasion the Jews could be turbulent, especially when their religious freedom was threatened. Under Claudius they were expelled from Rome because of an uprising, and there were serious riots in Alexandria later in the century. There is no evidence that they took any part in the Jewish war of A.D. 66 to 70, or that they offered any protest against the siege and capture of Jerusalem. Their apparent indifference to their national status even while they were exiles among the Gentiles is part of the paradox of the millennia which is the Jew.

*Part II*

**THE GOSPELS**

# THE GOSPELS

## The Records of the Life of Christ
### The Period of Inception
### 6 B.C. to A.D. 29

---

The Gospels as Literary Works

The Gospel of Matthew

The Gospel of Mark

The Gospel of Luke

The Gospel of John

The Synoptic Problem

The Life of Christ

# CHAPTER VI

# The Gospels as Literary Works

Christianity as a movement owes its origin to the person and work of Jesus Christ, its Founder and its Head. Except for a few fragmentary statements, the authentic records of His life are contained only in the four Gospels of Matthew, Mark, Luke, and John, which have been regarded as canonical by the Christian church from the earliest period of its history. Although there were numerous other Gospels which purported to recount facts concerning His life that are not recorded in the famous four, the apocryphal Gospels, as they are called, are generally of later date and of doubtful reliability. They contain little information that is not a duplication of what the canonical Gospels impart and much of what they add is obviously fanciful and legendary. Furthermore, they often betray by their language that they were written to bolster the views of some particular sect that did not represent the main stream of historic Christianity, but that was really a divergence from it or a rebellion against it.

Tatian, a Syrian Christian of the second century (A.D. 170), who devised the first harmony of the Gospels of which any trace has survived, used for his work only the four, although he must have known of others. Irenaeus, bishop of Lyons and Vienne, who lived about A.D. 180, put forward a rather quaint theory concerning the Gospels:[1]

> It is not possible that the Gospels can be either more or fewer in number than they are. For, since there are four zones of the world in which we live, and four principal winds, while the Church is scattered throughout all the world, and the "pillar and ground" of the Church is the Gospel and the spirit of life; it is fitting that she should have four pillars, breathing out immortality on every side, and vivifying men afresh.

Irenaeus' reasons for believing that there should be only four Gospels may seem to be far-fetched, but even if they are not regarded as scien-

---

1. Irenaeus, *Against Heresies*, IV, xi, 8. Translation of Alexander Roberts and James Donaldson. *The Ante-Nicene Fathers*. (American Reprint. Grand Rapids, Mich.: Wm. B. Eerdmans Publishing Co., 1951) Vol. I, p. 428.

tifically valid, their context indicates that the content of the Gospel record was being debated in Irenaeus' day and that he defended vigorously the truthfulness of the canonical Gospels that appear in the Bible. He says, in fact:[2]

> But that these Gospels alone are true and reliable, and neither an increase nor diminution of the aforesaid number, I have proved by so many and such [arguments].

Both on the basis of internal and of external evidence these writings unmistakably stand in a class by themselves.

The initial approach to the Gospels in this book deals with them as separate writings by four different authors for four different constituencies. The problem occasioned by their coincidences and differences will be treated later. Obviously they were read separately when first published rather than studied as parts of a harmonistic ensemble, and each was regarded by its writer and by its audience as comprising a narrative complete for its purpose. Although each author realized that he was not writing a detailed chronicle of every single act that Jesus performed (*Cf.* John 20:30, 21:25), he did regard his work as sufficient to convey the message or impression that he had been commissioned to deliver (John 20:31, Luke 1:4). For this reason one may conclude legitimately that each of the Gospels should be studied initially as a literary unit, apart from its relation to any or all of the other three. There is a value in the harmonistic study of the life of Christ, which attempts to piece together the biographical parts of the Gospels into one continuous story; but sometimes the meaning of the individual Gospels is obscured when the narrative is stressed at the expense of its fourfold interpretation.

For the foregoing reason each of the Gospels will be treated as separate from the others and will be analyzed in its historical and literary context to ascertain what its peculiar genius is. The Gospels are not considered in the chronological order of their production or of their publication, but are treated in the sequence of their occurrence in the familiar modern versions. Each will be presented in its setting with a brief introduction and with a condensed analysis of its content.

---

2. *Op. cit.*, III, xi, 9.

# THE GOSPEL OF MATTHEW

# THE GOSPEL OF MATTHEW

Origin

Date and Place

Content

Outline

Emphasis

Characters

Special Features

# CHAPTER VII

# The Gospel of Matthew

## Origin

The First Gospel is traditionally ascribed to Matthew Levi, a tax collector or publican, whom Jesus called to be one of His twelve disciples (Matt. 9:9-13, 10:3). Practically nothing is known of him except his name and occupation. After the listing of the apostles in the book of Acts (Acts 1:13) he disappeared from the history of the church, except for allusions that are probably legendary. Nowhere in the First Gospel is he explicitly called its author, but the early writers of the church who discuss the authorship credit it to Matthew. Eusebius (c. A.D. 325) quotes Papias (c. A.D. 100) as saying that Matthew had composed in Aramaic the Oracles of the Lord which were translated into Greek by each man as he was able.[1] Irenaeus, about a century and a half earlier than Eusebius, stated that "Matthew also issued a written Gospel among the Hebrews in their own dialect, while Peter and Paul were preaching at Rome and laying the foundations of the church."[2]

Several inferences may be drawn from these early statements concerning the origin of the First Gospel. First, the Matthaean authorship was undisputed. Since Matthew was a comparatively obscure member of the apostolic band, there seems to be no good reason for making him the author of a spurious work. Any forger who sought fame for his production would have chosen to publish it under the name of a more renowned apostle. Second, the general agreement of early writers accords with the known character of Matthew. As a publican he must have been literate and accustomed to taking notes as a part of his business activity. Third, the tradition that this Gospel was originally written in Aramaic does not preclude the possibility that the author may have published later a Greek edition which quickly superseded the older writing.

1. Eusebius, *Historia Ecclesiae,* III, xxxix, 16.
2. Irenaeus, *Against Heresies,* III, i, 1.

151

## Date and Place

Just when the Gospel was written is unknown. It can scarcely have been written before the first dispersion of the Jerusalem Christians (Acts 8:4), for the local church in Jerusalem would not have needed a written Gospel since the apostles were physically present to answer all questions and to impart authoritative teaching. It is doubtful whether it were written subsequent to A.D. 70, because in the prophecy dealing with the overthrow of Jerusalem there is no allusion to the city's actually having fallen (Matt. 24:1-28). The testimony of Irenaeus, quoted above, would place its writing in the time of Nero "while Paul and Peter were in Rome." If this tradition be correct, it may have been composed by Matthew originally for non-Palestinian Aramaic-speaking converts, who did not have access to the apostles and who were consequently dependent for their knowledge of Jesus upon a written text.

The testimony of Papias has been frequently rejected, since no trace of an Aramaic original has survived and since the language of the Gospel bears no marks of being a Greek translation. Promiscuous translations such as Papias mentions would hardly yield the good Greek of the existing Gospel. On the other hand, it is possible that seeing the demand for written information about the life of Jesus, the author made a Greek edition for the Gentile churches, perhaps for Antioch in particular. Since the Greek churches quickly outstripped the Aramaic churches in numbers and in influence, the Aramaic original might have perished at an early date. Contradictory opinions have been expressed concerning the original language of this Gospel. In any case, the existing Greek text is early and should probably be regarded as an edition rather than as a translation from Aramaic.

Matthew's Gospel is admirably suited to a church which was still closely related to Judaism, though becoming increasingly independent of it. It breathes the atmosphere of Messianism, yet it has a message for "all the world." It preserves the essence of the Abrahamic covenant, which stressed God's benefits to Abraham and to his seed as a separate people, and yet added: "In thee shall all the families of the earth be blessed" (Gen. 12:3).

The place of writing could be Antioch. The quotations of the Gospels in the early patristic writings like those of Papias and of Ignatius agree most closely with the text of Matthew, and show that this first Gospel was probably the favorite of the Syro-Jewish church. Furthermore, the church at Antioch was the first to have a markedly Gentile constituency which spoke both Aramaic and Greek. While absolute proof that the Gospel originated at Antioch is lacking, there is no other place more suitable for it. It may, therefore, have been composed some time between A.D. 50 and A.D. 70 and have been circulated by those who worked in and from the church of Antioch.

## Content

The theme of the Gospel of Matthew is announced by its opening words: "The book of the generation of Jesus Christ, the son of David, the son of Abraham" (Matt. 1:1). The phraseology reminds one of the book of Genesis, which is divided into sections by the use of the same phrase, "the book of the generations of . . ." or "the generations of . . ." (Gen. 2:4, 5:1, 6:9, *et al*). Each occurrence of this phrase marked a stage in the development of the Messianic promise. The links in the history of God's people are carried forward through Genesis, and one appears in Ruth 4:18, where the Messianic line ends with David. Matthew picks up the genealogy at this point and illustrates its fulfilment in the person of Jesus.

The structure of Matthew is built around a double outline which can be traced by recurring phrases in the book. The first is biographical and is quite similar to the framework of the biography of Jesus as given in Mark and in Luke. There are two points of division: the first in Matthew 4:17, "*From that time* (italics ours) began Jesus to preach, and to say, Repent ye; for the kingdom of heaven is at hand," and the second in Matthew 16:21, "*From that time* (italics ours) began Jesus to show unto His disciples, that he must go unto Jerusalem, and suffer many things of the elders and chief priests and scribes, and be killed, and the third day be raised up." The former of these two passages indicates the rise of Jesus' preaching career which brought Him into public prominence. The latter passage marked the beginning of the decline of His popularity and pointed toward the culmination of His career at the cross. The fact that these two foci of His life are so clearly marked in the Gospel indicates the avowed purpose of the author to present two aspects of Jesus' biography, and shows that he had a unitary concept of that life as a whole. The Gospel is no mere aggregation of fragmentary sayings and random stories, but it is definitely organized to show how the Messiah discharged the calling for which He came into the world.

The other structure of Matthew is peculiar to this first Gospel. Whereas the previously mentioned outline is a biographical interpretation of the life of Jesus, this other outline is topical. The material is divided into five blocks of text, each of which is centered around one

Sidon

ABILENE

X Mt. Hermon

Tyre

ITUREA

Caesarea-Philippi

MEDITERRANEAN SEA

PHOENICIA

GALILEE

AURANITIS

Chorazin
Capernaum • Bethsaida
SEA OF GALILEE (TIBERIAS)
Magdala • Gergesa
Nazareth

Mt. Carmel X

DECAPOLIS

SAMARIA

RIVER JORDAN

PERAEA

Jericho •

Jerusalem • Bethphage
Bethany
Bethlehem •
Herodium •

Machaerus •

JUDAEA

Wilderness of Judaea

DEAD SEA

Masada

EGYPT

# THE GOSPEL
# OF MATTHEW

dominant theme, and each of which ends with the phrase, "When Jesus had finished . . ." With the introductory narrative and the concluding story of the Passion there are seven divisions in all, which are summarized in an Epilogue that confronts the reader with the consequences of Jesus' Messianic claims. The sharp contrast of the action of the priests on the report of the guard at the tomb, and the action of the disciples upon the revelation of the risen Lord compel the reader to choose for himself which attitude he will take. Either he must align himself with the Jewish leaders who repudiated Jesus and would not acknowledge His claims under any circumstances, or else he must himself become a disciple.

## Outline

### MATTHEW: THE GOSPEL OF THE MESSIAH

I. The Prophecies of the Messiah Realized
    The Advent                           1:1-4:11

II. The Principles of the Messiah Announced
    The Inaugural Address           4:12-7:29
        Challenge to Enter          (7:13, 14)

III. The Power of the Messiah Revealed
    The Miracles                    8:1-11:1
        Challenge to Follow        (10:34-39)

IV. The Program of the Messiah Explained
    The Parables                  11:2-13:53
        Challenge to Acceptance     (11:28)
        Challenge to Understanding  (13:51)

V. The Purpose of the Messiah Declared
    The Crisis of the Cross        13:54-19:2
        Challenge to Testify        (16:13-15)

VI. The Problems of the Messiah Presented
    The Conflicts with Opponents   19:3-26:2
        Challenge to Repentance    (23:37-39)

VII. The Passion of the Messiah Accomplished
    The Death and Resurrection   26:3-28:10

VIII. Epilogue
    Rumor and Reality           28:11-20
        Challenge to Action        (28:16-20)

The first of these sections acquaints the reader of the Gospel with the background of the Messiah. His genealogy stemming from Abraham, the initial recipient of God's promises, and from David,

155

divinely chosen founder of Judah's royal house, is first stated in the opening verse and then demonstrated. The account of the virgin birth follows, together with the baptism and the temptation that prepared Him for His public labors. In this section of three and one half chapters the phrase "that it might be fulfilled which was spoken by the Lord through the prophet," or some similar expression, occurs no less than five times. The advent of Jesus is thus depicted as the completion of the divine purpose which was revealed in the Old Testament and which was partially worked out in the historical process which preceded His coming.

The second section opens with the appearance of Jesus in Galilee after the imprisonment of John the Baptist. It is devoted largely to the declaration of the spiritual and ethical principles of the Messianic kingdom. Jesus summoned men to repentance and to faith in Him, and as He declared to them the realm in which He was Lord, He sought to point out what the nature of that realm would be and how it could be entered.

Matthew alone uses the phrase, "the kingdom of heaven," thirty-three times. Five times he speaks of "the kingdom of God" (6:33, 12:28, 19:24, 21:31, 21:43). The other Synoptics use the latter term in many passages where Matthew employs "kingdom of heaven." While Jesus asserted unmistakably that His kingdom would have an ultimate material manifestation (8:11, 13:40-43), He also made plain that it has a present spiritual existence (4:17, 12:28).

The spiritual principles of the kingdom were embodied in the Sermon on the Mount, of which Matthew gives the fullest record. It defined Jesus' position with regard to the law, for He said that He "came not to destroy, but to fulfil" (5:17). He demanded a righteousness that exceeded the standard of Jewish legalism, for it was inward not outward; spontaneous, not legalistic; gauged by a person, and not by a code. Its highest standard was God Himself: "Ye therefore shall be perfect, as your heavenly Father is perfect" (5:48). In this respect He went beyond the law when He said: "Ye have heard that it was said to them of old time . . . but I say unto you" (5:21, 22). The Sermon on the Mount is a direct assertion of His right to transcend the law. He did not revoke the law but He went beyond it by the sheer holiness of His person.

The criterion of righteousness in the Sermon on the Mount is not conformity with human ideals, but consists in knowledge of Christ, in hearing His sayings, and in doing them (7:23, 24). The full import of Christ's person and work was yet to be realized, but the necessity of making Him central to all of His teaching and to all of faith is stated here unmistakably.

In order that these principles might be validated in the thinking of potential believers, some proofs of Jesus' power were necessary. The third section of Matthew (8:1-11:1) is occupied first with a recital of miracles of various types which showed Jesus' power over disease (leprosy, 8:1-4; palsy, 8:5-13; fever, 8:14-17; paralysis, 9:2-8; issue of blood, 9:20-22; blindness, 9:27-31), demons (8:28-34, 9:32-34), the powers of nature (8:23-27), and death (9:18, 23-26). The commission to the twelve which is described in Matthew 10 may be regarded as Jesus' delegation of power to these men and as His reassurance to them as they set out to exercise it. The preaching of the Messiah was not just the proclamation of a new ideal, but was to be the demonstration of a new power — a concept which the book of Acts states became a reality in the later life of the church: "And with great power gave the apostles their witness of the resurrection of the Lord Jesus: and great grace was upon them" (Acts 4:33).

Such miraculous acts, whether of the Lord Jesus Christ Himself or of His disciples, were not a sporadic and aimless show of power. Jesus was seeking to teach the multitude and to inaugurate a program for His kingdom rather than to bewilder or to amaze the crowds.

Beginning with the fourth section of Matthew (11:2-13:53) the parables are featured strongly. Not all of them belong to this part of the Gospel, but the greatest single aggregation of them is here in the thirteenth chapter. In figures taken from everyday life they portray the nature and program of the kingdom of heaven, particularly with reference to the future.

Jesus declared that the parables were intended both to reveal and to conceal truth, for when the disciples asked Him why He used parables in speaking to the crowds, He said:

> *Unto you it is given to know the mysteries of the kingdom of heaven, but to them it is not given.* (Matt. 13:11)

Jesus intended that His instructions should be plain to those who were ready for it, and obscure to those who were rebellious.

In this list are eight parables:

| | |
|---|---|
| 1. The Soils | 13:1-23 |
| 2. The Wheat and the Tares | 13:24-30, 36-43 |
| 3. The Mustard Seed | 13:31, 32 |
| 4. The Leaven | 13:33 |

| | |
|---|---|
| 5. The Treasure | 13:44 |
| 6. The Pearl | 13:45, 46 |
| 7. The Net | 13:47-50 |
| 8. The Householder | 13:51, 52 |

The list is divided at verse 36, where it is said that Jesus withdrew from the multitudes and went indoors, so that four parables were designed for the populace and four for His disciples.

The first four, then, present the kingdom of heaven to the crowd. Its inception by sowing the word of God, its reception by various types of hearers, the contrast of real and spurious response in the wheat and the tares, the amazing growth of the kingdom from a tiny beginning to a large tree, the dynamic forces of the kingdom as compared to leaven — all these were factors which He wanted the populace to know.

The last four parables deal with inner aspects of the kingdom: the cost of building it, the double destiny of those affected by it, and the intermingling of new and of old elements in its teaching.

All of the parables indicate that Jesus was not thinking of Himself simply as a Jewish reformer, but as the sovereign of the earth and as a figure of world importance.

The eleventh and twelfth chapters, preceding the parables, contain additional discourses which bear on the nature and importance of His mission. The challenge of John the Baptist (11:2-19), Jesus' rejection by the Galilean cities (11:20-24), His authority over the Sabbath (12:1-14), and His authority over the demons (12:22-37) — all contribute to the understanding of His work as a supernatural person who had come to earth on an unusual errand.

The crisis of this mission is anticipated in the next section of Matthew (13:54-19:2). The rejection of Jesus by His fellow citizens (13:54-58), the threat of Herod in the death of John the Baptist (14:1-12), the obtuseness of the disciples (15:1-16, 16:5-12) indicated tensions that brought from Jesus a declaration of the imminence of the cross, and also the revelation of Himself in the transfiguration (16:21-17:8). From this point on in the narrative the cross loomed increasingly before Jesus and became the immediate objective of His earthly career.

The declaration of the Messianic purpose led to conflict. In chapters 19:3 to 26:2 the problems of the Messiah are described and His conflicts with His opponents appear in definite events, such as the debates with the Herodians, the Sadducees, and the Pharisees (22:15-

40). The denunciations of chapter 23 and the prediction of the desolation of Jerusalem in chapters 24 and 25 grew out of this conflict.

Conflict must come to a crisis, and in the life of the Messiah that crisis was the cross. Matthew 26:3 through 28:10 describes His passion, His death, and His resurrection. Matthew stressed the Messianic character of His death by emphasizing its relation to prophecy. Four times Jesus alluded definitely to the Old Testament as applying to the events of His Passion (26:31, 54, 56, 27:9), and in replying to Caiaphas' questioning He used of Himself the title, Son of Man (26:64), which in Daniel (Dan. 7:13, 14) was applied to a heavenly being.

The Epilogue is a summary of the whole Gospel, clinching its teaching by illustrating the two attitudes toward Jesus: rejection in unbelief, or worship because of acceptance.

Each of the sections contains a challenge to the disciples, spoken by Jesus, which is obviously intended by the author to be a challenge to his reader also. At the close of the didactic section containing the Sermon on the Mount, Jesus called upon the disciples to take the first step of entering the way which leads to life (7:13, 14). As soon as He had proved His power to them, He commissioned them as witnesses and challenged them to take up the cross and follow Him (10:34-41). In the section dealing with the explanation of His program there is a double challenge: one to the multitude to come to Him for rest (11:28) and one to the disciples asking if they had understood His words (13:51). He wanted to make sure that His claims brought both volitional and intellectual response. The prediction of the cross at the great turning-point in His life evoked a call for committal: "Who say ye that I am?" (16:15). His rejection by Jerusalem constrained Him to summon the rebellious city to repentance (23:37-39). With the denouement of the story, the Great Commission says, "Go ye therefore . . .," the final appeal of the Gospel as a whole. Each section is thus applied practically to the action of the reader as he makes his way progressively through the book.

### Emphasis

The Gospel of Matthew was written to show how Jesus of Nazareth enlarged and explained the revelation which had been begun in the Messianic prophecies of the Old Testament. Although it is strongly Jewish in its character, it was written also for the benefit of Gentiles, since the final commission enjoined the Twelve to make disciples "of all nations" (28:19). If it were originally composed for the benefit of the church at Antioch, where Gentile converts first came together in large numbers, the reason for its character would be plain. Matthew was seeking to show to these converts the meaning of Jesus' ministry in terms of the Old Testament which their Jewish colleagues believed, and from which they themselves had been taught.

Certain incidents are peculiar to Matthew. The vision of Joseph (1:20-24), the visit of the Magi (2:1-12), the flight into Egypt (2:13-15), the massacre of the infants (2:16), the dream of Pilate's wife (27:19), the death of Judas (27:3-10), the resurrection of the saints at the crucifixion (27:52), the bribery of the guard (28:12-15), and the baptismal commission (28:19, 20) appear nowhere else in the Gospels. Among the parables, the tares (13:24-30, 36-43), the hidden treasure (13:44), the pearl (13:45, 46), the drag-net (13:47), the unmerciful servant (18:23-35), the laborers in the vineyard (20:1-16), the two sons (21:28-32), the marriage of the king's son (22:1-13), the ten virgins (25:1-13), and the talents (25:14-30) are exclusively Matthean.

Only three miracles are peculiar to Matthew: the two blind men (9:27-31), the dumb demoniac (9:32, 33), and the coin in the fish's mouth (17:24-27). Matthew's use of miracles seems to be directed more to their use as proofs of Jesus' Messianic power than to the advancement of a narrative, even though he duplicates many that appear in Mark and in Luke.

Matthew's Gospel is didactic in emphasis. It contains the largest single block of discourse material found in the Gospels (chaps. 5, 6, and 7), and there are other long passages (chaps. 10, 13, 18, 23, 24, 25) which reproduce Jesus' teaching. These discourses comprise about three fifths of the entire Gospel. Matthew evidently wanted to stress the content of Jesus' teaching as related to His person and to the law in order that the full implications of the Messiah's coming might be clear.

## Characters

Matthew lays less stress upon the individual actors in his narrative than the other Synoptists do, nor does he introduce many whose names do not appear elsewhere. Joseph (1:18-25), Herod the Great (2:1-16) and the mother of James and John (20:20, 21) are given more space than in Mark and in Luke; but both Mark and Luke use character sketches more than does Matthew.

In general, the characters of Matthew's Gospel are identical with those of Mark, Luke, and John. John the Baptist, Mary (Jesus' mother), the twelve disciples, Caiaphas, the high priests, Pilate, Simon of Cyrene, Joseph of Arimathea, and many minor figures — all play their part in the narrative. They are, however, incidental to the teaching.

## Special Features

1. Matthew is the *Gospel of Discourse.*

In each of the sections is one long specimen of discourse, as the following table shows.

| Section | Discourse |
|---|---|
| I. The Prophecies Realized<br>1:1-4:11 | Preaching of John<br>3:1-12 |
| II. The Principles Announced<br>4:12-7:29 | The Sermon on the Mount<br>5:1-7:29 |
| III. The Power Revealed<br>8:1-11:1 | The Commission<br>10:1-42 |
| IV. The Program Explained<br>11:2-13:53 | The Parables<br>13:1-52 |
| V. The Purpose Declared<br>13:54-19:2 | The Meaning of Forgiveness<br>18:1-35 |
| VI. The Problems Presented<br>19:3-26:2 | Denunciation and Prediction<br>23:1-25:46 |
| VII. The Passion Accomplished<br>26:3-28:10 | (No discourse: action) |
| VIII. Epilogue<br>28:11-20 | The Great Commission<br>28:18-20 |

2. Matthew is the *Gospel of the Church.*

Matthew's Gospel is the only one in which the word "church" occurs (16:18, 18:17). Both of these passages were spoken by Christ, showing that He had a definite idea of the church as an institution to come. The very fact that these utterances of His are embodied in Matthew may indicate that it was written for a young and struggling church that needed encouragement and discipline.

3. Matthew is the *Gospel of the King.*

Not only is the doctrine of the kingdom emphasized in Matthew, but through all of the Gospel the royalty of Christ is prominent. The genealogy in the first chapter follows the royal line of Judah. The alarm of Herod was caused because the birth of Jesus introduced a political rival. The entry into Jerusalem stresses His arrival as king, riding peacefully upon an ass's colt (21:5, 7). In the eschatological discourse He predicts that He will sit "on the throne of his glory" (25:31). The inscription over the cross, placed by Pilate, was "This is Jesus the King of the Jews" (27:37).

161

# THE GOSPEL OF MARK

# THE GOSPEL OF MARK

Origin

Date and Place

Content

Outline

Emphasis

Characters

# CHAPTER VIII

# The Gospel of Mark

## Origin

Of the author of this Gospel comparatively little is known. Nowhere does the book mention him by name; and there are relatively few passages that give any hints concerning his interests and personality, to say nothing of his identity. Tradition identifies him as John Mark, the scion of a Christian family in Jerusalem, the assistant and understudy of Paul, of Barnabas, and perhaps of Peter. The date of his birth is unknown, but he was probably ten years younger than the apostles, which would have made him approximately twenty years old at the time of the crucifixion. He was the son of Mary, a friend of the apostles, who is mentioned in Acts 12. The prayer meeting for the deliverance of Peter was held in her house, and it is possible that her home was the headquarters of the Christian leaders in Jerusalem. Evidently Peter sought it out as his first point of call after the deliverance from jail (Acts 12:12), which may indicate that he felt sure of finding his colleagues there at that time. It may have been in this house that the "upper room" was located where Jesus and the disciples ate the last supper, and where the pre-Pentecostal prayer meeting was held. If so, Mark was well acquainted with the leaders of the Christian movement almost from its inception.

The family from which Mark came was well-to-do, for his mother owned the house and kept slaves. Hayes suggests that he was "the spoiled son of a wealthy widow."[1] Barnabas, his cousin, was evidently a man of some property; for he sold a field, "and brought the money and laid it at the apostles' feet" (Acts 4:37). Their original home was probably Cyprus; at any rate, Barnabas came from there (Acts 4:36). Mark seems to have been brought up in an environment that combined piety and culture.

He was introduced to the ministry by his cousin Barnabas, who, after the visit to Jerusalem with Paul recorded in Acts 11:30, returned

---

1. Doremus A. Hayes, *The Synoptic Gospels and the Book of Acts* (New York; The Methodist Book Concern, n.d.) p. 105.

165

to Antioch taking Mark with him (Acts 12:25). When Barnabas and Paul went on the first missionary journey, Mark went along as assistant or understudy (Acts 13:5). Mark stayed with them during their work in Cyprus, but when they left Cyprus for the mainland of Asia, he parted from them and returned to Jerusalem (Acts 13:13). The reason for this defection is not given, but the implication seems to be that either he did not feel called to this work or else that he suffered some emotional reaction. Perhaps he did not like Paul; perhaps he was not interested in the Gentile mission. The fact remains that he did not go on with the others.

After the return to Antioch and the subsequent Council of Jerusalem, Barnabas proposed that John Mark be taken on the next journey. Paul demurred because Mark "went not with them to the work" (Acts 15:37-39). The disagreement between them was so sharp that they severed connections. Barnabas took Mark and sailed to Cyprus, whereas Paul, with a new assistant, went on with the mission in Asia.

At this point, probably about the year 50, Mark disappeared from the New Testament narrative and did not reappear for ten years. In the Epistle to the Colossians, however, Mark had again joined Paul's company at Rome, and the latter had recommended him to the Colossian church. At a somewhat later time, Paul characterized him as "useful to me for ministering" (II Tim. 4:11). The old disagreement must have been adjusted; Mark had evidently recovered himself in Paul's estimation. It is quite likely also that he was associated with Peter about the same time (I Pet. 5:13). Unquestionably he had been in the church from its very beginning and had been connected with its active witness from Jerusalem to Rome in the years between A.D. 30 and 65. Tradition, preserved by Eusebius, says that he founded the churches of Alexandria.[2]

## Date and Place

The earliest witnesses to the Gospel of Mark generally connect it with the preaching of Peter in Rome in the seventh decade of the Christian era.

Papias (c. A.D. 115), as quoted by Eusebius (A.D. 375),[3] said:

> And John the Presbyter also said this — Mark being the interpreter of Peter, whatsoever he recorded he wrote with great accuracy, but not, however, in the order in which it was spoken

---

2. Eusebius: *Historia Ecclesiae*, II, 16.
3. *Op. cit.*, III, 39.

or done by our Lord, for he neither heard nor followed our Lord, but as before said, he was in company with Peter, who gave him such instruction as was necessary, but not to give a history of our Lord's discourses: wherefore Mark has not erred in anything, by writing some things as he has recorded them; for he was carefully attentive to one thing, not to pass by anything he heard, or to state any thing falsely in these accounts.

Eusebius[4] quoted also Clement of Alexandria (c. A.D. 180) to the effect that Peter's hearers urged Mark to leave a record of the doctrine which Peter had communicated orally, and that Peter authorized the Gospel to be read in churches. Origen, Clement's successor (c. A.D. 225), is alleged to have said that Mark wrote his Gospel as Peter explained it to him.[5] Irenaeus confirmed this tradition by saying that "after the death of Peter and Paul, Mark delivered to us in writing things preached by Peter."[6]

The reliability of these traditions may be open to question since they do not come directly from the first century, but it is noteworthy that they agree on the Markan authorship for the second Gospel and that they all connect it with the preaching of Peter. The traditions disagree concerning the relation of the Gospel to the lifetime of Peter. Irenaeus implies that the Gospel was written after the death of Peter, presumably between A.D. 65 and A.D. 68, whereas Clement and Origen indicate that it was perfected during Peter's lifetime and authorized by him. There can be no doubt that this Gospel was produced by a man who knew some of the apostolic band and who had long and direct contact with their preaching.

From the foregoing facts certain deductions may be drawn:

1. Mark was brought up in the religious atmosphere of Judaism.

2. He may have been an eyewitness of some of the facts recorded in the Gospel that bears his name.

3. He was a close associate of the apostolic leaders of the early church, and would have been fully acquainted with their preaching about Jesus, and with the "good news" which they propagated.

4. He himself had been a participant in the work of preaching, and had witnessed the beginning of the Gentile mission.

To these facts may be added one or two from a consideration of the Gospel:

1. The author stressed facts rather than themes or topics.

---

4. *Op. cit.*, II, 15.
5. *Op. cit.*, VI, 25.
6. Irenaeus: *Against Heresies*, III, i, 1.

2. Possibly he was a witness of the arrest of Jesus in the garden. In Mark 14:51, 52 a young man is mentioned who had followed along with Jesus. No hint of his identity is given, nor is his place in the sequence clear at all. As far as the narrative is concerned, the omission of reference to him would not break its continuity. It is difficult to resist the temptation to see here a personal reminiscence of an experience vivid to the author, but not significant to the main thread of the tale. Neither of the other Synoptics records this. If this does refer to Mark, then he was an eyewitness of the last hours of Jesus' life, and it is quite likely that posterity owes much of the records of those hours to him.

3. Again, in Mark 15:21, there is a reference to Simon the Cyrenian, "the father of Alexander and Rufus." These two men have no part in the story; they are mentioned only here. Why? Probably because they were known to the author and to his readers as personal acquaintances. If so, the date of the Gospel must be set within a generation of the cross, even if it is assumed that these men were children when the crucifixion occurred.

4. Another interesting fact emerges from a comparison of Peter's speech in Acts 10:34-43 with this Gospel. Tradition asserts that Mark was Peter's assistant for a time, and there is some confirmation of it in I Peter 5:13. It is noteworthy that the sermon as recorded in Acts follows closely the outline of the content of Mark. Did Mark, as tradition asserts that he did, record in his Gospel the oral preaching of Peter?

From these considerations it may be concluded that this Gospel is the product of one of the junior preachers of the apostolic age, who was thoroughly acquainted with the message concerning Jesus and who recorded it as he heard it, without elaboration or embellishments of any kind. He made no attempt at a biographical interpretation; he merely allowed the facts themselves to speak for him. If it were written toward the end of his career, his own experience would have deepened and enriched his presentation of the message concerning Christ.

The foregoing discussion of the author has already covered much of the existing evidence concerning the date of the Gospel. It can scarcely have been later than A.D. 70 and may have been composed considerably earlier, if by "composed" is meant the collection and use of material in it, but not necessarily its publication. The close accord of Mark with Matthew and Luke, in which Gospels most of the material in Mark can be found, has led many to believe that Matthew and Luke used Mark as a source of information and that the written document must have antedated the other two Gospels. Such a conclusion would compel one to believe either that Mark was early, or that the others were late. If, however, these Gospels are three different written presentations of the apostolic message concerning the Lord Jesus Christ as inspired by the Holy Spirit, drawn from the common material which the apostles and their associates preached, there is a good possibility that they may have been produced simultaneously. For a further discussion of the subject, see the section on the Synoptic Problem in chapter XI.

The Gospel of Mark is terse, clear, and pointed, a style which would appeal to the Roman mind that was impatient of abstractions and of literary inbreeding. There are many Latinisms in Mark, such as *modius* for "bushel" (4:21), *census* for "tribute" (12:14), *speculator* for "executioner" (6:27 A.V.), *centurio* for "centurion" (15:39, 44, 45) and others. For most of these there were Greek equivalents. Mark apparently used the Latin terms because they were more common or more familiar. The Gospel contains little emphasis on Jewish law and customs. When they are mentioned they are explained more fully than in the other Synoptics. The internal evidence of the Gospel fits fairly well the external tradition that the place of publication may have been Rome. At any rate, Mark was intended for the unevangelized layman of practical Roman mentality.

## Content

The Gospel of Mark is a historical narrative which sets forth a representative picture of the person and work of the Lord Jesus Christ. It is not primarily a biography, for it does not discuss the parentage, the early environment, the birth, the education, or the family of its principal character, nor does it attempt to furnish information about any particular phase of His life. It gives in close succession, probably in general chronological order, a series of episodes in Christ's career with some detail concerning the last week that He spent on earth. It is almost entirely objective in its approach. Little comment is offered; the narrative tells its own story. If the last twelve verses of the Gospel, which are widely regarded as non-Markan because they do not appear in the text of the oldest manuscripts, be detached, the Gospel ends with singular abruptness. It is brief, pictorial, curt, clearcut, and forceful. Like a snapshot album devoted to one person, it gives a series of characteristic poses of Jesus without attempting close continuity between them. Nevertheless Mark affords a satisfactory understanding of His person and work when the total impression of these individual episodes is put together.

The subject of the Gospel is adequately summed up in the opening verse, "The beginning of the gospel of Jesus Christ, the Son of God."[7] Whether the words are an ancient heading given to the Gospel, or whether they are the one chosen by the writer, they are an appropriate introduction to its content. The person of Christ dominates the narrative throughout its course. His works are the chief source of interest, and His death and resurrection in Jerusalem bring the story to a thrilling climax.

There is no attempt to hide or to exaggerate the supernatural element in His life. The miracles are almost always connected with some definite human need and are performed for the relief of some emergency, not for mere exhibitionism. There is a steady calm progress on the part of Jesus to the goal set for Himself, and there is more than a hint of the surprising dénouement in the resurrection (8:31, 9:31, 10:34). At the end the reader is left to make his own decision concerning the personality who is portrayed as man, and yet as more than man.

## Outline

An outline of Mark is difficult to construct because of the impressionistic character of the Gospel. For his effect upon the reader the author apparently relied more upon the total impact of the Gospel than he did upon the climactic sequence of sections. The following, however, will afford a fair guide to the structure of the book.

### MARK: THE GOSPEL OF THE SON OF GOD       Mark 1:1

| (Topical Outline) | (Place) | |
|---|---|---|
| I. The Preparation | | 1:2-13 |
| The Forerunner | Nazareth | 1:2-8 |
| The Baptism | to | 1:9-11 |
| The Temptation | Wilderness | 1:12, 13 |
| II. The Opening Ministry: | | |
| Credentials | | 1:14-5:43 |
| Introduction: Works | Galilee | 1:14-2:12 |

7. The words, "the Son of God," which appear in the text of the ARV, are omitted from Nestle's Greek text and from that of Westcott and Hort, notwithstanding the united support of manuscripts B and D.

The foregoing outline is given in somewhat more detailed fashion than that of Matthew for the purpose of correlating several elements in the structure of Mark. Unlike Matthew, which follows chiefly the theme of the Messiah, Mark is concerned with the activity of Jesus as the Son of God, who is also the Servant of God. The basic outline is built on the changes in the geographical localities of His ministry. This Gospel says little about any ministry in Jerusalem prior to the Passion, although Jesus must have been there several times before His last visit. Not until He came to the crisis of His ministry did He remove from Galilee and the Decapolis. The trips to Tyre and Sidon, or to Caesarea Philippi, were attempts to withdraw from the tumult and the conflict which attended His public ministry, in order that He might have opportunity to pray and to think alone, and to instruct His disciples in the truths which they perceived only too dimly.

The outline shows also a progression in the thought of Mark. The Greek word *euthus* or *eutheos,* translated "straightway," "immediately," "forthwith," "anon," is used forty-two times, more times than in all the rest of the New Testament. It conveys the impression that however varied and detailed Jesus' ministry may have been, He was hurrying toward some unseen goal which He envisioned, but which was hidden to most of His contemporaries and only faintly perceived by the disciples at those rare intervals when His words illumined their understanding.

The outline attempts to classify the material in Mark. The first section (1:2-13) may be called an introduction, but is more properly an abbreviated account of the preparation of Jesus for His great work. Mark's treatment of this period of Jesus' life is much briefer than that of Matthew and of Luke. There is no genealogy, the preaching of John is stated in its bare elements, and the temptation is not narrated in detail. The entire section deals with the credentials of Jesus, for He was endorsed by John, was anointed by the Holy Spirit, and was tested in the wilderness.

The second section (1:14-5:43) gives the initial impression of being simply a miscellany of representative events. Actually it contains a series of demonstrations of Jesus' authority. The miracle of the man sick with the palsy (2:1-12), which stands at the end of a list of healings, illustrated Jesus' power to forgive sins. The debate with the Pharisees over picking grain on the Sabbath (2:23-28), coupled with the healing of the man with a withered hand (3:1-6), established the principle of Jesus' lordship of the Sabbath. His authority over demons is mentioned in several passages (3:11, 20-30; 5:1-20). The storm on

172

THE
GOSPEL
OF
MARK

the lake of Galilee revealed His power over the elements of nature (4:35-41). The raising of Jairus' daughter demonstrated His power over death (5:21-24, 35-43). Along with these proofs of Jesus' superiority Mark records much of His teaching, but the chief stress in the first part of his narrative is on the right of Jesus to speak and to act as the Son of God and as the Son of Man.

The third section (6:1-8:26) continues the teachings and miracles of the second, but gives a much larger place to the element of conflict. The unbelief of His fellow-townsmen (6:6), the political pressure of Herod who had executed John the Baptist and who might consequently look upon Jesus with suspicion (6:27-29), the danger of popularity which could easily subvert His divine mission into demagoguery, and the traditionalism of the Pharisees (7:1-23) created pressures that Jesus had to resist. Finally, after one futile attempt to withdraw from the importunate crowds (6:31-34), He retired to Tyre and Sidon, Gentile territory where He would not be so well known (7:24). Even there He was asked for assistance. This section on the full ministry brings out the lights and shadows of Jesus' work. His compassion on the multitude, His readiness to minister to the needy, His wisdom in answering questions are contrasted with the unthinking greediness of the crowds.

The fourth section (8:27-10:31) commences with Jesus' retirement to Caesarea Philippi. Mark, like the other Synoptics, treats this as the pivotal point of Jesus' career. Jesus challenged His disciples to make a personal confession of faith in Him (8:27). He disclosed to them for the first time the necessity of His death, and then, in the transfiguration scene, revealed to them His real glory. Over and over again[8] He taught them that He must die and rise again, "but they understood not the saying, and were afraid to ask him" (9:32).

Section five enlarges upon the consequences of this turn in Jesus' affairs by treating the final journey to the cross. In the teaching which Jesus gave to the disciples (10:32-40), in the healing of Bartimaeus, who was singled out by being named personally (10:46-52), and in the popular presentation of the dramatic entry into the city (11:1-10), He showed His attitude of service toward God and man. In the controversy with the various religious groups and in the apocalyptic discourse spoken to the disciples on the Mount of Olives, Jesus laid down the principles of thought and predictions for the future that explained more perfectly the outcome of His mission. He emphasized particularly the divine viewpoint of human life, culminating in His

---

8. Mark 9:31, *edidaskon,* imperfect tense.

return at the close of the age. The tragedy of the cross is not minimized by Mark; but even before he recounts the events of the Passion, he indicates that Jesus would surmount triumphantly the apparent disaster that confronted Him.

The section on the Passion (14:1-15:47) does not vary greatly in its essential facts from the story told in the other Gospels. The last few days of Jesus' life are given in closer chronological sequence than any other period of equal length in His life. Certainly it was the most vivid period and the most important. Mark's plain factual style enhances the value of the narrative and makes one ask why so marvelous a person, with such tremendous authority, should have come to so untimely an end.

Two answers to this question are given in the Gospel itself. One is the declaration of Jesus in Mark 10:45:

> *For the Son of man also came not to be ministered unto, but to minister, and to give his life a ransom for many.*

The tragedy of the Gospel was an inevitable part of His service to men and of His redemption of them. The other answer is contained in the last section on the resurrection (16:1-8 [20]). The discovery of the empty tomb was proof that something had happened in Joseph's garden that could not be explained on any purely naturalistic basis. The positive testimony of the angel and the sudden terror of the women prove that the unexpected had happened and that Jesus had really risen.

The genuineness of the last twelve verses of Mark has been disputed on textual grounds, for several of the oldest and most generally reliable manuscripts omit them entirely. Several endings are in existence. though the one which is familiar is the best of all of them. In any case, it represents an account which can be traced back to the end of the second century, and it bears strong affinities to the other accounts of the resurrection, so that there is good reason for believing that it contains authentic information. If Mark himself wrote it, he probably added it as an epilogue, since it begins with a resumé of what he has already stated in the first eight verses. It stresses the disbelief of the disciples (16:11, 13, 14, 16), as if to say that even after the crowning demonstration of Jesus' authority over death many were still incredulous and needed an added exhortation to faith.

## Emphasis

As noted already, Mark is a Gospel of action. It has no prologue, except for the title. Direct citations from the Old Testament for purposes of prophetic interpretation are very few, although there are numerous quotations and allusions. Of seventy parables and parabolic utterances in the Gospels, Mark has only eighteen, though some of them comprise only a sentence apiece. For its size, however, Mark gives more space to the miracles than does any other Gospel for it records eighteen out of a possible total of thirty-five. Luke, for instance, in ninety-one pages of Greek text narrates only twenty miracles, whereas the eighteen of Mark are included in fifty-three pages of the same text. Plainly, Mark was more interested in deeds than in speculation.

Mark is a Gospel of personal reactions. All through its pages are recorded the responses of Jesus' audience. They were "amazed" (1:27), critical (2:7), afraid (4:41), puzzled (6:14), "astonished" (7:37), bitterly hostile (14:1). There are at least twenty-three such references. The narrative presents its own appeal, and in the reflection of the popular mind one can see the evaluation of modern attitudes to Jesus. Beside these incidental notes of popular response there are many recorded interviews of Jesus, and even observations of His personal gestures (3:5, 5:41, 7:33, 8:23, 9:27, 10:16).

All of these touches and others make Mark the Gospel of vividness. There are one hundred fifty-one uses of the historic present tense of the verb in Mark and many uses of the imperfect tense, both of which portray action as in process rather than simply as an event. Vivid phrases occur frequently: "The Spirit *driveth* him forth into the wilderness" (1:12); "when they had *broken it up* [the roof]" (2:4); "the unclean spirits . . . *fell down* before him" (3:11); "the waves beat into the boat, insomuch that the boat *was now filling*" (4:37); "he commanded them that all should sit down by companies *upon the green grass*" (6:39). The italicized phrases are a few samples taken at random from the text to illustrate the vigor and freshness of the Markan style — a style which shows unquestionably the oral testimony of an eyewitness who was telling exactly what he saw as it affected him and others.

The purpose of this Gospel seems to be primarily evangelistic. It is an attempt to bring the person and work of Christ before the public as a new message, "the gospel," without assuming much knowledge of theology or of Old Testament teaching on the part of the hearer. Its brief anecdotes, its epigrammatic sentences, its pointed applications of truth are just what a street preacher would use in telling of Christ to a promiscuous crowd. Although the Gospel is not primarily literary in style, it is integrated by the person of whom it speaks, and it gives a picture of Christ that is factual and inescapable.

## Characters

Mark does not specialize in character sketches, although many of the personalities in his pages are etched more sharply than are those in Matthew. The young man in the garden who escaped from the soldiery (14:51, 52), Alexander and Rufus (15:21), Simon the leper (14:3) are mentioned as acquaintances of the author, and possibly of the readers. The allusion to Alexander and Rufus is particularly intriguing, for it implies that Mark's readers knew these men and were their contemporaries. If Rufus be identical with the man mentioned in Romans 16:13, the dating of Mark somewhere between A.D. 56 and A.D. 66 and its origin at Rome might be confirmed. Mark, however, does not mention as many persons as does Luke, nor does he use them as patterns to the same extent that Luke and John do. He seems to have been more interested in the progress of his story than in the analysis of individual characters. The naming of these persons suggests that later they may have become celebrities in the Christian community prior to the writing of this Gospel.

# THE GOSPEL OF LUKE

# THE GOSPEL OF LUKE

Origin

Author

Date and Place

Content

Outline

Emphasis

Characters

# CHAPTER IX

# The Gospel of Luke

## Origin

Of the three Synoptic Gospels Luke affords the greatest amount of information concerning its own beginning. Its author, who does not give his own name, supplied a literary introduction stating his aims in writing it, the methods that he employed, and his relationships to his contemporaries who had attempted the same thing. This introduction (Luke 1:1-4) is the key to the book, and to the book of Acts also, if Luke-Acts be regarded as a unit.

From the introduction a number of inferences may be drawn as follows:

1. In the time of the writer a number of works were extant which contained only a partial, or possibly a garbled account of Jesus' life and work. The author would not have written a Gospel of his own had he been perfectly satisfied with any of those that he knew.

2. These accounts had attempted some systematic arrangement of available facts ("to draw up a narrative" — 1:1).

3. These facts were well known to the Christian world and were accepted independently of the narratives. Luke says that they "have been fulfilled among us" (1:1).

4. The author felt himself at least as well informed as the others and as capable of writing an account on his own responsibility ("it seemed good to me also").

5. His information came from competent official sources ("who from the beginning were eyewitnesses and ministers of the word" — 1:2).

6. He was conversant with the facts, either by observation or by inquiry, and he was certainly a contemporary of the main course of action in the sense that he lived in the generation of those who had witnessed it. The term translated "having traced the course of all things"[1] is the same as the one used in II Timothy 3:10, 11, where

---

1. Greek: *parekolouthekoti.*

181

Paul said that Timothy had "followed" his "teaching, conduct . . . what things befell me at Antioch, at Iconium, at Lystra." The language does not imply that Timothy was present with Paul at every occasion in these cities, but it does indicate that he was a contemporary of Paul and that he had some first-hand knowledge of these affairs.

The word *anothen,* translated "from the first" in the ARV, has been a source of some controversy. As used in the Johannine writings and in James (1:17) it means almost invariably "from above." It is used only twice by Luke, here, and in Acts 26:5. In the latter passage, which is a speech of Paul, it cannot possibly mean "from above," but must mean "beforehand," "from some time back." Knowling says that Paul was referring to the beginning of his public education in Jerusalem.[2] Singularly enough the only use of the word in the Pauline epistles (Gal. 4:9) means "back again," a reference to former time. While it could be rendered "from above" in Luke 1:3, such a translation is not necessitated by the context, and certainly would not be uniform with other Lukan and Pauline language.

The translation of an ambiguous term is always best determined by the current usage of the author; and since the rendering of the ARV is in accord with that usage, it is retained here.

On this basis it may be understood that the author is claiming a contemporary knowledge of facts that was not acquired recently. His knowledge of Christ went back over a number of years of his life, during which he had associated with apostles, eyewitnesses, and possibly with personal friends or relatives of the Lord Jesus. The urge of the Holy Spirit which made him an author controlled the choice of the incidents that he recorded and the language in which he wrote them.

7. Luke's knowledge covered all of the major facts. His Gospel contains many particulars that do not appear in the others and is the most generally representative life of Christ.

8. He professed to write accurately and in logical order. His use of the term "in order" does not necessarily presuppose chronological order; but it does mean that he had a definite plan of procedure and that he intended to adhere to it.

9. Luke's addressee was probably a man of the upper class who may be called here by his baptismal name, Theophilus, which meant literally

---

2. R. J. Knowling in *Expositor's Greek Testament* (New York: George H. Doran Co., n. d.), Vol. II, p. 501.

"lover of God" or "loved by God." The epithet "most excellent"[3] was generally applied only to officials or to members of the aristocracy. Perhaps he was a convert of Luke, or a patron who assumed responsibility for circulating Luke's works.

10. This addressee had already been informed orally concerning Christ, perhaps through the preaching that he had heard; but he needed further instruction to stabilize him and to convince him of the truth.

11. Luke's obvious purpose was to give to his friend complete knowledge of the truth.

From the foregoing deductions one may conclude that the author was a man who possessed literary gifts and who knew how to make use of them in presenting the message of Christ. Who was he?

## Author

The identity of the author depends upon the relation of the Third Gospel to the book of Acts. If Luke and Acts were written by the same person, one can apply to Luke such evidence concerning the author as may be internal to Acts, and vice versa. In Acts the author was undoubtedly a participant in many of the events that he described, for he used frequently the pronoun "we." The "we sections" have become a useful guide for determining the interests, character, and possible identity of the writer.

The first of these is found in Codex Bezae (D), a manuscript of the sixth century, whose readings are often exceptional, as is this one. It is located in Acts 11:28, and reads:

> And there was great rejoicing, and when we gathered together, one of their number, named Agabus, spoke, indicating that a great famine was about to take place over the whole world . . .

Since this reading occurs only in Codex Bezae it is generally rejected; but if it is genuine, it makes the writer a member of the early church at Antioch during the ministry of Barnabas and Saul.

The first generally accepted reference begins with Acts 16:10, at Paul's departure from Troas on his second missionary journey. The writer accompanied him from Troas to Philippi, where the references to the first person plural cease with the discussion of Paul's imprisonment (Acts 16:17, 19-34). Probably the writer was present at Philippi but was not arrested. The "we sections" reappear at Paul's return to Macedonia as recorded in Acts 20:6 ff. From this point the

---

3. Greek: *kratiste.* See Acts 23:26, 24:3, 26:25.

"we sections" remain throughout the book, although the writer does not seem to be in evidence during the imprisonment of Paul at Caesarea. Nevertheless, he accompanied Paul on the voyage to Rome (Acts 27:1, 2, ff.) and stayed with him until the end of the story.

The relation of Luke to Acts is close. Both documents are addressed to the same person, Theophilus. The introduction to Acts dovetails exactly with the content of Luke when it says that "the former treatise" concerned "all that Jesus began both to do and to teach" (Acts 1:1). The stress on the resurrection and on the teaching ministry of the forty days accords well with the content of Luke 24. The emphasis in Acts on the place of the Holy Spirit is exactly like that of the Gospel. Harnack has shown that in vocabulary and in style there is a close agreement between the two narratives.[4] The argument is too long and complicated to be reproduced here, but the case for the unity of Luke-Acts seems to be fairly established. Such facts, then, as are true of the writer of Acts will be equally true of the writer of Luke, and may legitimately be used to fix his identity.

Accordingly, the author of Luke-Acts may have been an Antiochian Gentile, converted in Antioch not more than fifteen years after Pentecost. He became a friend and associate of Paul and traveled with him on the second journey after meeting him at Troas (Acts 16:10). He remained at Philippi as pastor of the church while Paul pursued his itinerant ministry in Achaia and, after a visit to Antioch (18:22), in Asia Minor (19:1-41). When Paul returned to Philippi on the third journey, the author joined his company again (20:6). He went with him to the mainland of Asia, and thence accompanied him to Jerusalem.

The four years of Paul's imprisonment give no reference to the writer's activities during that time; but at the close of the period he accompanied Paul to Rome, where he was about to stand trial before Caesar.

This man, whose diary forms the best source for knowledge about the missionary travels of Paul, must have been a close associate of the great apostle. Of the known traveling companions of this period, none fits the requirements save Luke. Identification is established chiefly by process of elimination. The writer was not Timothy, nor any of those mentioned in Acts 20:4-6, for obviously the writer and Paul did not accompany these on their trip from Philippi to Troas, but went later. If the lists of associates in Colossians (4:7-17) and Philemon

---

4. Adolph Harnack, *Luke the Physician* (Translated by J. R. Wilkinson. *Crown Theological Library* London: Williams and Norgate; New York: G. P. Putnam's Sons, 1907).

(23, 24) be used, Aristarchus can be eliminated as one of the list in Acts 20; Mark is not the writer, since in Acts he is mentioned in the third person; Epaphras' field of labor was not Philippi, but the cities of Asia Minor; Demas ended his course in disgrace (II Tim. 4:10); Jesus Justus evidently was Jewish by ancestry, as the writer of Acts was not. Only Luke remains as a possibility.

Internal evidence has some bearing on this conclusion. The author possessed high literary ability and was probably well educated. His language shows a definite Greek turn of mind. For instance, his use of the word "barbarians" in Acts 28:2 does not imply that the inhabitants of Malta were crude savages, but it means only that they were not a Greek-speaking people. He was a keen observer, for the twenty-seventh chapter of Acts gives the best account of ancient shipping that has come down from antiquity. A comparison of Mark 5:25-26 with Luke 8:43 shows that he had some interest in a physician's viewpoint, which would confirm the title given to Luke in Colossians 4:14: "Luke, the beloved physician."

External tradition supports the conclusion that Luke, the physician and the friend of Paul, was the writer of the Third Gospel. Justin Martyr of the second century used this Gospel.[5] Tatian employed it in the Diatessaron. Marcion included a revised form of it in his canon; and from the end of the second century onward it was widely quoted as Lukan. Tertullian alone quoted or alluded to the Lukan text more than five hundred times.

Since the identity of the author is reasonably well established, some notice should be taken of his character and of his achievements.

Briefly, he was a Greek-speaking Gentile by birth, who had received a good education and who possessed considerable intellectual ability. He was probably one of the early converts of the first mission in Antioch. Nothing is known directly of his life until he met Paul at Troas, about A.D. 51. From Troas he went with Paul to Macedonia, where he became pastor of the Philippian church that was distinguished for its zeal and for its loyalty to the founder. Perhaps the "brother" mentioned in II Corinthians 8:22 is a reference to Luke. He may have been a blood-brother of Titus, who was himself connected with Antioch at an early date (Gal. 2:3). Corinthians suggests that this "brother" was of good repute in Achaia and that he was noted for his fame in the gospel. If the reference concerns Luke, he may have acted as Paul's representative all through Macedonia and Achaia while making headquarters at Philippi.

---

5. Cf. Luke 22:44 with Justin Martyr, *Dialogue with Trypho*, ciii.

When Paul returned to Philippi on his third journey, Luke rejoined him and went with him to Palestine. During Paul's stay in Jerusalem and the imprisonment in Caesarea no mention is made of Luke; but he cannot have been far away, for he shared the journey to Rome and wrote the record of the shipwreck (Acts 27). He is mentioned in the Prison Epistles (Col. 4:14, Phm. 24), where he was classed among the "fellow-workers." From this point the data are extremely fragmentary and uncertain. He seems to have been with Paul during the last imprisonment that immediately preceded his death (II Tim. 4:11).

Luke was no mere spectator, viewing Christian truth from outside, but was an active preacher and missionary himself. He was the first great church historian and literary apologist for Christianity. As an associate of Paul his work might be expected to reflect the knowledge of Christ that was used in the preaching to the Gentiles.

## Date and Place

Two termini fix within limits the time of the writing of Luke: it must have been written before Acts, and after the development of Christianity to the point where it would attract the attention of a Gentile inquirer like Theophilus. Acts was probably composed prior to the close of Paul's first imprisonment at Rome, since the abrupt ending of the book intimates that the author had no more to say. The Gospel was, of course, written after the close of the life of Jesus, and its prologue shows that already many others had attempted to write Gospels concerning the facts that were believed by a fairly extensive Christian community. Perhaps A.D. 60 would serve as a median date; for by that time Luke would have been a Christian at least ten years or more, and would have traveled in Palestine, where he could have met many of those who had known Jesus in the flesh. He may have occupied the time while Paul was in prison by investigating the background of the life of Jesus, concerning whom he had heard so much and for whom he himself had been a missionary.

Later datings have been assigned to Luke's Gospel on the ground of its alleged use of Mark, but the literary similarities between the Gospels can be explained on the basis of the common element of evangelistic preaching concerning Christ which was current in the apostolic church. Luke and Mark may have had personal contact at Antioch when John Mark first went there in the company of Barnabas and Saul. Although the date of A.D. 60 cannot be fixed dogmatically, it is as satisfactory as any later date would be.

**186**

No clue is given in this Gospel concerning its place of writing. Probably it was written outside of Palestine, though it may have been composed at Caesarea. Most suggestions, including Rome, Caesarea, Achaia, Asia Minor, and Alexandria are mere guesses. There is not even any good early tradition relating to the place of its origin. All that can be said is that it was written somewhere in the Hellenistic world by a man who worked among Gentiles.

## Content

In general organization the Gospel of Luke follows the main sequence of events as given in Matthew and in Mark, with many unique additions. The accounts of the birth of John the Baptist (1:5-25, 57-80) and of the birth and childhood of Jesus (1:26-56, 2:1-52), the genealogy (3:23-38), the preaching at Nazareth (4:16-30), the special summons to Peter (5:8-10), six miracles (5:1-11, 7:11-17, 13:10-17, 14:1-6, 17:11-19, 22:49-51), nineteen parables (7:41-43, 10:30-37, 11:5-8, 12:13-21, 12:35-40, 12:41-48, 13:6-9, 14:7-11, 14:16-24, 14:28-30, 14:31, 32, 15:8-10, 15:11-32, 16:1-13, 16:19-31, 17:7-10, 18:1-8, 18:9-14, 19:11-27), the story of the encounter with Zacchaeus (19:1-10), the mocking of Jesus by Herod (23:8-12), and the post-resurrection appearance of Jesus on the road to Emmaus (24:13-35) are all major additions in Luke's Gospel. There are many other features peculiar to Luke which are too detailed and too numerous to catalog.

## Outline

The material of Luke is organized around the central concept of Jesus as a member of humanity who lived the perfect and representative life of the Son of Man through the power of the Holy Spirit. The development of this concept is rooted in Luke 2:11, where the child was announced as "a Saviour, who is Christ the Lord." The first of these titles speaks of His mission; the second and third identify Him as the Messiah of Judaism.

LUKE: THE GOSPEL OF THE SAVIOUR OF MEN

The initial statement of Luke's preface declares that the Gospel was written to impart to its reader spiritual certainty concerning the things of which he had been orally instructed. The verb "instructed"[6] is generally used in the New Testament of information which is imparted formally rather than casually. Evidently Luke wanted to give

------

6. Greek: *katecheo.*

THE GOSPEL
OF LUKE

Theophilus an authentic basis in this Gospel for correcting the teaching with which he was already familiar.

On this assumption one may conclude that Luke took special care to present all of his facts accurately, as indeed he says (1:3), and that he would organize them into some framework that would leave an integrated impression on the mind of the reader.

The section on the preparation of the Saviour contains material that is not duplicated in the other Gospels. Matthew states that Jesus was born of a virgin, but he tells the story from the viewpoint of Joseph, whereas Luke tells it from the viewpoint of Mary. Nothing concerning the birth of John the Baptist can be found in Matthew or in Mark.

The third section, the introduction of Jesus to His full ministry, opened with a direct connection with history, as if to show that He was not an idealized religious figure, but a very real participant in the history of mankind who could be localized in time and space. The genealogy is traced from Adam, and emphasizes human descent rather than the royal line. The account of the temptation is closely akin to that of Matthew except in order. Luke calls attention to the fact that the devil had "completed every temptation" (4:13), as if he wished to indicate that Jesus met all the representative temptations of humanity.

In opening the fourth section on the ministry of the Saviour, Luke records the sermon in Nazareth in which Jesus announced His relation to prophetic Scripture. He set the proclamation of "the acceptable year of the Lord" as the goal of His ministry. The subsequent biographical material is quite similar to that which is found at this point in the other Synoptics, though Luke has added many individual touches.

The fifth section is peculiarly Lukan. With the exception of occasional paragraphs very little of the text between Luke 9:51 and 18:30 occurs in the other Gospels. The parables, the Good Samaritan (10:28-37), the Rich Fool (12:13-21), the Fruitless Fig Tree (13:6-9), the Seats at the Marriage Feast (14:7-14), the Great Supper (14:15-24), the Lost Coin (15:8-10), the Prodigal Son (15:11-32), the Unjust Steward (16:1-13), the Rich Man and Lazarus (16:19-31), the Pharisee and the Publican (18:9-14) are found only in Luke. Although they seem at first reading to be a random collection of Jesus' parables, they are illustrative of the meaning of His mission. Each parable or narrative is a specimen of Luke's use of fresh material from the life of Christ to explain His significance for Gentile readers.

Luke's narrative of the Passion contains no large single paragraphs that deviate greatly from the general pattern of the Synoptic narrative as a whole. The order of the last supper (22:19-23), Jesus' comfort of Simon Peter (22:31, 32), the episode of the bloodlike sweat (22:43, 44), the arrangement of events in the house of Caiaphas (22:63-71), the appearance of Jesus before Herod (23:4-16), Jesus' address to the women of Jerusalem (23:27-31), the penitent thief (23:39-43) add to the pictorial quality of the story, but do not alter its progress or meaning. The human sufferings and the human sympathies of Jesus were stressed by Luke as he showed how the Son of Man endured the cross in obedience to the Father.

The account of the resurrection is strikingly new and different. The reality is the same as in the other Gospels but the appearance of Jesus to the two men on the way to Emmaus clinches the argument of this Gospel for certainty. The actuality of Jesus' death, the despair of the disciples, the unexpected and convincing manifestation of His living presence, His interpretation of the Scriptures in terms of Himself, and the spiritual conviction which seized upon them as He spoke to them were all compelling evidence that in the person of Christ something new had happened on the earth. The concluding words of the Gospel connected the historical reality with doctrinal truth and show that the revelation through Christ is the basis for the preaching of repentance and of forgiveness of sins.

## Emphasis

Tradition says that Luke was an artist, and that he painted pictures for the early church. Whether he ever painted on canvas may be uncertain, but unquestionably he was an artist in words. His is the most literary of the Gospels; his stories as he took them from the lips of Jesus or as he told them himself are gems of expression and his vocabulary is rich and varied. Four beautiful songs or poems are imbedded in his work which have come down to the modern day as hymns of the Church: the *Magnificat* (1:46-55), the song of Mary when she went to visit Elizabeth; the *Benedictus* (1:67-79) spoken by Zacharias at the birth of John; the *Gloria in Excelsis* (2:14) of the heavenly host at the birth of Jesus; and the *Nunc Dimittis,* Simeon's prayer at the dedication of the infant Jesus (2:28-32).

Luke's Gospel is predominantly historical. No other writer gives dating for his narrative as Luke does in 1:5, 2:1, and 3:1, 2. No other attempts so complete a sketch of the career of Christ from birth to death, even though many periods of His life are not discussed in detail. There is no provincialism in his treatment of Christ; he looks at Him through the eyes of a cosmopolitan for whom there is neither

Jew nor Gentile, Greek nor barbarian, bond nor free. Luke is impartial in the best sense of that term. His history is not a dull chronicle of happenings, but is a live interpretation written into an integral whole by the inspiration of the Holy Spirit. Sir William Ramsay said:

> You may press the words of Luke in a degree beyond any other historian's, and they stand the keenest scrutiny and the hardest treatment, provided always that the critic knows his subject and does not go beyond the limits of science and justice.[7]

If Ramsay's praise seems exaggerated, one need only to contrast Luke's writings with some of those of his contemporaries to realize that for sobriety, insight, and accuracy they are quite superior. Luke-Acts was written to give a spiritual analysis of the rise and growth of the Christian church, and as such it must be historical in method.

Doctrine is emphasized in the Third Gospel. Luke could scarcely have traveled with Paul and have ministered as a pastor and missionary without being aware of the importance of doctrinal teaching. Although he does not discuss theology topically, his vocabulary reveals his knowledge of it and his interest in it. The person of Christ, the Son of God, who was acknowledged by the angels (1:35), by demons (4:41), by the Father (9:35), is presented both as deity and as humanity. Salvation is a prominent teaching in Luke: ". . . the Son of man came to seek and to save that which was lost" (19:10) is a key sentence in the book; and several of the parables, particularly those of the fifteenth chapter, illustrate the meaning of salvation. The word "justify"[8] which is used so frequently by Paul appears several times in Luke-Acts, though not always in a theological sense. In one instance, however, of the Pharisees and the publican (18:14), it was used unmistakably of a man's spiritual standing before God. Like the other Gospels, Luke lays a foundation for theology rather than developing it as a subject, but the doctrine of the person of Christ, the nature and meaning of repentance, salvation, sin, justification, redemption, and many others are patent to the reader.

The doctrine of the Holy Spirit is given special prominence; in fact, there are more references to the Holy Spirit in Luke than there are in Matthew and in Mark combined. All of the chief actors of the

---

7. Sir William Ramsay, *The Bearing of Recent Discoveries on the Trustworthiness of the New Testament* (Fourth Edition. London: Hodder & Stoughton, Ltd., 1920) p. 89.
8. Greek: *dikaioo*.

Gospel, John the Baptist (1:15), Mary (1:35), Elizabeth (1:41), Zacharias (1:67), Simeon (2:25, 26), and the Lord Jesus Himself (4:1) were empowered for their work by the Holy Spirit. The whole life of Jesus was lived by the Spirit. He was conceived by the Spirit (1:35), baptized by the Spirit (3:22), tested by the Spirit (4:1), empowered by the Spirit for His ministry (4:14, 18), cheered by the Spirit (10:21), and He expected that His disciples would complete His work in the power of the Spirit (24:49). Acts, of course, carried this theme to its fuller development by showing the nature and extent of the work of the Holy Spirit in the church.

Certain classes of people receive marked attention in this Gospel. Luke has much to say about women; the word "woman" occurs forty-three times, and only forty-nine times in Matthew and Mark combined. The character of Mary, Jesus' mother, is treated more fully in Luke than in Matthew. Elizabeth, the mother of John (1:5, 6, 39-45, 57), and Anna the prophetess (2:36-38), the company of women that traveled among Jesus' disciples (8:2, 3), the women who mourned His execution (23:27, 28), and the women who were present at the cross and at the tomb (23:55, 56, 24:1-11) were all noted. Children receive more prominence in Luke than is usual in the annals of antiquity. The birth and infancy of Jesus and of John are omitted completely by Mark; Luke gives three chapters to them. Thrice Luke notes that Jesus performed a miracle on an only child (7:12, 8:42, 9:38). In his pages Jesus appears as the champion of the poor and oppressed. Seven or eight of His parables either are concerned with the contrast of poverty and wealth or stress economic need (7:41, 43; 11:5-8; 12:13-21; 15:8-10; 16:1-13; 16:19-31; 18:1-8). All of these parables belong exclusively to Luke. The portrayal of the rich in the story of the rich man and Lazarus and in the parable of the rich fool is not complimentary, though it is not bitter. Although Luke himself belonged to the upper middle class, he associated voluntarily with the lower classes, and his Gospel was written to apply Christ to their needs.

A word should be said about Luke's skill in writing. Many of the parables of Jesus as Luke reproduced them would be noteworthy not only for their spiritual teaching, but also for their beauty of expression. The parable of the prodigal son in Luke 15 is one of the greatest short stories of all time, and its diction in the Greek is a marvel of combined simplicity and meaningfulness. No subject could be handled with more delicacy or sympathy than the account of Jesus' birth as given by Luke. The picture of the two on the road to Emmaus condenses the whole subject of the resurrection into a paragraph or two of exciting narrative, and includes also the essential teaching of the fact. Anyone who reads the Gospels as a literary critic would select Luke as outstanding.

## Characters

Several new characters appear in this Gospel. Zacharias and Elizabeth his wife, Simeon, Anna, Zacchaeus, and Cleopas are not mentioned elsewhere, and each is a distinct type. Luke's literary characters are as interesting as his historical characters. Who could forget the patient and loving father of Luke 15 and his sons, one wilful and irresponsible, the other haughty and unbending (15:11-32)? The Samaritan who risked life and purse to rescue the Jewish stranger beaten by robbers (10:30-37), the idle rich man who was gloating over his prosperity (12:13-21), the shrewd steward who rescued an income for himself from the wreck of his stewardship (16:1-13), and the snobbish Pharisee who prayed ostentatiously in the temple courts (18:9-14) are all types true to life. They may very well have been taken by Jesus from individual cases that He had observed, and have been preserved for us in Luke's vivid narrative.

The cumulative effect of Luke's Gospel is precisely that which is expressed in the purpose stated by the author. The narrative is so real and so well expressed that it makes one see Jesus as an actual figure of history, not just as the subject of an abstract essay. Luke 19:10, "For the Son of man came to seek and to save that which was lost," is amply illustrated by this Gospel. It portrays Jesus as the Son of man, showing how He lived among men, how He estimated them, and what He did for them.

# THE GOSPEL OF JOHN

# THE GOSPEL OF JOHN

Origin

Author

Date and Place

Content

Outline

Emphasis

Purpose

Characters

# CHAPTER X

# The Gospel of John

## Origin

The Gospel of John is the most unusual and perhaps the most valuable member of the quartet of canonical Gospels. Although it deals with the same broad sequence of events to be found in the pages of the others, it is quite different in structure and in style. It contains no parables and only seven miracles, five of which are not recorded elsewhere. The discourses of Jesus in it are concerned chiefly with His person rather than with the ethical teaching of the kingdom. Personal interviews are multiplied, and Jesus' relationship to individuals is stressed more than his general contact with the public. The Gospel is strongly theological, and it deals particularly with the nature of His person and with the meaning of faith in Him.

Because of the marked differences between John and the Synoptics, its truthfulness has been questioned. The answer lies in its origin and purpose. Traditionally it was written by John the son of Zebedee, the last surviving member of the apostolic band, while he was spending the declining years of his life at Ephesus. Although this opinion has been persistently attacked, it still remains as good a probability as any other hypothesis that can be offered. So little is known concerning the Christian churches at large in the end of the first century that the framework for this Gospel is exceedingly difficult to reconstruct.

The earliest evidence for its existence is to be found in Papias, as quoted by Eusebius.[1] In this passage he alluded to John, who was one of the disciples of the Lord, and also to an elder John, a disciple of the Lord, who was his contemporary. Eusebius deduced that the two persons were different individuals, and cited the existence of two tombs in Ephesus, both of which were called John's in his day. Since Papias' works are not now extant, no independent judgment can be formed on the meaning of this statement. Possibly Eusebius misunderstood him. There is no reason why an apostle could not have also been called an elder, and Papias may simply have been saying that whereas the ma-

---

1. Eusebius, *Historia Ecclesiae* III, xxxix, 124, 127.

jority of the apostles did not survive their oral testimony, one or two of them remained until his day as the last witnesses in the flesh of what Jesus had said and done.

The theory that the Fourth Gospel was the product of some unknown presbyter by the name of John and not of John the apostle cannot be regarded as established. All the testimony of the fathers from the time of Irenaeus is overwhelmingly in favor of the Johannine authorship. Clement of Alexandria (A.D. 190), Origen (c. A.D. 220), Hippolytus (c. A.D. 225), Tertullian (c. A.D. 200), and the Muratorian Fragment (c. A.D. 170) agree in attributing the Fourth Gospel to John, the son of Zebedee.

## Author

From the Gospel itself certain facts about its author may be educed. First, he was a Jew who was accustomed to thinking in Aramaic, although the Gospel was written in Greek. Very few subordinate clauses appear in its text, and not infrequently Hebrew or Aramaic words are inserted and then explained. The author was familiar with Jewish tradition. In 1:19-28 he referred to the Jewish expectation of a coming Messiah. He knew the Jewish feeling toward the Samaritans (4:9) and their exclusive attitude in worship (4:20). He was acquainted with the Jewish feasts, which he explained carefully for the readers.

Second, he was a Palestinian Jew, who had personal acquaintance with the land and especially with Jerusalem and its environs (9:7, 11:18, 18:1). He was familiar with the cities of Galilee (1:44, 2:1) and with the territory of Samaria (4:5, 6, 21). He seems to have been quite at home in the country which he described.

Again, he was an eyewitness of the events which he recorded. Both in 1:14, "we beheld his glory . . .," and in 19:35, where he spoke in the third person, "he that hath seen hath borne witness," he claims to be stating what had been part of his personal experience. Small touches scattered through the Gospel confirm this impression. The hour at which Jesus sat on the well curb (4:6), the number and size of the pots at the wedding of Cana (2:6), the weight and value of the ointment that Mary used on Jesus (12:3, 5), the details of Jesus' trial (chaps. 18, 19) are points which have little to do with the main narrative, but which indicate the observer's eye.

Who was the author? Evidently he was with Jesus from the very first of His career, for he mentions episodes that antedate the opening of the account of Jesus' ministry in the Synoptics. He must have belonged to the group of disciples mentioned in the narrative. According to the final chapter, he is to be identified with the "beloved disciple" who was a close associate of Peter, and who had been very near to Jesus at the last supper (13:23), at the trial (18:15, 16), and at the cross (19:26, 27). Only one of Jesus' most intimate associates would fit these circumstances. James was killed early in the history of the church (Acts 12:2). Peter, Thomas, and Philip are mentioned so frequently in the third person that no one of them could have been the author. Although the author did not name himself, he took for granted that his readers knew who he was and that they would accept his authority in the matters of which he wrote. John the son of Zebedee is the best remaining possibility, and on the assumption of his authorship of the Gospel the following conclusions are founded.

The biography of John is fragmentary like all other biblical biographies. He was one of the sons of Zebedee (Mark 1:19, 20), a fisherman of Galilee, and of Salome, who was probably the sister of Mary, Jesus' mother (Cf. Matt. 27:56, Mark 15:40, John 19:25). He grew to manhood in Galilee and was a partner with his brother and with Andrew and Peter in the fishing business. He may have belonged first to the disciples of John the Baptist, and possibly was the companion of Andrew mentioned in John 1:40. If so, he accompanied Jesus on His first tour in Galilee (John 2:2), and later with his partners quit the fishing trade to follow Him (Matt. 4:21, 22).

The episodes of Jesus' life in which John shared are too numerous to list and treat separately. He was with Jesus in Jerusalem during the early Judean ministry. Perhaps the interview with Nicodemus was held at his home. He was a participant later in the mission of the twelve, as described by Matthew (10:1, 2). He needed Jesus' counsel as much as any other of the twelve, for he and James seem to have possessed unusually ardent temperaments. Jesus called them "Sons of thunder," or, by a more literal rendering, "Sons of tumult" (Mark 3:17). Mark does not assign any reason for the giving of this name to them, but the usage of the Hebrew phrase "son of . . ." usually means that the term which completes it qualifies the man, as "sons of Belial" means "worthless fellows." Their bigotry and truculence were revealed in their readiness to rebuke the man casting out demons because he did not follow with them (Luke 9:49), and in their desire to call down fire from heaven upon the Samaritan villages that would not receive Jesus (Luke 9:52-54). Both rashly asked their mother to petition Jesus that He would grant them the seats of primacy in His kingdom (Matt. 20:20-28). These crudities of spirit, even though a motive of loyalty to Him and to His work may have activated them, were sharply rebuked by Jesus.

At the last supper John occupied a place of privilege and of intimacy next to Jesus (John 13:23). At the trial he obtained access to the court of the high priest because he was known to the family (18:15, 16). Perhaps he had been the representative at Jerusalem of his father's fishing company, and so had become acquainted with all of the prominent households of the city. Apparently he witnessed the trial and death of Jesus and assumed the responsibility for Jesus' mother, when Jesus committed her to his care (19:26, 27). He stayed with Peter during the dark days of the interment, and with him was one of the first visitors at the empty tomb. There, as he looked at the empty grave clothes, he "saw and believed" (20:8).

The Epilogue of this Gospel hints that he lived for a long time after the beginning of the Christian era, for an explanation of his long life would scarcely have been necessary otherwise. The Epistles show that he rose to a position of influence in the church and that he became a powerful expositor of the love of God as revealed in Christ. His death probably took place at the close of the first century.

From these scattered items of John's biography, woven into the general narrative of the life of Christ, one can see something of his personal spiritual experiences. Intense in nature, he gave to Christ an undivided loyalty which at times expressed itself crudely and rashly. As Christ tamed his ardor and purified it of unrestrained violence, John became the apostle of love whose devotion was not excelled by that of any other writer of the New Testament. The fire of his nature appears in the vigor of his language. John echoes the strictures of Jesus against unbelievers (8:44) when he calls them "children of the devil" (I John 3:10). The same man, however, said: "Beloved, let us love one another: for love is of God; and every one that loveth is begotten of God, and knoweth God" (I John 4:7). The two are not inconsistent to an intense nature. John is the example of a man who could have been a great sinner, out of whom Christ made a great witness.

## Date and Place

The date of the Fourth Gospel has been variously estimated from A.D. 40 to A.D. 140, or even later. It cannot be later than Tatian's Diatessaron, into which it was incorporated about the middle of the second century. The discovery of the Rylands fragment, which preserves a scrap from John 18:31-33, 37, 38, shows that John was probably in use in the first half of the second century.[2] Goodenough argues that John may have been written as early as A.D. 40,[3] though few scholars accept so early a date. The best solution seems to be that John was produced in Asia Minor, possibly in Ephesus, toward the close of the first century, when the church had achieved a measure of maturity, and when there was need for an advance in the teaching concerning the nature of faith. It was apparently written in Gentile surroundings, for the feasts and usages of the Jews are explained for the benefit of those who were unfamiliar with them (John 2:13, 4:9, 19:31).

## Content

The key to the content of the Gospel of John is the author's own statement in John 20:30, 31:

> *Many other signs therefore did Jesus in the presence of the disciples, which are not written in this book: but these are written, that ye may believe that Jesus is the Christ, the Son of God; and that believing ye may have life in his name.*

Three words are prominent in this brief passage: *signs, believe, life.* The first of these words contains a clue to the organization of the Gospel around a select number of miracles, parallel in general character to those which are recorded in the Synoptic Gospels, but called *signs* here because of their special meaning in this Gospel. Seven are named which were performed by Jesus publicly on other people or for the benefit of other people. They illustrate different areas of His power, and collectively bear witness to the central doctrine of the Gospel, His deity. They may be classified as follows:

| Title | Passage | Area of Power |
|---|---|---|
| The Changing of Water into Wine | 2:1-11 | Quality |
| The Healing of the Nobleman's Son | 4:46-54 | Space |
| The Healing of the Impotent Man | 5:1-9 | Time |
| The Feeding of the Five Thousand | 6:1-14 | Quantity |
| The Walking on the Water | 6:16-21 | Natural Law |
| The Healing of the Blind Man | 9:1-12 | Misfortune |
| The Raising of Lazarus | 11:1-46 | Death |

These seven miracles operated precisely in the areas where man is unable to effect any change of laws or conditions which affect

---

2. Frederick Kenyon, *Our Bible and the Ancient Manuscripts* (Revised Edition. New York: Harper and Bros., Publishers, 1940), p. 128.

3. Erwin R. Goodenough, "John a Primitive Gospel." *Journal of Biblical Literature*, LXIV (1945), 145-182. Philadelphia: Society of Biblical Literature and Exegesis, 1945.

his life. In these areas Jesus proved Himself potent where man is impotent; and the works that He did testify to His supernatural ability.

The second word, *believe,* is the key word in the Gospel, occurring ninety-eight times. It is customarily translated *believe,* though sometimes it is rendered *trust* or *commit* (see 2:24). It usually means acknowledgment of a personal claim, or else it stands for the complete commitment of the individual to Christ. In it is the full meaning of the whole Christian life, for the tense of the verb used in this passage implies the continuing process of belief, involving also progress. John defines belief in Christ as receiving Him (1:12), making Him a part of one's life. Convinced by the *signs,* which were proofs of the power of Jesus' person, the believer would logically move on to a settled faith.

The third word in the key to the Gospel is *life,* which, in Johannine language, is the sum total of all that is imparted to the believer in his salvation. It is the highest experience of which humanity is capable. "This," said Jesus, "is life eternal, that they should know thee the only true God, and him whom thou didst send, *even* Jesus Christ" (17:3). Life, according to John, is not just animal vitality or the course of human existence. It involves a kind of nature, a new consciousness, interaction with environment, and constant development. Christ is presented as the example of this life which is God's gift to the Christian and God's goal for the Christian.

These three words, *signs, belief, life,* provide logical organization for the Gospel. In the *signs* is the revelation of God; in *belief* is the reaction that they are designed to produce; in *life* is the result that belief brings.

## Outline

The development of the central theme of belief appears in the outline of the Gospel.

### JOHN: THE GOSPEL OF BELIEF

| | |
|---|---|
| I. The Prologue | 1:1-18 |
|     The Theme Stated: Belief | |
| | |
| II. The Period of Consideration | 1:19-4:54 |
|     The Presentation of the Object of Belief | |
| | |
|       The Testimony of John's Witness | 1:19-51 |
|       The Testimony of Jesus' Works | 2:1-22 |
|       The Testimony of Jesus' Words | 2:23-4:54 |

The structure of John's Gospel is so plain that its reader can hardly miss it. From beginning to end the theme of belief is followed consistently. Moreover, the Gospel is not an attempt to superimpose an artificial organization upon existing facts. The inspired writer has selected certain episodes and teachings which represent the character and progress of the revelation of God in Christ (1:19), and has

THE
**HOLY LAND**
— IN THE —
GOSPEL OF JOHN

arranged them in such a way as to sweep his reader along in the tide of spiritual movement toward an active confessional faith in Christ.

The Prologue (1:1-18) begins by using the term *word*[4] to introduce the person of Christ. This term differs from those used in the other Gospels, for it does not connote any particular religious background. *Christ* is Jewish; *Lord* is Gentile; *Jesus* is human; but *Word* or *Logos* is philosophical. John thus makes the subject of his Gospel a universal figure, the incarnation of the Eternal Reason who is God, who came from God, and who reveals God as a son reveals a father. He is to be apprehended by those who receive Him (1:12), and the conflict between those who receive Him and those who do not is likened to the conflict between light and darkness.

The Period of Consideration (1:19-4:54) presents the person of the Word made flesh as He appeared to His contemporaries and as He was received by them. First He is proclaimed in the witness of His forerunner, John, and in His dealing with John's disciples. His essential mission, "the Lamb of God," (1:29), and His method of appealing to the needs and desires of His would-be followers connects Him with preceding history and revelation. He utilized both the preaching of John and the prophetic Scriptures of the Old Testament to establish His position. In the works which He performed He demonstrated His inherent power over things, over men, and over institutions (2:1-22). The interviews that followed were fuller manifestations of His sufficiency for all men. The learned and gentlemanly Jewish teacher, Nicodemus, the sharp-tongued and cynical Samaritan woman, and the importunate nobleman of Galilee, probably a Gentile, were all directed to faith in Jesus by different arguments and by different methods.

From Jesus' public presentation of Himself arose controversy, for when He appealed to men to believe in Him, many refused. He did not ask for a blind or unreasoning faith, but He took care always to appeal to facts and to define clearly the issues at stake in belief and in unbelief.

The healing of the man at the pool precipitated the Period of Controversy (5:1-6:71) because the miracle was performed on the Sabbath. Jesus indicated that His action was a sample of what His Father was continually doing, and thus tacitly claimed deity as His prerogative. In the discussion that followed (5:19-47) He argued for belief in Himself on the basis of five witnesses: Himself, the Forerunner, the Father, the works which He had performed, and the Scripture. The

---

4. Greek: *logos.*

205

miracles of chapter 6, according to John, were directed chiefly to his disciples in order to evoke from them a committal to faith. These miracles and the discourses that followed are bound closely together, for the discourse is only the amplification of the truth enacted in the miracles. The appeal for belief is very strong in this section, as if Jesus were desirous of having the disciples commit themselves to Him before the heat of controversy might alienate them from Him.

The Period of Conflict (7:1-11:53) carries the trends of the Period of Controversy to their logical crisis. The growing though hesitant faith of the disciples is contrasted with the stark cynicism of Jesus' brethren, with the wavering allegiance of the bewildered multitude, and with the venomous opposition of the Jewish hierarchy. Jesus' own evaluation of the conflict appears in the history of the blind man, where He expressed the necessity of doing the works of God while He still had opportunity, and also in the raising of Lazarus, which He regarded as a supreme test of faith and as the climactic proof of His power. The discourse material which is included between these two miracles in the tenth chapter is Jesus' last extended public statement of His mission. It declares the purpose of His death as clearly as did His utterance to the disciples at Caesarea Philippi which is recorded in the Synoptics. The outcome of the conflict is predicted in His words: "I lay down my life, that I may take it again" (10:17).

In the Period of Crisis (11:54-12:36a) appear the various tensions which the conflict has created. Jesus retired from Jerusalem and its environs to Ephraim in order that He might be out of the storm center. The feeling of His friends was openly declared by the family of Bethany, who gave a dinner in His honor (12:1, 2). The pilgrim multitude, who were present in Jerusalem for the feast of the Passover, hailed Him enthusiastically (12:20, 21). Jesus Himself realized that the die was cast, and removed Himself from public contacts (12:36). Divine destiny, not popular vote, was the deciding factor in His life.

Up to this point Jesus' ministry was public; from here on it was private. The Period of Conference (12:36b-17:26) comprises the final instruction to the disciples after the last supper and also His prayer to the Father. The preparation of the disciples for the shock of the cross, and the report to the Father that He had finished His work concluded the earthly ministry of Jesus.

The Period of Consummation (18:1-20:31) brings the fulfilment of the two clashing principles of belief and of unbelief. In the betrayal and crucifixion unbelief was unmasked. The weakness of Peter, the treachery of Judas, the jealous malice of the priests, and the cowardice

206

of Pilate show how unbelief reaches its ultimate end. On the other hand, the constancy of the beloved disciple and the women, and the generous action of Joseph and of Nicodemus show how even an imperfect and uninstructed faith can maintain loyalty in spite of bewilderment and danger. The resurrection, of course, was the final justification of belief as well as the final vindication of the revelation through Jesus the Son of God.

## Emphasis

The Gospel of John has many special features which strengthen the presentation of its main theme. The claims of Jesus are set forth in seven major I AM's:

1. The bread of life                                6:35
2. The light of the world                     8:12, 9:5
3. The door (of the sheepfold)           10:7
4. The good shepherd                          10:11, 14
5. The resurrection and the life         11:25
6. The way, the truth and the life        14:6
7. The true vine                                     15:1

The personal relation of Jesus to man is stressed in John. Twenty-seven interviews are noted, some of which are extensive and some of which are very brief. Included in the list are passages which can be classified under other headings, such as the miracle of the nobleman's son (4:46-54), or the trial before Pilate (18:28-19:16). On occasions like these the interest of Jesus in the individual is prominent rather than the action itself. In the Synoptics, for example, the trial before Pilate is an important feature of the dénouement of Jesus' life, while in the Gospel of John Jesus' personal interest in Pilate and His effort to bring Pilate to a recognition of His claims are much more plain.

The Johannine vocabulary is so unusual that only a verse or two from this Gospel, quoted apart from its context, is easily recognizable. Certain key words are repeated constantly, not because the writer is limited in scope of thought, but because the central truths of the Gospel, like diamonds, need to be viewed from the angle of each facet. Some of these terms, like "life," "light," "darkness," "work," "world," "believe," "flesh," "hour," are either figurative or else have a special technical meaning in this Gospel. Others are abstract and somewhat philosophical in content: "truth," "true," "hate," "receive," "love" (two different verbs), "take away," "send," "beginning," "know" (two different verbs), "glory," "glorify," "witness" (verb and noun), "abide," "the Father." John's Gospel shows by its vocabulary that teaching on the Christian life had already crystallized into certain definite concepts which were expressed in fixed phraseology, and which then, as today, represented a whole new pattern of spiritual truth.

The Gospel of John emphasizes the deity of Jesus Christ, the Son of God. Although no Gospel portrays more clearly His humanity, there is no other that asserts so directly the prerogatives of deity: "The Word was God" (1:1); "I and the Father are one (10:30); "Before Abraham was born, I am" (8:58); "He that hath seen me hath seen the Father" (14:9); and Thomas' ejaculation, "My Lord and my God" (20:28).

The humanity of Jesus is also emphasized. He was weary (4:6), thirsty (4:7), impatient (6:26), wistful (6:67), severe (8:44), sorrowful (11:35), appreciative (12:7), troubled (12:27), loving (13:1), loyal (18:8), courageous (18:23). To His contemporaries who met Him casually He was "the man that is called Jesus" (9:11); to those who lived with Him He became "the Holy One of God" (6:69).

## Purpose

As already stated, the purpose of this Gospel is apologetic. All of the Gospels were designed to inculcate belief in those who read them or who heard them read. This Gospel was planned for those who had already some philosophical predilections, as the Prologue shows, and who were looking for an answer to Philip's demand: "Lord, show us the Father, and it sufficeth us" (14:8).

It is possible that John's Gospel was written as a conscious attempt to supplement the current accounts of the life and work of Jesus which had found written expression in the canonical Synoptic Gospels. One cannot state dogmatically that John knew and read Matthew, or Mark, or Luke. Nevertheless, the general omission of Jesus' Galilean ministry, the almost total absence of the parables, the definite reference to selectivity in the miracles (20:30), and the dovetailing of some of John's historical data with that in the Synoptics make one feel that the author was trying to give to the public fresh information that had not previously been used in writing. For instance, in the account of the last supper, John described the foot-washing scene and explained how Jesus wished to provide an object lesson in humility for the disciples. Apart from the assumption that such a lesson might be salutary for general application, he assigned no definite reason for it. Luke, however, told how the disciples were arguing among themselves "which of them was accounted to be greatest" (Luke 22:24). The two accounts thus interlock in meaning, and one may speculate whether John were not explaining how Jesus met the situation which Luke described as a personal addition to the Lukan account.

## Characters

One peculiarity of John's Gospel is its development of character in sketches separated by intervals of text. Nicodemus (John 3:1-15, 7:50-52, 19:39), Philip (1:43-46, 6:5-7, 14:8-11), Thomas (11:16, 14:5, 6, 20:24-29), Mary and Martha (11:1-40, 12:2-8), Mary, the mother of Jesus (2:1-5, 19:26-27), and others are mentioned naturally and easily as they are recalled in connection with the main narratives, and yet when the separate allusions to them are combined, they make a complete snapshot portrait of the person concerned. To some extent this procedure is true in the other Gospels, but it is largely confined to a few prominent characters such as Peter or Judas, whereas the Fourth Gospel uses both prominent and obscure characters as examples of belief and of unbelief.

# THE SYNOPTIC PROBLEM

# THE SYNOPTIC PROBLEM

Definition
Origin
Proposed Solutions

# CHAPTER XI

## The Synoptic Problem

### Definition

A study of the Gospels would not be complete without a few observations on the chief literary problem that has engaged the attention of New Testament scholars for the last century and a half. The Synoptic problem, so called, is briefly this: If the three Synoptic Gospels are totally independent of each other in origin and development, why do they resemble each other so closely, even to exact verbal agreement in many places? If, on the other hand, they have literary relationship with each other, how can they be three independent witnesses to the deeds and teachings of the Lord Jesus Christ? Neither part of this dilemma can rightly be suppressed or neglected. Facts must be explained by the best and most reasonable hypothesis available. Nevertheless, a purely naturalistic answer will not do justice to the origin of the Gospels or to any other part of Scripture. The Bible is supernatural in its revelation, in its ethics, and in its power, and cannot therefore be explained on any basis other than that of divine inspiration.

### Origin

As a sample of the type of passage which illustrates the problem one might take the healing of a leper, as described in Matthew 8:1-4, Mark 1:40-45, and Luke 5:12-16. All of them are narrating one event, for the action is alike in all of them. To a great extent the language is identical also, for the core of the story is told in the same way by all three Gospels. The major differences are in the setting of the accounts.

How shall the verbal agreements be explained? Two school papers with as close an agreement between them as is exhibited in the Synoptics would instantly arouse suspicion on the part of the teacher that the writers either had copied from each other, or else that they had collaborated. Did the writers of the Gospels copy each other, or did they collaborate?

213

One should recognize first that the passages where the Synoptics agree most fully are the quotations of the words of Christ. Such a phenomenon is natural, because the words of Jesus would be most likely to be repeated verbatim, while the setting in which they were placed could be expressed in varying ways. Moreover, there is no reason why He might not have repeated the same teaching under different circumstances which would be severally reported by the different evangelists.

Still another prominent question is the relation of Mark to the other two Synoptics. Practically all of Mark's material with the exception of about fifty verses can be found embedded in Matthew and in Luke. Of 1068 verses in Matthew, about 500 are similar to Mark, and out of 1149 verses in Luke, about 320 resemble Mark. Furthermore, Matthew and Mark may agree against Luke, or Luke and Mark may agree against Matthew, but Matthew and Luke never agree against Mark where any considerable body of text exists that is common to all three. Did these writers know and use Mark's work, or are these phenomena purely accidental?

There are also a number of passages common to Matthew and to Luke which Mark does not contain at all, chiefly sayings and parables of Jesus. As these occur in the two Gospels they have a high degree of verbal similarity. Do they represent some "common source"?

## Proposed Solutions

Many theories have been propounded to account for these phenomena.[1] One which has found great favor with many modern scholars is the "Two-Document Hypothesis," which holds that the Gospel of Mark and a lost collection of the sayings of Jesus called "Q," from the German "Quelle," meaning "source," were the main sources from which Matthew and Luke composed their works. Mark, as already noted, is largely paralleled in Matthew and in Luke, and there is a strong resemblance in many of the Matthean and Lukan records of the sayings of Jesus that lends seeming plausibility to the theory that there was a "Q."

In spite of the fact that many reputable and even some conservative scholars have adopted this theory, it cannot be received as fact. "Q" has never been identified with any existing document, and while it is not inconceivable that such a manuscript would have perished after

---

1. See H. C. Thiessen, *Introduction to the New Testament* (Grand Rapids, Mich.: Wm. B. Eerdmans Co., 1951), pp. 101-129.

having been copied extensively, there is no good objective proof of its existence.

Again, the appearance of parallels to Mark in Matthew and in Luke does not necessitate the knowledge or absorption of Mark as a document. Luke and John Mark were personally acquainted, perhaps in the early years of the church at Antioch of Syria, and certainly they knew each other later at Rome. Whether Matthew ever knew Mark is uncertain, but he may well have talked with the young man whose home was in Jerusalem in the days immediately after Pentecost. Living contact and exchange of knowledge may have entered into creating the common pool of facts which the Synoptists had at their disposal.

Another factor entering into the solution of the Synoptic Problem is the oral preaching of the early church. Before the Gospels were written at all the life of Jesus was the core of apostolic preaching, as appears in Peter's address on the day of Pentecost (Acts 2:22-32), in his sermon in the house of Cornelius (10:36-43), and in Paul's address in Antioch of Pisidia (13:23-33). The Synoptists could not have been ignorant of this "oral tradition," as it is called; in fact, the preface to Luke's Gospel implies that the writer knew what had been handed down "by ministers of the word" (Luke 1:2). While the theory of oral tradition may not explain all of the Synoptic problem, it is worth more attention than has been accorded to it in recent years.

Finally, the purposes of the Evangelists should be taken into account. Granting that they possessed much material in common, they put it to different uses, and organized it into different frameworks under the direction of the mind of the Spirit. The very differences between the writers speak of independence; the similarities reflect a common background of information, a common subject of writing, and the common inspiration of God.[2]

---

2. Since a technical discussion of the Synoptic problem does not properly belong in a study in New Testament survey, the foregoing statement deals with the topic only in barest outline. For a fuller statement of the author's viewpoint, see M. C. Tenney, *The Genius of the Gospels* (Grand Rapids, Mich.: Wm. B. Eerdmans Co, 1951), pp. 1-119. An excellent small treatise of more general nature is F. F. Bruce, *Are The New Testament Documents Reliable?* (Grand Rapids: Wm. B. Eerdmans Publishing Co., 1954), pp. 28-47. The bulk of critical literature on this subject is enormous, of which relatively little has been written from a conservative standpoint.

# THE LIFE OF CHRIST

# THE LIFE OF CHRIST

# CHAPTER XII

## The Life of Christ

One would naturally expect that the Lord Jesus Christ would be sufficiently important to receive ample notice in the literature of His time, and that extensive biographical material would be available. He was observed by multitudes of people, and His own followers numbered into the hundreds (I Cor. 15:6), whose witness was still living in the middle of the first century. As a matter of fact, the amount of information concerning Him is comparatively meager. Aside from the four Gospels, and a few scattered allusions in the Epistles, contemporary history is almost silent concerning Him.

### The Secular Sources of Information

There are, however, a few references to Christ or to Christianity that can be cited.

Josephus, in his *Antiquities*,[1] made the following statement:

> Now there was about this time Jesus, a wise man, if it be lawful to call him a man, for he was a doer of wonderful works, a teacher of such men as receive the truth with pleasure. He drew over to him both many of the Jews, and many of the Gentiles. He was [the] Christ. And when Pilate, at the suggestion of the principal men among us, had condemned him to the cross, those that loved him at the first did not forsake him; for he appeared to them alive again the third day; as the divine prophets had foretold these and ten thousand other wonderful things concerning him. And the tribe of Christians so named from him are not extinct at this day.

Tacitus, a Roman historian of the second century, in writing of the reign of Nero, alluded to the death of Christ and to the existence of Christians in Rome:[2]

---

1. Josephus, *Antiquities* XVIII, iii, 3. See Philip Schaff, *History of the Christian Church* (Wm. B. Eerdmans Publishing Co., 1950), Vol. I, pp. 92ff., for an evaluation of this passage. It is considered by many to be a Christian interpolation into the text of Josephus.
2. Tacitus, *Annals* xv, 44. The Oxford Translation, Revised. (New York; Harper & Bros., Publishers, 1858) p. 423.

But not all the relief that could come from man, not all the bounties that the prince could bestow, nor all the atonements which could be presented to the gods, availed to relieve Nero from the infamy of being believed to have ordered the conflagration. Hence, to suppress the rumor, he falsely charged with the guilt, and punished with the most exquisite tortures, the persons commonly called Christians, who were hated for their enormities. Christus, the founder of that name, was put to death as a criminal by Pontius Pilate, procurator of Judea, in the reign of Tiberius: but the pernicious superstition, repressed for a time, broke out again, not only through Judea, where the mischief originated, but through the city of Rome also . . .

Suetonius' testimony is brief:[3]

Punishment [by Nero] was inflicted on the Christians, a class of men given to a new and mischievous superstition.

The younger Pliny, who was a correspondent of Trajan, spoke in one of his letters of the Christians as he had met them in Asia:[4]

They affirmed, however, the whole of their guilt, or their error, was, that they were in the habit of meeting on a certain fixed day before it was light, when they sang in alternate verses a hymn to Christ, as to a god, and bound themselves by a solemn oath, not to any wicked deeds, but never to commit any fraud, theft, or adultery, never to falsify their word, nor to deny a trust when they should be called on to deliver it up . . .

Lucian, the satirist of the second century, spoke scornfully of Christ and of the Christians.[5] He connected them with the synagogues of Palestine, and alluded to Christ as

. . . the man who was crucified in Palestine because he introduced this new cult into the world . . . Furthermore, their first lawgiver persuaded them that they are all brothers one of another after they have transgressed once for all by denying the Greek gods and by worshipping that crucified sophist himself and living under his laws.

---

3. Suetonius, *The Lives of the Caesars, Nero,* xvi. Loeb Classical Library. English Translation by J.C. Rolfe, Vol. II. (London: William Heinemann; New York: G. P. Putnam's Sons), p. 111.

4. Pliny: *Letters,* X, xcvi. Loeb Classical Library. English translation by William Melmoth, revised by W. M. L. Hutchinson. (London: William Heinemann; Cambridge, Mass.; Harvard University Press, 1935) Vol. II, p. 403.

5. Lucian, *The Passing of Peregrinus,* 12, 13. Loeb Classical Library. English translation by A. M. Harmon. (London: William Heinemann, Ltd.; Cambridge, Mass.; Harvard University Press, 1936) pp. 13, 15.

These brief notices of Christ and of Christianity were penned by men who were ignorant of the history of the movement and who were hostile to its tenets. They show that Christianity was already widespread by the second century and that the historic existence of Christ was generally acknowledged even by His foes. The nature of these references prove that He was regarded as an obscure fanatic whose cult had attained a prominence far greater than might rightfully have been expected. Up to the time of Nero, and in the circle of the court, Christianity was looked upon by Romans in much the same way that Americans would appraise an importation of Japanese Shintoism.

## The Periods of Jesus' Life

Since the data afforded by the four Gospels are not complete in the sense that they are exhaustive, a full biography of Jesus cannot be reconstructed from them. Of the four, Luke is perhaps the most representative, but he does not include the early Judean ministry which is mentioned by John. No one of these attempts a physical description of Jesus' person, although some facts about it must have been known to the writers. Only Luke gives a glimpse of His youth; for the most part, the thirty years of His life are passed over in silence. John alone follows any definite chronological scheme which is traceable to his allusions to the feasts which Jesus attended; and one of those is ambiguous (John 5:1). The order of narration in any Gospel is not necessarily chronological, for each Gospel has its own objective and organizes its material for effect rather than for temporal sequence. It is an interpretation, not a chronicle. For this reason there are some differences of opinion on the preferred order of events in the life of Christ. The following outline agrees with the consensus of most scholars and treats the larger blocks of material in the Gospels rather than the smaller questions of detail which belong properly to a specialized study. The periods follow the conventional arrangement as given by Burton and Goodspeed,[6] Huck,[7] and others.

---

6. E. D. Burton and E. J. Goodspeed, *A Harmony of the Synoptic Gospels*, (New York: Charles Scribner's Sons, n.d.) pp. xv, 279.

7. Albert Huck, *A Synopsis of the First Three Gospels*, (Ninth Edition. Revised by Hans Lietzmann. English Edition by Frank Leslie Cross. Tubingen: J. C. B. Mohr, 1936) pp. xx, 213.

## Chart of the Harmony of the Life of Christ

| Period | Gospel Content | | | |
|---|---|---|---|---|
| | Matthew | Mark | Luke | John |
| **I. Parentage and Infancy** | | | | |
| Genealogy | 1:1-17 | | 3:23-38 | |
| Birth of John the Baptist | | | 1:5-25 57-80 | |
| Annunciation | 1:18-25 | | 1:26-38 | |
| The Birth of Jesus | 2:1 | | 2:1-7 | |
| The Angels | | | 2:8-20 | |
| The Circumcision and Presentation | | | 2:21-39 | |
| The Wise Men | 2:1-12 | | | |
| The Flight into Egypt | 2:13-23 | | | |
| Childhood and Visit to Jerusalem | | | 2:40-50 | |
| The Silent Years | | | 2:51, 52 | |
| **II. Preparatory Action** | | | | |
| The Ministry of John | 3:1-12 | 1:1-8 | 3:1-20 | 1:19-37 |
| The Baptism of Jesus | 3:13-17 | 1:9-11 | 3:21, 22 | |
| The Temptation | 4:1-11 | 1:12, 13 | 4:1-13 | |
| **III. The Early Galilean Ministry** | | | | |
| The Wedding at Cana | | | | 2:1-12 |
| **IV. The Early Judean Ministry (Passover)** | | | | |
| A Cleansing of the Temple | | | | 2:13-25 |
| Interview with Nicodemus | | | | 3:1-21 |
| Competition with John the Baptist | | | | 3:23-36 |
| Withdrawal through Samaria | | | | 4:1-44 |
| **V. The Return to Galilee** | | | | |
| The Arrival | 4:12 | 1:14 | 4:14 | 4:43-45 |
| Healing of the Nobleman's Son | | | | 4:46-54 |
| The Imprisonment of John and | | | | |
| The Move to Capernaum | 4:12-16 | | | |
| The First Galilean Tour | 4:17 | | | |
| The Call of the First Disciples | 4:18-22 | 1:16 | | |
| A Day of Work | 8:14-17 | 1:21-34 | 4:31-41 | |
| Traveling and Preaching | | 1:35-39 | 4:42-44 | |
| Miracles and Discourses | 8:1-4 9:1-17 12:1-21 | 1:40-3:12 | 5:1-6:19 | |

## The Periods of Jesus' Life

| Period | | Gospel Content | | |
|---|---|---|---|---|
| | Matthew | Mark | Luke | John |
| The Appointment of the Twelve | | 3:13-19a | 6:12-16 | |
| The Sermon on the Mount | 5:1-7:29 | | (6:20-49) | |
| The Centurion's Servant | 8:5-13 | | 7:1-10 | |
| The Widow's Son | | | 7:11-17 | |
| The Inquiry of John the Baptist | 11:2-30 | | 7:18-35 | |
| The Anointing of Jesus | | | 7:36-50 | |
| Another Preaching Tour | | | 8:1-3 | |
| The Protest of the Family | 12:46-50 | 3:31-35 | 8:19-21 | |
| Parables | 13:1-53 | 4:1-34 | 8:4-18 | |
| Miracles | 8:18, 23-34 9:18-26 | 4:35-5:43 | 8:22-56 | |
| VI. A Third Tour: The Peak of the Ministry | | | | |
| Rejection at Nazareth | 13:54-58 | 6:1-6 | | |
| The Tour of the Twelve | 9:36-11:1 | 6:7-13 | 9:1-6 | |
| The Death of John | 14:1-12 | 6:14-29 | 9:7-9 | |
| The Return of the Twelve | 14:13 | 6:30-32 | 9:10 | |
| The Feeding of the 5000 | 14:13-21 | 6:33-44 | 9:11-17 | 6:1-13 |
| The Retirement and the Walking on the Sea | 14:22-33 | 6:45-52 | | 6:14-21 |
| The Discourse in the Synagogue | 15:1-20 | 7:1-23 | | |
| VII. The Retirement to the North | | | | |
| In Tyre and Sidon | 15:21-28 | 7:24-30 | | |
| In Decapolis | 15:29-31 | 7:31-37 | | |
| Feeding of the 4000 Discourse | 15:32-16:12 | 8:1-21 | | |
| Healing of the Blind Man | | 8:22-26 | | |
| The Revelation of His Person | 16:13-26 | 8:27-37 | 9:18-25 | |
| The Transfiguration | 16:27-17:13 | 8:38-9:13 | 9:26-36 | |
| Healing of the Demoniac | 17:14-21 | 9:14-29 | 9:37-43 | |
| Prediction of Death and Resurrection | 17:22, 23 | 9:30, 32 | 9:43-45 | |
| VIII. The Last Ministry in Galilee | 17:24-18:35 | 9:33-50 | 9:46-50 | 7:1-9 |
| IX. The Later Judean Ministry | | | | |
| The Journey to Jerusalem | 19:1, 2 | 10:1 | 9:51-62 | 7:10 |
| via Samaria | 8:19-22 | | | |

| Period | Matthew | Mark | Luke | John |
|---|---|---|---|---|
| Gospel Content | | | | |
| The Feast of Tabernacles | | | | 7:11-52 |
| The Woman Taken in Adultery | | | | 7:53-8:11 |
| Argument with Pharisees | | | | 8:12-59 |
| The Man Born Blind | | | | 9:1-41 |
| Discourse on Good Shepherd | | | | 10:1-21 |
| The Mission of the Seventy | | | 10:1-24 | |
| The Parable of the Good Samaritan | | | 10:25-37 | |
| Mary and Martha | | | 10:38-42 | |
| "The Lord's Prayer" | | | 11:1-13 | |
| Controversy with Pharisees | | | 11:14-54 | |
| Public Teachings | | | 12:1-59 | |
| The Feast of Dedication | | | | 10:22-39 |
| X. The Perean Ministry | | | | 10:40-42 |
| Warnings | | | 13:22-35 | |
| Dinner with a Pharisee | | | 14:1-24 | |
| Challenge to the Multitude | | | 14:25-35 | |
| Teaching Publicans and Sinners | | | 15:1-32 | |
| Teaching the Disciples | | | 16:1-17:10 | |
| The Raising of Lazarus | | | | 11:1-44 |
| The Withdrawal to Ephraim | | | | 11:45-54 |
| XI. The Last Journey to Jerusalem | | | | |
| Ministry in Samaria and Galilee | | | 17:11-18:14 | |
| Ministry in Perea | | | | |
| Teaching on Divorce | 19:1-12 | 10:1-12 | | |
| Teaching on Children | 19:13-15 | 10:13-16 | 18:15-17 | |
| The Rich Young Ruler | 19:16-20:16 | 10:17-31 | 18:18-30 | |
| Prediction of Death | 20:17-19 | 10:32-34 | 18:31-34 | |
| Ambition of James and John | 20:20-28 | 10:35-45 | | |
| Approach to Jerusalem | 20:29-34 | 10:46-52 | 18:35-19:28 | |
| Arrival at Bethany | | | | 11:55-12:11 |
| XII. The Passion Week | | | | |
| Sunday | | | | |
| The Triumphal Entry | 21:1-9 | 11:1-10 | 19:29-40 | 12:12-19 |
| Jesus' View of the City | 21:10, 11 | 11:11 | 19:41-44 | |
| Monday | | | | |
| Cursing of the Fig Tree | 21:18,19 | 11:12-14 | | |

| Period | Matthew | Mark | Luke | John |
|---|---|---|---|---|
| | | | Gospel Content | |
| Cleansing of the Temple | 21:12, 13 | 11:15-19 | 19:45-48 | |
| Healings in the Temple | 21:14-17 | | | |
| Tuesday | | | | |
| The Withered Fig Tree | 21:19-22 | 11:20-25 | | |
| Controversy | 21:23-22:46 | 11:27-12:37 | 20:1-44 | |
| Condemnation of Scribes and Pharisees | 23:1-39 | 12:38-40 | 20:45-47 | |
| Jesus' Observation of the Widow | | 12:41-44 | 21:1-4 | |
| The Visit of the Greeks | | | | 12:20-36 |
| Jewish Rejection of Jesus | | | | 12:37-50 |
| The Apocalyptic Discourse | 24, 25 | 13:1-37 | 21:5-38 | |
| Prediction of the Cross | 26:1-5 | 14:1, 2 | 22:1, 2 | |
| Anointing by Mary | 26:6-13 | 14:3-9 | | 12:2-8 |
| The Betrayal | 26:14-16 | 14:10, 11 | 22:3-6 | |
| Wednesday — no record | | | | |
| Thursday | | | | |
| The Passover Meal | 26:17-29 | 14:12-25 | 22:7-30 | 13:1-38 |
| Farewell Discourse | | | | 14:1-31 |
| Discourse on way to Gethsemane | | | | 15, 16 |
| The High Priestly Prayer | | | | 17 |
| In the Garden | 26:30, 36-46 | 14:26, 32-42 | 22:39-46 | 18:1 |
| Betrayal and Arrest | 26:47-56 | 14:43-52 | 22:47-53 | 18:2-12 |
| Trial before Annas | | | | 18:12-14, 19-23 |
| Trial before Caiaphas | 26:57, 59-68 | 14:53,55-65 | 22:54, 63-65 | 18:24 |
| The Denial of Peter | 26:58, 69-75 | 14:54,66-72 | 22:54-62 | 18:15-18 25-27 |
| Trial before the Sanhedrin | 27:1 | 15:1 | 22:66-71 | |
| Death of Judas | 27:3-10 | | | |
| Friday | | | | |
| Trial before Pilate | 27:2, 11-14 | 15:1-5 | 23:1-5 | 18:28-38 |
| Before Herod | | | 23:6-12 | |
| Return to Pilate | 27:15-26 | 15:6-15 | 23:13-25 | 18:39-19:16 |
| Mockery by Soldiers | 27:27-30 | 15:16-19 | | |
| The Way to Calvary | 27:31-34 | 15:20-23 | 23:26-32 | 19:16,17 |
| The Crucifixion | 27:35-56 | 15:24-41 | 23:33-49 | 19:18-30 |
| The Burial | 27:57-60 | 15:42-46 | 23:50-54 | 19:31-42 |
| Saturday | | | | |
| The Women at the Tomb | 27:61 | 15:47 | 23:55, 56 | |
| The Guard | 27:62-66 | | | |
| XIII. The Resurrection | | | | |
| Sunday | | | | |
| The Women's Visit | 28:1-8 | 16:1-8 | 24:1-12 | 20:1-10 |

| Period | Gospel Content | | | |
| --- | --- | --- | --- | --- |
| | Matthew | Mark | Luke | John |
| The Appearances of Jesus | | | | |
| Mary Magdalene | | 16:9-11 | | 20:11-18 |
| Other Women | 28:9-10 | | | |
| Report of the Guard | 28:11-15 | | | |
| The Two Disciples | | 16:12,13 | 24:13-32 | |
| Peter | | | 24:33-35 | |
| The Ten Apostles | | 16:14 | 24:36-43 | 20:19-25 |
| The Eleven Apostles | | | | 20:26-31 |
| By Sea of Galilee | | | | 21:1-14 |
| Conversation with Peter | | | | 21:15-25 |
| Disciples in Galilee | 28:16-20 | 16:15-18 | | |
| Eleven at Olivet | | | 24:44-49 | |
| The Great Commission and Ascension | 28:18-20 | 16:19,20 | 24:50-53 | |

A review of the foregoing sketch of biographical material shows that there is a great deal of overlapping in the accounts. Much material is given at least three times by the Synoptics and is sometimes repeated by John. The sections in which all three agree are usually narrative portions concerning miracles or parables. Certain outstanding events, such as the baptism, the temptation, the feeding of the five thousand, the transfiguration, and the passion week are recorded by all three of the Synoptics.

Luke and John have the largest amount of text which is not duplicated elsewhere. The section in Luke 9:51 to 18:14 is unique in its content, except as certain of the sayings are paralleled in Matthew for content, though not necessarily for context. Most of the Johannine material is different from that of the Synoptics, even when there is a general historical parallelism in sequence.

The Gospels are much more concerned with presenting a person than with writing a story. Not the completeness or the order of the account, but its significance is important. The difference between the varying reports indicate that they are supplementary, and probably undesignedly so as far as the human authors are concerned. The agreement of the accounts warrants amply the conclusion that a solid core of knowledge about Jesus was part of the fixed teaching of the early church, and that it was based upon the valid testimony of eye-witnesses.

Much has already been said under the separate treatments of the Gospels that need not be repeated. Discernible in all of them, irrespective of their individual approach to the biography of the Lord, is a rise in His appeal to the public, a crisis at which He is rejected by the leaders, abandoned by the populace, and not well understood by His disciples. At the death of John the Baptist and the return of the Twelve from their preaching tour one can see that Jesus' ministry had passed its peak in popular appeal and that He slowly began the conscious descent to the cross. The retirement to the north and the later ministries in Judea and in Perea were increasingly filled with controversy. Jesus' reactions to it indicated that He had little hope of convincing His enemies of His message, but He used it as a means for teaching the disciples who clung to Him until the last.

The resurrection is the crowning event of Jesus' career. He predicted it on several occasions. Of the truthfulness of the Gospels and of their intent to proclaim that Jesus had physically risen from the dead there can be no legitimate doubt. All agree that the tomb was found empty on the first day of the week and that he appeared in tangible and recognizable form to His followers on numerous occasions.

No one of these periods is chronicled exhaustively, not even the Passion week, in which Wednesday seems to have been omitted from the chronological account.

## The Geography of Jesus' Life

The active life of the Lord Jesus was spent within the confines of Palestine, a territory comprising not more than ten thousand square miles. In infancy He was taken into Egypt by Joseph and Mary in order to escape the threat of Herod's anger (Matt. 2:13, 14), and at the crisis of His ministry He visited Tyre and Sidon (Matt. 15:21); but most of His travels were on the roads between Galilee and Jerusalem. If He crossed the Jordan to the east, He probably stayed in the cities and villages that bordered the river, so that He did not go far into the trans-Jordanian country.

The land of Palestine is located at the eastern end of the Mediterranean Sea which washes its entire western shore. From Mt. Lebanon on the north to the southern end of the Dead Sea is a distance of approximately one hundred seventy-five miles. From the coast to the Sea of Galilee on the north is only twenty-eight miles; from the coast to the Dead Sea on the south is about fifty-four miles. From north to south the land is divided by the Jordan river which rises in the springs at the foot of Mt. Hermon and then flows southward through Lake Huleh and the Sea of Galilee to its terminus in the Dead Sea.

The land is divided into four general sections: the coastal plain, which extends northward from the desert along the Mediterranean up to Mt. Carmel; the hill country which is rugged and largely barren; the valley of the Jordan, a deep gorge which, at the Dead Sea, is twelve hundred seventy-five feet below sea level; and a mountainous plateau east of the Jordan which is bordered on the east by the desert.

These four divisions provided Palestine with a variety of climate and of material resources. The coastal plain had a few good harbors, but Joppa (the modern Jaffa) and Ptolemais, north of Carmel, were embarkation points for the ships that plied the sea-borne trade of the eastern Mediterranean. Along the coastal plain ran the road which had from time immemorial been the communicating link between Egypt and the kingdoms to the north and east. The climate along the shore was temperate and mild and the soil was fertile, so that agriculture flourished.

The hill country, where the Israelites had lived since the conquest of the land under Joshua, was rocky and barren. Jerusalem, near the end of the Dead Sea, and Samaria, near Mt. Ebal and Mt. Gerizim, were the two most important centers. The high elevation of the hill country gave it a moderate climate. Small farming, including the culture of grapes, small grains, and cattle, formed the principal occupation of the people.

Beginning at Mt. Carmel the plain of Esdraelon extended along the Kishon valley from the northwest in a southeasterly direction to the foot of Mt. Gilboa and thence connected with the valley that led to the Jordan. Because it was the sole good line of communication between the coastal plain and the center of the land, it was a military prey of great value and the plain was often the battleground for opposing armies of north and south when they fought for the possession of Palestine. Megiddo, the key city of the region, gave its name to Har-Magedon, the Hill of Megiddo, or Armageddon, the site of the predicted last great conflict of this age (Rev. 16:16).

Within the hill country the majority of the population of Palestine lived. In the north was Galilee, the home country of Jesus. It was rugged terrain, but here and there the valleys gave opportunity for farming, while on the lake the fishing industry throve. The plain of Gennesaret which bordered the lake on the west was fertile and the lake was ringed with towns which had sprung up because of the business that grew there. Trade routes to the east passed through Galilee. Nazareth, Jesus' early home, was on one of these caravan routes. Many Romans and Greeks settled along the lake because of the healthy climate and because of business opportunities. Bethsaida, Chorazin, Capernaum, Magdala, the home of Mary, and Tiberias were some of these towns that Jesus frequented. Nazareth and Cana were farther inland.

South of Galilee was Samaria, the former center of the northern kingdom of Israel. The country is rough and hilly, less cultivable than Galilee. The twin mountains of Ebal and Gerizim, a center of worship since the days of the conquest, dominated the landscape. The Plain of Shechem, where Jacob settled and dug his well (John 4:5), supported a farming population.

South of Samaria was Judea, somewhat similar in terrain to Samaria. The lowlands bordering on the coastal plain were watered by occasional streams from the hills and by the winds which brought moisture from the Mediterranean. The center of the land was too rocky for much farming and the eastern part of Judea was almost wholly barren desert. The southern part, or the Negeb as it is still called, was fertile but dry, much like parts of the western United States. Irrigation has opened this territory to farming in recent years, though in the time of Christ it was practically uninhabitable.

The valley of the Jordan is one of the most unusual geological phenomena in the world. It is part of a rift that extends from the Taurus mountains in the north down through Arabia and the eastern tongue of the Red Sea into Africa. From its headwaters to the Dead Sea which has no outlet the Jordan has a fall of approximately three thousand feet. Lake Huleh into which it flows first is a small body of water about three miles wide, located in the middle of a large swamp of reeds. From Huleh it flows eleven miles into the Sea of Galilee, called by the Romans the Lake of Tiberias. The lake is fourteen miles long, nine miles wide at its greatest expanse and six hundred eighty-two feet below sea level. Because of the winds which often descended on it through the chimney-like defiles in the hills the lake was subject to sudden violent storms. On the eastern side the banks were steep and the country was wild; on the western side there were broad cultivable slopes and a number of towns and cities dotted the shore.

From the Sea of Galilee the Jordan winds a tortuous course to the Dead Sea. The gorge of the Jordan is narrow with steep sides, and is tropical in climate. The river is augmented by two other streams, the Jarmuk which enters from the east four miles south of the lake, and the Jabbok which joins it from the east about twenty miles north of the Dead Sea. The actual bed of the river is usually from one to two hundred feet wide, but in the rainy season the entire inner gorge is often flooded with its muddy waters. In ancient times there were no bridges at all, but the river could be crossed by fords in a few places.

The Dead Sea was called in the Old Testament the Salt Sea, or the Sea of the Arabah (Josh. 3:16, II Ki. 14:25). Because it has no outlet it is really a gigantic evaporating basin in which minerals and salts have been collecting for centuries. The water is extremely bitter to the taste and is so impregnated with chemicals that one cannot sink in it. The cities of the plain which perished in the overthrow of Sodom and Gomorrah probably lie below the water of the southern tongue of the Dead Sea. The rocky desert to the south and southeast where Edom was located contained mineral deposits which were worked occasionally by the inhabitants.

Some farming was carried on in the Jordan valley wherever it was wide enough to allow for settlement. Its tropical climate permitted the raising of fruits and crops that would not thrive in the colder highlands.

Across the Jordan valley lay the eastern plateau which stretched away to the Arabian desert. Toward the north was the Anti-Lebanon range of mountains while toward the south bordering the Jordan were the hills of Gilead and of Moab. On the slope of the Anti-Lebanons lay Damascus, the oldest continuously inhabited city in the world. South of it came the grasslands of Bashan, famous for their cattle. The northern section of this territory was known as Iturea in Christ's day, and the southern section was called Gaulanitis, from the city of Golan. Gilead which extended from the Jarmuk river to the head of the Dead Sea and the upper part of Moab, between Gilead and the Arnon river, were the Perea of the New Testament.

In the time of Christ Palestine and Syria were closely linked together by Roman rule and by settlements. The province of Syria included Phoenicia to Mt. Carmel and a strip of the coastal plain south of Joppa. The Roman governors of Syria kept a watchful eye on developments in Palestine and intervened occasionally if the local ruler or the Roman procurator did not seem to be acting wisely.

The Decapolis, a region south and east of the sea of Galilee, originally a federation of ten cities settled by Greek-speaking people, contained a large foreign population. They did not constitute a single political unit for they were under different rulers, some from Syria, some under Philip. They brought into Palestine a western type of civilization which was quite different from that of the Hebrew people and which must have familiarized even the rural population with

Hellenistic customs and institutions. Although Jesus lived much of His life in Galilee, He could not have been unfamiliar with the language, customs, and beliefs of the Gentile peoples who dominated the world outside of Palestine.

The routes by which Jesus traveled and the places that He visited are located on the individual maps which appear with the discussion of the Gospels. He and His disciples toured Galilee and apparently visited most of the villages of the district. The majority of the cities which He entered are identifiable. Bethlehem and Nazareth are still flourishing villages. Cana where He performed His first public miracle (John 2:1-11), Nazareth where He spent His early years engaging in the carpenter's trade (Luke 4:34, Mark 6:3), Chorazin and Capernaum where He preached frequently (Matt. 11:21, 23), Magdala the home of Mary Magdalene (Matt. 27:56), and Nain where Jesus restored the widow's son to life were all within twenty-five miles of each other. The site of Bethsaida is uncertain, but quite likely it was at the head of the lake of Galilee east of the Jordan. The description of its location in John indicates that it was on the opposite side of the lake from Capernaum and Tiberias (John 6:1, 17, 25).

On the east side of Galilee was the region of Gerasa where Jesus cured the demoniac (Luke 8:26, 37). Probably it is to be identified with Kersa or Gergesa which was located at a rather wild spot on a precipitous shoreline rather than with Gerasa, the modern Jerash, southeast of Galilee in the Decapolis.

Jesus' ministry in Judea was confined to the city of Jerusalem itself and to a few outlying villages. Bethany where He ate with Mary and Martha was a mile to the eastward on the slope of the mount of Olives. Ephraim, to which He retired when the hostility became too great, was near the wilderness (John 11:54). Bethphage (Luke 19:29) was probably near Bethany. Emmaus, to which He walked with the two disciples after the resurrection, was about seven and one half miles west of Jerusalem on the road to Joppa. The site is disputed, but a reference in Josephus[6] states that there was such a place called Emmaus only sixty stadia from Jerusalem, which accords exactly with Luke's description of the distance (Luke 24:13).

To Jerusalem itself the references in the Gospel are numerous. The temple, the pools of Siloam and of Bethesda with its porticoes (John 5:2), the valley of the Kidron between the city and the mount of Olives (John 18:1), the garden of Gethsemane located on the side of the

6. Josephus, *Wars of the Jews*, VII, vi, 6.

mount of Olives (Luke 22:39), Golgotha, "The skull" (Luke 23:33), were all landmarks familiar to Jesus and to the writers of the Gospels.

## The Teaching of Jesus

In Mark's description of the activity of the Lord Jesus Christ there are fourteen references to the fact that He was engaged in teaching the multitude or His disciples. Luke and Matthew also speak frequently of His teaching work. Instruction was His delight, and its effectiveness is well attested by the way in which His disciples remembered His words and repeated them to others.

### Methods

The method of teaching which Jesus used was not entirely novel. Some of the rabbis of His day, like Hillel, were famed for their wisdom and for their ability to hold the attention of their people. All of the pedagogical devices which they employed were doubtless known to Him, and He used them; but He used them far more effectively than they did. The people "were astonished at his teaching: for he taught them as having authority, and not as the scribes" (Mark 1:22). There was a directness, a freshness, and an authority in the teaching of the Lord Jesus Christ that made Him more effective than His contemporaries. He was a master teacher whose skill in instructing the ignorant and the wayward was unsurpassed. What were His methods?

The method of teaching for which He is best known is the parable. A parable is an extended metaphor, the description of some common action or object as an illustration of spiritual truth. It is unlike an allegory because the latter may be purely fictitious, whereas the parable is always connected with ordinary, though perhaps unidentified, occurrences. Jesus' parables of the new and old wineskins (Mark 2:22), the seed that fell in different kinds of soils (Mark 4:2-8), the salt (Matt. 5:13), the good and bad fruit trees (Matt. 7:16-20), the wise and foolish virgins (Matt. 25:1-13), and the unfaithful steward (Luke 16:1-8) are excellent examples of this type of teaching. Each situation was taken from daily life, well-known to Jesus' hearers. Each narrative was simply told with a minimum of detail. The point of the parable was clear and was sometimes applied by a concluding sentence, as in the parable of the ten virgins: "Watch therefore, for ye know not the day nor the hour" (Matt. 25:13).

The parable as a medium of teaching served several purposes. The average hearer would readily understand it because he would instantly recognize its relation to his daily life. Jesus may have taken some of His parables from current affairs so that his audience thought they could recognize the person of whom He spoke. The parables could easily be remembered, for they were neither lengthy nor abstract. Their spiritual application was always relevant to the hearer's need. Occasionally parables were given in sequence in order to present different aspects of the same subject, like those of Matthew 13 on the kingdom of heaven or like those of Luke 15 concerning God's reclamation of sinners.

A second method that Jesus used was the epigram, — a terse, pungent statement that would stick in the mind of His hearer like a barbed arrow. In this category belong the Beatitudes (Matt. 5:3-12), or the statement: "He that findeth his life shall lose it; and he that loseth his life for my sake shall find it" (Matt. 10:39). Many of these epigrams contain paradoxes which make them all the more striking.

Occasionally Jesus employed argument in His teaching; but when He did so, He usually argued from the basis of Scripture rather than from abstract premises or assumptions. In this regard He differed from the Greek philosophers who usually tried to establish some axiomatic truth by common agreement, and then developed its implications into a system. In Matthew 22:15-45 there are recorded debates which Jesus conducted with the Pharisees and the Sadducees. In each case His opponents introduced the argument; when He finally posed a question of His own, the argument was founded on a biblical statement. Jesus did not argue for argument's sake. When He did engage in debate, His logic was irresistible.

Another of the Master's favorite methods was that of question and answer. His questions were never trivial, but they were generally related to the deepest human problems. Sometimes they were startling: "For which is easier, to say, Thy sins are forgiven; or to say, Arise, and walk?" (Matt. 9:5) "For what shall a man be profited, if he shall gain the whole world, and forfeit his life?" (Matt. 16:26). Questions make men think, whether they are direct or rhetorical. The questions of Jesus always brought His hearers to an alternative, especially those that concerned Himself, such as "Who do men say that I am? . . . But who say ye that I am?" (Mark 8:27, 29) Jesus encouraged His disciples to ask questions also. His teaching involved free discussion (John 13:31-14:24), in which they posed their problems and He answered them.

On some occasions Jesus used object lessons. He took a little child to illustrate humility (Matt. 18:1-6), and from the action of the widow who was contributing to the treasury He drew a lesson in giving (Luke 21:1-4). All the parables were implied object lessons, though the material of which Jesus spoke was not always present when He made the comparisons.

These samples of Jesus' method illustrate its variety and its success. He created the parable as a means of teaching, although approximations to it can be found in the Old Testament (Judg. 9:7-15, Isa. 5:1-7), and although the rabbis now and then employed the same general technique. He knew how to make the truth simple and cogent; His parables have lived when the others have been forgotten.

## Purpose — MORAL + SPIRITUAL PURPOSE

All of the teaching of Jesus had a moral and spiritual purpose that was bound up with the mission on which He had been sent by the Father. "The words that I say unto you I speak not from myself: but the Father abiding in me doeth his works" (John 14:10). He regarded His teaching not simply as good advice or as hopeful speculation on universal theories. To Him it was a declaration of moral and spiritual finalities. "Every one therefore that heareth these words of mine, and doeth them, shall be likened unto a wise man, who built his house upon the rock ..." (Matt. 7:24). Jesus taught in order to give to men the authoritative word of God on which their destiny depended.

## Content

The body of teaching is scattered throughout the Gospels, and there is scarcely a page in any one of them which does not contain didactic utterances of Jesus. Some of it appears in blocks. The ethical teaching is concentrated in the sermon on the mount (Matt. 5, 6, 7). The parables of the kingdom have been gathered in Matthew 13; the eschatological teaching concerning the end of the age is found mostly in Matthew 24 and 25, and in the parallel passages in Mark 13 and Luke 21. John is filled with discourse: the teaching about His person (John 5:19-47), the Bread of life (6:32-59), the nature of His person and of His mission (8:12-59), the shepherd and the sheep (10:1-30), and the farewell to the disciples, in which He sought to prepare them for His death (13:31-16:33). Some of these, such as the last one, were spoken on one occasion only; others, like the sermon on the mount, may have been repeated many times. Jesus made many preaching tours and undoubtedly He often gave His parables and epigrams in various places as the need called for them.

234

The subjects which Jesus treated were varied. Social adjustments (Matt. 5:21-26), sex morality (5:27-32), oaths in speech (5:33-37), attitude toward evil (5:38-42), bestowal of charity (6:1-4), prayer (6:5-15, 7:7-12), fasting (6:16-18), economic life (6:19-34), marriage and divorce (19:3-12), relation to government (22:15-22), the nature of God (John 4:21-24), and others were discussed in turn. There is no hint that He ever sought to codify all of the teachings into one law to be obeyed, or into a philosophic system that would be logically impregnable. They were not organized around a system but around Himself, and their value depends upon what He is. Notable in the sermon on the mount is the phrase, "I say unto you," which marks the authority which Jesus possessed and constantly asserted. To some His teaching may seem like an unsystematic collection of unrelated sayings, but in the light of His person these sayings take on new meaning. They are the flashing facets of a divine personality.

## Doctrine

Certain teachings deserve special mention because of their doctrinal importance. Jesus presented God as a heavenly Father, whose fatherhood should be defined primarily in terms of His own relationship to God. "All things have been delivered unto me of my Father: and no one knoweth the Son, save the Father; neither doth any know the Father, save the Son, and he to whomsoever the Son will reveal *him*" (Matt. 11:27). Nowhere in the Gospels did Jesus say "Our Father" and include Himself with His disciples in the first personal pronoun. On the contrary, He said to Mary Magdalene at the tomb: "I ascend unto my Father and your Father, and my God and your God" (John 20:17). In the model prayer which He gave to His disciples He taught them to pray, "Our Father" (Matt. 6:9), expressing man's moral relationship to God. The divine fatherhood meant more to Him than it did to them, since He was in a unique sense the Son of God. He was the Son of God by nature; the disciples could become sons of God only by receiving Him (John 1:12).

The term "father," however, expressed God's attitude toward men. It connoted His love and justice (Matt. 5:44, 45), His interest and concern in His creation (10:29, 30), His forethought and purpose (20:23), His forgiving attitude (Luke 15:11-32), and His final determination of their destiny (John 14:2). The Gospel of John has more references to Jesus' teaching concerning "Our Father" than any one of the others, for the term appears more than one hundred times, and is Jesus' usual form of address to God.

235

Perhaps the one greatest single topic that Jesus discussed was the kingdom. There has been an unusual amount of debate concerning its exact nature. Is it to be equated with a spiritual domination over the lives of men? Was Jesus speaking solely of restoring the independent Jewish monarchy? Is the kingdom identical with the church, or with the millennial reign, or with some revolutionary economic order that He sought to establish? All of these questions have been asked and each has been answered in the affirmative by one group or another.

Apart from all speculation, certain facts are apparent in the Gospels. All of them mention the kingdom (Matt. 6:33, Mark 1:15, Luke 4:43, John 3:3), saying that Jesus preached it. John's Gospel speaks of it on two occasions only: in Jesus' interview with Nicodemus (3:3, 5) and in the trial before Pilate (18:36). To Jesus the kingdom was the entire sphere of the rule of God. Unquestionably it is spiritual in nature and not primarily political, but its full manifestation has not yet come, and shall not come until the King returns personally to reign (Matt. 25:1, 31).

In the teaching of Jesus no sharp difference is discernible between the meaning of the kingdom of heaven, a phrase used exclusively by Matthew, and the kingdom of God. Both were proclaimed by Jesus to be "at hand" (Matt. 3:2, Mark 1:15); the "mysteries" of both are mentioned in the parables (Matt. 13:11, Luke 8:10); both were preached from the days of John the Baptist (Matt. 11:12, 13, Luke 16:16); the two phrases were used indifferently in the invitation to little children (Matt. 19:14, Mark 10:14). If any distinction can be drawn between them, one might say that the kingdom of heaven was used as a Jewish term, possibly in order to avoid offense by unnecessary repetition of the name of God, and that the teaching connected with it concerns the outward manifestation of the kingdom. Most of the passages dealing with the inward aspects of the kingdom use the expression "the kingdom of God" (Luke 17:20, John 3:3, 5, Luke 22:16, 18, 23:51).

The doctrine of the kingdom was linked with the Old Testament. In its ethic it called for repentance (Matt. 4:17), for obedience to the commandments of the law (Matt. 5:19), for the whole-hearted doing of the will of God (Matt. 7:21). This was not synonymous with legalism, however; for Joseph of Arimathea, one of the earliest disciples, is described as "looking for the kingdom of God" (Luke 23:51). Jesus Himself regarded the kingdom as yet to come in its fulness after His death and resurrection (Luke 22:16). The kingdom, then, is that rule which God shall establish over the earth when Christ returns. Its

236

principles will conform to the highest spirit of holiness which is contained in the revealed law, and its perfection will come only through the work of Christ who is both redeemer and king.

The teaching of Jesus concerning Himself is of great significance. As a boy He informed Joseph and Mary of a peculiar obligation to His heavenly Father (Luke 2:49). He questioned His disciples concerning their belief in Him (Matt. 16:15) and accepted with approval Simon's reply that He was "the Son of the living God" (Matt. 16:16). Before His enemies He used language that predicated both preëxistence and deity (John 8:42, 58, 10:30-33, 36, Matt. 22:41-45). When believers worshiped Him, He did not demur (John 9:38, 20:28, 29), as Paul did on one occasion (Acts 14:11-18). The indirect implications of His teachings are equally conclusive, for He placed Himself above the law (Matt. 5:21, 22), and claimed authority to forgive sins (Mark 2:9-11). If the Gospel records are trustworthy at all, they declare unmistakably not only that Jesus was supernatural in His origin, but also that He claimed to be deity.

His estimate of His own mission is important. He came to preach the gospel of the kingdom (Luke 4:43), to call sinners to repentance (Matt. 9:13), to seek and to save the lost (Luke 19:10), to minister, and to give His life a ransom for many (Mark 10:45). He was sent by the Father (John 20:21), and just before His death He reported to the Father that He had accomplished His mission (John 17:4). Revelation and redemption had both been committed to Him and He completed both. He predicted on many occasions His death and resurrection (John 2:19, 3:14, 6:51, 12:24, Matt. 16:21, Mark 10:33, 34), and also His return to judgment (Matt. 25:31-46).

The many spiritual and ethical topics on which Jesus made pronouncements are too numerous to treat here. One common characteristic of His discourses is noteworthy: they were all based on the assumption that He had come to proclaim God's truth, that He had full authority to do so, and that man was obligated to follow His teaching. He represented Himself as the Son of God, and as the Son of God His word is final.

237

# PART III

# THE RECORDS OF THE EARLY CHURCH

# THE RECORDS OF THE EARLY CHURCH

The Period of Expansion
A.D. 29 to 60

---

The Establishment of the Church
The Transition
The Gentile Church
 and the Pauline Mission
The Pauline Program
The Pauline Imprisonment

# THE ESTABLISHMENT OF THE CHURCH

# THE ESTABLISHMENT OF THE CHURCH

The Record: Acts

Outline

Content

The Foundation

Pentecost

Early Preaching

Organization and Leaders

The First Dispersion

# CHAPTER XIII

# The Establishment of the Church

## Acts 1:1 to 8:3

Between the ministry of the Lord Jesus Christ and the church as it emerged into the full current of history there is a tremendous gap. How did it happen that the followers of Jesus, who were obscure provincial Galileans and Judeans, became world figures? What changed the timidity that drove these men to denial and flight at the crucifixion into a boldness that made them stalwart apologists for a new faith? How did preachers who were confessedly "unlearned and ignorant men" (Acts 4:13) make such an impact upon the world that they created an entirely new culture which reshaped the face of all western civilization? What was the origin of the theological truths contained in the New Testament and preached by the early missionaries? How is the teaching of the Epistles related to the teaching of the Gospels? How did it happen that a movement that began among Jews, that centered in a Jewish Messiah, and that was founded on the Jewish Scriptures became a religion espoused largely by Gentiles, as it is today?

These, and other similar questions are answered by the book of Acts, which is the only existing link between the ministry and teaching of Christ and the Christianity that appears full-blown in the Epistles of Paul and of the other New Testament writers.

## The Record: Acts

Acts in itself is not a unit, for it is obviously designed as a sequel to Luke. The author speaks of "the former treatise" (Acts 1:1), and his address to Theophilus indicates a relationship to the Gospel which is addressed to the same person. The summary of that former treatise, as Acts gives it (1:1, 2), accords exactly with the content of Luke and resumes the narrative at the point where Luke dropped it. There can be no reasonable doubt that Acts and Luke are two volumes of the same work. They were designed to fulfil the same general purpose of confirming personal faith and to provide an understandable historical

243

record of God's revelation to men in the work of Christ, both through His personal career and through His church. Historically and spiritually Acts holds the answer to these problems.

## Outline

Acts can be divided into five main sections:

I. Introduction        1:1-11
II. The Origin of the Church: Jerusalem    1:12-8:3
III. The Period of Transition: Samaria    8:4-11:18
IV. The Expansion to the Gentiles    11:19-21:14
      The Pauline Mission: Antioch and the Empire
V. The Imprisonment and Defense of Paul:   21:15-28:31
      Caesarea and Rome

Acts is constructed logically around the outline of geographical development given in 1:8: "ye shall be my witnesses both in Jerusalem, and in all Judea and Samaria, and unto the uttermost part of the earth." The first section after the introduction deals with the beginnings in Jerusalem. The second gives glimpses of work in Samaria, in the coastal plain, and in Caesarea. The last two sections take the message to the cities of the Mediterranean world, ending with Rome, the capital. The geographical expansion of the church was like waves of the tide, which rise higher after every recession, and move farther and farther up the beach.

The book of Acts may also be outlined by its record of growth. In 2:47, 5:14, 6:7, 9:31, 12:24, 16:5, 19:20 there are notations of increase in numbers or in quality of spiritual life which show that Acts is concerned with the progressive development of the group. In the last part of the book from 19:20 to the end the emphasis is more personal than general. It stresses the events in the life of Paul as an individual rather than the church as an institution.

Acts may also be outlined by the personalities that appear in it. Chapters one to five center about Peter; chapters six and seven, about Stephen; chapters eight through twelve introduce several personalities, chief of whom are Barnabas, Philip, and Saul of Tarsus; and from chapter thirteen to the end Paul is the dominant figure. A comparison between Peter and Paul is drawn in several instances: both were leaders, one to the Jews, one to the Gentiles. Peter labored largely in Jerusalem; Paul, in the Gentile world. Each had at least one discourse reproduced in full, which gives a summary of his preaching:

ACTS 1 - 11

Peter, on the day of Pentecost (2:14-40) ; Paul, at Antioch of Pisidia (13:16-42). Both performed miracles : Peter healed a lame man (3:1-10), and so did Paul (14:8-10). Peter brought swift judgment on Ananias and Sapphira (5:1-11), and Paul smote Elymas with blindness (13:6-11). Peter was freed from prison in Jerusalem (5:19-21, 12:1-11) ; Paul was released from jail at Philippi by divine intervention (16:19-30). Both stressed the work of the Holy Spirit (2:38, 19:2-6), and both made the resurrection a primary doctrine of their preaching (Peter: Acts 2:24-36, 3:15, 26, 4:2, 5:30, 10:40, 41; Paul: 13:30-37, 17:3, 18, 31, 24:15, 21, 25:19, 26:8, 23.) As one was the champion of the early church in Jerusalem, so the other was the founder of the first Gentile churches. There is, however, no intimation of antagonism between the two, nor was the work of either confined to one class of hearers. Peter brought the gospel to the house of the Gentile Cornelius, and Paul spoke to the Jews on every occasion that he could find.

The reliability of Acts has often been challenged, but it has never been successfully impugned. There are difficulties to be encountered in equating its chronology with that of the Epistles, and not all of the historical allusions in Acts can be confirmed because in many cases the requisite data are lacking. In those instances, however, where positive archaeological and literary data can be produced, Acts has been vindicated. John Knox, who thinks that "there is ample reason for being doubtful about some of the details" in Acts, admits that "there is every reason for trusting the essential historicity of the final chapters."[1]

### Content

The very fact that Luke was desirous of writing an explanatory treatise on the development of Christian teaching and on the Christian mission implies that he possessed some insight into its over-all significance. He was not merely a chronicler who drudgingly noted dry events on paper. He had the instincts of a historian, and he presented his facts with reference to the continuity of the theme that interested him. That theme was the growth of the church, particularly the transition from Judaism to Gentile Christianity. In this transition he took an active part, as his use of "we" indicates, and he was well qualified to deal with the theme of which he wrote.

Acts, then, does not pretend to be an exhaustive account of all the events that took place in the growth of the early church. No word is

---

1. John Knox, *Chapters in A Life of Paul* (New York: Abingdon-Cokesbury Press, n.d.), p. 43.

said of the expansion southward and eastward from Palestine, although there must have been Christians in Egypt and in Syria from a very early date. There were believers in Damascus before Paul's conversion, but no account is given of the progress of the church there. The main narrative of Acts is concerned with the mission which took the gospel northward through Antioch to Asia Minor and thence to Macedonia, Achaia, and Rome.

The probable reason for this restriction is twofold. First, the writer himself was best acquainted with that aspect of the expansion of Christianity and consequently could use it best as illustrative of his main theme. Second, his main purpose was to instruct his reader in the certainty of the gospel. The continuity of that gospel from Jesus through the disciples to the hour at which he wrote must be demonstrated. Since Paul was the leader of the Gentile mission, he deserved primary attention, and the explanation of the transition from Jew to Gentile, from law to grace, and from Palestine to the empire did not call for a comprehensive survey of all that took place in the missionary growth of the Christian church. For Luke's purpose the presentation of this one phase was sufficient.

The chronological period covered by Acts extends from the crucifixion of Christ about A.D. 29 to the close of Paul's imprisonment in Rome in A.D. 60. The datings of events in Acts have been variously set by different scholars, but the figures given here will represent a fair average of their findings. Ancient writers did not date events by a calendar but by the accession or by the reign of officials. Absolute exactitude to the month and day is sometimes impossible to achieve. Certain fixed points of chronology stand out in Acts.

| | | |
|---|---|---|
| 1. The death of Herod Agrippa I | Acts 12:20-23 | |
| 2. The famine under Claudius | 11:28 | |
| 3. The proconsulship of Sergius Paulus | 13:7 | |
| 4. The expulsion of Jews from Rome under Claudius | 18:2 | |
| 5. The proconsulship of Gallio | 18:12 | |
| 6. The proconsulship of Felix | 23:26, 24:27 | |
| 7. The accession of Festus, Felix' successor | 24:27 | |

On this rather slender framework the arrangement of Acts depends. The allusions are made incidentally, as if the author took for granted that his reader would know the time well enough to fit events into their proper places without further detailed references. Their equation with the years of the first century is as follows:

| | |
|---|---:|
| Death of Herod | A.D. 44 (spring) |
| Famine under Claudius | 44-48 |
| Proconsulship of Sergius Paulus | Before 51 |
| Expulsion of Jews from Rome | Probably 49 |
| Proconsulship of Gallio | Probably 52-53 |
| Proconsulship of Felix | 52-56 |
| Accession of Festus | 57-60 |

The most doubtful of these points is the accession of Festus. Eusebius places it in the reign of Nero, and with this dating most of the available sources agree.[2] Felix was tried in Rome for malfeasance, but could not have come to trial before Nero's accession. In that case, Festus was not appointed until after Nero's reign began. The summer of A.D. 57 is the most probable date for Festus' arrival in Palestine, and the hearing of Paul followed shortly afterwards. If, allowing for time of travel, Paul reached Rome about the summer of A.D. 58, the narrative of Acts closed in A.D. 60.

The other events help to locate some of the important periods of the book of Acts. The death of Herod synchronized with the rise of the Gentile church, for Acts 12:1 states after describing the beginning of the work in Antioch that "about that time Herod the king put forth his hands to afflict certain of the church," and not long after the persecution his death took place. The famine under Claudius (11:28) occurred about the same time between A.D. 44 and A.D. 48.

The proconsulship of Sergius Paulus in Cyprus, if before A.D. 51, means that Barnabas and Saul began their mission not later than A.D. 50, and probably earlier.

The accession of Gallio gives a fairly accurate point of reference for Paul's ministry in Corinth. The language of Acts 18:12 marks not only the dating of Paul's arrest and hearing before the proconsul, but also it seemingly implies that the Jews took advantage of Gallio's recent assumption of office in order to ask for a favor. If so, Paul's ministry may have preceded Gallio's arrival in the city, and although he did not leave Corinth immediately (18:18), it came toward the end of his stay of a year and a half (18:11). The ministry in Ephesus of two years and three months (19:8, 10) and the time of travel necessary to reach Jerusalem would bring Paul to the latter destination about the summer of A.D. 55 or of A.D. 56, and would end the two years' imprisonment at Caesarea at the time of Festus' administration.

Luke's interest was not primarily chronological, although he paid more attention to such details than did most of the writers of the New

---

2. Eusebius, *Historia Ecclesiae,* II, xxii, 1.

Testament. Acts stressed the gradual decline of the Jewish church and the rise of Gentile Christianity.

The first question that the disciples asked the risen Lord concerning His program was "Dost thou at this time restore the kingdom to Israel?" (1:6) The audience at Pentecost was Jewish (2:5), and the preaching was addressed to "men of Israel" (2:22). The church at Jerusalem was predominantly Jewish, although there were two groups among them, the Hebraists of Palestine, and the Hellenists of the Dispersion (6:1). The preaching was in Jewish terms and consisted of the presentation of Jesus as the Messiah who had risen from the dead.

Throughout this first period of the apostolic mission the church was established in Jerusalem. At the outset it was characterized as "the Way" (9:2), or "the sect of the Nazarenes" (24:5), a subordinate group in Judaism, perhaps in a category similar to that of the Essenes. The preaching of Stephen, which brought a violent reaction on the part of the Jewish leaders and the consequent dispersion of the disciples, compelled the leaders to seek other fields. The evangelization of Samaria, of Antioch, and of the Gentile world at large followed.

The period of transition (Acts 8:4 to 11:18) is not covered in detail. Only the work of a few of the refugees from persecution is given, but enough is told to show how spontaneously the Gentile trend began and how effective it was. The conversions of the Ethiopian eunuch and of Cornelius, both probably Gentile proselytes, and the enthusiastic response of the Samaritans to the preaching of Philip marked the new trend away from the establishment of the Messianic kingdom to the growth of the visible church.

The Gentile mission (11:19 to 28:31) began with the establishment of the church at Antioch. There the disciples were called Christians and took a new place in the world. They were known not just as a sect of Judaism, but as an independent body maintaining a different kind of faith (11:26). The Antioch church became a center of teaching, and from it the first mission to the Gentiles went forth. At Antioch was fought out the battle for Gentile freedom, which culminated in the decision of the council at Jerusalem that exempted the Gentile converts from observance of the ceremonial law.

The Pauline program described in Acts 15:35 to 21:14 was illustrative of the development of the church. Although Paul generally appealed "to the Jew first" (Rom. 1:16), the greatest response came from Gentile proselytes and heathen, and the churches that sprang up in the wake of his mission included both Jew and Gentile. On several

249

occasions Paul made unmistakably clear that he was turning to the Gentiles (13:46, 18:6, 19:9, 10, 21:19, 26:20, 23, 28:28). The general rejection of the message by the Jews confirmed the appointment as an apostle to the Gentiles (26:16-18), accelerated the growth of the church independently of the synagogue, and brought the final severance between Judaism and Christianity.

By this review of the growth of Christianity is revealed the pattern of church life: its power, its objective, its methods, its essential organization and discipline, and its missionary expansion. Acts is not only a history of a given period in the life of the church; it is a handbook for Christians. It illustrates the procedure and the effectiveness of a church built on the principles which the Holy Spirit administers.

Another aspect of Acts is its apologetic character. The relation of Christianity to the Roman government is traced from its origin to the time of Paul's hearing in Rome. Since the writer was a friend of Paul and a companion of the final journey to Rome, one cannot help wondering whether he were not trying to prove to his reader that Christianity was not a source of political danger, but that it was wholly a spiritual movement. J. Ironside Still in his work, *St. Paul on Trial*,[3] argued that Acts was written as a brief for the defense when Paul appeared before Caesar. Although his theory is not generally accepted, his recognition of the apologetic character of Luke-Acts deserves consideration. Theophilus to whom Luke-Acts was directed would not have needed certainty if there had been nothing to make him uncertain. Perhaps the disfavor exhibited toward the gospel by the Jews and Gentiles alike had made him look upon it with suspicion. In any case, Luke-Acts demonstrated that a new supernatural revelation had invaded the field of history. It was not confined to any one nationality or group, nor was it confined to any existing faith. Nurtured within Judaism it perpetuated its truth but transcended it by proclaiming that the Messiah had come. Since it was non-political in character it deserved to be treated as a permitted religion, at least on a plane of tolerance equal with the other religions of the empire. For Theophilus, of course, the apologetic was more direct than this, and could be stated in the words of Acts 4:12:

> *And in none other is there salvation: for neither is there any other name under heaven, that is given among men, wherein we must be saved.*

---

3. J. Ironside Still, *St. Paul on Trial* (New York: G. H. Doran Co., n.d.).

## The Foundation: Acts 1:1 to 8:3

The first period in the history of the early church can be characterized as that of establishment. At the outset there is no evidence that the believers broke sharply with Judaism. Pentecost was a Jewish feast before it became a Christian anniversary. The preaching of the apostles interpreted the Old Testament scriptures and stressed Jesus' Messianic office, even avowing that if the nation repented, the Messiah Jesus would return (3:19, 20). The addresses of Peter were gauged for a Jewish audience, and so was the great appeal of Stephen. When the apostles went to worship they went to the temple (3:1), and Stephen debated in the synagogues (6:9, 10) of the foreign residents in Jerusalem.

Nevertheless the church was not simply a natural outgrowth of Judaism, a new prophetic movement centered about the person of the Galilean Jesus. Luke's Gospel makes unmistakably plain that the career of Jesus from birth to death was miraculous and that He came among men as the Son of God (Luke 1:35). The opening of Acts says that ". . . he . . . showed himself alive after his passion by many proofs, appearing unto them by the space of forty days" (1:3). The resurrection is paramount all through Acts and is the foundation of doctrinal preaching. The church, according to Luke, is a new thing among men.

Within the five years more or less that elapsed between the death of Christ and the persecution that rose about Stephen the church had become a distinct body of men with its own peculiar organization, beliefs, and purpose.

### *Pentecost*

The birthday of the church was Pentecost. The eleven disciples, Mary, the mother of Jesus, His brethren, a number of the women who had followed Him, and a large group of unnamed believers, totaling about one hundred twenty, were gathered for prayer in accordance with the command of Christ. Judas, who had already died, had been replaced by Matthias. On the day of Pentecost, as they were assembled in one place, the Holy Spirit came upon them with visible and audible signs. They spoke with new languages, so that their hearers were able to understand in their own dialects "the mighty works of God" (2:5-13) which had been done in Christ.

The coming of the Spirit was the fulfilment of the prediction of John (Luke 3:15, 16) and of the promise by Jesus (Luke 24:49). Peter declared it to be a fulfilment of the prophecy of Joel (Acts 2:16-21) and a proof of the resurrection of Christ (2:32-36). It fused the believers into one group, giving them a unity which they had not previously possessed, and it emboldened them to brave the perils of persecution (2:4, 4:8, 31, 6:8-15).

### Early Preaching

The preaching during this early period of the church's life was centered in the life and person of Christ. Unlike modern preaching which is usually either the logical development of some topic or the elaboration of a single text, the apostolic preaching was a narration of the life and work of Jesus, with a defense of His resurrection, and was followed by a call to repentance and faith in His name. The sermons of Peter and of Stephen that are recorded in this part of Acts were apologetic in character, because they are answers to challenges which were flung at the preachers by a curious or hostile audience.

The apostolic preaching was strongly biblical in content. The New Testament had not been written at this time, but the addresses were saturated with Old Testament quotations and prophecies. Peter introduced his sermon at Pentecost with a long quotation from Joel, and he made another long quotation from the Psalms to show the Messianic promise of the resurrection. Stephen's address was a historical review of the unbelief of the nation which culminated in the rejection of Jesus. Both the precepts and the precedents of Scripture constituted the foundation of the apostolic message.

The burden of this preaching was the necessity of belief in the risen Messiah, repentance both personal and national, and the receiving of the Holy Spirit (2:38). It was accompanied by instruction, so that as the number of the believers increased, they were bound together in common knowledge and in common action (2:42).

### Organization and Leaders

The first church in Jerusalem was not a highly organized body, owning property and maintaining a strong ecclesiastical system. The apostles, because of their preaching and teaching functions, were naturally the leaders, but the government of the church was essentially democratic. When complaints were voiced that the widows of the Hellenistic Jews were being neglected in the distribution of daily food, the apostles suggested the appointment of qualified men to oversee this part of the church's activity. The choice was made by the "multi-tude" (6:5), and the new officials were duly appointed.

Much has been said about the so-called communism of the early church, by which a redistribution of goods was made for the benefit of the poor (2:45, 4:34, 35). It is true that the multitude "had all things common," but the giving was voluntary, not compulsory, and was apparently calculated for the emergency in Jerusalem where there were many "poor among the saints" (Rom. 15:26). There is no record that a similar system was maintained in other churches, although relief of the poor was a general practice.

Meetings were held both in the temple and in private homes (2:46), at which there was teaching, accompanied by breaking of bread and prayer (2:42).

The leaders of the early period were Peter, John, Stephen. Of the three, John was least prominent, being mentioned only in company with Peter. Peter was the preacher who dominated the scene. He made the opening address on the day of Pentecost, and he defended the position of the Christian believers before the Sanhedrin when he and John were accused (4:5-8). Peter's boldness and spiritual power were an amazing contrast to his vacillation at the time of his denial of Jesus.

Stephen, who was one of the seven appointed for relief work, and who became the outstanding apologist of the early church, was not one of the original twelve disciples. If his name has any bearing upon his background, he was a Hellenistic Jew who probably came to Jerusalem as a pilgrim, and after his conversion stayed with the church. As a debater in the foreign synagogues he was without a peer (6:9, 10). He did not confine his activities to social work, but became an apologist and an evangelist as well as the church's first martyr.

## The First Dispersion

At the violent death of Stephen and because of the sternly repressive measures taken by the Jewish leaders to crush the new movement, the majority of the Christians in Jerusalem were scattered abroad through Judea and Samaria. From this point to the last chapters of Acts little is said of the Jerusalem church. It was strongly Judaistic in character and maintained some observance of the law, as the later controversies showed (15:1, 21:17-26). The scattering of its adherents, however, resulted in numerous missionary projects, of which a few are narrated in the next section on the transition (8:4-11:18).

# THE TRANSITION

# THE TRANSITION

# CHAPTER XIV

## The Transition

### Acts 8:4 to 11:18

The sudden persecution which burst like a storm at the death of Stephen marked a sharp change in the affairs of the church. Up to this time the believers had been tolerated, or else the arrests, interrogations, and imprisonments had been spasmodic. The genuineness of the miracles which had been performed (4:15, 16) and the popular favor which they enjoyed (2:47) prevented the ruling priesthood from treating the church too drastically. Stephen's arraignment of the nation for the rejection of Christ, however, so enraged them that they did not wait for legal action but stoned him on the spot (7:54-60). The fall of this leader and the bitter hostility of the Jewish officials might have brought the church to an end had not God's intervention saved the day.

### The Preaching in Samaria

Evidently the seven who had been appointed to care for the widows of the Jerusalem church had not been content to remain servers of tables. Stephen became an apologist; Philip became an evangelist. Driven from Jerusalem, Philip made his way to Samaria, where he opened a preaching campaign.

Samaria was inhabited by a population of mixed ancestry. When the northern kingdom of Israel fell before the Assyrians in 721 B.C. they deported to Assyria a large number of people, replacing them by settlers from other lands. In the resulting mixture of population both the Jewish blood and the Jewish worship were affected. The Samaritans were half Gentile by descent, and they retained some of the features of heathen worship, although they adhered to Jehovah also (II Kings 17:24-33). In the time of the restoration under Ezra and Nehemiah they maintained a separate commonwealth (Neh. 4:1, 2, 7, 8) which was a serious rival of the group in Judea. They maintained a temple in Mt. Gerizim which the Jews regarded as schismatic (John 4:20, 22). The tension between the two peoples was so strong that

257

the Jews who traveled between Judea and Galilee usually avoided Samaria by crossing the Jordan and by using the roads on its eastern bank.

Philip's preaching among the Samaritans was, therefore, a surprising action for a Jew. It showed that he had a vision of the possibilities of his message for other peoples than his own. The response was amazing. The Samaritans forsook their superstitions and believed on Christ.

The mission of Philip was reinforced by the aid of Peter and John who visited Samaria to see what had been accomplished and to make sure that the Samaritans received the Holy Spirit. The book of Acts recounts four occasions on which the Holy Spirit came to man in a spectacular manner: to the disciples at Pentecost (2:1-4), to the Samaritans (8:17), to the Gentiles in the house of Cornelius (10:44-46), and upon the disciples of John the Baptist at Ephesus (19:6). Each of these instances represents the introduction of the Holy Spirit to a different class of people. Collectively they mark the beginning of the Spirit's work in the lives of individual believers at the opening of the church era. (The gift of the Holy Spirit was the proof of conversion (Rom. 8:9) and was the stamp of divine approval upon the apostles' work.)

### The Ethiopian Eunuch

The eunuch was an official of the Ethiopian court who was probably a proselyte returning from a pilgrimage to Jerusalem. The interview of Philip with this man was illustrative of several principles in the growth of the church. As in the case of the Samaritans, racial backgrounds and prejudices were overcome, the ministry to an individual was proved to be as important in the eyes of God as a mass revival, and the method of preaching Jesus from the Old Testament was demonstrated. Acts does not relate the consequences of this interview and makes no allusion to the effect of the gospel in Ethiopia. It does indicate that the period of transition from Jerusalem as the center of Christianity to the Gentile world involved a large number of contacts and that the message went in many directions.

### The Conversion of Paul

The ministry of Philip illustrated the outreach of the church to new localities and groups; the conversion of Saul of Tarsus was the provision of a new leader. (Next to the work of Christ Himself, the conversion of Saul was probably the most important event in the history of Christianity, for it not only removed an active enemy of the gospel, but also it transformed him into one of its chief propagators.

Saul of Tarsus appeared first in the pages of Acts as a young man holding the garments of those who stoned Stephen and "consenting unto his death" (8:1). Three separate accounts of his conversion are given in Acts: one by Luke in chapter nine as an integral part of the general historical account, and two which are included in quoted speeches of Paul (22:1-21; 26:2-23). Each had a different emphasis. The first account is historical, as part of the movement of the church; the last two are personal, and were given as defenses of Paul's life and doctrine before hostile or questioning audiences. Taken together with certain passages from his epistles,[1] they afford the sum total of available data concerning the great crisis of his life.

Saul, or Paul as he is generally known, was born into a strict Hebrew family near the beginning of the first century. His native city was Tarsus, a busy metropolis in Cilicia, situated on the north east corner of the Mediterranean Sea. From Tarsus a land road went north and west through the pass in the mountains known as the Cilician Gates, and the docks of the city were a center of shipping. The university of Tarsus was noted for its courses in philosophy and medicine, and the temple of Aesculapius, the god of healing, served as a hospital and clinic for the use of the medical students. Whether Paul ever attended the university is doubtful, but he can scarcely have escaped its influence on the thinking and life of the city.

He was educated strictly in good Jewish fashion, learning the Hebrew language and the Scriptures, and also the trade of tentmaking (18:3). He was acquainted with Aramaic, which he probably spoke at home, and with Greek, which was the prevalent language of Tarsus. Possibly he knew a little Latin also, though proof of his knowledge is lacking.

At the age of twelve he was sent to Jerusalem to study with Gamaliel (22:3), and according to his own testimony he made good progress in his studies (Gal. 1:14). By conviction he was a Pharisee, and his zeal was measured by the intensity with which he persecuted the church (Acts 26:9-11). By the time that he came to manhood he was already a leader in Judaism. The language of Acts 26:10, ". . . I gave my vote against them," if it is taken literally, implies that he was a

---

1. For full data see Frank J. Goodwin, *A Harmony of the Life of Paul* (Grand Rapids, Mich.: Baker Book House, n.d.) pp. 19-25.

member of the Sanhedrin. If that be so, he must have been thirty
or more years of age at the martyrdom of Stephen, since a man was
not eligible for membership in that body until he had attained maturity.

The moral antecedents of his conversion are suggested by his account of his inner life as given in Romans 7. Plagued by the consciousness of sin which was aroused by the law, he found that the good that
he wanted to do he could not produce, and the evil that he sought
to avoid was always present with him (Rom. 7:19). Whether Romans
7 applies to the converted or to the unconverted man has been long
debated by theologians, but there can be little doubt that it refers to
man under the law as Paul was. Certainly the law itself could produce the consciousness of sin even apart from the gospel. Paul's zeal
for persecution, then, may have been the effort of a misguided con-
science to do something for God which would compensate for the evil
in his soul.

The death of Stephen was also a rankling thorn in his mind. According to Paul's way of thinking, Stephen was a blasphemer and stood
condemned by the law. Nevertheless, Stephen's argument was essentially sound and could not be refuted. Furthermore, the vision
of the risen Christ which Stephen professed to have and the joy which
illumined his face in spite of impending death gave his life a reality
which the legalistic arguments of Saul could not shake. He alluded
to this event in his speech from the castle of Antonia (22:19, 20) an
experience which he could not forget. His conversion may not
have been caused by it, but it made part of the foundation for the
transformation which took place on the road to Damascus.

The conversion itself was distinctly a supernatural revelation of the
risen Christ to this implacable persecutor. Paul classes it as the last
of Jesus' post-resurrection appearances (I Cor. 15:8). No theory of
disease or hallucination can account for it adequately. Luke notes
that it took place at a definite locality near Damascus (9:3); that it
was accompanied by a great light (9:3) which Paul says was brighter
than the noonday sun (26:13); that an audible voice spoke to Paul
which was heard by the men with him (9:7), although they did not
understand what was said (22:9). Paul himself suffered physical
effects (9:8) which could be observed by those who accompanied him.
The objective character of the conversion is above doubt.

The subjective factor deserves some attention also. When the unknown voice spoke to him from the blazing light of the heavenly
glory, Paul's natural question was "Who art thou?" (9:5). The answer,
"I am Jesus" (9:5), would have been unbelievable to him had not his

experience with Stephen prepared him for it. In one flash of revelation he saw that Stephen was right, that all of the arguments of Judaism against Stephen and the disciples had been wrong, and that a new world of revelation had been opened to him. Parallel with the reversal of his theological thinking came a call to service in the Gentile world. He acceded and was filled with the Spirit for his new task (9:10-19).

The ministry of Paul began immediately in Damascus. Galatians says that he visited Arabia at this time (Gal. 1:17). Probably he did so between his initial testimony in the synagogues (9:22) and his final departure from Damascus (9:23-25). Quite possibly the shock to his thinking was so great that he had to retire for a while to readjust his beliefs to the new light that had come in Christ. His sudden reversal of position was as disconcerting to him as it was to his associates.

Paul's new faith in Jesus as the Messiah brought him into a clash with his former Jewish colleagues in Damascus (9:23), and for his own safety he was obliged to flee the city. In Jerusalem he was regarded with cold suspicion by the disciples who, logically enough, looked upon him as a wolf who was adopting the sheep's garb in order to raid the flock. Under the sponsorship of Barnabas, however, he was accepted into the apostolic circle (9:27). He maintained a bold program of preaching, especially among the Hellenistic Jews, quite similar to the work that Stephen had done. So great was his success and so violent was the reaction against him that the church sent him away to Tarsus (9:30) where the opposition that he aroused would endanger them less.

Paul, according to all testimony (9:15, 22:21, 26:17, Rom. 15:16, Gal. 1:16, 2:7, 8, Eph. 3:1-7), was God's choice as the apostle to the Gentiles. His conversion was part of the transition from the Jewish-centered church of Jerusalem to the Gentile church of the Roman world.

## The Preaching of Peter

The conversion of Paul brought into the church a new personality who was destined to become the outstanding apostle to the Gentiles, but the Spirit of God was working also with the personalities within the church, chief among whom was Peter. Beginning with the period of transition, he began to enlarge his ministry by preaching in the coastal plain of Sharon, where his activities were concentrated in the cities of Lydda and Joppa (9:32-43).

The important case in this period was the conversion of Cornelius, a Roman centurion, who was in command of a military detachment at Caesarea. Evidently he had already been interested in Judaism, for he is called "a devout man, and one that feared God with all his house" (10:2). Probably he was an adherent of the Jewish faith who had not formally become a proselyte but who had put his trust in Jehovah, the only God, and who had attached himself to the synagogue. He was typical of many Gentiles of that time who, disgusted with the irrationalities and excesses of paganism, had sought something better elsewhere. In Judaism he found a loftiness of theology and a purity of ethic that were missing in his previous experience, and so he embraced it enthusiastically.

The divine direction of Peter to the house of Cornelius is important in the history of Acts for a number of reasons. First, it indicated that God's provision of salvation was not to be confined to one race or people. Cornelius, the Roman Gentile, had as much right to hear the message of Christ as any Jew in the synagogues of Palestine.

Second, the conversion of Cornelius was the opening wedge for bringing Gentiles into the church. Peter's initial reaction to the divine command was a refusal to participate in anything that was unclean (10:14, 11:7-12). At God's behest he went to a Gentile home, preached, and subsequently remained for a few days (10:48). The conversion of these Gentiles was so convincing that Peter proposed their baptism and accepted them into fellowship (10:44-48).

The reception of these Gentiles precipitated a question within the church that remained a point of controversy for some time thereafter. Should a Jewish Christian eat with the uncircumcised Gentiles who did not observe the law? If the Gentiles became believers, how much of the law should they observe? Was legal observance the final criterion of righteousness or of a right relation with God? Not all of these questions were raised immediately by the conversion of Cornelius, but the whole principle of law versus grace was brought forward in the thinking of the church by the accession of the Gentiles, and the subsequent missionary movement made it even more acute.

The immediate answer of Peter illustrates the point that the history of Acts seeks to teach. The transition from law to grace was not an evolutionary drift, nor was it the policy of expediency, nor a whim of a few leaders. It was prompted by the Holy Spirit (10:19), explained by Spirit-led preaching (10:43), and confirmed when the Spirit came upon the Gentile believers (10:44, 11:15-18). "To the Gentiles also [had] God granted repentance unto life."

The sermon of Peter in the house of Cornelius is an excellent example of evangelistic preaching in the apostolic age. It is really a brief historical summary of the life of Christ, which places its major emphasis upon His death, His resurrection, and His coming to judgment. In general substance it is virtually an outline of the gospel narrative. The novel element in it is universality: "To him bear all the prophets witness, that through his name *every one that believeth* (italics ours) on him shall receive remission of sins" (10:43). Up to this time Peter had been preaching to the "men of Israel" (2:22), the descendants of Abraham, Isaac, and Jacob (3:13, 25), the "rulers and elders" (4:8). Here he adapted the message to an audience that did not possess the heritage of the covenant and of the law, and he said that it was directed "to every one that believeth." The implications of this message were more fully developed later by Paul, but the rule of grace and the doctrine of justification by faith were certainly latent in Peter's preaching.

The period of transition was thus marked by a change in the geographical scene of operations from Jerusalem to the wider sphere of Palestine as a whole, including Samaria and extending to Syria and Damascus. There was a change in constituency, for the Samaritans, the Ethiopians, and even Roman Gentiles were included. The preaching message began to expand as the purpose of God in reaching the Gentiles became increasingly evident, and the center of its thought shifted from the restoration of the kingdom to forgiveness of sins. The church began to face the problem of the interpretation of the law as it should — or should not — be applied to the Gentiles. A new leadership was provided for the missionary expansion that came as a result of the persecution and that was accelerated by the response to the preaching of this period. A new stage of growth was opening before the church, for which the period of transition had been a preparation.

# THE GENTILE CHURCH AND THE

# PAULINE MISSION

# THE GENTILE CHURCH AND THE PAULINE MISSION

The Church at Antioch

The Mission to the Gentiles
Cyprus
Antioch of Pisidia
Iconium, Lystra, and Derbe

The Council of Jerusalem

The Literature of Protest

The Epistle of James
The Author
Outline
Problems

The Epistle to the Galatians
Destination
Date
Content
Outline
Evaluation

## CHAPTER XV

# The Gentile Church and the Pauline Mission
### Acts 11:19 to 15:35

The missionary movement to the Gentiles as portrayed in Acts began with the establishment of the church of Antioch in Syria. The founding of this church was part of the sudden expansion that came in the period of transition. There is a definite link between Acts 8:4 and 11:19, for the latter says:

> They therefore that were scattered abroad upon the tribulation that arose about Stephen travelled as far as Phoenicia, and Cyprus, and Antioch, speaking the word to none save only to Jews. But there were some of them, men of Cyprus and Cyrene, who, when they were come to Antioch, spake unto the Greeks also, preaching the Lord Jesus.
>
> (Acts 11:19, 20)

The Cypriote and Cyrenian believers who preached at Antioch departed from the general exclusive procedure of their fellows by preaching to Greek Gentiles. Luke's comment here indicates that his presentation of the period of transition emphasized the exceptions rather than the usual procedure of preaching. Antioch, which was evangelized in that period, was so exceptional that it became the fountain-head of an entirely new missionary enterprise.

## The Church at Antioch

The city of Antioch was founded by Seleucus Nicator in 300 B.C. Under the early Seleucid kings it enlarged rapidly. The earliest city was purely Greek, but in later days Syrians settled outside the walls and were taken into the city as it grew. The third element of the population was Jewish, many of whom were descendants of colonists imported from Babylon. They possessed equal rights with the Greeks and maintained their own synagogue worship. Under Roman rule Antioch prospered, for it was the military and commercial gateway to the Orient, ranking next to Rome and Alexandria in size.

The year of founding the church in Antioch is not stated. Apparently it took place not long after the death of Stephen, probably between A.D. 33 and A.D. 40. Some time would be required for the church to attain sufficient importance in size and in character to bring it to the attention of the church in Jerusalem (11:22). They delegated Barnabas to visit Antioch, where he labored for an indeterminate period, and then went to Tarsus to ask Paul to become his assistant (11:22-26). They labored together for at least a year after that (11:26) before Agabus prophesied the famine which came to pass "in the days of Claudius" (11:28). The implication of the text is that the prophecy was given before the accession of Claudius in A.D. 41, and that the famine came later. Another chronological note is afforded by the reference to Herod Agrippa I (12:1) who died in A.D. 44. Probably the work in Antioch began around A.D. 33 to 35. If the "famine relief" took place about A.D. 44, Barnabas may have begun his connections with Antioch about A.D. 41, which would mean that Paul first came on the scene in A.D. 42.

While this chronology cannot be considered as final, it fits fairly well with Paul's known movements. If he were converted in A.D. 31 or even 32, and spent three years in the region of Damascus (Gal. 1:18), he could have returned to Jerusalem before A.D. 35. If he spent a year or two in Jerusalem before returning to Tarsus (9:28-30), he could have been engaged with preaching in Tarsus and Cilicia for five years before Barnabas persuaded him to join him in his new undertaking. This seems a rather long silence, but Luke's silence on other matters of equal interest shows that it is not exceptional.

The church at Antioch was important because it possessed certain distinctive features. First, it was the mother of all the Gentile churches. The household of Cornelius could scarcely be called a church in the sense that the group at Antioch was, for it was a household rather than a general congregation. From the Antioch church went the first recognized mission to the unevangelized world. At Antioch began the first controversy over the status of Gentile Christians. It was a center where the leaders of the church met. At one time or another, Peter, Barnabas, Titus, John Mark, Judas Barsabbas, Silas, and, if the Western text is correct,[1] the author of Acts himself were all connected with this church. It is noteworthy that practically all of these men were engaged in the Gentile mission and were mentioned in Paul's Epistles as well as in Acts.

---

1. Acts 11:28, Codex D: *sunestrammenon de hemon ephe heis ex auton*, translated, " . . . and when we were gathered together, one of them said . . . " According to this text, the writer of Acts included himself among the Antiochenes.

The written Gospels may have originated at Antioch. The possibility of contact between Mark and Luke as well as the fact of their later association at Rome may have some bearing on the much discussed Synoptic problem. Ignatius, bishop of Antioch at the close of the first century, seems to have quoted almost exclusively from Matthew when he alluded to the Gospels, as if Matthew were the only Synoptic Gospel that he knew. Streeter[2] argues at length for the Antiochene origin of Matthew on the basis of its use by Ignatius and in the *Didaché,* both of which he identifies as Syrian documents. If these three Gospels struck their roots into the living oral teaching of the church at Antioch, their ministry to the world is in a measure the legacy of this church to the Gentile believers of yesterday and today.

The church at Antioch was distinguished also for its teachers. Of those mentioned in Acts 13:1, only Barnabas and Paul were known from later references, but their ministry must have made the church famous as a center of teaching. Antioch virtually superseded Jerusalem as the home of Christian preaching and as the headquarters of evangelistic missions.

Perhaps the ascendancy of Antioch was hastened by the persecution of Herod in A.D. 44. The church at Jerusalem had always been financially weak, since many of the poorer members had to be subsidized by gifts. The famine must have weakened it still further, in spite of relief from Antioch (11:28-30). The persecution under Herod brought the death of James, the son of Zebedee (12:2), and Peter barely escaped with his life (12:17). The interlude of 12:1-24 gives only a brief glimpse of the situation in Jerusalem, but it shows a devout church under tremendous pressure, struggling to maintain its very existence.

The most outstanding fact about the church at Antioch was its testimony. "The disciples were called Christians first in Antioch" (11:26). Previously the believers in Christ had been looked upon as a sect of the Jews, but with a Gentile constituency and with a growing system of doctrine that was quite different from that of the Mosaic law, the world began to see the difference and to label them accordingly. "Christian" meant "belonging to Christ" as "Herodian" meant "belonging to Herod." The name was probably given in derision, but the character of the disciples and the testimony that they bore gave it a complimentary meaning.

2. Burnet H. Streeter, *The Four Gospels* (New York: The Macmillan Company, 1925), pp. 12, 500-523.

## The Mission to the Gentiles

By the year 46 or thereabouts the church at Antioch had grown into a stable and active group. They were instructed in the faith; their reputation was so well established in the city that they were given a classification of their own as Christians; and they had sponsored a relief expedition to Jerusalem to carry a contribution for those who were suffering because of famine. In the course of regular worship there came a call to "separate Barnabas and Saul" (13:2) for a special work. In obedience to this direction of the Holy Spirit the two men were consecrated by the church to the new task and were sent on their mission.

### Cyprus

The first sphere of activity was Cyprus, which was Barnabas' native soil (4:36). The church may have had some interests there, since the first evangelists in Antioch included in their number "men of Cyprus" (11:20). Barnabas and Saul, with John Mark as their assistant, visited the synagogues and there preached the new message. In the conflict with Elymas for the attention of the proconsul, Paul came to the fore. Recognizing the diabolical character of Elymas' sorcery, he rebuked him publicly and pronounced judgment upon him. The proconsul, amazed at the swift retribution that fell upon Elymas, "believed" (13:12).

No statistical results of the campaign in Cyprus are given, but one important change took place. In Acts 13:2 the team is described as "Barnabas and Saul," giving Barnabas the place of prominence as the senior missionary, and calling Paul by his Jewish name. In Acts 13:13 the phraseology changes to "Paul and his company," using Paul's Gentile name. From this turn in the narrative Paul is in the place of prominence. The ministry in Cyprus brought out his qualifications for leadership and placed him in undisputed command of the mission.

At this same period two other things happened. Paul left Cyprus and moved to Asia Minor, and John Mark withdrew from the party and returned to Jerusalem. For Paul it was the beginning of a world-wide project of carrying the gospel to untrodden regions. For Mark it may have seemed to be an unwarranted deviation from an established program. Whether he were jealous for his relative, Barnabas, who had been relegated to second place, or whether he were afraid of entering the wild territory of central Asia Minor, or whether

*John Mark*

he had some doctrinal difference with Paul is not told. In any case he refused to go farther and turned back.

## Antioch of Pisidia

The address of Paul in the synagogue at Antioch of Pisidia is quoted at length by Luke (13:16-43). In its general style it is quite similar to that of Stephen, for its approach is the historical review of God's dealing with the nation of Israel. The central theme is introduced in verse 23: "Of this man's seed hath God according to promise brought unto Israel a Saviour, Jesus . . ." The development of the theme does not vary greatly from the apostolic preaching recorded in the early chapters of Acts, but when Paul came to the climax of this address he introduced one element that was new:

> Be it known unto you therefore, brethren, that through this man is proclaimed unto you remission of sins: and by him every one that believeth is justified from all things, from which ye could not be justified by the law of Moses.

(Acts 13:38, 39, emphasis ours)

Although the resurrection and the forgiveness of sins through Christ had been proclaimed by Peter (2:32, 36, 38, 3:15, 19, 5:30, 31, 10:40, 43), not until this time had anyone preached so explicitly that men could be justified individually before God solely on the ground of faith. To be justified means to be declared righteous, or to be regarded as legally righteous. To obtain by faith a standing with God that would enable one to possess assurance of salvation would mean that the works of the law were unavailing and unnecessary. It was a new and a bold advance in the truth concerning Christ.

The immediate result was twofold. There was a tremendous response to Paul's preaching, for "the next sabbath almost the whole city was gathered together to hear the word of God" (13:44). On the other hand, Jewish opposition became bitter and stooped to jealousy and slander (13:45). The ultimate result was that Paul announced that he would turn to the Gentiles, of whom a number believed (13:48). The Gentiles, rather than the Jews, became the core of the new church in Antioch of Pisidia.

## Iconium, Lystra, and Derbe

The same situation was duplicated in the town of Iconium, situated a little to the southeast of Antioch. A flourishing church was built in the synagogue, but the division of opinion became so strong that the preachers were expelled from the city and took refuge in the outlying cities of Lystra and Derbe.

In Lystra Paul encountered paganism. The priest of Jupiter-before-the-city (14:13), seeing the healing of the cripple that Paul performed and thinking that Paul and Barnabas were gods come down to earth, attempted to offer sacrifice to them. Paul's horrified protest against the error affords an insight into his method of approaching the pagan mind, which was ignorant of the Old Testament. He and Barnabas appealed to the one God who had given "rains and fruitful seasons" (14:17), a point of contact that the simple agriculturalists of that region would appreciate whether they had any formal theology or not.

The stay at Lystra was terminated by the incursion of Jewish agitators from Pisidian Antioch and Iconium, who persuaded the ignorant and fickle people that Paul was a dangerous propagandist. Stoned and dragged out of the city as dead, he recovered consciousness and went on to Derbe to preach there. Having gathered a group of believers in that city, Paul and Barnabas retraced their steps, strengthening and organizing the churches that they had founded. They returned to Syrian Antioch to report on the things that God had done with them, and to show how ". . . he had opened a door of faith unto the Gentiles" (14:27).

The importance of this itinerary can scarcely be exaggerated. It brought Paul into the foreground as a leader of the church and placed him on a par with the apostles (Cf. Gal. 2:7-9). It contributed to the education of John Mark, even though he seems to have made a conspicuous failure. Initial contact with Timothy probably dated from this journey, for Paul alluded to his experience in this region when he wrote to Timothy many years later (II Tim. 3:11). Above all, it marked a new departure in the theological thinking of the church, for out of the events of this journey came the Pauline doctrine of justification by faith.

### The Council of Jerusalem

The rapid growth of the Gentile church under the mission of Paul and Barnabas brought into focus a new problem. If the Gentiles became believers in Jesus as the Messiah, and if they accepted Him as Saviour and Lord, to what extent should they be required to observe the precepts of the law? The Lord Jesus Christ had placed Himself and His teachings above the law and had indicated that He was superior to Moses and to the prophets as a son is superior to the servants in the household. The full import of his words had not gained immediate recognition, but the slow trend within the Christian movement under the leadership of the Holy Spirit had been away from legalism and toward faith. With the mission to Gentiles who knew nothing of the law and who had entered into the Christian fellowship solely by belief, the division of opinion within the church became acute. Peter's debate with the Jewish Christians in Jerusalem after his visit to the house of Cornelius was an early sign of the tension. Only when he reported that the Holy Spirit came upon the Gentiles as He had upon the Jewish believers at Pentecost did the Jewish Christians admit that Gentiles might be saved at all (11:18).

The legalistic element in the Jerusalem church remained active, however. After Paul and Barnabas returned to Antioch and told of the success of their preaching, ". . . certain men came down from Judea and taught the brethren, *saying,* Except ye be circumcised after the custom of Moses, ye cannot be saved" (15:1). To the Gentiles this teaching must have been a shock. They had not been brought up on the law, and their spiritual experience since their conversion had proved quite satisfactory without the observance of all the ceremonies. Furthermore, they had found in Christ a deliverance from the legalism and from the ceremonialism of their own religions. Why should they now put themselves back under another bondage?

*false prophets*

The Judaizers, on the other hand, argued that circumcision had been established by the law of Moses as a sign of God's covenant (Exod. 12:48), and that the Divine will had insisted on it rigidly. As a matter of fact, it antedated the Mosaic law, for God had required it of Abraham as a mark of the covenant that was established through him (Gen. 17:9-14). The outward significance of the rite was applied to the inward life even under the law, which speaks of being circumcised in heart (Deut. 10:12-16), but in actual practice it had probably become a routine ceremony.

The argument became so sharp that the church at Antioch decided to send delegates to discuss the matter with the apostles and elders at Jerusalem. Paul, Barnabas, and some others went to Jerusalem and were welcomed by the church. They gave a full report of their successful work among the Gentiles. Opposition came from a group of Pharisees who contended naturally enough for the strict observance of the law.

A free discussion followed in which both sides participated. Three decisive contributions are noted by Luke.

The speech of Peter carried weight because he spoke as the initial leader of the church in Jerusalem and as one that had already experienced the practical aspects of the question. He pointed out that (1) it was God's choice that the Gentiles should hear the message of Christ (15:7); (2) that they had been given the Holy Spirit without any discrimination against them (15:8); (3) that the ceremonial law was an unbearable yoke upon the Jews themselves (15:10); and (4) that salvation was by grace for the Jew as well as for the Gentile (15:11). Peter's argument from church experience brought the matter up to date.

Paul and Barnabas reported on the work among the Gentiles, stressing the "signs and wonders" which had been effected (15:12). The implication of their argument was that God would not have prospered their mission if He had not approved their methods. Their appeal was pragmatic.

The final speech was given by James, who was generally considered to be a champion of the strict observance of the law (Gal. 2:12). He pointed out the Scriptural argument that God had intended to save the Gentiles, who would seek after Him. James recommended that they be not required to keep all the law, but that they be requested to abstain from certain practices which would be particularly offensive to their Jewish brethren; namely, (1) idolatry, (2) fornication, (3) eating of meat from strangled animals, and (4) eating of blood. These regulations were suggested more as a basis of fellowship than as a platform of ethics, although the first two dealt with moral issues which had to be faced irrespective of Jewish law.

In some of the manuscript texts of Acts the third phrase, ". . . and from what is strangled," is omitted.[3] Should this reading be correct, the last term, ". . . and from blood," might be interpreted to mean bloodshed or murder. In that case all three requirements would be ethical or moral, and the regulation would mean that these standards would be expected of the Gentiles as essential to moral character.

James called attention to the additional fact that if any Gentiles really desired to adopt Judaism, there had been synagogues in every major city of the empire for generations. It would be easy to ascertain the meaning of the law from them. His suggestion encouraged the assumption that the Christian message, though akin to that of the synagogue in many ways, nevertheless had new and distinctive features of its own. Such an admission on James' part took him out of the

---

3. Omitted by D, gig, Irenaeus lat., Ephraem Syrus.

category of the Judaizers who claimed his authority for insisting upon the necessity of circumcision.

The decision that followed the discussion favored the recommendation of James. Not only the "official board," but also the whole church agreed to send back delegates to Antioch with Paul and Barnabas, bearing written record of the proceedings of the group (15:22, 23). The communication contained several important provisions: (1) a repudiation of the initial group of Judaizers who had begun the controversy (15:24); (2) approbation of Barnabas and Paul (15:25); (3) the authorization of Judas and Silas as delegates (15:27); and (4) the decision of "the Holy Ghost and us" to insist upon the "necessary" abstinence from idolatry, from blood, from things strangled, and from fornication.

The decision was well received by the church at Antioch. Judas and Silas remained for a little time to participate in the work (15:32, 33) and finally returned to Jerusalem. Paul and Barnabas resumed their work of teaching and peace descended upon the church.

## The Literature of Protest

The controversy over circumcision for Gentiles was no mere tempest in a teacup that affected only the superficial peace of the churches at Jerusalem and at Antioch and that was settled by a few concessions to Jewish prejudice. Several deeper questions were involved. What was the place of the law in the plan of God? Was obedience to the law in addition to faith in Christ necessary for salvation? If the Gentiles did not need to keep the law, just what relation existed between salvation by faith and ethical behavior? What connection is there between faith and works? These and similar problems were reflected in many of the books of the New Testament that were written in the decade between A.D. 50 and A.D. 60, but two of these writings dealt so clearly with this subject that they may be called the literature of protest.

The date of these books is a disputed subject. The clues which are used by one group of commentators as proof for an early date may be used by the opposing school to argue for a late date. While a complete discussion of this topic does not lie within the scope of this book, reasons for the earlier date of writing will be given in treating each epistle. They represent in any case a trend of thought closely connected with the period centering around the council of Jerusalem.

## The Epistle of James

The Epistle of James is ascribed traditionally to James, the brother of the Lord, who was moderator of the council. The author's name appears in the salutation, and his Jewish interest is immediately apparent in his greeting to the twelve tribes of the Dispersion. Throughout the epistle there is little reference to systematic Christian doctrine. The name of Jesus Christ appears only twice (1:1, 2:1), and there is a possible reference to Him in 5:8. The synagogue is mentioned as the place of meeting rather than the church (2:2). The illustrations are taken from the Old Testament, or else are drawn from rural life. In style and in content the Epistle of James bears a striking similarity to the teachings of Jesus, particularly to the Sermon on the Mount. The same proverbial epigrammatic statements of truth, the same homely figures of speech drawn from everyday country life, the same directness of address, and the same topics of discussion appear in James. The scantiness of James' Christological discussion, the heavy emphasis on ethics, and the obvious parallels with the teaching of Jesus seemingly indicate that the epistle was written at a time when the church was still within the general circle of Judaism before it had become an independent religious movement.

If it be objected that the epistle is addressed to the Dispersion who would not have been converted at so early a date, one need only recall that there were synagogues in Jerusalem that represented the Dispersion as early as the time of Stephen (Acts 6:9), and that James had a wide acquaintance with the pilgrims who came annually from all parts of the world to celebrate the various feasts (21:20, 21). While one may not be able to prove conclusively that the book of James was written as early as A.D. 45 to 50, its content fits that era fairly well.

### The Author

If James were the brother of Jesus mentioned in the Gospels (Mark 6:3), their exact relationship remains to be defined. Was James a child of Joseph by a former marriage, which would make him to be really a stepbrother, or was he a half brother, a son of Joseph and Mary, or was the word "brother" loosely used to mean "cousin"? All three theories have been advanced at various times, and usually the first and third have been defended by those who have argued for the perpetual virginity of Mary. The third seems to be the least likely to be acceptable, for the references to Jesus' sisters and brothers (Mark 6:3, Matt. 13:55, John 2:12, 7:3, 10) imply a contact between them and

Jesus that was within rather than without the immediate family. If they were older than Jesus, and not sons of Mary, the patronizing and unbelieving attitude which they took is all the more explicable (John 7:3-5). The fact that Jesus committed His mother to John rather than to some of the brethren would easily be accounted for by the fact that none of them would have a sufficient interest in their stepmother to assume responsibility for her. On the other hand, the fact that they came with her to remonstrate with Jesus concerning His public preaching (Matt. 12:46-50) may show that they were her sons.[4]

In any case, James was brought up in the same environment as Jesus and was in close touch with Him all during the years that led up to His ministry. His background would be practically the same as that of Jesus. As an interpreter of truth he would have the advantage of knowing its historical and geographical context thoroughly. James, while not a believer during the life of Jesus (John 7:2-8), was a witness of the resurrection (I Cor. 15:7) and was among those waiting for the Spirit on the day of Pentecost (Acts 1:14). Upon the withdrawal of Peter from Palestine (Acts 12:17) he took over the leadership of the Jerusalem church. He was noted for strict adherence to the law (Gal. 2:12) and was later the champion of the Jews who had felt uneasy about Paul's reputation (Acts 21:17-26). It would be extreme to say that he was opposed to Paul, but he stood for a stricter application of the law to the life of the Christian than Paul did in his ministry to the Gentiles.

There is no indication that James opposed Paul's teaching as a matter of principle. According to Galatians he gave Paul the right hand of fellowship (Gal. 2:9, 10), and in Acts his demeanor was certainly not that of an antagonist. He was solicitous to remove all misapprehensions the Jews might have concerning Paul's real attitude. On the other hand, he may have feared that with release from the system of the law there might come lax and careless behavior that would dishonor the name of the Christian believers. His epistle was written to foster a practical ethical life just as Paul wrote the practical applications of his epistles for the same reason.

## Outline

The Epistle of James is difficult to outline because of the variety of topics discussed in it and because these topics do not seem to follow

---

4. A very satisfactory brief treatment of this subject may be found in A. T. Robertson, *Practical and Social Aspects of Christianity* (Second edition, New York: Geo. H. Doran Co., n.d.), pp. 16-18.

any fixed pattern. There is, however, a basic structure in James which accords generally with the following pattern.

## JAMES: THE TRUE STANDARDS OF LIVING

James, like the book of Proverbs in the Old Testament, deals with practical application of truth to everyday situations. In vivid homely language it sets forth the ethical requirements of the Christian life.

## Problems

The second chapter of James, which says, "Ye see that by works a man is justified, and not only by faith" (2:24), has been a puzzle to many people. Martin Luther called James "an epistle of straw" because it seemed to contradict the teaching of Romans and of Galatians on justification by faith alone. James is not really an attack upon faith, but it is a protest against the hypocrisy of pretending to have faith without demonstrating it in works. "Show me thy faith apart from *thy* works, and I by my works will show thee *my* faith" (2:18). Every truth has its perversion, and the doctrine of salvation by faith may easily have degenerated into the acceptance of a creed without a corresponding holiness of life. James does not deny the necessity of faith. He insists that faith must produce results. Like Paul, he took his illustration from the life of Abraham, the founder of the Jewish race and the first beneficiary of God's covenant relations with His people. Paul cited this instance of Abraham's response to God's promise as proof that salvation is by faith, not by works (Rom. 4). James used Abraham's sacrifice of Isaac to prove that faith must be manifested through works in order to be real (James 2:21-24). The two instances are not contradictory, for Abraham had to exercise faith to come into relationship with God at the outset, and that faith was manifested by his obedience in doing what God had commanded him to do. The two principles are supplementary, not contradictory.

## The Epistle to the Galatians

The second piece of writing which emerged from the general controversy over keeping the law was Paul's Epistle to the Galatians. As James was written from the standpoint of a strict Jew who worked to avoid all semblance of looseness and license in the use of ethical freedom, "the perfect law of liberty" (James 1:25), so Galatians was written by a champion of freedom who saw that neither Gentiles nor Jews could be delivered from their sins by self-effort in keeping a set of ethical principles. Galatians accordingly has been called "the Magna Charta of spiritual emancipation"[5] because it declared that "Christ redeemed us from the curse of the law, having become a curse for us . . . that we might receive the promise of the Spirit through faith" (Gal. 3:13, 14).[6]

### Destination

Galatia is the name that was given originally to the territory in north central Asia Minor, where the invading Gauls settled in the third century before Christ and maintained an independent kingdom for many years. Gradually the Gallic population was absorbed into the other peoples living there, and after a number of political changes, the territory became the property of Rome in 25 B.C. The Romans incorporated this northern section into a larger division of land which

5. See F. W. Farrar, *Messages of the Books of the Bible* (London: Macmillan & Co., Ltd., 1909), Vol. I, p. 258.
6. For a full discussion of Galatians and its antecedents, see the author's book on *Galatians: The Charter of Christian Liberty*. (Grand Rapids, Mich.; Wm. B. Eerdmans Co., 1951) p. 200.

they made a province and called by the name of Galatia. Galatia, then, under Roman rule, could mean Galatia proper, which the Gauls had founded, or it could be applied to the whole province which included the southern cities of Antioch, Iconium, Derbe, and Lystra.

To which of these did Paul refer when he wrote his epistle to the churches of Galatia (Gal. 1:2)? The usage of the New Testament appears in seven passages. In Galatians 1:2 and in 3:1 the people of the churches are addressed, but no hint is given of their location beyond the mere use of the name. In I Corinthians 16:1 Paul spoke of "the churches of Galatia" whom he had asked for a contribution for the poor in Jerusalem. In the same context he referred to Macedonia (16:5), to Achaia (16:15), and to Asia (16:19). Since these last three names refer to Roman provinces, it seems probable that Galatia in the context should also mean the province as a whole.

The two other passages which allude to Galatia are found in Acts. The former of the two, Acts 16:6, says, "And they went through the region of Phrygia and Galatia . . ." The expression is peculiar and could be translated better "the Phrygian and Galatian region," or "the Phrygio-Galatic country." Since Paul and his company were on their way westward, the territory must have been adjacent to Asia and Mysia, which they were prevented from entering. The second allusion occurs in Acts 18:23, "the region of Galatia, and Phrygia, in order." Here the same terms are used, but in reverse order. Perhaps both refer to the mountainous country which lay on the borders of Galatia and which had been ethnically Phrygian. Whether the Lukan and Pauline usages of these terms coincided exactly or not, both referred to the same general region included within the bounds of the Roman province of Galatia. The problem is this: Was Galatians written to the churches in the south of the province which Paul and Barnabas evangelized on the first journey, or was it written to a group of churches in Galatia proper, which were founded on the second and third journeys?

The latter of these views, which is the older, has been defended by J. B. Lightfoot[7] and by a number of other scholars. It assumes that Paul's visit to Galatia proper began on the second journey when he left the southern territory of Derbe, Lystra, and Iconium, and traveled through "the region of Phrygia and Galatia" mentioned in Acts 16:6. According to this view, Paul traversed the territory of old Galatia, including the cities of Pessinus, Ancyra, and Tavium, and finally reached

---

7. J. B. Lightfoot, *St. Paul's Epistle to the Galatians* (Tenth Edition, London: Macmillan & Co., 1890), pp. 18-35.

Troas after a long journey. A second similar trip on the third journey is stated in Acts 18:23.

The South Galatian theory, as the other view is called, was championed by Sir William Ramsay,[8] who contended that "the churches of Galatia" were those of Antioch of Pisidia, Iconium, Derbe, and Lystra which Paul established on his first missionary journey. They were subsequently revisited on the later journeys (Acts 16:1-6, 18:23). The second tour of these southern churches did not preclude completely a northern swing in his last itinerary; for the language of Acts 16:2, 4, and 6 shows that Paul covered the territory around Derbe and Lystra, and then that he went along the Phrygio-Galatic border to Mysia and Bithynia, at which point he turned westward to Troas.

The importance of the difference of interpretation is that the South Galatian theory allows for an earlier dating of Galatians and for a better explanation of its historical setting. If Galatians were not written until after Paul toured the Galatic territory on his second or third journey, and consequently long after the council of Jerusalem, it is difficult to explain why he made no appeal to the decision of that council in settling the controversy of law versus grace. Irrespective of whether the decision were regarded as a concession by the Jewish church to the Gentiles in order that the latter might make their own decisions, or whether it were an expression of an authoritative dogma, it could have been quite useful in convincing the Galatians that the teaching of the Judaizing faction was insupportable. The fact that no action of the council is so much as mentioned probably indicates that it had not yet taken place.

This conclusion is strengthened by the internal evidence of Galatians. Paul reviewed his biography up to the time of writing. He spoke of his conversion and call (1:15, 16), his stay in Damascus (1:17), his first visit to Jerusalem (1:18), his ministry in Syria and Cilicia (1:21), and the visit to Jerusalem with Barnabas (2:1-10) which has been equated with the "famine visit" of Acts 11:30, or with the council of Acts 15. If it were the latter, there is a strange silence of Galatians concerning many of its important features that would have been quite pertinent to the argument of the letter. If the visit of Galatians 2 were the "famine visit," it explains why Barnabas and Paul felt that they had such a free hand in Antioch, and why Paul included relief for the poor in his subsequent missions. The episode of Peter's defection (Gal. 2:11 ff.) can be much more easily explained if it preceded the

8. W. M. Ramsay, *A Historical Commentary on St. Paul's Epistle to the Galatians* (New York: G. P. Putnam's Sons, 1900), pp. xi, 478.

PAUL'S FIRST JOURNEY

council, for the confusion and discussion which it precipitated could hardly have taken place in Antioch after the decision had been rendered and after the letters had been sent to the Gentile churches.

## Date

If, then, the South Galatian theory be adopted, it means that Paul and Barnabas on their first tour preached in the cities of southern Galatia, and on their return trip organized the converts into church groups (14:21-23), closing their mission about the year A.D. 48. After their return to Antioch, Peter paid a visit to the city, and openly fellowshiped with the Gentile converts. He had not been there long before some men came down from Jerusalem who professed to follow the strict observance of the law that James practiced, and who argued that unless the converts were circumcised, they could not be saved (Acts 15:1). Peter, overawed by their attitude, withdrew from eating with the Gentiles. In the meantime the same controversy had broken out in Galatia, agitated perhaps by local Jewish influences which were quite strong (Acts 14:2). Paul therefore on the eve of the council wrote this letter to the Galatian churches, in order to settle for them by correspondence the question which he expected to debate in the coming assembly in Jerusalem. This conclusion is confirmed somewhat by a comparison of Peter's speech in Acts 15:7-11 with the structure of Galatians as a whole. His emphasis on his personal calling and experience, on theological argumentation, and on the practical development of grace parallels the general outline of Galatians and also reflects Paul's conversation with him as reported in Galatians 2. If Galatians can be fitted into this situation, it was written from Antioch, just prior to the council in A.D. 48 or 49.

Not all scholars agree with this solution, and admittedly it involves some difficulties. The chronological problems are great. If the "famine visit" with which Galatians 2:1-10 has been equated took place fourteen years after Paul's first trip to Jerusalem, and if his conversion were three years before that, he must have been converted about A.D. 31. The relief journey to Jerusalem cannot have been much later than A.D. 46, and even allowing for counting fractions of years as whole years, the interval between it and his conversion must have been at least fifteen years. In that case, his conversion occurred about three years after the crucifixion of Christ. If the passage in Galatians 2:1-10 be interpreted as a private aspect of the council, the chronological and psychological difficulties are sharpened. The following diagram will give a fairly satisfactory perspective of the chronology involved.

## Chart of Early Pauline Chronology

| EVENT | REFERENCE | TIME |
|---|---|---|
| Resurrection: Pentecost | Acts 1:3, 5, 2:1 | A.D 29 |
| Conversion of Paul at Damascus | Acts 9:1-18 | 31 |
| Visit to Arabia | Gal. 1:17 | |
| Return to Damascus | | |
| Paul's First Visit to Jerusalem | 1:18 | 33 |
| Interview with Cephas | | |
| Spent 15 days in city | | |
| Departure to Syria and Cilicia | 1:21 | |
| Early ministry in Antioch | | |
| Second Visit to Jerusalem | 2:1-10 | 46 |
| Accompanied by Barnabas and Titus | | |
| Motivated by revelation | | |
| Private interview | | |
| Complaint about "false brethren" | | |
| Agreement with James, Cephas, and John | | |
| First Missionary Journey | | No interval stated in text |
| Return to Antioch | 2:11 ff. | |
| Visit of Cephas | | |
| Controversy | | |
| Writing of Galatians | | |
| Council of Jerusalem | Acts 15:1-35 | 48/49 |

## Content

Galatians was not written as an essay in contemporary history. It was a protest against corruption of the gospel of Christ. The essential truth of justification by faith rather than by the works of the law had been obscured by the Judaizers' insistence that believers in Christ must keep the law if they expected to be perfect before God. When Paul learned that this teaching had begun to penetrate the Galatian churches and that it had alienated them from their heritage of liberty, he wrote the impassioned remonstrance that is contained in this epistle.

The tone of the book is warlike. It fairly crackles with indignation though it is not the anger of personal pique but of spiritual principle. "Though we, or an angel from heaven, should preach unto you any gospel other than that which we preached unto you, let him be anathema" (Gal. 1:8), cried Paul as he reproved the Galatians for their acceptance of the legalistic error.

## Outline

The structure of Galatians is symmetrical and logical. Its outline is as follows:

### GALATIANS: THE DEFENSE OF CHRISTIAN LIBERTY

## Evaluation

If the early date for Galatians is correct, the book is the earliest of Paul's extant writings. It summarizes the heart of "the gospel which [he preached] among the Gentiles" (Gal. 2:2). In it he showed that man's chief problem is obtaining a right standing with God. Since he is incapable of establishing this himself because "a man is not justified by the works of the law" (Gal. 2:16), it must be provided for him by another. Christ has given this standing, for He "gave himself for our sins, that he might deliver us out of this present evil world" (1:4). His provision is available to those who put their full trust in Him, for "the promise by faith in Jesus Christ [is] given to them that believe" (3:22). This standing is not simply a legal fiction, applied only externally or ceremonially, but it becomes part of the inner life through union with Christ. "I have been crucified with Christ; and it is no longer I that live, but Christ liveth in me: and that *life* which I now live in the flesh I live in faith, *the faith* which is in the Son of God, who loved me, and gave himself up for me" (Gal. 2:20). Salvation is thus not only the application of a new life, but is also its impartation.

The books of James and Galatians thus illustrate the two aspects of Christianity which from the very beginning have seemed to be conflicting, though in reality they are supplementary. In James there is a stern insistence upon the ethic of Christ, a demand that faith prove its existence by its fruits. Nevertheless James, no less than Paul, emphasizes the need of the transformation of the individual by the grace of God; for he says, "Of his own will he brought us forth by the word of truth, that we should be a kind of firstfruits of his creatures" (Jas. 1:18). Galatians stresses the dynamic of the gospel which produces the ethic. "Christ redeemed us from the curse of the law, having become a curse for us . . . that upon the Gentiles might come the blessing of Abraham in Christ Jesus; that we might receive the promise of the Spirit through faith" (Gal. 3:13, 14). Nor was Paul less concerned than James about the ethical life, for he says: "*Use* not your freedom for an occasion to the flesh, but through love be servants one to another" (5:13). Like the two sides of a coin, these two aspects of Christian truth must always accompany each other.

Thus the Gentile mission, with its enlarged declaration of Christian truth was launched. The doctrine of justification by faith apart from the law was recognized by the church and was accepted. Christianity was ready for a new era of development.

V

# THE PAULINE PROGRAM

# THE PAULINE PROGRAM

The Second Mission to Asia Minor

The Mission to Macedonia
Philippi
Thessalonica
Beroea

The Thessalonian Letters

I Thessalonians
Content
Outline
Evaluation

II Thessalonians
Content
Outline
Evaluation

The Mission to Achaia
Athens
Corinth

The Mission to Asia

Ephesus

The Corinthian Correspondence
Background
The "Lost Letter"

I Corinthians
Date
Content
Outline
Evaluation

II Corinthians
Content
Outline
Evaluation

The Last Visit to Corinth

The Projected Mission

The Epistle to the Romans
Background
Content
Outline
Evaluation

The Mission Concluded

# CHAPTER XVI

## The Pauline Program
### Acts 15:36 to 21:16

After the close of the council of Jerusalem, Paul and Barnabas returned to Antioch and spent some time in teaching and in preaching (15:35). Probably the dispute over the question of circumcision had resulted in intellectual confusion within the church which could be disentangled only by careful instruction. The missionary incentive, however, had not been forgotten and before long a new enterprise was begun.

A comparison of Acts 15:36 with 13:1, 2 will show that the new mission was Paul's suggestion, whereas the original mission to Cyprus was proposed by the church as a whole. The leadership which Paul had assumed halfway through the former journey (13:13) had now become an established fact. Furthermore, the proposal of Paul disclosed an important aspect of his missionary policy:

> Let us return now and visit the brethren in every city wherein we proclaimed the word of the Lord, and see how they fare.

Evangelization should be followed by consolidation through instruction and organization of the converts.

Unfortunately a dispute arose between Barnabas and Paul which, for the time being at least, severed their partnership. Barnabas desired to take with them his cousin John Mark, whose service had been unsatisfactory on the previous trip. Doubtless he wanted to give the young recruit a second chance. Paul, realizing the seriousness of the task which they were about to undertake, thought that Mark would be a bad risk, and refused to accept him as a colleague. Both men were right in a measure. Mark was too valuable a man to be thrown aside for one mistake; and at the same time the life of the young churches should not be jeopardized by a careless or unreliable worker. The solution which they reached was the best possible one for the circumstances. Barnabas took Mark with him to Cyprus, his home territory, where any possible defection on Mark's part would do less harm and where Mark would not be subjected to so great a strain as in the pioneer

289

country of Asia. Paul chose Silas, one of the men who had been a delegate to Antioch from the Jerusalem council, and struck north through Syria and Cilicia toward the frontiers of Asia Minor.

At this point Barnabas disappeared from the narrative of Acts. Apparently Paul did not break fellowship with him completely, for later he mentioned him (I Cor. 9:6) as still engaged in the work of the Lord and as still within the circle of his acquaintance at the time when he wrote I Corinthians. The episode is illustrative of how two good men can differ on an important issue, and yet be right on both sides of it. Barnabas' sponsorship of Mark was vindicated by the favorable spiritual growth of the latter, and Paul's jealousy for the pioneer fields brought many new laborers into the work and probably averted a second disappointment similar to Mark's withdrawal from Perga.

## The Second Mission to Asia Minor

The expedition set out on its journey in A.D. 49, after the interval of teaching in Antioch. They traveled by land "through Syria and Cilicia, confirming the churches" (15:41). In this way each of the two groups began by revisiting the churches that had previously been founded: for Paul had labored a long time in these regions before he was summoned to Antioch. Still traveling overland, they made their way northward from Tarsus through the Cilician Gates, and then westward along the caravan route that lay through southern Galatia. Probably it was late spring or early summer before they left the parched plains and ventured to cross the mountains into the hinterland.

Eventually they reached Derbe and Lystra, which had been the last outposts of their previous tour. Here occurred an unusual event. Paul found Timothy, a young convert, whose mother was a Jewess and whose father was a Greek. His mother was probably a convert of Paul's previous visit. Timothy had been thoroughly trained in the Old Testament Scriptures by his Jewish mother and grandmother (I Tim. 1:5, 3:14, 15) and was highly regarded by the Christians of the region. Recognizing Timothy as a potential leader and as a valuable assistant for work in that territory, Paul decided to add him to his company.

The status of Timothy, however, posed a new problem for Paul. As the son of a Gentile father, and uncircumcised, he might be rejected by the Jewish population who had already proved hostile to Paul and to his message. On the other hand, if Paul had him circumcised, would he not seemingly be making a concession to the Judaizers who had

PAUL'S SECOND JOURNEY

already plagued Galatia and whose position Paul had already attacked in his epistle? On this very journey Paul was publicizing the results of the council of Jerusalem (16:4), and the circumcision of Timothy would seem inconsistent with all for which he had contended. Nevertheless he did have him circumcised. Timothy was half a Jew by birth and wholly a Jew by training. The act was not a repudiation of the principle that Gentiles need not submit to the law, for Timothy was not rated as a Gentile. It was a personal concession which violated no principle, but which removed an obstacle to further work among the Jews of this region. The Gentile converts would probably not be greatly disturbed, since they would class Timothy as a Jew anyway and since they were not compelled to submit to the rite themselves.

Apparently the epistle and the personal visit of Paul brought peace to the Galatian churches. No details are given of this trip except that "the churches were strengthened in the faith, and increased in number daily" (16:5).

Having completed the visitation of Galatia, Paul looked for new fields to enter. He preached along the western border of Galatia, which was Phrygian in nationality ("the Phrygio-Galatic region"), as he proceeded along the road toward Asia (16:6). Being directed not to enter Asia, he looked northward to Mysia and Bithynia, but these provinces also were closed to him. In perplexity he made his way to Troas, the westernmost port of Asia, wondering what his next move should be.

### The Mission to Macedonia

Two important events occurred at Troas. First of all, there came a night vision of a Macedonian man beseeching Paul: "Come over into Macedonia, and help us" (16:9). Instantly Paul accepted the vision as the answer to his perplexity, believing it to be the call of God. This decision was momentous. Had Paul turned eastward, it is conceivable that today the Western world might have been receiving missionaries of the gospel from the Orient instead of sending them thither. The evangelization of Europe and all of the effect of the gospel upon western civilization began with Paul's response to the Macedonian call.

Again, at Troas he was joined by Luke, the missionary diarist and writer of Luke-Acts. The tenth verse of the sixteenth chapter contains an abrupt change in person which shows that the author at this point became a participant in the action. "And when he had seen the vision, straightway *we* sought to go forth into Macedonia . . ." (16:10, italics ours). Although the author never named himself in the account that he wrote, the use of the first personal plural pronoun betrayed his presence and enables the reader to reconstruct to some extent the relation between the author and the episodes that he described.

## Philippi

Leaving Troas, probably in the month of August, Paul and his company crossed the Aegean Sea to Neapolis in Macedonia, the seaport of Philippi. Philippi lay ten or twelve miles inland up the river Gangites. The city was named for Philip, the father of Alexander the Great, who had founded it as a center for mining the gold and silver that were available nearby. Through it passed the trade that flowed from Neapolis along the great Egnatian highway to its western terminal at Dyrrhachium, the port on the Adriatic Sea.

Philippi was the leading city of its district and was a Roman colony (16:12). Colonial status made its inhabitants citizens of Rome, privileged to vote in Roman elections and to have a Roman type of government. Such cities guarded their political privileges jealously and sought to avoid any action that would bring them into disfavor with Rome. Knowing this sentiment, Paul wrote to them later, saying, "For our citizenship is in heaven," or, as Moffatt translated it, "For ye are a colony of heaven" (Phil. 3:20), as if to say that spiritually they were as much a part of the eternal city as politically they were attached to Rome.

Since there was no large colony of Jews in Philippi, there was no synagogue where Paul could begin his preaching. A small prayer meeting outside the city by the river was the only nucleus that he could find, and he resorted thither. Lydia, a Thyatiran dealer in dyestuffs and textiles, and a proselyte, opened her home to him as headquarters.

During his ministry in the city he expelled a demon from a slave girl, a clairvoyant who had been a source of wealth to her masters. Angered by the loss of their business, they accused Paul and Silas of teaching "customs which it is not lawful for us to receive, or to observe, being Romans" (16:21). This appeal to political prejudices resulted in the imprisonment and beating of Paul and Silas who were released from jail by an earthquake. Their claim of Roman citizenship exempted them from further punishment but their ministry in Philippi was ended, and they left for other fields. Here in the story the "we-section" ends, and a fair inference may be drawn that the writer remained in Philippi. His obvious interest and pride in the city, his knowledge of detail concerning it, and the fact that with the return of Paul to Philippi at a later date the "we-sections" are resumed constitute fair proof that he remained to act as pastor for the new church and perhaps to serve as an evangelist for Macedonia.

## Thessalonica

Traveling along the Egnatian highway from Philippi, Paul and his companions passed through Amphipolis and Apollonia enroute to Thessalonica, the modern Saloniki. It was founded about 315 B.C. by Cassander, who named it in honor of his wife, the half sister of Alexander the Great. It was a free city, with officers called *politarchs* (17:6), a seaport and a center of trade.

The Jewish colony in Thessalonica had a synagogue where Paul preached for three weeks. Luke defined briefly but carefully the type of message that Paul gave to men of Jewish background. Its major premise was that the Messiah of the Scriptures must die and rise again from the dead — a new idea to the Jews who thought of the Messiah only as a king. The minor premise was that Jesus of Nazareth fitted the prophetic description and should be identified with the Messiah (17:3). The conclusion is not stated, but its content is obvious. If Jesus of Nazareth is the predicted Messiah He should be accepted instantly by all true Jews.

A sharp division of opinion followed. Some of the Jews believed and there was a great response among the proselyte Greeks. Paul, alluding to this instance in the first letter that he wrote to the church, said that they accepted his message "not *as* the word of men, but, as it is in truth, the word of God" (I Thess. 2:13), and that they "turned unto God from idols, to serve a living and true God" (I Thess. 1:9). Several times in the Thessalonian epistles he referred to the tension between the converts and the Jews who had refused his message, and he could not hide his exasperation over the petty jealousy that made them hinder his giving the gospel of Christ to the Gentiles (I Thess. 2:15, 16). The opposition became so intense that the evangelists could not remain in the city. They fled by night to Beroea where they began again their preaching in the synagogue.

## Beroea

The visit to Beroea was more peaceful than that in Thessalonica. The Jews received Paul's message and diligently examined the Scriptures to see whether or not he were telling the truth. Although they may not have been any more ready to accept his preaching than their fellow-religionists of Thessalonica (17:11), they were at least more candid in their attitude. Believers were multiplying when a delegation from Thessalonica descended upon them and commenced to attack Paul. Realizing that nothing could be done, the believers sent him on his way as if he were to take ship at the sea; but instead of proceeding to a port, he turned south and went to Athens where he was beyond the reach of the Jews.

In spite of persecution the Thessalonian church flourished as the Pauline correspondence shows. When Paul left Beroea, Silas and Timothy remained behind to complete the work that he could not finish. Evidently Timothy joined him at Athens and brought news of the turmoil in Macedonia which had involved the churches in affliction and temptation. Paul promptly sent him back to encourage the church and to prepare a report as to how they were standing the test (I Thess. 3:1-5). Silas also probably returned to Macedonia, perhaps to Philippi. At any rate, Paul was left alone in Athens and did not see his helpers again until they joined him later at Corinth (Acts 18:5).

## The Thessalonian Letters

### I Thessalonians

#### Content

Although these letters belong chronologically to Paul's stay in Corinth about the end of A.D. 51, they are considered here because of their relation to the church. They were written within a few months of each other while Paul was engaged in the ministry in Achaia. The first letter was writen upon the receipt of the report that Timothy brought back to Corinth, and it included his name and that of Silas in its greeting. Its content is generally twofold: praise for the steadfastness of the Thessalonians under persecution by the Jews and the correction of certain errors and misunderstandings that had grown up among them. The main doctrinal theme concerned the return of Christ, a topic which is scarcely mentioned in Galatians unless it appears in Paul's allusion to waiting for the hope of righteousness (Gal. 5:5). It was no novelty in apostolic preaching; for Peter intimated that Jesus Christ had been received into the heavens until the time of restoration of all things spoken by the prophets (Acts 3:21), and Paul himself in his speech in Athens said that Christ would be the judge of the world (17:31). James, also, had spoken of the coming of the Lord (Jas. 5:7, 8). The Thessalonian epistles, however, have the earliest full discussion of this truth in Christian literature.

*Outline*

I THESSALONIANS: THE GROWTH OF A NEW CHURCH

*Evaluation*

The problems in this epistle are quite different from those mentioned in Galatians. In general they reflect the problems of Gentile converts, not those of Jewish believers. The questions of fornication and of idleness were much less likely to appear in a Jewish community because the law, which was instilled into Jewish children from their earliest years, settled these questions in advance. The Gentiles had no such background. Sex relations were governed chiefly by pleasure and by convenience; and although the pagan moralists set certain limits upon license, they did not speak with an authoritative "Thus saith the Lord." The social solidarity which the Jew possessed because of his family and because of his loyalty to the commonwealth of Israel did not characterize the Gentile converts who by their very conversion had been cut loose from such social bonds as paganism had to offer. To create a sense of brotherhood and of mutual responsibility the Thessalonians were commanded to labor industriously and to behave discreetly "toward them that are without" (I Thess. 4:12).

The teaching on the Lord's coming was not entirely new, for Paul spoke later of having taught these things while he was with them (II Thess. 2:5). He may have known some of the teachings of Christ

296

on this subject; for he says, "This we say unto you by the word of the Lord" (I Thess. 4:15), and he used the figure of the thief in the night (I Thess. 5:4), which Jesus used for the same teaching (Matt. 24:43, Luke 12:39, 40). The first part of the discussion concerning the translation of the living and the resurrection of the dead (I Thess. 4:13-18) was evidently prompted by the concern of the Thessalonians for those who had died. They believed that the Lord would come, but what would happen to those who died before He came? The second part of the discussion (5:1-11) was evoked by the desire to know when Christ would return. Paul replied that the answer lay in spiritual consciousness rather than in speculative calculation. If they were alert and active, waiting eagerly for the return of Christ, they would be preserved from wrath and would not need to fear.

## II Thessalonians
### Content

The second epistle to the Thessalonians was written to remove the misapprehension that "the day of the Lord is just at hand" (II Thess. 2:2). Perhaps the vehemence with which Paul preached the doctrine had led to a misunderstanding of his preaching or of the allusions contained in his first letter. It may be that they had received some teaching from a spurious source; for he urged them not to be "quickly shaken from your mind . . . either by spirit, or by word, or by epistle *as from us*" (II Thess. 2:2, italics ours), which may mean that he was repudiating some teaching falsely attributed to him by others. In any case, he undertook to provide for them definite criteria by which they might recognize the approach of "the day of the Lord."

Unfortunately the criteria which were clear to Paul and to the Thessalonians are not so easily understandable today. The veiled reference to the "hinderer" (II Thess. 2:6, 7) is difficult of interpretation. Apparently there are three major events which will presage the Lord's coming: (1) a sudden acceleration of apostasy from godliness (2:3), (2) the removal of some restraining influence (2:6, 7), and (3) the complete unveiling of the incarnation of evil who will be animated by Satan and who will oppose and exalt himself above all that is called God (2:4, 9). Nowhere else in the Pauline epistles does this particular aspect of eschatological teaching occur. It was, however, an integral part of Paul's current instruction and was preached by him in the churches. The passage indicates that the mystery of lawlessness and the mystery of Christ develop concurrently in the world, and that there will be ultimately an inevitable clash in which Christ must and

297

will triumph. The triumph itself will be His personal return to earth
to destroy the antichrist and to reward His saints.

The exhortation of the third chapter is an expansion of the charge
given in I Thessalonians to "study to be quiet, and to do your own
business, and to work with your hands" (I Thess. 4:11). Some of
the Thessalonians had become so enamored of the idea that the Lord's
coming could release them from the evils and tensions of the world
that they had given up working and were waiting for the appearance
of the Deliverer. They were out of step with the rest of the church
and were dependent upon others for their support (II Thess. 3:6-11).
Paul urged them to earn their own living and to mind their own
business.

*Outline*

## II THESSALONIANS: THE EXPECTATION OF THE CHURCH

|  |  |
|---|---|
| I. Salutation | 1:1, 2 |
| II. Expectation in Persecution | 1:3-12 |
| Thanksgiving for Growth | 1:3, 4 |
| Explanation of Purpose | 1:5 |
| Expectation of Outcome | 1:6-10 |
| **Prayer** | 1:11, 12 |
| III. Explanation of Events | 2:1-17 |
| Alarms Quieted | 2:1, 2 |
| **Apostasy Predicted** | 2:3-7 |
| Antichrist Revealed | 2:8-12 |
| Attitude of Faith Encouraged | 2:13-17 |
| IV. Exhortations to Readiness | 3:1-15 |
| To Prayer | 3:1-5 |
| To Industry | 3:6-15 |
| V. Benediction and Salutation | 3:16-18 |

*Evaluation*

First and Second Thessalonians are among the first of Paul's writings. They testify to the fact that the message which Paul preached
was no novelty, but that it had already been a settled body of faith for
some time. Paul's reference to his preaching among them (II Thess.
2:15) the same things that he wrote in his letter shows that he had
a well-defined system of belief and his use of the word "tradition"

298

(II Thess. 2:15, 3:6) corroborates this impression. "Tradition" did not mean to Paul a loosely transmitted rumor of doubtful authenticity. It meant rather a body of instruction which may have been oral, but which was carefully preserved and exactly formulated. He used the cognate verb in describing his transmission of the facts of the life of Christ which for him constituted the gospel (I Cor. 15:3: *delivered*), and Luke used the same verb to describe the narration of the facts of the life of Christ by eyewitnesses (Luke 1:2). The "tradition" must have included ethical precepts, for he implied that it was a rule of conduct which the brethren could follow (II Thess. 3:6).

This tradition, furthermore, was not only authentic but authoritative. In Galatians Paul said that his gospel was exclusive in its truth and that no other could be substituted for it. In II Thessalonians 3:14 he said:

> *And if any man obeyeth not our word by this epistle, note that man, that ye have no company with him, to the end that he may be ashamed.*

If he were insisting upon his authority as purely personal, he could scarcely escape being called a religious egotist and tyrant. If, on the other hand, he had received his message from God, so that his utterance was the word of God mediated through him by the Holy Spirit (I Thess. 2:13), he had a right to his authority.

Practically every major doctrine in the catalogue of faith is represented in these two small epistles. Although they were not written as doctrinal treatises, nor primarily to present the author's general theological views, they contain a well-rounded body of theological teaching.

Paul and those who received his epistles believed in one living God (I 1:9), the Father (II 1:2), who has loved men and has chosen them to enjoy His salvation (II 2:16, I 1:4). He has sent deliverance from wrath through Jesus Christ, His Son (I 1:10), and has revealed this deliverance through the message of the gospel (I 1:5, 2:9, II 2:14). This message has been confirmed and has been made real by the power of the Holy Spirit (I 1:5, 4:8). The gospel concerns the Lord Jesus Christ, who was killed by the Jews (I 2:15). He rose from the dead (I 1:10, 4:14, 5:10). He is now in heaven (I 1:10), but He will come again (I 2:19, 4:15, 5:23, II 2:1). To Him is ascribed deity, for He is called Lord (I 1:6), God's Son (I 1:10), and the Lord Jesus Christ (I 1:1, 3, 5:28, II 1:1). Believers (1) receiving the word of God (I 1:6), (2) turn from idols, serve God and wait for the return of Christ (I 1:9, 10). Their normal growth is in sanctification (I 4:3, 7,

II 2:13). In personal life they are to be clean (I 4:4-6), industrious (I 4:11, 12), prayerful (I 5:17), and cheerful (I 5:16). Theoretically and practically the Thessalonian letters embody all the essentials of Christian truth.

# The Mission to Achaia

## Athens

The city of Athens was one of the wonders of the ancient world. In its golden age, the fourth century B.C., it had probably held within its walls more literary genius, more philosophical brilliance, and more architectural beauty than any other city of antiquity. In the time of Paul its political and commercial importance had declined greatly, but a faint aura of intellectuality and of culture still hung over it. The people of Athens were deeply conscious of their heritage and they prided themselves on their past. Many of the finest buildings of Athens' heyday, such as the Erectheum and the Parthenon, were still intact. The intellectual atmosphere of the city preserved the philosophical tradition, and if the teachers who frequented the porticoes and street corners lacked the creative genius of Plato and of Aristotle, they had at least an appreciation of the thinkers of the past that could not be duplicated readily elsewhere.

While Paul was awaiting at Athens the arrival of Silas and Timothy from Macedonia, he gave himself as usual to the ministry. Two spheres of activity were open to him: the synagogue, where he met the usual congregation of Jews and proselytes, and the market place, where he encountered the pagan thinkers. Here he met a new type of opponent, the educated and cynical pagan, who was ready to hear anything and unready to believe it. Luke devoted considerable space to the singular clash of the Jewish Christian Paul, whose passionate hatred of idolatry collided with the skeptical tolerance of pagans who might not take their own gods seriously, but who would not take his message seriously either.

Paul's preaching intrigued their curiosity and they took him to the Areopagus for a hearing. Literally, the Areopagus was Mars' Hill, a small rocky elevation in Athens where there was an area large enough for a public conference. Ramsay contends with some show of reason that *Areopagus* here means not so much the place as the group that took its name from the place, the governing council of the city that controlled educational policies and passed upon the licensing of foreign teachers.[1] There is no indication that he was on trial because a charge had been made against him. He was simply making an official statement of the chief tenets of his teaching.

The speech itself (17:22-31) was a masterpiece of condensation. Beginning with the point of contact furnished by the lavish display of architecture and statuary that adorned the city, most of which was dedicated to the worship of the gods, he made a plea for the one God who made the heavens and the earth and who governs the destinies of men. In contrast to the vague absentee deity of Epicureanism he spoke of God as immanent; in contrast to the pantheistic Logos of Stoicism he emphasized God's personality and the necessity for repentance, which was the opposite of Stoic fatalism.[2] The contemptuous interruption of the crowd prevented his progressing to the more detailed aspects of Christian revelation, so that the speech remained unfinished. There were a few converts.

Apparently the ministry in Athens was a disappointment to Paul. He created no great stir in the synagogue, and the pagan population dismissed him with ridicule. He was accustomed to being thrown out of town, but he was not used to being subjected to contemptuous indifference. Evidently it cut deeply into him; for he wrote to the Corinthians concerning his arrival among them after leaving Athens: "I was with you in weakness, and in fear, and in much trembling" (I Cor. 2:3). Possibly this timorous attitude had physical causes, but it seems more likely that the unusual dismissal which Athens gave him unnerved him and caused him to rethink his whole procedure in apologetics.

## Corinth

From Athens Paul went to Corinth, a city of totally different character. The city had been sacked and burned by the Romans in 146 B.C. In 46 B.C. it was rebuilt by Julius Caesar and became the acknowledged political capital of Achaia, which was a senatorial province. Corinth was the residence of the governing proconsul, as Acts 18:12 states.

Located in the isthmus that connected the Peloponnesus to the mainland, between the Gulf of Lechaeum on the west and the Aegean Sea on the east, Corinth became a center of trade. Rather than sailing

---

1. William Ramsay, *St. Paul, the Traveler and the Roman Citizen* (New York: G. P. Putnam's Sons, 1909), pp. 243-248.
2. For a description of Epicureanism and Stoicism, see pp. 106-108.

around Cape Malea on the southern tip of the Peloponnesus, where navigation was dangerous, many shipmasters preferred to transship their cargoes at Corinth and to send them westward from Lechaeum to the Adriatic ports of Italy. Corinth, with its two seaports, Lechaeum on the west and Cenchrea on the east, enjoyed a monopoly of trade and rapidly grew wealthy.

In government it was a Roman colony like Philippi. Its population was cosmopolitan. The inhabitants had been killed or displaced when the city was first destroyed, and when it was rebuilt new elements settled there. Jews came for the trade; Romans were there on official business or were descendants of the original colonists; Greeks gravitated toward the city from the countryside; and the commerce brought the usual miscellany of sailors, salesmen, bankers, and peoples from every corner of the Mediterranean world.

Rapid growth in wealth promoted a false culture. Corinth was a "boom town," which sought luxury, display, sensuality, and sport. Morally, Corinthians were regarded as inferior even according to the loose standards of paganism. They were usually represented on the Roman stage as drunk. "To live as do the Corinthians" was a euphemism for the vilest kind of life. The temple of Aphrodite in Corinth at one time lodged one thousand priestesses who were professional prostitutes, and the ebb and flow of travel and commerce brought to the city a floating population that included the scum of the Mediterranean. Wealth and dire poverty, beauty and wretchedness, culture and squalor rubbed elbows at Corinth.

Since Paul had spent no great length of time at Athens, his arrival at Corinth may be dated in the fall of the same year that he left Macedonia. The administration of Gallio before whom he was tried probably began with the opening of the proconsular year in July of A.D. 52. Paul's total stay in Corinth was a year and a half (18:11), but how much of that preceded his trial and how much of it followed is uncertain. Luke says that after Gallio dismissed his case he remained in the city for "many days" (18:18). Perhaps the most acceptable dating would bring him to Corinth in the fall of A.D. 51, and would place his departure from the city in the early spring of A.D. 53.

As already noted, the scorn with which his message was greeted at Athens brought him to Corinth in a depressed frame of mind. His colleagues had not returned from Macedonia, and his funds were probably running short. When he reached Corinth, he found employment at his old trade of tentmaking with Aquila and Priscilla, who had been expelled from Rome by the edict of Claudius. Whether they were converts to Christianity before they came to Corinth, or whether they became believers through contact with Paul is not known. In any case, he found shelter, employment, and fellowship with them.

In a short time Silas and Timothy returned from Macedonia bringing the news of the growth of the churches. At this time may have come the contribution to Paul's support of which he spoke in the Philippian letter:

> . . . *when I departed from Macedonia, no church had fellowship with me in the matter of giving and receiving but ye only; for even in Thessalonica ye sent once and again unto my need.*
>
> (Phil. 4:15, 16)

This passage implies that the Macedonian churches gave more generously after he left. Encouraged by the good tidings and by the support from Macedonia, his preaching became more vigorous and more definite that Jesus was the Messiah (18:5).

The reaction in the synagogue was such that Paul withdrew, vowing that he would leave them to their unbelief and go to the Gentiles. He quit the synagogue, transferring his headquarters to the home of a proselyte, Titus Justus, who lived nearby. The ruler of the synagogue became a believer and many of the Corinthians believed and were baptized.

Paul's ministry in Corinth at this time seems to have been under a considerable strain. He was reorganizing his missionary procedure, for he said in I Corinthians that he "came not with excellency of speech or of wisdom, proclaiming . . . the testimony of God" (I Cor. 2:1). He could not recall exactly how many he baptized (I Cor. 1:16). The eighteen months of pioneering in this corrupt and idolatrous city must have taken heavy toll of his physical and nervous strength. It may be that his return from Achaia to Palestine was occasioned by illness, though Luke says nothing of it.

In company with Aquila and Priscilla, Paul left Corinth and set out for the east. They stopped at Ephesus enroute, where Aquila and Priscilla took up new headquarters and began their ministry. Paul preached in the synagogue, but only for a short time since he was desirous of reaching Palestine quickly.

No details are given of his journey and there is only the barest mention of his arrival at his destination. He landed in Caesarea; greeted "the church" (18:22), whether at Caesarea or at Jerusalem is not clear; and then proceeded to Antioch — his last visit to the church that had originally commissioned him. Probably the eastern part of the

PAUL'S THIRD JOURNEY

journey consumed most of the summer, so that by the fall of A.D. 53 he was once again on the road westward (18:22, 23).

Late summer and early fall may have been spent in the tour of Galatia and Phrygia. The disturbance in the Galatian churches which began at the time of the Council (A.D. 48 or 49) may not have died down completely, so that Paul had to "establish" the disciples. Before winter set in, Paul was back at Ephesus where he began his mission in Asia that was the longest and perhaps the stormiest ministry of his experience.

## The Mission to Asia

### Ephesus

The city of Ephesus was one of the oldest of the settlements on the west coast of Asia Minor and was the leading city of the Roman province of Asia. Its origin is shrouded in antiquity, but it was a prominent settlement in the eighth century B.C. and was at an early date taken over by the Greeks. It was located about three miles from the sea on the Cayster river, which at that time was navigable, so that Ephesus was a seaport. The valley of the Cayster penetrated far inland, making a caravan route to the East. Roads from Ephesus communicated with all the other large cities of the province and with the lines of commerce that connected with the north and east. It was a strategic point for evangelism, since workers from Ephesus could maintain contact with the whole Asian hinterland.

The outstanding feature of Ephesus was its great temple of Artemis, a local deity who was later identified with Artemis of the Greeks and with Diana of the Romans. Her image was a many-breasted figure with a female face, having instead of legs a solid block of stone. The first temple was probably begun in the sixth century B.C., but was not finished until 400 B.C. It was burned to the ground in 356 B.C. and replaced by a newer and larger structure, four hundred twenty-five feet by two hundred twenty feet, which was subsidized by contributions from all of Asia. It was considered to be one of the wonders of the world and was an outstanding center for pilgrims who came to worship at its shrine.

Not only was the temple a center for religious worship, but because its halls and grounds were regarded as sacred and inviolable, it became also an asylum for the oppressed and a depository for funds.

A crude picture of the temple appeared on Ephesian coins, accompanied by the very title which is used in Acts for the city, NEOKOROS, or "temple-sweeper" of Artemis (19:35). Contrary to much of the routine state worship of the ancient world, the inhabitants of Asia and of Ephesus in particular exhibited an almost fanatical devotion to Artemis. Its intensity appeared in the action of the mob in the amphitheatre, which for two hours shouted "Great *is* Diana of the Ephesians" (19:34).

Ephesus was rated as a free city and maintained its own government. The ultimate authority lay in the popular assembly when legally convoked (19:39), while the leaders or senate of the city acted as the central legislative body. The secretary or "town clerk" was the responsible officer who was instructed with keeping records and with presenting business to the assembly (19:35). The influence of labor was also strong; for it was the guild of silversmiths who protested that Paul's evangelizing activities had imperiled their trade in religious souvenirs, the silver shrines that were miniature copies of the temple.

There were several important problems which Paul encountered in Ephesus. The first was the question of the survival of the teaching of John the Baptist, whose disciples were still active after John's life had closed. Apollos, an educated Alexandrian Jew, had already been preaching in Ephesus concerning Jesus, "knowing only the baptism of John" (18:24, 25). Undoubtedly he knew that the Messiah was coming, that He had already been anointed to serve God, and that preparation for His ministry must include repentance and faith. His knowledge was not so much false as partial; he had not gone far enough. He was preaching in the synagogues and apparently evoked some response.

Under the tutelage of Priscilla and Aquila his understanding was broadened. A contrast of phrases here is enlightening: Luke says that he "had been instructed in the way of the Lord" (18:25), but that "Priscilla and Aquila . . . expounded unto him the way of God *more accurately*" (18:26, italics ours). Leaving Ephesus with the recommendation of the believers there, he went over to Achaia and became a strong apologist for the Christian faith, especially among the Jews (18:28). Later he became one of Paul's trusted friends and colleagues (I Cor. 16:12, Titus 3:13).

Apollos departed from Ephesus before Paul arrived, but others like him were there. These men, disciples of John the Baptist, were deficient in personal spiritual experience. So obvious was this fact that when Paul came into contact with them, he asked them if they had received the Holy Spirit when they believed. Their answer was that they had not so much as heard whether the Holy Spirit had come. In view of John's prediction that Jesus would baptize with the Holy Spirit, it seems inconceivable that they had never heard His name; but they might never have heard of the fulfilment of the promise at Pentecost. The reply of Paul proved that the baptism of John was insufficient to produce a full Christian experience; for the believer must not only repent of sin, but he must be filled with the Spirit. The first problem at Ephesus, then, was to bring sincere but immature believers up to date.

A second important problem of the Asian mission was the occult. The Jewish exorcists represented by the seven sons of Sceva, and the hundreds of nameless persons who burned their books of magic are proof of the wide extent to which superstition and demonology prevailed. The answer to this problem was twofold. On the positive side, the power of Christ was demonstrated to be greater than that of the exorcists and of demon cults. The sick were healed, the obsessed were delivered, and those who practiced the occult arts were so convicted of the evil of their ways that they voluntarily destroyed the books of magic on which they had relied (19:19). On the negative side, the exclusive character of the gospel was demonstrated. A Christian did not *add* his Christianity to his other religions; it displaced them. Christianity was essentially intolerant of all rivals, and nowhere is this principle better demonstrated than at Ephesus.

The ministry of Paul in Ephesus was singularly effective. For more than two years (19:8, 10) he was able to preach unhindered, first in the synagogue and later in the school of Tyrannus (19:9). He performed special miracles (19:11) and reached the populace of Ephesus and of the province as a whole more thoroughly than he did the people of any other place. Luke notes that "all they that dwelt in Asia heard the word of the Lord, both Jews and Greeks" (19:10), that "mightily grew the word of the Lord and prevailed" (19:20), and that so many had believed that idolatry suffered economic loss (19:26, 27). The church at Ephesus became a missionary center and was for centuries one of the strongholds of Christianity in Asia Minor.

## The Corinthian Correspondence

### Background

During Paul's stay in Ephesus he maintained relations with the churches of Achaia which he had founded on the preceding journey. The church at Corinth was a vexing problem to him because of its instability. Since it was largely composed of Gentiles who had no training in the Old Testament Scriptures, and whose religious and moral antecedents were the exact opposite of Christian principle, much teaching was required to bring them up to the place of spiritual maturity (I Cor. 3:1-3).

The ministry of Apollos among them was helpful in many ways. He attracted many of the Corinthians by his learning and by his polished presentation of truth. He was especially effective in dealing with Jews, since he knew the Old Testament well and could argue publicly in convincing fashion (Acts 18:27, 28). Paul appreciated his ministry and commended him (I Cor. 16:12).

It is possible that Peter may have visited Corinth, although no detail is given concerning his work. Paul mentioned his name as known to the Corinthians (I Cor. 1:12) and implied that he also was engaged in itinerant preaching (I Cor. 9:5). It is scarcely probable that a certain faction in the Corinthian church would claim him as their champion had there not been some contact with him personally at that time.

### The "Lost Letter"

While Apollos and possibly Cephas were visiting Corinth and preaching there, Paul was on the tour that took him back to Palestine and thence to Ephesus. During this period, or shortly after his return to Ephesus, he wrote a letter to which he alluded in I Corinthians 5:9: "I wrote unto you in my epistle to have no company with fornicators . . ." The moral atmosphere of Corinth was such that an absolute separation from evil was necessary if the church were to survive. Evidently there had been some misunderstanding of his injunction; for in I Corinthians he explained that he was not advocating withdrawal from the world, but that there should be separation from professing Christians who persisted in this sin.

The full content of the previous letter will never be known, since it has been lost. An ingenious hypothesis has been offered that fragments of this "lost letter" were preserved in the manuscript collection at Corinth, and that I Corinthians 6:12-20 and II Corinthians 6:14-7:1 are parts of it which were incorporated into the body of the later epistle.[3] The hypothesis rests solely upon subjective impression; and however plausible it may seem, there is no good external evidence to support it. It is certain that the problem of moral purity was of supreme importance at Corinth, as it was elsewhere throughout the

---

3. See David Smith, *Life and Letters of St. Paul* (New York: George H. Doran Co., n. d.), Appendix I, p. 654.

Gentile world, and that it was one of the earliest issues with which Paul had to deal

# I Corinthians

## Date

The response to the first letter was quite unsatisfactory. Apollos and Cephas had removed to other fields, and the church, bereft of adequate leadership, had fallen into confusion. Disquieting rumors concerning it began to drift back to Ephesus through slaves of a Corinthian family who were in Ephesus on business. Finally three members of the church, Stephanas, Fortunatus, and Achaicus brought a contribution to Paul and also a letter containing certain questions which the Corinthians wanted clarified. In response Paul wrote I Corinthians. It was composed near the end of his sojourn at Ephesus, for he had already formulated his plans for leaving Asia and for making an extended visit to Macedonia and Achaia (I Cor. 16:5-7). It must have been composed during the winter or in the fall, for he spoke of staying at Ephesus until Pentecost because of the success which was attending his work (I Cor. 16:8). He was engaged in raising the contribution for the poor in Jerusalem, which he took with him on his last journey to that city (Acts 24:17), so that he contemplated returning to Palestine again in the near future. Probably it was written in the winter of A.D. 55, during the prosperous peak of his work at Ephesus.

## Content

I Corinthians is the most varied in its content and in its style of all the epistles of Paul. The topics discussed range from schism to finance and from church decorum to the resurrection. Every literary device known to writing is employed in its pages: logic, sarcasm, entreaty, scolding, poetry, narration, exposition — in short, it is written in the same style as Paul would have carried on a conversation with the elders of Corinth had he been present with them. It is thoroughly informal in its approach rather than being a set essay on theological subjects. There is, however, a central theme. Findlay has called it "the doctrine of the cross in its social application."[4] It reflects the conflict which took place when Christian experience and Christian ideals of conduct came into conflict with the concepts and practices of the pagan world.

---

4. G. G. Findlay, *The First Epistle of Paul to the Corinthians* in *The Expositors' Bible* (Grand Rapids, Wm. B. Eerdmans, repr. 1947) Vol. II, p. 739.

The problems discussed in it are by no means outdated, for they are still to be found wherever Christians come into contact with a pagan civilization.

## *Outline*

The structure of I Corinthians depends upon the order of topics which had been brought to Paul's attention by the visitors from Corinth and by the letter which the Corinthians had written. How much news had been imparted by Apollos and by the trio who brought the contribution is not told. He made direct reference to "them *that are of the household* of Chloe" (I Cor. 1:11) who had informed him of the parties that had grown up within the church and of the immorality and litigation that disturbed their peace. These topics he discussed at length in the first six chapters. Beginning with the seventh chapter a new phrase appears: "Now concerning the things whereof ye wrote . . ." (7:1), and its subsequent repetitions (7:25, 8:1, [11:2,] 12:1, [15:1,] 16:1) mark off the subdivisions of his reply to their written questions.

## Evaluation

I Corinthians affords a better insight into the problems of a pioneer church than almost any other writing in the New Testament. Each problem was met by applying a spiritual principle rather than by recommending a psychological expedient. For schism, the remedy is spiritual maturity (3:1-9); for fornication, church discipline until the offender repents and is restored (5:1-5); for litigation there should be arbitration within the Christian community (6:1-6). In the case of marriage between a believer and an unbeliever, the concern of the believer is to save the unbeliever, not to alienate him or her (7:16); for the problem of the unmarried virgins, self-control or lawful marriage (7:36, 37). In the casuistic questions of food offered to idols and of details of worship, the relation of the believer to God is the deciding factor (10:31, 11:13, 32). Similarly the gifts are administered by God (12:28) within the church.

I Corinthians contains some allusions to church life and practice that are puzzling to modern Christians. The status of the "virgins" in chapter 7, where the word "daughter" (7:36-38) does not occur in the original text, the "delivering unto Satan" (5:5) in church discipline, and baptism for the dead (15:29) are usages for which no explanation is given, although they were evidently well known to Paul and to his readers. The mention of them does not mean that they were widely practiced. Baptism for the dead, too, may have been a local custom in the Corinthian church which was not necessarily approved, but which was used by Paul as a practical point of appeal in his argument for the resurrection.

I Corinthians was despatched to its destination by Timothy (16:10). Paul had tried to persuade Apollos to undertake the task of straightening out the church's problems, but he declined. Perhaps he thought that his presence could only increase the schismatic tendency among the followers. Paul had some misgivings concerning Timothy's effectiveness, for he urged the Corinthians not to frighten him or to despise him (16:10, 11).

Nothing is said concerning the outcome of Timothy's mission, but it seems to have been a failure. In II Corinthians Paul spoke twice of his plans and said, "This is the third time I am ready to come to you" (II Cor. 12:14, 13:1). Since his first visit to Corinth was the founding of the church, and since his letter was written from Macedonia after leaving Ephesus where he was waiting to come to Corinth, there must have been an unrecorded visit somewhere between Timothy's visit and Paul's departure from Asia. Such a call need not have occupied any great length of time, for transit from Ephesus to Corinth could be made easily. Luke does not record any such trip in Acts, but neither does he record many other episodes which might have been equally interesting or important. A survey of II Corinthians will show that Paul doubtless did go to Corinth to attempt to accomplish what Timothy had not been able to do, and that while there he had been grossly insulted and his counsel had been rejected. Rival self-styled "apostles," who drew their support from the churches and who boasted of their Jewish ancestry and of their activity as ministers of Christ, had invaded Corinth and had belittled Paul to the church (See II Cor. 10 and 11). Furthermore, the offending members of the church had been decidedly unrepentant (II Cor. 12:21). The situation was tense.

Paul decided that he would not return again to Corinth until the church adopted a different attitude (II Cor. 1:23). He had hoped that he might raise some money in Achaia for the Jerusalem collection. In anticipation of carrying through the original plan of a final visit to Macedonia and Achaia, he sent Titus ahead to deal with the church, while he closed the work at Ephesus and went to Troas enroute westward.

Perhaps Paul wrote once again to Corinth at this time. There has been some speculation as to whether II Corinthians represents one epistle or two. In II Corinthians 2:4 Paul spoke of a previous letter which he wrote "with many tears," and which was intended to convince the Corinthians of his love for them. I Corinthians does not seem to fit the description, and II Corinthians as it stands was written subsequently. A number of scholars have suggested that II Corinthians 10 through 13 may be a third epistle, written between I Corinthians and II Corinthians 1 through 9, which Paul wrote to defend himself and which he sent to the church by the hand of Titus (II Cor. 7:8-13).[5] Others have contended that the intermediary severe letter was lost.[6] As in the case of the first letter, there is no satisfactory external evidence for partitioning II Corinthians. Every manuscript of the Pauline

---

5. For a full exposition of this view, see David Smith, *The Life and Letters of St. Paul* (New York: George H. Doran Co., n. d.), pp. 325-371. Compare also James Moffatt, *Introduction to the Literature of the New Testament* (New York: Charles Scribner's Sons, 1911), pp. 119-123.

6. See H. C. Thiessen, *Introduction to the New Testament* (Grand Rapids, Mich.: Wm. B. Eerdmans Publishing Co., 1951), pp. 209, 210.

Epistles contains it as it is, so that its integrity cannot be challenged on grounds of manuscript variation. If chapters 10 through 13 do represent a third epistle, while chapters 1 through 9 represent a fourth, there is no trace of original separation in the manuscript tradition.

When Paul reached Troas after leaving Ephesus, he looked eagerly for Titus, but Titus did not appear (II Cor. 2:12, 13). Paul, oppressed with worry over what might have happened at Corinth, went across to Macedonia, where his troubles multiplied (II Cor. 7:5). While he was laboring there and arranging with the Macedonian churches for their gifts to Jerusalem, Titus suddenly arrived with the good news that a revival had broken out in the Corinthian church and that its attitude had changed from one of carelessness and obstinacy to one of repentance. With joy Paul sat down and penned II Corinthians as a preparation for a third visit which he hoped would have only happy consequences. If the whole epistle were written at this time, he included a lengthy defense of his ministry (2:14 to 7:4) and the financial request for the Corinthians and their colleagues of Achaia to match the Macedonian contributions to Jerusalem (Chaps. 8, 9).

## II Corinthians

### Content

The content has already been discussed in some measure. The epistle differs from I Corinthians in dealing with personal matters rather than with doctrinal teaching or with ecclesiastical order. The human Paul is much in evidence: his feelings, desires, dislikes, ambitions, and obligations are all spread before his readers. This epistle contains less systematic teaching and more personal expression of feeling than even I Corinthians; nor is its structure as clear-cut as is that of the former epistle.

### Outline

II CORINTHIANS: THE EPISTLE OF PAUL'S MINISTRY

|  |  |
|---|---|
| I. Salutation | 1:1, 2 |
| II. Explanation of Personal Conduct | 1:3-2:13 |
| III. The Defense of the Ministry | 2:14-7:4 |
| The Nature of the Ministry | 2:14-3:18 |
| The Sincerity of the Ministry | 4:1-6 |
| The Perseverance of the Ministry | 4:7-15 |
| The Prospect of the Ministry | 4:16-5:10 |
| The Sanctions of the Ministry | 5:11-19 |
| The Example of the Ministry | 5:20-6:10 |
| The Appeal of the Ministry | 6:11-7:4 |

313

## Evaluation

Second Corinthians affords an insight into the career of Paul that none of the other epistles give. It was written not only to defend him against the occasional criticisms of the Corinthian church, but also against the slanders and accusations that his enemies raised against him wherever he was preaching. The controversy which began in Galatia had created a powerful group of Judaizing opponents, who did not scruple to use any methods, fair or foul, in order to discredit him. He had to contend not only with the spiritual inertia and with the evils of the traditional paganism, but he had to face also the active malice of jealous and prejudiced leaders who professed to be Christians.

The accusations brought by his opponents were numerous. They charged him with walking "according to the flesh" (10:2). They said that he was a coward, for he wrote letters that resounded like thunder, but in actual presence he was about as authoritative as a mouse (10:10). He did not maintain himself in dignity by taking support from the churches, but demeaned himself by working (11:7). They claimed that he was not one of the original apostles, and so was not qualified to teach (11:5, 12:11, 12), and that he had no credentials that he could show (3:1). They attacked his personal character by saying that he was fleshly (10:2), boastful (10:8, 15), deceitful (12:16), and they insinuated that he embezzled the funds that were being entrusted to him (8:20-23).

The accusers themselves were apparently Jews (11:22) who were "ministers of Christ" (11:23), and who, by means of the clever use of recommendations from other churches (3:1) had obtained entrance into the Pauline churches. Doubtless they were responsible for some of the schism in Corinth. They were haughty and domineering (11:19, 20), but were not ready to do pioneering work or to suffer for Christ (11:23 ff.). They were, in short, "false brethren."

This picture, drawn from inference from the language of Paul, shows that the church of the apostolic age had its struggles and its sins. The marvel is not that it was imperfect; the marvel is that it survived. Only a divine dynamic could have given enduring vitality to so weak and sensual a group as the Corinthian church.

The positive teaching of the epistle makes it one of the most valuable in the New Testament. Its picture of the ministry, its statement of the prospects beyond death (chap. 5), and its teaching on giving (chaps. 8 and 9) are all outstanding passages.

## The Last Visit to Corinth

The arrival of Titus in Macedonia with the reassuring word of a change in the attitude of the Corinthian church (II Cor. 7:6-16) enabled Paul to pursue his journey without fear. Luke simply says that he spent three months in Achaia, but gives no details. In the spring of A.D. 56 he made plans to return to Jerusalem with the offering, when he learned that a plot against his life had been hatched by his Jewish enemies (Acts 20:3). Realizing that they would easily do away with him on shipboard, he dispatched his companions to Troas, while he, in company with Luke, went north to Philippi by the land route, and then sailed for Troas just after the close of the Feast of Unleavened Bread, which came immediately after the Passover.[7]

The way in which the "we-section" reappears at this point in Acts (20:5, 6) indicates that Luke had been traveling with Paul in Achaia. Robertson[8] suggests, following an ancient tradition, that perhaps Luke is identical with "the brother whose praise in the gospel *is spread* through all the churches; and . . . who was also appointed by the churches to travel with us in *the matter of* this grace" (II Cor. 8:18, 19). No name is mentioned, and the anonymous person could be any one of the companions of Paul listed in Acts 20:4. On the other hand, the definite article when used with terms denoting members of a family may be translated as a possessive pronoun. If Titus and Luke were brothers, the early connection of both of them with Antioch and the silence concerning both in the book of Acts could be explained more easily. At any rate, Luke at this time was Paul's active helper in the campaign throughout Macedonia and Achaia, and he became Paul's closest associate in the years of imprisonment that followed.

## The Projected Mission

Paul had planned the return to Jerusalem to be only an interlude in a larger mission. Already he had his eyes on a grander goal than any

7. Supra, p. 126.
8. A. T. Robertson, *Luke, the Historian in the Light of Research* (New York: Charles Scribner's Sons, 1923), p. 21.

of the cities that he had evangelized previously. Rome beckoned him; for he was a citizen of the empire. If he could reach Rome with the gospel, it could easily be disseminated to all parts of the empire, for all roads led to Rome.

With true missionary statesmanship he laid out his course of action. Luke says that "after these things were ended [the ministry at Ephesus], Paul purposed in the spirit, when he had passed through Macedonia and Achaia, to go to Jerusalem, saying, After I have been there, I must also see Rome" (Acts 19:21).

## The Epistle to the Romans

### Background

In preparation for this next step in his missionary enterprise, he wrote the Epistle to the Romans. It was sent from Corinth, which is the traditional view, or from Philippi, just prior to sailing for Troas,[9] for Paul states in its closing chapters that he had concluded his preaching as far as Illyricum (Rom. 15:19); that he had in hand the offering which the churches of Macedonia and Achaia had taken for the poor at Jerusalem (15:26), and that he was on the eve of sailing to Jerusalem to deliver it (15:25). He expected that his presence in Judea might not be well received by some; but he intended to return shortly in order to visit Rome, and even to go to Spain (15:24, 28, 32). Granting that Romans 16 is an integral part of the epistle, it was sent to Rome by Phoebe, a deaconess of the church of Cenchrea, who was traveling in that direction (16:1).

Paul had numerous friends at Rome. He had tried frequently to visit them, but had been hindered (15:22, 1:13) on each occasion. The church could not have been a large one and probably it consisted chiefly of Gentiles, since in addressing them he classed them as Gentiles (1:13), and since the later account of his visit to Rome as given by Acts indicates ignorance concerning Christian truth on the part of the Jews. They had heard of the movement, but had not investigated it for themselves, nor had any others reported to them about it (Acts 28:21). The Gentile church of Rome had in it a small minority of Jews at the most; and the Jews who lived in Rome, having come to the city since the expulsion under Claudius, had not made the acquaintance of those who were in the church.

9. See Theophilus M. Taylor, "The Place of Origin of Romans," in *Journal of Biblical Literature* LXVII (1948), 281-295.

The origin of the church in Rome is unknown. There were present at Jerusalem on the day of Pentecost "sojourners from Rome" (Acts 2:10) who may have returned with the message of Christ. Aquila and Priscilla had come from Rome, and, according to Romans 16:3, had returned thither. No hint is given in the New Testament that Peter had anything to do with the founding of this church. It seems to have been one that began spontaneously among believers, the majority of whom had probably migrated to Rome from other parts of the world.

Paul had several reasons for being interested in this church. His desire to see the imperial city, the need of the Christians for instruction, his wish to forestall any Judaizing activity in a group of great potential importance, and his hope of support from them as he undertook a tour to Spain (15:24) — all contributed to his resolve to spend some time with them.

Romans was written as a substitute for immediate personal contact and as preparatory for making the Roman church a missionary center comparable to Antioch, Ephesus, Philippi, and the other cities where Paul had labored. Romans, therefore, unlike Corinthians, is not devoted so much to the correction of errors as to the teaching of truth. Although it does not comprise all the fields of Christian thought — for eschatology is notably lacking in its content — it does give a fuller and more systematic view of the heart of Christianity than any other of Paul's epistles, with the possible exception of Ephesians. Most of the Pauline epistles are controversial or corrective in nature; Romans is chiefly didactic.

## Content

The central theme of Romans is the revelation of the righteousness of God to man, and its application to his spiritual need. Its theme is thus basic to all Christian experience, for man cannot do business with God until a proper approach has been established. The epistle is directed particularly to Gentiles. Paul stated that he was an apostle to the Gentiles (1:5); he sketched the religious history of the Gentile world as the prelude to revelation (1:18-32); he asserted that God's salvation is for "Gentiles also" (3:29) and that there is "no distinction" between Jew and Greek in the way of faith. Romans avers that salvation is universal in its scope.

The development of this theme of the righteousness of God can best be seen in the outline.

317

*Outline*

## ROMANS: THE GOSPEL OF GOD'S RIGHTEOUSNESS

## Evaluation

Romans has long been the mainstay of Christian theology. Most of its technical terms, such as justification, imputation, adoption, and sanctification are drawn from the vocabulary of this epistle, and the structure of its argument provides the backbone of Christian thought. Its logical method is obvious. First, the theme is announced: ". . . the gospel . . . is the power of God unto salvation to every one that believeth" (1:16). The need for that power is shown by the fall of the world, Jew and Gentile alike, so that "there is none righteous, no not one" (3:10). If, then, all are helpless and condemned, relief must come from without by providing for them both a legal and a personal righteousness. This is found in Christ, "whom God set forth *to be* a propitiation, through faith, in his blood, to show his righteousness because of the passing over of the sins done aforetime" (3:25). Since the sinner cannot earn his salvation, this righteousness must be accepted by faith. Individually and racially man is restored to his right position before God through the grace manifested in Christ.

Chapters six through eight deal with the personal problems that rise out of the new spiritual relationships. "Shall we continue in sin, that grace may abound?" (6:1) "Shall we sin, because we are not under law, but under grace?" (6:15) "Is the law sin?" (7:7) "Who shall deliver me out of the body of this death?" (7:24) All these questions are answered by the description of the personal life in the Spirit given in chapter 8.

The section comprising chapters nine through eleven deals with a broader question. Has God, by instituting salvation for all by faith, invalidated the covenant with Israel which was established through the law? Paul points out that the choice of the Gentiles is quite in keeping with God's original procedure of choosing Jacob rather than Esau. It is no less right for God to choose the Gentiles for salvation than it was right for Him to choose Israel to be the vehicle of His revelation. His will is ultimate; beyond it there is no court of appeal. Furthermore, Israel's unbelief had forfeited her standing, so that the Gentile is now being given his day before God. The time may come when the Gentiles' opportunity will close (11:25), and then the believers of Israel shall enter into their heritage. The present dealing of God with Gentiles is neither arbitrary nor accidental, but is in full accordance with the divine plan.

The practical section of Romans makes close ethical application of the salvation described in the first eleven chapters. The redeemed individual is obligated to live a righteous life: "whether we live . . .

319

or die, we are the Lord's. For to this end Christ died and lived *again,* that he might be Lord of both the dead and the living" (14:8, 9). The conclusion (15:14-33) expresses Paul's own sense of debt to Christ for making known the gospel "not where Christ was *already* named" (15:20). He translated the obligation of the gospel of righteousness into missionary terms.

Romans is a superb example of the integration of doctrine with missionary purpose. Had Paul not believed that men were lost and that God had provided a righteousness for them, he would not have been a missionary. Had he not been an active missionary, he never would have formulated so systematic a presentation of truth as Romans. It illustrates what he did when he "established" the converts in his churches.[10]

## The Mission Concluded

Two brief stops on the way to Palestine are described at some length by Luke in Acts 20. The first was the meeting in Troas at which Paul preached. It is one of the earliest existing descriptions of Christian worship. The meeting was on the first day of the week, in the evening. The disciples gathered to break bread together, presumably the love-feast, or *Agape,* which culminated in the Lord's Supper, described in I Corinthians 11:17-26. Preaching or discourse was a part of the service. In this case Paul preached and taught through the night because he was leaving on the next day and might not return.

The second stop was at Miletus, a sizable port on the west coast of Asia. Paul had taken a fast ship that bypassed Ephesus, in order that he might reach Jerusalem by Pentecost. When the ship touched at Miletus, he summoned the elders of the church at Ephesus in order to give them a farewell message. Luke used the speech to epitomize Paul's missionary policies and achievements up to date. It is the utterance of a great soul who had given his life unreservedly into the hands of Christ and who had been fully directed by the Holy Spirit in his ministry. It discloses his own consciousness that trouble awaited him at Jerusalem (Acts 20:22, 23) and that his work in Asia was ended (20:25), for he contemplated going farther west on his next trip. Perhaps he realized that old age was beginning to overtake him, and that there would not be time to retrace his first steps as he had done in former journeys for the purpose of confirming the believers. With an affectionate farewell he parted from them (20:36-38).

10. Compare the language of Rom. 1:11 and Acts 18:23. Apparently the word "establish" (Greek: *sterizo*) had the connotation of "instruction."

## The Mission Concluded

The remainder of the voyage was uneventful, except for repeated warnings to Paul to stay away from Jerusalem (21:4, 10, 11). In spite of the pleas of his friends, Paul persisted in his original plan, and the others assented reluctantly, saying, "The will of the Lord be done" (21:14).

With this visit to Jerusalem closed the most active part of Paul's missionary career. In a little less than a decade he had won the freedom of the Gentile believers from the yoke of legalism. He had built a strong chain of churches from Antioch of Syria and Tarsus of Cilicia straight across southern Asia Minor to Ephesus and Troas, and thence through Macedonia and Achaia to Illyricum. He had chosen and trained companions like Luke, Timothy, Silas, Aristarchus, Titus, and others who were well qualified to maintain the work with him or without him. He had commenced an epistolary literature which already was regarded as a standard for faith and practice. In his preaching he had laid the groundwork for future Christian theology and apologetics, and by his plans he pursued a statesmanlike campaign of missionary evangelism. His plans for a trip to Rome and Spain showed that he wanted to match the imperial commonwealth with an imperial faith. Notwithstanding his bitter and active enemies, he had established the Gentile church upon a firm foundation and had already formulated the essence of Christian theology as the Spirit of God revealed it to him.

# THE PAULINE IMPRISONMENT

# THE PAULINE IMPRISONMENT

Jerusalem

The Epistles

Philemon
    Background
    Content and Outline
    Evaluation

Ephesians
    Background
    Content
    Outline
    Evaluation

Colossians
    Background
    Content
    Outline
    Evaluation

Philippians
    Background
    Content
    Outline
    Evaluation

Results of the Pauline Imprisonment

# CHAPTER XVII

## The Pauline Imprisonment

### Acts 21:17 to 28:31

The last section of Acts, containing the account of Paul's imprisonment, trials, and voyage to Rome, seems almost like an anti-climax. About one quarter of the entire book is given to the discussion of events which seemingly had no bearing upon the doctrinal or missionary advance of the church. Instead of showing how the church expanded into Rome and Spain, the account leaves Paul under custody in his own hired house and tells nothing of the hearing before the emperor nor of Paul's subsequent ministry if the hearing ended in release. The story ends abruptly, and, to the usual way of thinking, unsatisfactorily.

The abruptness of Acts' ending may be accounted for by assuming that the author wrote all that he knew. If he were attempting to bring Theophilus up to date, he would want to inform him as quickly as possible; and, having given him the latest developments in Paul's career, there would be nothing left to say. The disproportionate emphasis on the imprisonment may mean that Luke could write more freely and fully of what he himself had witnessed, but there is probably an even better reason for the detail concerning the period. Christianity had become increasingly separate from Judaism, and its independence was more and more apparent to the observant public. The view that Rome took of it would have a very important effect upon its future; for if it were to be regarded as a dangerous revolutionary movement, immediate suppression would follow. In this account written for Theophilus, who was possibly a Roman official, Luke desired to show that Christianity had no political pretensions and that its relations with the Roman power had always been friendly. Persecution had come from the Jews on religious grounds; but all charges that it was subversive of Roman authority, as at Philippi (Acts 16:20, 21), were false. Furthermore, these chapters of Acts have great biographical and theological value because they reveal more of the inner thought and teaching of Paul than do most of the other passages in Acts.

PAUL'S VOYAGE TO ROME

## Jerusalem

Paul's arrival in Jerusalem brought an immediate clash within the Jewish church in spite of his attempts at pacification. At the suggestion of James, Paul undertook the financial responsibility of helping some Jewish Christians to discharge the Nazirite vow (21:23, 24).[1] Paul himself had undertaken the vow on a previous occasion (18:18), and James thought that it would afford him a good means of demonstrating that he had no aversion to keeping the law voluntarily. By so doing he could stop the various rumors that were being circulated about him that he was teaching all the Jews of the Dispersion not to circumcise their children nor to keep the customs of the law (21:21).

The project was well under way when the inevitable clash occurred. The Jews from Asia, who had been his bitter opponents at Ephesus and elsewhere, assuming that he had brought his Gentile companions into the forbidden sanctuary of the temple, accused him publicly of so doing and mobbed him. The ensuing riot took on such proportions that the Roman military tribune had to intervene with his armed cohorts. They rescued Paul from the fury of the mob and conducted him to the Castle of Antonia for further examination.

Paul gained permission from the tribune to speak from the castle steps (21:40) and, addressing the crowd in Aramaic, made his defense. The crowd listened respectfully as he told of his conversion. No objection was voiced to the reality of the blinding light, which to a Jewish mind would connote Shekinah glory of God,[2] nor to the glorification of Jesus, nor to the concepts of baptism and repentance. Only when Paul mentioned a call to the Gentiles did the hatred of the mob burst into flame and he had to be withdrawn from the castle for safety.

In the examinations and hearings that followed, two facts were brought into prominence: Paul's innocence of any political or criminal offense, and his Roman citizenship. He was in protective custody for four years. Two years were spent in Caesarea, because Felix hoped to extort a bribe from Paul for releasing him (24:26). He failed to discharge him when his procuratorship ended for he thought that thus he could curry favor with the Jews (24:27). At the accession of Festus, Paul, realizing that the Jews would never relent in their hatred nor withdraw their accusations, feared that Festus would listen to them and leave him to languish indefinitely in prison. To take the case out of Festus' hands, he appealed to Caesar (25:10-12). Festus,

---

1. For the nature of the vow, see Numbers 6:1-20.
2. The Shekinah was the brilliant glory that accompanied the manifest presence of God. See Exodus 3:1-5, II Chronicles 7:1-3, Isaiah 6.

knowing that Paul was a Roman citizen, was obligated to comply with his demand, and dispatched him to Rome to stand trial. Waiting for the hearing consumed another two years (28:30). Whether Paul were released because the case had not come to trial within the prescribed time, or whether he were tried and discharged as innocent is not told.

This period of enforced inactivity was by no means fruitless. Even in Jerusalem Paul was not forbidden to maintain contact with the outside world (23:16), and in Rome he dwelt in his own hired house where he carried on a ministry to all who called on him there (28:30, 31). He could not travel, but he had liberty to teach and to write within the limits of his own cell or house.

The epistles that were written during this period testify that the growth of the church was not brought to a halt by Paul's imprisonment, and that the literature which Paul produced was of more solid and didactic nature than anything he had written up to that time, with the possible exception of Romans. The Prison Epistles as a group deal more with general teaching and less with individual questions than do the earlier Travel Epistles. They reveal a church which was not simply the initial aggregation of converts, eager, uncertain, perplexed by current problems and somewhat disorganized, but a church which was maturing rapidly. There are indications that the second generation of Christians was beginning to emerge, whose problems were those of complacency rather than of confusion. They had already been instructed in the elements of the faith, and they needed to receive the deeper teaching which would enlighten and stabilize them.

In spite of the change in Paul's plans which the imprisonment effected, his sense of destiny and his faith that the purpose of God was sending him to Rome did not alter. The vision in Jerusalem that came just after his appearance before the Sanhedrin said: "As thou hast testified concerning me at Jerusalem, so must thou bear witness also at Rome" (23:11). The promise was renewed in the midst of the peril of the shipwreck by the angel of God, who said: "Fear not, Paul; thou must stand before Caesar" (27:24), and Paul's response was characteristic: "I believe God" (27:25). The entire period is an exemplification of the slow but sure operation of divine providence in Paul's ministration of the gospel.

The development of his message is also indicated by the repeated allusions in his defense to the resurrection of Christ. Allowing for the fact that the addresses in this section are apologetic rather than didactic, they show that in Paul's thinking the resurrection had taken a central place.  In his defense before the Sanhedrin he said, "Brethren, I am a Pharisee, a son of Pharisees: touching the hope and resurrection of the dead I am called in question" (23:6).  In the hearing before Felix he defined the belief of the "sect" to which he belonged by saying that he hoped "that there shall be a resurrection both of the just and unjust" (24:15).  Even Festus, the Roman governor, who could hardly be called theologically minded, introduced Paul to Agrippa declaring that the Jews "had certain questions against him of their own religion, and of one Jesus, who was dead, whom Paul affirmed to be alive" (25:19).  In the reply to Agrippa's invitation to speak for himself, Paul asked, "Why is it judged incredible with you, if God doth raise the dead?" (26:8)  Following the account of his conversion, which presupposed the activity of a risen Christ, Paul avowed that his message was founded on prophecy, "how that the Christ must suffer, *and* how that he first by the resurrection of the dead should proclaim light both to the people and to the Gentiles" (26:23).

This stress on the resurrection is, of course, evident in all of Paul's epistles from the very first (Gal. 1:1, I Thess. 1:10, 4:14, I Cor. 15:1-8, II Cor. 5:15, Rom. 1:4).  The amplification of its meaning for the believer is developed in the sixth and eighth chapters of Romans, but its claims upon his ethical and devotional life appear most clearly in Colossians and Ephesians.  It may be that during the enforced retirement of his imprisonment Paul was able to contemplate more fully the meaning of the truth that was familiar to him and to formulate in greater detail its consequences for the Christian life.

## The Epistles

The four "prison epistles," Philippians, Colossians, Ephesians, and Philemon were the product of this period from A.D. 56 or 57 to A.D. 60 or 61.  Some critical questions have been raised concerning them.  Were they written at Caesarea, or at Rome?  Are they all genuinely Pauline?  What was their destination?

There is no doubt that they were written during the period of imprisonment for all of them make reference to Paul's bonds (Phil. 1:12, 13, Eph. 3:1, 4:1, 6:20, Col. 1:24, Phm. 1).  Probably the traditional view that they were written from Rome is correct, for the allusions to Caesar's household (Phil. 4:22) and to the praetorian guard (Phil. 1:13) would apply better to Rome than to Caesarea.  He seemed to be in a center of travel, where his friends came and went with ease, which would be much more characteristic of Rome than of Caesarea.

Some question has been raised in recent years concerning the genuineness of Ephesians. Goodspeed and others contend that it was written by a man who first collected and edited the Pauline epistles in order to provide an introduction for the collection. The letter, however, bears the name of Paul; the personal references are all in keeping with the known facts of his life; and its close resemblance to Colossians may be accounted for by the fact that both were written approximately at the same time so that the prevailing ideas of both were similar. There is no convincing external evidence that Ephesians was written by another than Paul, and the internal evidence that is cited is susceptible of more than one interpretation.[3] It is possible that Ephesians was an encyclical letter, written not only to Ephesus, but generally for the churches of Asia which had been the field of Paul's last extended ministry before the imprisonment. The phrase *at Ephesus* of 1:1 is lacking in some of the oldest manuscripts.[4] One wonders why there are no personal greetings appended to this letter which was traditionally sent to a church where Paul labored for three years, unless he intended it for general reading by many churches. Its broad teaching, which does not deal with specific situations in a local church confirms this impression. If it were a circular letter to the churches of Asia, undoubtedly one copy was sent to Ephesus. Since Ephesus was the largest church of the province, the copy in its possession would be the most accessible and the one most frequently reproduced. The destination of each of the other Prison Epistles is clearly indicated by the superscription which it bears, and has never been a subject of argument.

## Philemon

### Background

Philemon was written at the same time and under the same circumstances as Ephesians and Colossians. Onesimus, a slave of Philemon who was a business man of Colosse, had absconded with some of his master's property and had gone to Rome to lose himself in the crowds of that great city. In some way he came in contact with Paul and was converted (Phm. 10).

Realizing the necessity of making right the wrong that he had done, Paul sent him back to his former master with this note, requesting that

---

3. The strongest case for the non-Pauline authorship of Ephesians has been proposed by Edgar J. Goodspeed in his *An Introduction to the New Testament* (Chicago: The University of Chicago Press, n. d.), pp. 222-239. His argument, however, is based almost wholly on internal evidence.

4. *En Epheso* does not appear in P46, B*, or Aleph.

he be received and forgiven. Paul agreed to pay for the financial loss that Onesimus had caused (Phm. 18, 19). He added that he hoped for release in a short time, after which he planned to visit the churches again.

## Content and Outline

Although this epistle is intensely personal rather than theological, it contains the finest picture of the meaning of forgiveness that can be found in the New Testament. The outline will be a sufficient summary.

PHILEMON: A PICTURE OF CHRISTIAN FORGIVENESS

| | |
|---|---|
| I. Salutation: The Family | 1:1-3 |
| II. The Fellowship | 1:4-7 |
| III. The Favor | 1:8-20 |
| IV. The Farewells | 1:21-25 |

## Evaluation

In this letter are found all the elements of forgiveness: the offense (11, 18), compassion (10), intercession (10, 18, 19), substitution (18, 19), restoration to favor (15), and elevation to a new relationship (16). Every aspect of the divine forgiveness of sin is duplicated in the forgiveness which Paul sought for Onesimus. It is a practical lesson in the petition of the prayer, "Forgive us our debts as we also have forgiven our debtors."

# Ephesians

## Background

The necessity for the writing of Philemon and of sending a letter back to Asia afforded an opportunity to send others also. Ephesians, as a general encyclical to be distributed through the Ephesian church, and Colossians, a direct communication to the church at Colosse, were composed at this time, probably in A.D. 60 or 61. The messenger was Tychicus, whom Onesimus accompanied (Eph. 6:21, Col. 4:7-9). With Paul at the time of writing were Aristarchus, who had been one of the delegates to Jerusalem (Acts 20:4), Epaphras, an Asian, Luke "the beloved physician," and Demas. Mark had rejoined Paul at this time and was evidently contemplating a journey to Asia (Col. 4:10), for Paul commended him to Colosse. Jesus Justus, a Jewish colleague, is otherwise unknown. The fact that these men are mentioned both in

Colossians and in Philemon indicates that the epistles were written about the same time.

Ephesians was written after many churches had been founded, and after Paul had opportunity to contemplate the meaning of the new organism that had come into being. It is the one writing in the New Testament in which the word "church" means the church universal rather than the local group. It was intended to inform the Gentiles of their new calling, and it disclosed the mystery of the body of Christ in which there is neither Jew nor Gentile, bond nor free.

## Content

Throughout the Epistle to the Ephesians runs the one theme of the church. The epistle was not directed to novices in the Christian faith, but to those who, having achieved some maturity in spiritual experience, wished to go on to fuller knowledge and life. Certain themes recur constantly in the book. The sovereign purpose of God in establishing the church permeates the first half of the epistle (1:4, 5, 9, 11, 13, 20; 2:4, 6, 10; 3:11) in which the divine plan of redemption is elaborated. In the second half the conduct of the believer is emphasized in the word "walk," which describes his model for conduct (4:1, 17; 5:1, 8, 15) as contrasted with his former behavior in the world (2:1). The sphere of the Christian's activities is "in the heavenlies" (1:3, 10, 20; 2:6; 3:10; 6:12), a phrase which refers to spiritual rather than to geographical locality. The dynamic of the church's life is the Holy Spirit, who is the seal of acceptance (1:13), the means of access to God (2:18), the source of revealed truth (3:5), the secret of universal power (3:16), the bond of unity (4:3, 4), the mentor of thinking and of speech (4:30), the stimulus of joy (5:18), and the armorer for conflict (6:17).

The textual divisions of Ephesians given below follow each other logically, leading the Christian from an understanding of the origin of his salvation in the thought and action of the Triune God to the practical application of that salvation in everyday life.

## Outline

EPHESIANS: THE EPISTLE OF THE CHURCH

| | |
|---|---|
| I. Introduction | 1:1, 2 |
| II. The Constitution of the Church | 1:3-14 |
| By the Father | 1:3-6 |
| In the Son | 1:6-12 |
| Through the Spirit | 1:13, 14 |

*Deuteronomy 33:27*
*The eternal God is Thy refuge, and underneath are the EVERLASTING ARMS.*

III. The Consciousness of the Church: A Prayer   1:15-23
     Of hope of calling
     Of inheritance in saints
     Of greatness of power
     Of leadership of Christ

IV. The Creation of the Church      2:1-10
     Material: from children of wrath
     Means: by grace
     Purpose: for good works

 V. The Concord of the Church      2:11-22
     Union of Jew and Gentile in Christ

VI. The Calling of the Church      3:1-21
     To reveal the wisdom of God     3:1-13
     To experience the fulness of God: a prayer  3:14-21

VII. The Conduct of the Church      4:1-6:9
     Its ministry: diversity in unity     4:1-16
     Its moral standards     4:17-5:14
     Its corporate behavior toward the world    5:15-21
     Its domestic standards     5:22-6:9

VIII. The Conflict of the Church      6:10-20

 IX. Conclusion      6:21-24

## Evaluation

If Romans is a sample of the kind of teaching that Paul would give to churches upon his first visit to them, Ephesians is a specimen of his "Bible conference" technique. Much of its material can be duplicated in his other epistles, and there is little theology or ethics in Ephesians which cannot be found in essence elsewhere. The total complex, however, is integrated into a new picture of the church as a single functioning body, created out of Jew and Gentile, equipped with standards of its own, and engaged in a spiritual conflict. Its goal is "the unity of the faith, . . . the knowledge of the Son of God . . . the measure of the stature of the fulness of Christ" (4:13).

## Colossians

### Background

Colossians and Ephesians are twin epistles; in fact, their resemblance is so great that some who doubted the Pauline authorship of Ephesians have averred that it is only a copy of Colossians with additions. The town of Colosse was located in the hinterland of Asia on a rocky ridge overlooking the valley of the Lycus river, not far from the cities of Hierapolis and Laodicea. During the period of the Persian Wars in the fifth century B.C., Colosse had been a town of considerable importance; but as Hierapolis and Laodicea grew, its commerce declined. It had been especially noted for the glossy black wool that was grown by the shepherds in the adjoining hill country. In Paul's day it was decadent, although still a good-sized city.

Paul himself had probably not visited Colosse or its neighboring cities, since he says that they had "not seen [his] face in the flesh" (Col. 2:1). It must have been evangelized during his stay in Asia, perhaps by Timothy and Epaphras (1:7) who itinerated while Paul preached in Ephesus.

The heresy of Colosse which evoked this epistle was a local development which arose because of the peculiar situation of the city. Colosse was on the trade route from the East, along which Oriental religions as well as Oriental merchandise were transported to Rome. The Colossians were Phrygian Gentiles (1:27), whose religious antecedents were highly emotional and mystical. They were seeking to attain the fulness of God; and when teachers came among them with a philosophy that promised a mystic knowledge of God, they were entranced by it. Among its tenets were voluntary humiliation, probably by ascetic practices (2:18, 20, 21), the worship of angels, who may have been reputed intermediaries between God and man (2:18), and abstinence from certain foods and drinks, and the observance of feasts and ceremonial days (2:16). It is quite likely that in these teachings there was also a strain of Jewish legalism, brought in from contacts with the Jewish population of Asia Minor. Paul's references to ceremonialism (2:11) and to the fact that the ceremonies and feasts were a shadow of things to come (2:17) sound more like Judaism than heathenism. The Colossian heresy, then, was of the same order as the Galatian heresy, except that it centered about the person of Christ rather than about salvation by grace versus salvation by works.

The answer to this heresy lay not in extended argument, but in a positive presentation of the person of Christ. Paul pointed out that all philosophies, spiritual powers, ceremonial observances and restrictions were secondary to the preëminence of Christ.

## Content

Outstanding in Colossians is the passage from 1:14 to 22, which sets forth Paul's Christology. Curiously enough, it was not a separate treatise, but was part of a prayer with which Paul opened the paragraph in 1:9. Beginning with a relative clause explanatory of the phrase, "the Son of his love" (1:13), it continued with a description of Christ in terms which could be applied only to deity, summarized finally in the astounding statement that "in him dwelleth all the fulness of the Godhead bodily" (2:9). In creation, redemption, in the church, and in personal life Christ must be preëminent.

Redemption is prominent in the teaching of Colossians. In Christ men have forgiveness of sins (1:14). Through the blood of His cross they are reconciled to God (1:20, 22). The bond written in ordinance that was against us has been abolished in the cross (2:14). The subjective application of death and resurrection is also taught in Colossians: "If ye died with Christ . . . why . . . do ye subject yourselves to ordinances? If then ye were raised together with Christ, seek the things that are above, where Christ is, seated on the right hand of God" (2:20, 3:1).

## Outline

### COLOSSIANS: CHRIST PREEMINENT

| | |
|---|---|
| I. Salutation | 1:1, 2 |
| II. Christ Preëminent in Personal Relationships | 1:3-2:7 |
| In Personal Contacts | 1:3-8 |
| In Personal Presentation | 1:9-23 |
| In Personal Purpose | 1:24-2:7 |
| III. Christ Preëminent in Doctrine | 2:8-3:4 |
| False Philosophy versus Christ | 2:8-15 |
| False Worship versus Christ | 2:16-19 |
| False Asceticism versus Christ | 2:20-3:4 |
| IV. Christ Preëminent in Ethics | 3:5-4:6 |
| Negatively: "Put off . . ." | 3:5-11 |
| Positively: "Put on . . ." | 3:12-17 |
| In Family Relationships | 3:18-4:1 |
| General | 4:2-6 |
| V. Concluding Personal Greetings | 4:7-18 |

## Evaluation

Colossians was written as an antidote to a blasé intellectualism which prated of mysteries, secret knowledge, and wisdom, while discounting Christ by a false philosophy. Paul shows that in Christ is God perfectly pictured (1:15); that in Him all the fulness of deity resides

(1:19); and that in Him are hidden all the treasures of wisdom and knowledge (2:3). Moreover, the ethical demands of the Christian life are closely linked with its intellectual standards. "Set your mind on the things that are above, not on the things that are upon the earth" (3:2). The practical section of the book that follows this injunction (3:5-4:6) is connected to it by a "therefore," which establishes the relation of conscious effect between knowledge and behavior. Paul was no purveyor of idle theories. For him the gospel had clear ethical consequences.

## Philippians

### Background

Philippians is the most personal of all the epistles of Paul that were not written to individuals. In the four pages that it occupies in an ordinary size Bible there are not less than one hundred uses of the first personal pronoun. Paul was not talking about himself in any boastful spirit, nor was he engaged in defense of his personal ministry, as in II Corinthians. The Philippian church had been intensely loyal to him, and he felt that he could speak to them freely of his tribulations and of his spiritual ambitions.

Practically a decade had passed since Paul, Silas, and Luke had first entered Philippi. From the very beginning there had been response to his message. This church included many women, possibly friends of Lydia, who had labored with him in the gospel (Phil. 4:3). Some of them, like Syntyche and Euodia, did not always agree among themselves (4:2). At the outset of his ministry in Macedonia the church had supported him; but as his travels had taken him farther afield, they had not done so much for him. The news of the disaster in Jerusalem and his consequent imprisonment in Rome had revived their sympathetic interest (4:10-14), and they had again made a contribution to his need. Epaphroditus, their messenger, had brought to Paul their gifts, and he, in turn, had been taken seriously ill. Paul counted his recovery an answer to prayer (2:25-27), and was sending him back to Philippi with the letter which he wrote (2:28, 29). He stated that Epaphroditus had risked his life to bring the gifts, though the nature of the danger was not revealed. Perhaps he incurred infection of disease through his travels and contacts; perhaps he laid himself open to suspicion by communicating with a man who was a political prisoner.

The date of Philippians is uncertain, but it seems most reasonable to believe that it was written toward the close of Paul's two years in Rome. Lightfoot thinks that it may have been earlier than the Asian epistles, because its language has greater affinity with that of the Travel Epistles than with that of the others.[5] Language affinity is a very tenuous argument, since an author may change his style and vocabulary not only with the advance of his years but also with the needs of the situation for which he was writing. While it is true, as Lightfoot points out, that Philippians does resemble Romans more in its vocabulary and general style than it does Ephesians or Colossians, it was intended for a church that was more European than Asian and that was not affected by the mysticism and legalism that plagued Colosse.

Several other factors enter into the background. Some time must be allowed for the news of Paul's arrival in Rome to reach Philippi, and for the church there to send Epaphroditus to him with the gift. Paul's reputation among the pretorian guard (1:13) and the penetration of the gospel among the members of Caesar's household (4:22) required an interval of time. The two factions among the preachers, those that envied and disliked Paul, and those that stood with him (1:15, 16) did not develop over night. Furthermore, his view of his trial shows that he was uncertain of the outcome and that while he was resigned to whatever might happen, he appeared confident that he would be released for further service (1:23-26, 2:17, 24).

There seems to have been no particular schism or heresy within the Philippian church itself that called for disciplinary action. The references to the Judaizers in chapter 3:2 picture them as a potential rather than as a present danger; and while Paul's language is vehement, his main purpose is not so much to refute their error as to arouse the Philippians to walk worthily of their heavenly citizenship (3:17-21).

## Content

Two topics predominate in the text of Philippians. One is the *gospel,* which Paul mentions nine times. He speaks of "the fellowship in the gospel" (1:5, Greek text), the "confirmation of the gospel" (1:7), "the progress of the gospel" (1:12), "the defence of the gospel" (1:16), "worthy of the gospel" (1:27), "striving for the faith of the gospel" (1:27), "service in the gospel" (2:22, Greek text), "labor in the gospel" (4:3), "the beginning of the gospel" (4:15). Paul used the term as denoting a body of faith, a message, and the sphere of activity bounded by preaching. No definition of the gospel is given in Philippians, but the heart of the gospel is contained in two phrases that give respectively the historical and the personal aspects: he be-

5. J. B. Lightfoot, *St. Paul's Epistle to the Philippians* (Eighth Edition, London: Macmillan and Co., 1888), pp. 30-46.

came "obedient *even* unto death, yea, the death of the cross" (2:8), and "having a righteousness . . . which is through faith in Christ" (3:9). The former is the good news that Christ died for men; the latter assures men that they can possess His righteousness before God. These are the two aspects of the gospel.

The second topic in Philippians which Paul stressed is *joy.* The outlook for him in Rome certainly was unpleasant, since his enemies were seeking to undermine his work, and since sudden execution was a possible outcome for the trial. Philippians is anything but pessimistic. Paul rejoiced in every remembrance of the Philippians (1:3), because Christ was preached whether sincerely or hypocritically (1:18), in the growth of humility in his followers (2:2), in his personal sacrifice for Christ (2:17), and in the gifts and good will of his friends (4:10). All through the epistle there is a brilliant joy of faith contrasted with the somber background of untoward circumstance and of impending disaster.

### *Outline*

PHILIPPIANS: THE PERSONAL EPISTLE

## Evaluation

Philippians is a note of thanks for favors received and an expression of the personal Christian life of Paul. The two outstanding passages in this epistle, 2:5-11 and 3:2-15, express respectively the supreme obedience of Christ to the will of God and the supreme passion of His servant, Paul, to achieve the goal for which Christ had called him. The former passage was not written primarily as an essay in Christology, but was given incidentally to illustrate the nature of humility to which Paul was exhorting the Philippians. The very fact that Paul took its truth for granted in using it as an illustration confirms the theological truth that it contains. Men take for granted what they believe in common; they argue when disputable differences arise.

Much ink has been spilled over the meaning of the phrase, he "emptied himself" (2:7). To what extent did Christ relinquish the prerogatives of deity when He came among men? The Lord Jesus Christ voluntarily divested Himself of visible glory in order to take upon Himself the garment of humanity, and in order to meet the penalty of human sin on human ground; but He did not cease to be deity. Along with Colossians 1, Hebrews 1 and 2, and John 1, this is one of the outstanding passages relating to the doctrine of the incarnation.

The other passage, Philippians 3, provides an insight into the driving motive in the life of Paul. His amazing devotion and unflagging zeal place him among the great leaders of history who have devoted their lives to a cause in which they believed utterly. To him, however, all of life was summed up in Christ. To "gain" Him, to "know" Him, to "be found" in Him, to attain the goal set in Him engaged all of Paul's attention. Philippians depicts a totalitarian life in Christ.

## Results of the Pauline Imprisonment

The outcome of the period of imprisonment is not difficult to assess, even though there may be some questions as to whether Paul were released or not. In spite of his confinement at Caesarea and at Rome, Paul's ministry was not ended. Through his assistants and friends, who are mentioned in the salutations to his epistles, he maintained constant communication with the churches. The enforced retirement provided more time for prayer and for contemplation, out of which came the priceless revelation of the Prison Epistles. His appeal to Caesar brought Christianity directly to the attention of the Roman government and compelled the civil authorities to pass upon its legality. If it was to be allowed as a *religio licita,* a permitted cult, the persecution of it would be illegal, and its security would be assured. If, on the other hand, it were adjudged to be a *religio illicita,* a forbidden cult, then the ensuing persecution would only advertise it and offer an opportunity for a demonstration of its power. In the decade of the Gentile mission from A.D. 46 to 56, and in the four years of Paul's imprisonment, the church came out from under the banner of Judaism and formed its own ranks as an independent movement. It was now ready for even greater advances in missionary expansion.

# Part IV

## THE PROBLEMS OF THE EARLY CHURCH

# THE PROBLEMS OF THE EARLY CHURCH

The Period of Consolidation
A.D. 60 to 100

---

The Institutional Church:
   The Pastoral Epistles

The Suffering Church: I Peter

The Break from Judaism: Hebrews

The Growing Heresies: II Peter;
   Jude; I, II, III, John

The Expectant Church: Revelation

# THE INSTITUTIONAL CHURCH:

# THE PASTORAL EPISTLES

# THE INSTITUTIONAL CHURCH:
# THE PASTORAL EPISTLES

Background

I Timothy
        Timothy's Biography
        Outline
        Content

Titus
        Background
        Outline
        Content

II Timothy
        Background
        Outline
        Content

Evaluation

# CHAPTER XVIII

# The Institutional Church: The Pastoral Epistles

## Background

No single consecutive history is available which gives in written form the fortunes of the church from the close of the book of Acts to the end of the first century. Only the individual books of the canon, with such additional hints as may be gleaned from the writings of the early church fathers, can supply any knowledge of events in this period. The uncertainty of placing exactly the dates and places of origin of these writings adds to the problem, so that a consistent picture of this era is almost impossible to reconstruct.

A definite change took place after the imprisonment of Paul. The man himself was different; for although he was unready to quit the ardent pursuit of his calling, as Philippians showed (Phil. 3:12), time was against him. In Philemon he described himself as "Paul the aged" (Phm. 9), and in Philippians he indicated that death might not be far distant (Phil. 1:20, 21). He was relying increasingly upon the aid of his younger associates, who were still free and better able than he to carry on the work of preaching.

The Pastoral Epistles, I Timothy, Titus, and II Timothy, belong at this stage in his career. Their genuineness has been disputed because of the differences between them and the general body of Pauline literature in vocabulary, in style, and in content. They still bear Paul's name, and their connection with his known biography is sufficiently strong to warrant their acceptance, since his vocabulary and style may vary with age and circumstances. There is a marked difference in both between the Prison Epistles and the Travel Epistles, so that a further difference between the others and the Pastoral Epistles is not surprising.

The biographical data which they supply seemingly indicate that Paul must have been acquitted on his first hearing before the emperor and that he enjoyed thereafter a short period of free ministry. His original plan had been to deposit the offering of the Gentile churches at Jerusalem, and then to hasten westward in order to strengthen the church in Rome, from which he would proceed to Spain. Four years at least had elapsed since he had been the master of his own plans, but finally he was released. The allusions to his movements in the Pastorals bear no relation to the account given in Acts, and in many particulars do not correspond with it at all. The inevitable deduction is that the three epistles must have been written later, when Paul was traveling again.

The chronological relations of the Pastorals to the Prison Epistles seem clear from their reference to Paul's companions. Many of these are identical with those of the Prison Epistles, but are located in places which show that they had left Paul's immediate vicinity. Timothy had been left at Ephesus while Paul was enroute to Macedonia (I Tim. 1:3), whereas on the last trip that Timothy took with Paul the order of procedure was from Macedonia to Asia (Acts 20:4-6), and Timothy did not remain in Ephesus. Demas had deserted Paul (II Tim. 4:10), whereas the Prison Epistles included him among the group at Rome (Phm. 24). Titus was left in Crete (Titus 1:5), and then went to Dalmatia (II Tim. 4:10); but on none of the journeys in Acts did Paul go to Crete, nor did he have Titus with him when he finally did go there during the voyage to Rome. Mark was in Asia (II Tim. 4:11) where Paul had recommended him in one of the Asian letters (Col. 4:10). Luke was still with him (II Tim. 4:11). Tychicus had gone on his errand to Ephesus (II Tim. 4:12). Paul himself had visited Ephesus (I Tim. 1:3), Crete (Titus 1:5), Nicopolis (Titus 3:12), Corinth (II Tim. 4:20), Miletus (4:20), and Troas (4:13), and was presently located in Rome (II Tim. 1:17). He was in prison (II Tim. 1:16) and was quite sure that the end of his life was not far away (II Tim. 4:6, 7). Altogether the situation was very different from that described by the Prison Epistles.

Within the range of the Pastoral Epistles there was probably some lapse of time. I Timothy pictures Paul as traveling and active, counseling his young lieutenant concerning his pastoral duties. Titus is quite similar in its outlook. II Timothy, however, is definitely a terminus, for Paul evidently was confident that he would not survive the winter (II Tim. 4:21). His first hearing, at which nobody defended him, had ended favorably (4:17); but accusers had become more vicious (4:14), and his condemnation and execution would be only a matter of time. The temper of Nero was very uncertain, and the chances of further clemency from him would be small.

The Pastorals belong together. If vocabulary and style can be used as a criterion for estimating their relationship to each other, they certainly must have been written by the same man and under the same general circumstances. They are, therefore, a fair basis for judging the state of the church in the seventh decade of the Christian era.

# I Timothy

Assuming that Paul was acquitted in A.D. 60 or 61 after his appeal to the emperor, he resumed his missionary activities. Contrary to his original expectations (Acts 20:38), the way was open for him to revisit the Asian churches. There had been some defection among them, for Paul counseled Timothy to "charge certain men not to teach a different doctrine, neither to give heed to fables and endless genealogies . . ." (I Tim. 1:3, 4). They had desired to be teachers of the law, though they were inexperienced and untaught in its mysteries (1:7). In addition to those who were intellectually confused stood those who were morally abandoned, such as Hymenaeus and Alexander (1:20), who had been put under stringent discipline. Profitless argument (1:6) and spiritual shipwreck had followed these trends.

The organization of the church had increased in complexity. Offices had become fixed and were sought by some as affording desirable eminence, so that the prestige of the office rather than its usefulness became the chief objective. Bishops, deacons, and elders are all mentioned, though probably the first and third of these classes may be identical.[1] Widows who were supported by the church were "enrolled," and they assumed some responsibility for the social service of the church (5:9). The services had certain regular features: prayer with uplifted hands (2:8), modesty and unobtrusiveness on the part of the women (2:11), reading, preaching, and teaching (4:13), the laying on of hands to confer a spiritual gift (4:14). As the second and third generations of believers arose the theology of the church was increasingly taken for granted and became decreasingly vital. Wrangling and argument developed over points of difference; heresy became a growingly imminent danger.

## Timothy's Biography

Timothy himself is an interesting study. Born in Lystra of a Greek father and of a Jewish mother, he was brought up in the Jewish faith and was taught the Scriptures from childhood. Paul made him an understudy in his second journey (Acts 16:1-3), and Timothy remained with him ever after. He shared in the evangelization of Macedonia and Achaia and aided Paul during the three years of preaching at Ephesus, where he became thoroughly acquainted with the city and with the needs of the local church. He was one of the delegates appointed to Jerusalem (Acts 20:4) and probably went with Paul all

---

1. Cf. Acts 20:17 and 28. The persons mentioned belonged to Ephesus.

the way back to that city. He was with Paul in Rome during the first imprisonment, for his name appears in the headings of Colossians (1:1) and of Philemon (1). After the release he traveled with Paul and evidently was left at Ephesus to straighten out the tangle that had developed there, while Paul went on to visit the churches in Macedonia. At the end of Paul's life he joined him at Rome (II Tim. 4:11, 21), and himself suffered imprisonment (Heb. 13:23), from which he was later released.

Timothy was a trustworthy but not a forceful character. He gave the impression of immaturity, although he must have been at least thirty years of age when Paul assigned him to the pastorate at Ephesus (I Tim. 4:12). He was timid (II Tim. 1:6, 7) and was subject to stomach trouble (I Tim. 5:23). The epistles which bear his name were intended to encourage him and to strengthen him for the tremendous task which Paul had bequeathed to him.

## Outline

### I TIMOTHY: ADVICE TO A YOUNG PREACHER

| | |
|---|---|
| I. Salutation | 1:1, 2 |
| II. Preamble | 1:3-17 |
| The Emergency at Ephesus | 1:3-11 |
| The Experience of Paul | 1:12-17 |
| III. The Official Commission | 1:18-4:5 |
| Its Purpose | 1:18-20 |
| Concerning Prayer | 2:1-8 |
| Concerning Worship by Women | 2:9-15 |
| Concerning the Office of Bishop | 3:1-7 |
| Concerning the Office of Deacon | 3:8-13 |
| Parenthesis | 3:14-16 |
| Concerning Apostasy | 4:1-5 |
| IV. The Personal Admonitions | 4:6-6:19 |
| Concerning Personal Conduct | 4:6-16 |
| Concerning Relationships with Groups | 5:1-6:2 |
| Widows | 5:1-16 |
| Elders | 5:17-19 |
| Backsliders | 5:20-25 |
| Bondslaves | 6:1, 2 |
| False Teachers | 6:3-8 |
| Avaricious Persons | 6:9-10 |
| Concerning Personal Confession | 6:11-16 |
| Concerning Use of Wealth | 6:17-19 |
| V. Concluding Salutation | 6:20-21 |

## Content

An integrated outline of this epistle is difficult to achieve because of its conversational style and because of its intensely personal tone. Some sentences seem irrelevant to their context, such as the injunction to "be no longer a drinker of water" in 5:23. These are just the sort of sayings that one might expect in casual conversation where the speaker interjects them as he thinks of them without planning a formal essay. The preamble (1:3-17) sketches the emergency for which Paul had left Timothy at Ephesus. He recalls for Timothy his own experience, which serves as a pattern of the call to the ministry. He reminds Timothy frequently of the responsibility of this calling (1:18, 4:6, 12, 16, 5:21, 6:11, 20), as if to keep him from quitting a difficult task. The official commission, introduced by the phrase, "This charge I commit unto thee . . ." (1:18), deals with matters of organizational importance in the church. The corporate devotional, official, and doctrinal problems are aired and pastoral administrative policies are outlined. Under the section on personal admonitions (4:6-6:19) Paul outlines the relation of the preacher to his own ministry and to the groups in the congregation, showing how to deal with each one of them. The final appeal to Timothy as a man of God is a classic, and in the four imperatives, *flee, follow, fight, keep* (6:11, 12, 14), Paul sketched the elements of personal ministerial life.

# Titus

## Background

In order of time Titus followed I Timothy. Paul, having left Ephesus, went to Macedonia and perhaps sailed thence to Crete, where he had been a visitor on his voyage to Rome. On this occasion he spent some time there, but left Titus to complete the establishment of the church and to rectify its errors. One wonders whether Paul felt that his time was short and that he wanted to return to Ephesus, for he spoke of sending Tychicus to Crete (3:12) at a later date. His ultimate goal was Nicopolis (probably in Epirus), where he planned to winter.

The situation in Crete was discouraging. The church was unorganized, and its members were quite careless in behavior. If the injunctions of chapter 2 are any indication of what the churches needed, the men were lax and careless, the older women were gossips and wine-bibbers, and the young women were idle and flirtatious. Perhaps the preaching of the gospel of grace had given the Cretans the impression that salvation by faith was unrelated to an industrious and ethical life. Six times (1:16, 2:7, 14, 3:1, 8, 14) in this short epistle good works are urged upon Christians. Although Paul says that salvation cannot be earned by good works (3:5), he affirms with equal vigor that believers must be careful to maintain good works.

The disturbance in Crete had been caused by a combination of the ethical laxity which sprang from the natural tendencies of the Cretans (1:12, 13), accentuated by disputation over Jewish fables and commandments which were promoted by a Judaizing group (1:10) who were godless (1:16), unruly (1:10), divisive (1:11), and mercenary (1:11). These teachers differed from those that troubled the Galatians because their error was moral perversity, whereas that of the Galatians was stringent legalism. Both are condemned by this epistle.

Both I Timothy and Titus were written to counsel an understudy who was working out the problems of a difficult pastorate. Titus, the recipient of this epistle, had been an acquaintance and associate of Paul for fifteen years or more. He was a Gentile convert of the early days in Antioch, whose conversion was so convincing that he served as Exhibit A of the uncircumcised Gentile believers when Paul and Barnabas went up for the conference at Jerusalem (Gal. 2:1, 3). He must have been with Paul during his third journey, for he acted as Paul's emissary during the trying days of the church's rebellion in Corinth, and he was successful in bringing them back to penitence and loyalty (II Cor. 7:6-16). He had traveled widely in Macedonia to collect the funds that Paul was raising and had his hearty approval (II Cor. 8:16, 19, 23). He may have been included in the "us" of Acts 20:5, though he is not mentioned by name anywhere in Acts. The last allusion to him in the New Testament states that he had gone to Dalmatia (II Tim. 4:10). He seems to have been a stronger character than Timothy and better able to cope with opposition.

### Outline

## TITUS: THE SOUND DOCTRINE

I. Salutation: The Source of Sound Doctrine 1:1-4

II. The Administration of Sound Doctrine   1:5-16
    The Appointment of Elders   1:5-9
    The Exposure of False Teachers   1:10-16

III. The Preaching of Sound Doctrine   2:1-15

| | |
|---|---|
| Application | 2:1-10 |
|     To aged men | |
|     To aged women | |
|     To young women | |
|     To young men | |
|     To himself | |
|     To slaves | |
| Definition | 2:11-15 |
| IV. Counseling by Sound Doctrine | 3:1-11 |
| V. Concluding Salutations | 3:12-15 |

## Content

The general content of Titus is like that of I Timothy, except for a stronger emphasis on creedal formulation. In two passages Paul states the closest approach to a formulated creed in the whole New Testament (2:11-14, 3:4-7). Note the elements contained in these passages:

1. The personality of God (2:11, 3:6).
2. The qualities of His love and grace (2:11, 3:4).
3. His title of Saviour (2:10, 3:4).
4. The saviourhood of Christ (2:13, 3:6).
5. The Holy Spirit (3:5).
6. The implication of the Triune Being of God (3:5, 6).
7. The essential deity of Christ (2:13).
8. The vicarious atonement of Christ (2:14).
9. The universality of salvation (2:11).
10. Salvation by grace, not by works (3:5).
11. The incoming of the Holy Spirit (3:5).
12. Justification by faith (3:7).
13. Sanctification (purification) of His own people (2:14).
14. Separation from evil (2:12).
15. Inheritance of eternal life (3:7).
16. The return of Christ (2:13).

The foregoing points constitute a fair digest of New Testament theology.

Titus is a good summary of the doctrinal teaching of the church as it emerged into the institutional stage. Although it was written to a pioneer missionary, he represented a church that had passed the pioneer era and that had settled policies and faith. The word "sound" implies

351

that a recognized standard of doctrine had been acknowledged, t
which correct life and teaching must conform.

## II Timothy

### Background

Whether Paul ever fulfilled his desire to visit Spain is not know
Clement of Rome (A.D. 95) said in his letter that Paul ". . .taug
righteousness to all the world, and when he had reached the limits
the West he gave his testimony before the rulers . . ."[2]  If Clemen
was writing from Rome, it would be as strange for him to refer
Rome as "the bound of the west" as for a man living in Chicago
call that city the western boundary of the United States.  Clement d
not mention Spain, and it is possible that he was simply surmisin
what Paul had done on the assumption that he had fulfilled his avowe
intention.  It would be interesting to know whether Paul actually d
preach there, and whether the early churches in North Africa an
Britain might have been founded by his converts.

Any trip to Spain at this time, then, must be purely speculativ
and its appearance on the map is at best a probability.  If Paul
travels follow rigidly the lines marked out in the Pastorals, he stoppe
at Corinth (4:20), where Erastus chose to remain, at Miletus, wher
he left Trophimus sick, and at Troas (4:13).  The exact order
these steps is not prescribed by the narrative.  He did not stop
Ephesus, but sent Tychicus thither.  He must have been arreste
suddenly and taken to Rome, for he left his plans unfinished.  Th
books which he dropped at Troas he may have intended to retrie
later, but he had no opportunity to do so.  The place of his arre
is uncertain; it might have been Troas or Nicopolis.

The cause of his arrest is also uncertain.  If Alexander the coppe
smith mentioned in II Timothy 4:14 be identical with the Alexande
of Acts 19:33, one might venture a guess that he was a Jewish meta
lurgist who was disgruntled with Paul on two counts: Paul's preach
ing of free grace for Gentiles, and the decline of the trade in shrine
at Ephesus because of Paul's vigorous inroads into heathenism.  The sit
uation at Ephesus had been tense.  Paul spoke in II Corint'.ians 1:8
"our affliction which befell *us* in Asia, that we were weighed dow
exceedingly, beyond our power, insomuch that we despaired even
life."  In Acts 20:19 he referred to "plots of the Jews" which had bee
formed there.  Perhaps Alexander, still rankling over Paul's escap

---

2. I Clement V, 7. See Kirsopp Lake, *The Apostolic Fathers* (London: Willia
Heinemann, 1919), Vol. I, p. 17.

from Ephesus and over the loss of trade which his fellow workmen had suffered, denounced him to the Roman authorities and finally brought about his condemnation. Alexander was known to Timothy also, and Paul's counsel to beware of him implies that he was operating where Timothy was, perhaps in Ephesus.

The general tone of the Pastoral Epistles reveals a church that was fighting for its life against the malicious jealousy of a frustrated Judaism and against the corrupt indifference of a decadent paganism. Paul, the representative of the passing generation of missionary pioneers, was delegating his responsibilities to younger and more vigorous assistants, some of whom, like Titus and Timothy, were worthy successors, and others of whom, like Demas, were recreant (II Tim. 4:10). II Timothy was his last message to his helpers and friends before he passed off the scene.

## Outline

### II TIMOTHY: THE FAREWELL MESSAGE

## Content

The content of this last epistle is an intermingling of personal sentiment and of administrative policy, of reminiscence and of instruction, of sadness and of confidence. Its main purpose was to strengthen Timothy for the arduous task which Paul himself was about to relinquish. He laid down the pastoral pattern by first reminding Timothy of his own personal experience, and by including him in it: "who saved *us,* and called *us* with a holy calling . . . according to his own purpose and grace" (II Timothy 1:9, italics ours). With this calling in mind, he urged Timothy to undertake his problems as a soldier goes to war (2:3), trusting his general to plan the campaign, and serving wholeheartedly and uncomplainingly in the ranks wherever he is needed. In personal life and in public relations with the church he should always be the Lord's servant, not contentious, but ready to help all men to understand the truth of God.

The picture of the last days, like the similar passage in I Timothy 4:1-3, was a piece of prophecy characterizing the conditions to which the church might look forward. The antidote that Paul prescribed for the influx of evil was the knowledge of the Scriptures, "which are able to make thee wise unto salvation through faith which is in Christ Jesus" (II Tim. 3:15).

The final charge (4:1-6) is a classic, and should be studied carefully by every candidate for the ministry.

## Evaluation

The Pastoral Epistles as a group are the most valuable source extant for the understanding of the life of the church in the transition period between the close of the pioneer days and the emergence of the institutional organization that is portrayed in the Epistles of Ignatius. Two or three tendencies are worthy of notice.

For one, the growth of heresy is more apparent. Opposition to truth and doctrinal divergences appear in all of the Pauline Epistles. Galatians attacks legalism; I Corinthians states that some did not believe in the resurrection of the body; Colossians reflects the inroads of some philosophic cult. These, however, were sporadic and local, with the possible exception of the Judaizing tendency, but even that varied in its character and in its intensity in different places. In the Pastorals these same errors appear, but they are intensified and constitute a future menace which the younger preachers must meet.

Because of this menace, there is a greater stress on formulated creed in the Pastorals than in the earlier writings. The specific doctrinal formulas in Titus, the injunction to "hold the pattern of sound words which thou hast heard from me" (II Tim. 1:13), and the frequent sentences of creedal form (I Tim. 1:15, 2:3-5, 3:16, 4:10, II Tim. 1:10, 2:8, 3:16) impress the reader that the Pastorals were written to a church that was beginning to put its faith into articulate terms. Such creedal expressions were current, for the formula "Faithful is the saying" is used to introduce a number of them as if they were commonly employed in the oral teaching of the church (I Tim. 1:15, 3:1, 4:9; II Tim. 2:11, Titus 3:8). The phrase "sound doctrine" occurs frequently also (I Tim. 1:10, 6:3, II Tim. 1:13, 4:3, Titus 1:9, 2:1, 2:8). The word means literally "healthful" and is usually connected with good works as well as with correct principles. Creed and life are never divorced in the Bible.

Although the self-consciousness of the church as an institution had begun to emerge (I Tim. 3:15), it had not become a fixed hierarchy or a machine organization. Spiritual vitality and conduct were more important than ritual and politics, and the missionary motive was still keen. In spite of incipient persecution and heresies, the church was still growing apace.

# THE SUFFERING CHURCH: I PETER

# THE SUFFERING CHURCH: I PETER

Background
Author
Outline
Content
Evaluation

# CHAPTER XIX

# The Suffering Church: I Peter

## Background

Thus far in the New Testament little has been said about the relation between Christianity and the Roman government. The few political references in the Gospels deal with the local rule of the Herods rather than with the imperial system, with the exception of Jesus' famous utterance: ". . . Render therefore unto Caesar the things that are Caesar's; and unto God the things that are God's" (Matt. 22:21). Acts invariably represents the contacts between Christianity and the Roman officials in a favorable light, but it gives the impression that those contacts were few. The epistles of Paul do not discuss political theory and merely enjoin the Christians to be subject to the powers that be, because they are ordained of God (Rom. 13:1-6).

This comparative silence concerning political relations which under a totalitarian government could hardly have been unimportant may be explained in several ways. First, Christianity was primarily spiritual, not political. "My kingdom is not of this world," said Jesus to Pilate: "if my kingdom were of this world, then would my servants fight . . ." (John 18:36). The application of the principles which Jesus taught had political consequences, but neither He nor the apostles were revolutionists or agitators.

Again, as has been observed, Christianity grew up within Judaism, which was a *religio licita,* a cult permitted and protected by the state. Rome's policy was tolerance wherever religious observances did not conflict with the state's claims. As long as the Christians created no disturbance, they were simply ignored.

The Christians who did come into contact with Rome in the earlier part of the first century left a favorable impression upon the Roman authorities. Paul stood on his rights as a citizen on at least two occasions and demanded recognition for them (Acts 16:36-39, 22:24-29) but he could also say that he had never been guilty of subversive activities or of raising insurrection (24:12). The church had followed a policy of peaceful penetration of society with the message of Christ.

Toward the close of the sixth decade the situation began to change. The Christians had separated from Judaism and were recognized as a

THE PROVINCES OF ASIA MINOR
THE SEVEN CHURCHES OF ASIA

different group.  Their firm adherence to belief in an invisible God and in a risen Christ excited the suspicion and the contempt of the public, while their talk of a coming judgment and overthrow of the existing world created misunderstanding and hatred.  The reaction against them in Rome under Nero was the product of this popular dislike, activated by Nero's spiteful accusations.  The close of the Pastoral Epistles shows that Paul's death marked a turn in the policy of the government from casual tolerance to hostile criticism.

When the churches began to realize this change in attitude, they became apprehensive of what might befall them.  They could not organize resistance, for by so doing they would violate their own principle of peaceful obedience to the government, and would only give occasion for further charges against them.  Were they faced with extinction? What would the outcome be?  Would the brutalities of Nero be duplicated in the provinces?  They looked to their leaders to answer their questions for them.

I Peter was written in reply to this situation as it affected the churches of northern Asia Minor in the provinces of Pontus, Galatia, Cappadocia, Asia, and Bithynia.  Two of these provinces, Pontus and Cappadocia, are not mentioned in Acts among those evangelized by Paul; Bithynia he attempted to reach, but was forbidden to do so (Acts 16:7).  Galatia and Asia he did evangelize, but the way in which these provinces are listed gives the impression that Peter was addressing only those Christians living in the northern sections.

The origin and constituency of these churches are not well known. Men from Cappadocia and Pontus were present on the day of Pentecost (Acts 2:9) and may have returned to their homes with the news of the coming of the Messiah and of the outpouring of the Holy Spirit.  It is possible that Peter had preached in these regions, for he had worked with the church at Antioch (Gal. 2:11), and had traveled in the Mediterranean world while Paul was preaching during the European campaign (I Cor. 9:5).  While there is no statement on record that Peter founded or even visited these churches, there is nothing to preclude his doing so.  Perhaps Paul refrained from undertaking a mission in these provinces because he knew that somebody else had already been there.

The epistle is addressed to "the elect who are sojourners of the Dispersion . . ." (1:1).  This salutation, together with the references to the Gentiles (2:12, 4:3), conveys the impression that the "elect" were converts from the Dispersion and that these groups were predominantly Jewish in character.  The question may legitimately be raised whether these terms are literal or figurative. "Gentile" had come to mean not only non-Jewish in the racial sense, but also in the spiritual sense. To a Jew, a Gentile was a man who did not know the true God. When the Christians took over Jewish phraseology, "Gentile" thus became the equivalent of the modern term "heathen." This use of the word in I Peter is confirmed by one or two other passages. I Peter 1:14 commands the hearers to set their hope on Christ "as children of obedience, not fashioning yourselves according to your former lusts in *the time of* your ignorance." Those who had been brought up as Jews with the knowledge of the Scriptures could hardly have been called ignorant. Again Peter spoke of the "vain manner of life handed down from your fathers" (1:18). He said that they were "called . . . out of darkness" (2:9), and in the second passage where the Gentiles are mentioned, he told them that "the time past may suffice to have wrought the desire of the Gentiles, and to have walked in lasciviousness, lusts, winebibbings, revellings, carousings, and abominable idolatries" (4:3). While these churches, like those that Paul established, may have contained a large nucleus of Jews of the Dispersion and of proselytes, there seems to be no doubt that they included Gentiles also. The language of Peter may apply to either for the most part; but the allusion to "abominable idolatries" (4:3) demands some Gentile background.

The ominous shadow of persecution was the occasion for this letter. Suffering is one of the keynotes of the epistle, being mentioned no less than sixteen times. The churches have "been put to grief in manifold trials" (1:6); some of their members were "suffering wrongfully" (2:19); there was a possibility that they might have to "suffer for righteousness' sake" (3:14), even for doing what is right (3:17). Darker days might be ahead; for a "fiery trial" was coming upon them in which they would be classed with murderers, thieves, and evildoers. Peter urged them not to be ashamed if they "suffer as Christians" (4:12-16). These sufferings were not to be exclusively their misfortune, for Christians in the whole world would be affected (5:9). All must bear these trials as bravely as they can. The letter was a warning and an encouragement preparatory to the coming emergency.

## Author

Simon Peter, the author of the epistle, is the best known of the apostles of Christ. Like most of his comrades, he was a Galilean, a fisherman by trade, who was brought to Christ early in His ministry (John 1:41, 42). Simon was his given name; Peter (Rock) was a nickname conferred on him by Jesus who predicted that his impulsive and vacillating nature would become as stable and as reliable as a rock. Simon left the fishing boats at Jesus' summons (Mark 1:16-20) and joined His company as He toured Galilee. He was a natural leader (Mark 1:29) and often was spokesman for the twelve (Mark 8:29, John 6:67, 68, Matt. 19:27). Jesus placed him in the inner circle of the disciples (Mark 5:37, 9:2, 14:33) and gave him special attention on several occasions (Luke 5:10, Matt. 16:17, Luke 22:31, 32, John 13:6-10). He was impulsive, vacillating, and selfish, hasty in action and quick in recoil. His denial of Jesus was not the result of premeditated malice but of sudden panic, of which later he repented bitterly (Matt. 26:69-75). Nevertheless there was in his soul a deep undercurrent of loyalty (John 13:36-38, 18:10, 15). He was deeply concerned over the disappearance of Jesus' body from the tomb (John 20:2-6), and rejoiced to see the risen Lord (John 21:7, 15-21).

*Peter's Character*

On the day of Pentecost Peter, in company with the others who shared in the prayer meeting, was filled with the Holy Spirit. Instantly he became the leader of the group. His sermon set the keynote for the new enterprise, and his preaching, healings, and discipline dominate the first five chapters of Acts. With the outbreak of persecution by the Sanhedrin he went farther afield into the coastal plain of Palestine and to Samaria and Antioch. With the passage of the years he traveled widely in an itinerant ministry much like Paul's. Tradition says that he was crucified head downward in Rome during the persecution under Nero, not later than A.D. 68.

I Peter states that it was written from "Babylon" (5:13). There are three possible interpretations of this location: (1) the historic Babylon in Mesopotamia, where there was a Jewish settlement until much later in the Christian era, and where Peter could well have founded a church; (2) a town in Egypt; and (3) a mystic name for Rome, by which Christians applied to it all the evil connotations that had been historically associated with the Babylon on the Euphrates, and by which they could vent their feelings without being detected.

There is no tradition that Peter had ever been in Babylon in Egypt, nor was it a place of sufficient importance to warrant his attention. Babylon on the Euphrates is a better possibility, since it was the home of many Jewish people from the captivity until the times of the Talmud. There is, however, no evidence that Peter was ever in this region, and though a number of commentators have favored his residence in the region of Babylon, their reasons are not very cogent.

Several facts seemingly lend support to the idea that "Babylon" meant Rome. John Mark, who was with Peter at the writing of the epistle, was in Rome at the time of Paul's imprisonment (Col. 4:10). The provinces are named in an order which hints that the messenger bearing the letter would make a circuit terminating in the west rather than in the east. If he were making his way back toward the source of the letter, Rome rather than Babylon would be a more logical end for his travels. Uniform patristic evidence places Peter in Rome at the end of his life. For these reasons, it seems wisest to conclude that the epistle was composed in Rome.

If this conclusion is correct, it does not imply that Peter had founded the church at Rome or that he had ministered there for any great length of time. Neither Acts nor Romans gives any hint that Peter had been in Rome prior to A.D. 60. If he did write from Rome, he was probably paying the city a casual visit in much the same way that he had called at Corinth at an earlier date.[1]

I Peter is much like the epistles of Paul in its general style, and resembles Romans and Ephesians in its language and structure. A Pauline influence on Peter would not be surprising, since both men had been acquainted with each other for years, and since Paul's influence on the thinking of Peter is affirmed in Galatians 2:11-21. Peter was familiar with Paul's epistles (II Pet. 3:15, 16). Furthermore, if Silvanus, Peter's amanuensis (5:12), is identical with Silas, Paul's associate and helper, Peter could easily have learned much concerning Paul's teaching from him.

In addition to the theme of suffering that pervades the epistle there is the counter-theme of "the true grace of God" (5:12). Suffering should be met with grace and should develop grace in the individual. The term appears in the greeting (1:2), as the summary of the message of the prophets (1:10), as the expectation of the future (1:13), as the pattern for conduct under abuse (2:19, 20, Greek text), as the fulness of the blessings that come in answer to prayer (3:7), as the equipment for spiritual service (4:10), and as the favor which God shows to those who wait on Him humbly (5:5).

---

1. For a thorough discussion of this question, see Paton J. Gloag, *Introduction to the Catholic Epistles* (Edinburgh; T. & T. Clark, 1887), pp. 144-160, and Elmer T. Merrill, *Essays in Early Christian History* (London: Macmillan & Co., Ltd., 1924), pp. 275-353.

## Outline

## Content

The personal experience of Peter with Christ is reflected in this epistle to his friends who were imperiled by impending persecutions. He had known the feeling of helplessness when he realized that Jesus was dead, but his hope had become living when Jesus rose (1:3). His reference to love for Christ (1:8) recalls Jesus' challenge to him, "Lovest thou me more than these?" (John 21:15 ff.), and His exhortation to "tend the flock of God" (5:2) is an echo of Jesus' injunction to him to do the same thing (John 21:15-17). The command, "gird yourselves with humility" (5:5) means "to put on a slave's apron," which recalls Jesus' girding Himself with a towel to wash the feet of the disciples (John 13:4). Five times he speaks of the sufferings of Christ (2:23, 3:18, 4:1, 4:13, 5:1) as if the scene of Gethsemane and the crucifixion left an indelible impression upon him.

One notable feature of the structure of the epistle is its use of imperatives. Beginning with 1:13, which follows the opening paragraph of

thanksgiving, there is a continuous chain of commands that runs all the
way to the end of the book.

| | | |
|---|---|---|
| 1. | Be sober | 1:13 |
| 2. | Set your hope . . . on grace | 1:13 |
| 3. | Be holy | 1:15 |
| 4. | Pass the time . . . in fear | 1:17 |
| 5. | Love one another | 1:23 |
| 6. | Long for the spiritual milk | 2:2 |
| 7. | Be subject to every ordinance of man | 2:13 |
| 8. | Honor all men | |
| 9. | Love the brotherhood | 2:17 |
| 10. | Fear God | |
| 11. | Honor the king | |
| 12. | Servants, be in subjection | 2:18 |
| 13. | Wives, be in subjection | 3:1 |
| 14. | Ye husbands, dwell with your wives . . . | 3:7 |
| 15. | Finally *be* ye all . . . | 3:8 |
| 16. | Fear not | 3:14 |
| 17. | Neither be ye troubled | 3:14 |
| 18. | Sanctify in your hearts | 3:15 |
| 19. | Arm yourselves | 4:1 |
| 20. | Be of sound mind | 4:7 |
| 21. | Be sober . . . | 4:7 |
| 22. | Think it not strange | 4:12 |
| 23. | Rejoice | 4:13 |
| 24. | Let none of you suffer | 4:15 |
| 25. | Let him not be ashamed | 4:16 |
| 26. | Let him glorify God | 4:16 |
| 27. | Let them . . . commit their souls | 4:19 |
| 28. | Tend the flock of God | 5:2 |
| 29. | Be subject unto the elders | 5:5 |
| 30. | Gird yourselves with humility | 5:5 |
| 31. | Humble yourselves | 5:6 |
| 32. | Be sober | 5:8 |
| 33. | Be watchful | 5:8 |
| 34. | Withstand the devil | 5:9 |

These numerous imperatives give the epistle a directness and an
informality which resemble a preaching style. Peter was speaking
from his heart, not writing a formal essay. All of the stronger and
better qualities of his nature, the result of being born "again unto a
living hope by the resurrection of Jesus Christ from the dead" (1:3),
appear in this work. It is Peter at his regenerate best.

## Evaluation

The chief value of the epistle is that it shows Christians how to live out their redemption in a hostile world. Salvation may involve suffering, but it brings a hope also, as the grace of God is amplified in the individual life.

The paragraph in 3:18-22 has always been a difficult passage to interpret. Does it mean that Christ preached in the unseen world of spirits between His death and His resurrection? If so, did He offer them a "second chance," or did He simply announce to them the results of His Passion? Does this passage mean that these "spirits in prison" were the disembodied persons who died in the Flood? Does it mean that baptism in itself can bring salvation? The passage bristles with questions to which innumerable answers have been given. Every commentator has his own solution.

The language does not imply any doctrine of a "second chance." The word "preach" means literally "to announce." It is not the word which means to preach the gospel as an invitation to come to God. If in the realm of spirit Christ visited the unseen world, He did so to declare the result of His Passion. As to baptism, Noah and his sons were not saved *because* of the water, but *through* it. The water itself was their greatest peril, but in obedience to God they were carried through it. The water of baptism does not save men. It is rather by passing through the water as emblematic of death and of resurrection that the believer enters into a life of glory. As Peter states in 2:24, baptism recalls the atonement of Christ, "who his own self bare our sins in his body upon the tree, that we, having died unto sins, might live unto righteousness." The passage is really a parallel of Paul's figure in Romans 6.

# THE BREAK FROM JUDAISM: HEBREWS

# THE BREAK FROM JUDAISM: HEBREWS

Background
Author
Date
Outline
Content
Evaluation

# CHAPTER XX

# The Break From Judaism: Hebrews

## *Background*

The rapid growth of the Gentile church which was independent of Judaism both by heritage and by conviction could only result in a sharp and final separation between the two. The members of the Jewish church still clung to the observances of the law, though they trusted for their salvation in Jesus, the Messiah. The tension between Jews and Gentiles which appeared all through the first thirty years of Christian history became stronger as the church rivaled the synagogue in its number of adherents and in its growth through the world. Jewish rejection of the Christian message finally came to the point where even Paul abandoned any hope of national repentance. Although he had said, "I could wish that I myself were anathema from Christ for my brethren's sake, my kinsmen according to the flesh . . ." (Rom. 9:3), he turned from them and declared, "Be it known therefore unto you, that this salvation of God is sent unto the Gentiles: they will also hear" (Acts 28:28).

This breach was widened by two other factors. From the very first, when Peter had said unto a Jewish audience in Jerusalem, "To you (Jews) is the promise, and to your children, and to all that are afar off, *even* as many as the Lord our God shall call unto him" (Acts 2:39), the universality of the gospel had been proclaimed. The Jew was exclusive, and the idea of uniting with the Gentiles in a bond of common fellowship which did not involve their becoming complete Jews was repugnant to him. The second factor that made the breach complete was the fall of Jerusalem in A.D. 70. Judaism as a religion and Judaism as a political system were one; and when the political system fell so that the Jew was without a land, a temple, and without a government of his own, he lost much of his essential system. When Judaism was forced to relinquish these means of outward expression, it became solely the worship of God through the study of the law, and consequently its legalism was strengthened more than ever.

For Jewish Christians this tension posed some unusual problems. All Christians believed in the divine authority of the Old Testament Scriptures and used them as the basis for their faith and practice. How, now, should those Scriptures be interpreted? Should they follow the rabbis into a static interpretation, or should they, as Christians, view the entire body of writings in the light of the new revelation of Jesus the Messiah?

What stand should they take on the national situation? If they believed the words of Jesus, who said in His Olivet discourse that not one stone of Jerusalem should be left upon another (Matt. 24:2, Luke 19:41-44), they could only accept the overthrow of the city as the inevitable judgment of God for the rejectors of the King. If, however, they turned from the law to grace, and from Jerusalem as a center of worship to their own churches, they would be regarded as traitors by their countrymen who were loyal to the law. If they went back to legalism, they would be abandoning Christ and would lose all that He came to bring.

It was not an easy decision to make, and many of them, both in Palestine and in the Dispersion, wavered in their thinking. The decision was important, because it affected the fate of the church. Jewish Christians had, on the whole, a more solid training than the Gentile Christians and consequently possessed a more intelligent faith, since they already knew the Scriptures. Their loyalty or their defection would have a powerful influence on the outcome of the missionary enterprise. For their own sake, and for the sake of the growing church, they must be shown that God was about to do a new thing, and that they must advance with Him in faith rather than draw back.

The book of Hebrews was written to meet this dilemma. Its exact destination is unknown; for it contains no formal salutation, and in the oldest manuscripts its title is simply "To the Hebrews." The people to whom it was sent were schooled thoroughly in the Old Testament and in its sacrificial system. They had been acquainted with the gospel and had heard it preached by men who were eyewitnesses of His life and who possessed the gifts of the Spirit (Heb. 2:3, 4). They themselves had been staunch believers, enduring emotional and physical persecution for their new faith (10:32-34). They were not novices.

Their geographical location is a matter of dispute, and depends largely upon the interpretation of one phrase in the thirteenth chapter (13:24): "They of Italy salute you." Does it mean that the author was *in* Italy, sending greetings back to these Hebrew Christians, wherever they were? Or does it mean that they lived in Italy, and that their friends who were *from* Italy in the sense of traveling or residing away from home, sent greetings to the homeland? The preposition *apo*, translated "from," would support the latter conclusion.

On this slim basis and because the earliest known quotation of this epistle occurs in I Clement, which was written from Rome, some scholars have concluded that it was sent to the Hebrew Christians in Rome who were uncertain whether to persist in their profession of Christ or to go back to the synagogue.[1] The older theory is that it was written to the Jewish Christians of Palestine for the same reason.[2]

## Author

An even greater puzzle is the authorship. The writer does not give his own name, nor does he refer to any circumstances or connections that would identify him with absolute certainty. A study of the epistle shows that he was a man of high literary ability, with a style that approached more nearly that of classical Greek than that of any other writer of the New Testament. He was not an immediate disciple of Christ (2:3). He was well versed in the Old Testament, which he quoted from the Septuagint version. He may have been a Jew, since he frequently used the first person plural in addressing his Jewish audience. He was a friend of Timothy and probably belonged to the Pauline circle (Heb. 13:23). His use of the quotation from Habakkuk 2:4, "The righteous shall live by his faith," accords with Paul's usage in Romans 1:17 and Galatians 3:11.

Several hypotheses have been advanced concerning his identity, though none has behind it the same unanimity of tradition that supports the Lukan authorship of the Third Gospel and Acts. The Eastern church from early days considered the epistle to be the product of Paul, but probably indirectly. Eusebius stated that Clement of Alexandria claimed that Paul wrote it in Hebrew and that Luke translated it into Greek.[3] Origen frequently quoted it as Paul's and admitted that it was generally received as his; but when giving his own opinion said, "If then, any church considers this epistle as coming from Paul, let it be commended for this, for neither did those ancient men deliver it as such without cause. But who it was that really wrote the epistle,

---

1. E. J. Goodspeed: *An Introduction to the New Testament* (Chicago: University of Chicago Press, n. d.), pp. 253-259; James Moffatt, *Introduction to the Literature of the New Testament* (New York: Charles Scribner's Sons, 1910), pp. 446, 447.
2. B. F. Westcott, *The Epistle to the Hebrews* (Second Edition, London: Macmillan and Co., 1892). P. xli.
3. Eusebius, *Historia Ecclesiae* VI, 14, quoting Clement's *Hypotyposes*.

God only knows."[4] The general line of argument and the style and diction of the book are not Pauline.

Many other names have been suggested for the author, chief among whom are Barnabas, to whom Tertullian attributed it,[5] and Apollos, a guess of Martin Luther. In favor of Barnabas are the facts that he was a Jew, a Levite, a friend of Paul whose teaching must have resembled Paul's closely, and one who could minister to Jew and to Gentile alike. His long experience at teaching would fit with the character of the epistle, which is didactic. For Apollos there is no early tradition whatsoever. He too was a Jew, an Alexandrian learned in the Scriptures, and singularly successful in his ministry among Jews. He was a friend of Paul and was still active in his ministry toward the end of Paul's life (Titus 3:13).

In no hypotheses do the conclusions amount to final proof. One thing is certain: as Hayes says,[6] "If the authorship of this epistle is uncertain, its inspiration is indisputable."

### Date

The epistle was written during the lifetime of the second generation of Christians (2:1-4) and at a considerable interval after the conversion of the recipients (5:12). They had forgotten the "former days" (10:32) and their leaders had died (13:7). Timothy had been imprisoned (13:23), but was still living and had been liberated. The allusions to the priesthood imply that the temple was still standing, but the removal of Jewish institutions was not too far distant (12:27). Persecution was imminent (10:32-36, 12:4). The epistle seems to fit best into the situation of the late sixties, when the church at Rome was fearing persecution and when the fall of the Jewish commonwealth was imminent.

### Outline

The entire theme of the epistle is built around the word "better," which is used in a series of comparisons to show how God's revelation in Christ is superior to the revelation that came through the law, especially as the law was applied through the Levitical priesthood. The revelational quality and the validity of the law for its own time is not

---

4. Quoted from Origen by Eusebius, *op. cit.*, VI, 25.
5. Tertullian, *De Pudicitia*, XX.
6. D. A. Hayes, *The New Testament Epistles* (New York: The Methodist Book Concern, n. d.), p. 76.

denied at all; on the other hand, much of the argument of Hebrews is founded on the Old Testament. The new revelation in Christ has superseded the old; the coming of the substance has made the shadow obsolete.

In structure the book consists of the aforesaid series of comparisons, after each of which is a warning and an exhortation, usually contained in a parenthesis. It is like an oration which begins with a proposition, which proceeds with an argument applied periodically to the needs of the readers, and which ends with a tremendous climax. Except for the thirteenth chapter it is not at all epistolary in style and could better be described as a speech.

HEBREWS: THE EPISTLE OF BETTER THINGS

## Content

The foregoing argument was intended to encourage a group of people who were tempted to abandon their faith because of the pressure of persecution and because of their attachment to the older revelation of the law. The writer showed them that the same God who delivered the law to Moses by the hand of angels has since spoken historically in His Son, who has been made temporarily lower than the angels in order that He might enter perfectly into the sphere of human life as a participant in it (2:9, 10, 14-18). Because He is both divine and human, He is qualified to serve as a high priest, in which capacity He is superior to the Aaronic priesthood. Death cannot terminate His tenure (7:24), and His sphere of service is in the heavenly sanctuary, the very presence of God (9:11, 12). Furthermore, the sacrifice that he offers does not need to be repeated. He Himself is the offering as well as the priest, completely acceptable to God, potent to remove the guilt of transgressions under the law and under grace (9:15, 10:10, 19). The eternal salvation which He has thus purchased is attainable by faith, the same kind of faith that was exercised by the men of the Old Testament who were the spiritual leaders of their generation. This faith, applied under the conditions in which the readers were living, would bring them assurance, endurance, and the ultimate entrance into the unshaken kingdom.

Progressive warning may be found in the list of perils besetting the believers. Each of them is a more radical step away from faith than the one preceding it. First is the peril of neglect, characterized by the word "drift away" (2:1). It connotes indifference, not opposition. The second, the peril of unbelief, is epitomized in the quotation of Psalm 95, which in turn describes the attitude of the Israelites toward the promise of entrance into Palestine. By exaggerating the opposition before them and by ignoring the manifest power of God in their

376

previous experience they failed to claim their rightful heritage, and so lost the blessing which God had prepared for them. Coupled with unbelief and practically synonymous with it is the peril of disobedience. Unwillingness to obey the new revelation would be fatal to spiritual progress.

The peril of immaturity and the peril of rejection are much alike. Both have occasioned considerable theological controversy. The warnings seemingly indicate that once a man refuses to obey, or abandons his position of faith, he can never be restored (6:6, 10:26). Both passages refer to a deliberate and purposeful rejection of Christ, a wilful abandonment of truth, rather than to a sudden lapse or error which the doer himself might lament. Without minimizing the danger of carelessness, one may say that these warnings relate to voluntary apostasy rather than to unconscious decline. The last peril is climactic and involves point-blank refusal to heed God's revelation in the Son. "See that ye refuse not him that speaketh" (12:25). The reference is to the blood of Jesus, "which speaketh better things than that of Abel" (12:24) because it invites to salvation rather than invoking vengeance. If that voice be refused, doom is final.

Parallel with the warnings which appear periodically in the text are exhortations that add a positive quality to the argument. In the Greek text they are clearly marked by the use of the first person plural hortatory subjunctive, which is consistently translated in English "Let us . . ." The subjoined list will show how these exhortations are distributed in the book.

| | |
|---|---|
| 1. Let us fear . . . | 4:1 |
| 2. Let us therefore give diligence to enter | 4:11 |
| 3. Let us hold fast our confession | 4:14 |
| 4. Let us draw near . . . to the throne of grace | 4:16 |
| 5. Let us press on unto perfection | 6:1 |
| 6. Let us draw near | 10:22 |
| 7. Let us hold fast the confession of our faith | 10:23 |
| 8. Let us consider one another | 10:24 |
| 9. Let us . . . lay aside every weight | 12:1 |
| 10. Let us run the race | 12:1 |
| 11. Let us have grace | 12:28 |
| 12. Let us therefore go forth unto him | 13:13 |
| 13. Let us offer up sacrifice of praise | 13:15 |

With the exception of the first, which describes fear, a negative emotion, every one of these exhortations summons the believer to a higher stage of spiritual perfection, culminating in "Let us therefore go forth unto him without the camp, bearing his reproach," the final test of allegiance to Christ and to His Cross. Eight out of thirteen of these occur in the last three chapters, for with the conclusion of the argument the application is strengthened. The other five are connected with the severer warnings to offer a word of encouragement to what would otherwise be only a negative deterrent.

## Evaluation

The greatest single value of the book of Hebrews is its teaching on the present ministry and priesthood of Christ. There are many references in the New Testament to His ascension and to His place at the right hand of the Father, but with the exception of Romans 8:34 none of these explains what He is now doing. Hebrews, by its interpretation of the Messianic reference in Psalm 110:4, "Jehovah hath sworn, and will not repent: Thou art a priest forever, after the order of Melchizedek," has given a whole new ground of assurance to the believer in Christ. As the Aaronic priesthood by its sacrifices and intercession ministered to the Old Testament believer who obeyed the law, so Christ, in a fuller measure, though invisible, ministers now to those under grace. Those who witnessed the passing of the Jewish priesthood and who felt that with it a divinely ordained system of salvation had vanished, must have been greatly reassured by the teaching that this man "for ever hath his priesthood unchangeable" (7:24).

Hebrews is an excellent specimen of teaching in the early church. Unlike many of Paul's epistles, it was not taken up with a variety of questions which had no particular relation to each other, nor was it an evangelistic sermon addressed to a promiscuous audience. It is an exposition of one theme, the new revelation of God, based upon the passages in the Old Testament that contain the latent truth and developed in orderly rhetorical fashion to a climax. Its use of quotations gives a good idea of the passages and the methods of interpretation that were used by the Christian teachers of the first century.

Doctrinally Hebrews accords with the Pauline epistles, although it is not patterned according to their phraseology. Its theme, like that of Romans and Galatians, is salvation by faith in the sacrifice of Christ. The illustration of Abraham's faith is given more space in Hebrews than any other instance, thus bringing it into line with Paul's use of it. In the few casual references to the earthly life of Christ there are some resemblances to Luke (2:3, Luke 1:2; 2:18, Luke 4:13; 5:7, Luke 22:43; 12:2, Luke 9:51; 12:24, Luke 22:20), although they are

not close enough to prove anything with regard to authorship. Hebrews
is a good witness to the growing independence of the Gentile church
and to the enlargement of universal revelation that came through
Christ.

In its Christology, Hebrews adds much to the doctrine of the atonement, which it places in a covenantal relationship. This book explains
the meaning of the new covenant more fully than did Jeremiah, whom
it quotes (Heb. 8:8-12, Jer. 31:31-34), or than did Jesus Himself.
Hebrews connects the incarnation with the atonement (2:14-17).

In the study of the Old Testament Hebrews is an excellent guide to
the meaning of typology and to an understanding of the lasting significance of the Levitical ritual. It does not purport to give a detailed
exposition of all the features of the offerings and feasts, but its confirmation of their prophetic function in pointing forward to Christ is a
valuable key for unlocking the treasures of the Old Testament. It is
the best commentary available on these subjects.

The most familiar passage in Hebrews is, of course, the eleventh
chapter which sketches the progress of faith by the use of Old Testament illustrations. Romans, taking the text from Habakkuk, explains
the meaning of *just* and shows who is justified and how he is justified.
Galatians shows what the life under grace really is, an exercise of
spiritual liberty, and so expounds the idea of *live*. Hebrews demon-
strates the meaning and progress of *faith*. By its warnings, by its
exhortations, and by its gallery of examples it seeks to show what
faith is, how it functions, and what results it achieves. These three
books, Romans, Galatians, and Hebrews form a trilogy explaining the
heart and essence of the Christian life of faith.

# THE PERIL OF HERESIES:

## II Peter; Jude; I, II, III John

# THE PERIL OF HERESIES

II Peter
>  Background
>  Content
>  Outline
>  Evaluation

Jude
>  Background
>  Place and Date
>  Content
>  Outline
>  Evaluation

I, II, III John
>  Background

>  I John
>>  Content
>>  Outline

>  II John
>>  Background
>>  Content and Outline

>  III John
>>  Content and Outline
>>  Evaluation

# CHAPTER XXI

## The Peril of Heresies:

### II Peter; Jude; I, II, III John

Such evidence as survives from the last four decades of the first century reveals that the churches were "by heresies distressed" as well as "by schisms rent asunder." Digressions from truth occurred in every direction and constant vigilance was necessary if the Christians were to keep their faith pure.

The rise of false doctrines was neither new nor unanticipated. The Judaizing controversy which began at Antioch and which plagued Paul throughout his ministry was a harbinger of many other errors that have existed in the church ever since. Among the Corinthians were those who said that there was no resurrection of the dead (I Cor. 15: 12). Perhaps the errorists still claimed to be Christians and felt that their denial of the physical resurrection was of minor importance. Paul, however, showed that it struck at the very heart of all Christian faith. When he made his farewell address at Miletus, he told the Ephesian elders that after his departure grievous wolves would enter in, not sparing the flock; and from among their own number men would arise, speaking perverse things, to draw away the disciples after them (Acts 20:29, 30). In the epistles to Timothy and Titus he laid great stress on doctrinal correctness, and he predicted that in later times some would fall away from the faith, listening to seducing spirits and to demoniacal doctrines (I Tim. 4:1). Furthermore, he predicted that the churches themselves would degenerate to the point where they would not endure the sound doctrine, but, having itching ears, would turn away from the truth unto fables (II Tim. 4:4). Although the complete demonstration of this tendency may still await fulfilment in the culmination of this age, the trend became apparent within the first century.

Five short epistles, II Peter, Jude, I, II, and III John, were written to cope with these trends toward false doctrines within the church. Controversy was not their sole aim, nor was their subject matter devoted entirely to attacking heresy. Their approach was positive rather than negative, as their outlines will show. They are, however, all colored by the dangers of the times, which threatened the church quite as much by the subtle infiltration of paganism into its thinking as by the frontal attacks of persecution from without.

Whether the errors which these epistles sought to combat can be identified with those that appear in the works of the church fathers may be debatable. Some, for instance, have seen in the Johannine writings the reflection of Docetism, a heresy which held that Christ was not historically real but was a phantom that appeared in human guise and then vanished. Perhaps the full-blown heresies of the second century are not historically identical with those intimated in the strictures of the later New Testament books, but the trends are the same and the essential errors are the same. Error, like human nature, does not vary greatly through the centuries. The labels change; the delusions are persistent.

Individually, then, each of these books must be considered in its own setting. The dates for them are somewhat uncertain, but unquestionably they all belong to the period after A.D. 60.

# II Peter

## Background

There is less external evidence for the Petrine authorship of this epistle than there is for the traditional authorship of any other book of the New Testament. None of the early fathers quote it definitely, although there are occasional points of similarity to it in *Hermas, I Clement,* the pseudo-*II Clement,* and the *Didache.* Eusebius quotes Origen (c. A.D. 220) as saying that "Peter . . . has left one epistle undisputed. Suppose also the second one left by him, for on this there is some doubt."[1] Unquestionably Origen knew of its existence, and his statement does not necessarily imply that he rejected its genuineness. The fullest conclusion that could legitimately be drawn from his statement is that II Peter was not generally received by all the church.

Such a situation, however, is not unique to II Peter. In the same context Origen affirmed that II and III John were not accepted by all the churches, but he dismissed the debate as inconsequential because of the brevity of these epistles. The small content of these letters, and the fact that they have been sent to an obscure destination possibly prevented wide circulation at the first, and may have caused

---

1. Eusebius, *Historia Ecclesiae,* VI, xxv, 8.

some of the churches to question their validity when they appeared before the public at a later date.

Assuredly II Peter is not anonymous and the biographical touches that it contains accord with Peter's known life. He spoke with feeling of being cleansed from old sins (1:9). There is a clear allusion to approaching death (1:13) which was predicted by Christ Himself (1:14; cf. John 21:18, 19). The transfiguration was cited as a landmark in the life of the author and of his colleagues (1:16-18). A previous epistle sent to the same destination is mentioned (3:1). The recipients had also received letters from Paul, which Peter had found puzzling, but which he acknowledged to be "scriptures" (3:15, 16). This last allusion might require a late date for the epistle, since it presupposes the writing and the circulation of the Pauline letters, were it not for the intimate phrase, "our beloved brother, Paul" (3:15). The writer treats Paul as a respected equal and contemporary, not as a canonized saint of a bygone day.

There is a decided difference of vocabulary and style between I and II Peter. The second epistle is written in a more labored and awkward Greek. Perhaps a different amanuensis was employed, or possibly Peter transcribed it himself.

While the external evidence for the genuineness of II Peter is not so clear and convincing as it is for other books of the New Testament, the internal evidence creates at least a presumption of authenticity. The epistle bears no traces of heresy; there is nothing in it which Peter could not have written; and it is not embellished with biographical details which are obviously imaginative, as so many apocryphal works are. Since conclusive proof of spuriousness is lacking, it will be treated here as genuine.

If it was written by Peter, the internal allusions to his career fit into the background of his life. It was his last extant work sent shortly before his death to the churches with which he had communicated in his first epistle. The threat of persecution seems to have passed away; for the suffering of Christians is not stressed at all. Perhaps if the epistle were dispatched from Rome about A.D. 65 to 67, Peter realized that the disturbance which originally threatened to affect the provinces had proved to be only local in its scope. New problems had arisen that demanded attention; the danger to his churches was now less from without than it was from within.

The peril confronting the churches was that of doubt and error arising from the false teachings of those who professed to be leaders. "There shall be false teachers, who shall privily bring in destructive heresies, denying even the Master that bought them" (II Pet. 2:1). The nature of this departure from the norm of faith was not outlined completely. It seems to have involved a denial of the redemption and lordship of Christ (2:1), adding a complete abandonment of all moral standards and a bold self-assertiveness which was the accompaniment of spiritual ignorance (2:10-12).

The full manifestation of these conditions was still future to Peter (2:1), although he saw the danger of the existing ignorance and uncertainty in the minds of the people of the church. Twice he asserted that they needed to be reminded of the truths which had been taught them (1:12, 3:1, 2); first, that in the Scriptures, which were not the product of human ingenuity or opinion, there was an authoritative revelation by the Holy Spirit (1:19-21); and second, that the coming of the Lord, which had begun to seem vague and distant, would be "as a thief" (3:10). II Peter was designed as a stimulus to loyal faith and as an encouragement to those Christians whose expectation of the Lord's coming was failing because of its apparently unreasonable delay.

## Content

As the central theme of I Peter was *suffering,* so that of II Peter is *knowledge.* If the errorists were magnifying their knowledge as the basis of their superiority, Peter wanted to show that the answer to false knowledge is true knowledge. The words *know* and *knowledge* appear sixteen times, six of which refer to the knowledge of Christ. The recurring theme unifies the epistle and lends progression to its thought.

As the following outline shows, it can be divided into three main sections. The first discusses the nature of true knowledge which is bestowed as a gift of God through His power (1:3) and through His promises (1:4). This makes the believer a partaker of the divine nature, and the ensuing growth prepares him for the fuller experience of the heavenly kingdom yet to come. The basis of this knowledge is to be found in the personal testimony of those who know Christ and in the revelation of the Scriptures which came through the direct impartation and control of the Holy Spirit.

The second section is prophetic denunciation of errorists whose advent in the church is expected. Their divisive mistakes have in common the denial of the lordship and redemptive work of Christ, and are accompanied by moral looseness. Historic precedent is cited to show how God has judged such perversions in the past, and the pictorial language in 2:10b through 19 describes vividly their activities and their false premises. Their ultimate doom, "it were better for them not to have known the way of righteousness, than, after knowing it, to turn back" (2:21) recalls the words of the Lord Jesus concerning Judas: "Good were it for that man if he had not been born" (Matt. 26:24).

The prevailingly eschatological character of II Peter appears most clearly in the last chapter. The references to death in chapter 1 indicate that Peter had an eternal perspective, and the allusion to prophecy (1:21) implies a relation to the future. The second section speaks explicitly of error and declension to come. The third chapter points out that the only hope for the future lies in the true knowledge of God's program, and in patience while it is being carried out. The mockers will deny the truth of the Lord's coming which the prophets and the apostles, among whom the writer classed himself (1:1), had spoken with assurance. The precedent of the past has shown that absolute uniformity in nature does not prevail and that catastrophic judgments have occurred. In like manner, the day of the Lord will come as a thief in the night — the same phraseology that Paul used (I Thess. 5:2) — and the ensuing dissolution of the existing order will usher in "new heavens and a new earth, wherein dwelleth righteousness" (3:13).

## Outline

### II PETER: THE TRUE KNOWLEDGE OF GOD

## Evaluation

The chief contribution of II Peter to the teaching of the New Testament is its statement concerning the Scriptures: "No prophecy of scripture is of private interpretation. For no prophecy ever came by the will of man: but men spake from God, being moved by the Holy Spirit" (1:20, 21). The crucial words in the passage are "private," "interpretation," and "moved." "Private" (*idias*) may be translated as "its own," "belonging peculiarly to itself." "Interpretation" (*epiluseos*) contains the idea of explanation or illumination. This does not mean that an individual may not attempt to interpret the Scripture, but it is a warning that no single text can be taken by itself, or out of its spiritual context, because the Holy Spirit is the real author and only He is capable of being the final interpreter. The word "moved" (*pheromenoi*) means "borne along," carried as a ship is carried on a tide, the full power of its propulsion being utilized within the larger realm of the resistless ocean current. The allusion to Paul's epistles as "scriptures" in 3:16 indicates the beginning of the canon of the New Testament, though Peter claims no more for Paul's writings than Paul did for his own (I Thess. 2:13). II Peter unites with II Timothy 2:15 and 3:16 to show that the written revelation of the Old Testament was the disclosure of God's mind and will; and that in a day of theological controversy and of moral decline it was the accepted standard of faith and practice.

# Jude

## Background

The literary relation of Jude to II Peter is an important factor in determining the background. There can be no doubt that the two are separate epistles, and yet the similarities of occasion, of thought, and of vocabulary between the two can hardly be accidental. A comparison of the Epistle of Jude with the second chapter of II Peter will convince any reader of the English text or of the Greek text that some connection exists between them. What is the relationship?

Four different answers have been proposed:

1. II Peter and Jude have no relationship save as they are addressed to people who have the same situation facing them. This solution does not explain adequately the minute verbal similarities.

2. II Peter and Jude were paraphrased from some common source. This solution is improbable; for both authors were capable of originating the content of their epistles, and predicating a third unknown epistle only adds to the confusion.

3. II Peter took much of the data from Jude. Jude's references to history are more exact and circumstantial, and his organization is clearer. It would seem that the shorter epistle would be used by the longer, rather than that the shorter should be condensed from the larger.

4. Jude was stimulated to write his epistle by seeing Peter's, but organized his independently.

The last of these views seems most reasonable and has the eminent support of Zahn.[2] The epistle states explicitly that its author intended to write to his constituency concerning "our common salvation" when his purpose was suddenly changed by some new stimulus that prompted an apologetic rather than a theological or a devotional work (Jude 3). He said that "certain men crept in privily," who had already been described, and that they were running rampant in the church. In verses 17 and 18 he quoted verbatim from II Peter 3:3, which he attributed to "the apostles of our Lord Jesus Christ." From these passages it would be reasonable to conclude that the second epistle of Peter had fallen into Jude's hands and that he had written to his hearers concerning the apostasy which Peter had predicted and which was already beginning in the church.

The greater explicitness of references and the closer organization of structure are part of Jude's independent style.

The author was doubtless the brother of James, the moderator of the church of Jerusalem, and the half-brother of Jesus who is mentioned in Mark 6:3. Like James he must have believed on Jesus as the Messiah after the resurrection and was numbered among the waiting group on the day of Pentecost. He seems to have taken no prominent part in the affairs of the apostolic church. In style and in vocabulary the Epistle of Jude bears a resemblance to that of James. Both are terse and graphic in expression. Both depended largely on figures of speech taken from outdoor life. Both are characterized by a certain ethical sternness. The writer did not class himself among the apostles (17).

## Place and Date

No clear indication is afforded by the epistle as to where or when it was written. If Jude ministered to the Jewish churches of Palestine, it may well have been sent to them in the period just prior to the fall of Jerusalem. One might guess that what Peter had predicted for

---

2. Theodor Zahn, *Introduction to the New Testament* (Translated from the third German edition. New York: Charles Scribner's Sons, 1909), II, 262-270.

the part of the church to which he wrote had begun already to take place in the church for which Jude was responsible. If Peter's epistle had just been circulated, Jude's may well be dated around A.D. 67 or 68. If, on the other hand, Jude's appeal to the memory of the people (17) means that the text of II Peter had been long in circulation, the obvious conclusion is that Jude may have been issued as late as A.D. 80. Jerusalem could not have been the destination at this later date.

## Content

Jude announced that his purpose was to urge his readers to "contend earnestly for the faith which was once for all delivered unto the saints" (3). The necessity for this emergency was the infiltration into the Christian ranks of men who were "turning the grace of our God into lasciviousness and denying our only Master and Lord, Jesus Christ" (4). The phraseology defining the heresy accords with that of Peter, but it is more specific. It sounds as if the error were a type of anti-nomianism, which made license out of liberty and which repudiated the lordship of Christ. So far had the heresy swung away from legalism that it observed no restraints and it possessed no fixed moral standards. It was idle intellectual speculation, accompanied by fancy oratory, with no duties attached.

In his general argument Jude follows the order of II Peter, but his pictures are sharper and more cameo-like. Three historic examples of judgment are cited: the destruction of the unbelieving group who came out of Egypt, but who would not enter the land of Canaan; the angels "who kept not their own principality"; and the cities of Sodom and Gomorrah. In each case the irrevocable judgment of God fell on those who had sinned blatantly and inexcusably. To these three groups of egregious sinners are likened the apostates, marked out in Jude by the pronoun *these* (8, 10, 12, 14, 16, 19). Their irreverence, ignorance, treachery, emptiness, and egotism are pilloried in Jude's vigorous language. The nature of their error is described by their likeness to the three great rebels of the Pentateuch: the way of blood-less sacrifice — Cain; the error of thinking that God is the minister of man's convenience rather than the Lord of his destinies — Balaam; and the arrogance of a self-devised faith — Korah.

With the last section of Jude the pronoun changes from *these* to *ye,* and the antidote to apostasy is presented to the readers. First, *remember* the words of Christ given by His apostles, echoing Peter's statement that he felt he ought to "put them in remembrance" of the truth that he possessed. Second, Jude commanded them to *keep* themselves in the love of God by prayer and by constructive action (20, 21). Last of all, preservation from apostasy includes the *rescue* of others from the errors that surround them, so that their doubt may not lead them ultimately to disaster (22, 23).

## Outline

### JUDE: A WARNING AGAINST APOSTASY

| | | |
|---|---|---|
| I. | Salutation | 1, 2 |
| II. | The Announcement of Emergency | 3, 4 |
| III. | The Appeal to Historic Precedents | 5-7 |
| IV. | The Arraignment of Apostate Teachers | 8-16 |
| V. | The Advice to Believers | 17-23 |
| VI. | Concluding Benediction | 24, 25 |

## Evaluation

One of the curiosities of this small epistle is its fondness for triads of thought. It has six main sections, which are arranged in three pairs: the first two introduce the thought; the second two discuss the apostasy; and the last two state the conclusion. The author described himself in three ways: his proper name, Jude; his function, a servant of Jesus Christ; his relation to the Christian community, the brother of James. He salutes his readers as "called," "beloved," and "kept"; and his greeting wishes them mercy, peace, and love. There are many other "threes" employed by the author which the student can find for himself. Probably they have no special significance beyond marking a mental trait of the author.

The use of apocryphal literature has occasioned some questioning of this epistle. The reference to Enoch in verse 14 agrees verbatim with a passage in the book of *Enoch* and the reference to the dispute between Michael and the devil for the body of Moses appears in *The Assumption of Moses*. Both of these writings were produced early in the first century by Jewish writers, who sought to advance the teachings of their sect or party by appeal to the authority of Old Testament leaders. The quotations pose a dilemma: for if Jude was inspired, did his quotations of these works give equal authority to them? If, on the other hand, they were random quotations which carried no authority, why should he quote them at all? There is a fair analogy in Paul's address at Athens when he quoted the Greek poet Aratus (Acts 17:28) to substantiate a point of his address because he knew that it would carry weight with his audience, not because he regarded the Greek poet as inspired or authoritative in the realm of theology. In like manner the apocryphal works were sometimes used to illustrate certain principles for those who regarded them with reverence. In the early Christian church some of these were highly esteemed and were deemed profitable reading. Jude's audience must have been familiar with this literature, for he made extensive allusions to it even apart from the express quotations.[3]

The epistle shows that by the time it was written, quite certainly not later than A.D. 85, there was a recognized body of belief that could be called Christianity. Doctrinal formulation is a slow process, and the history of Christianity for the last nineteen hundred years is the history of the rise and fall of doctrinal patterns and emphases, some of which were extreme, others of which were erroneous, but all of which belonged to the general stream of thought that is called Christian. One would be tempted to think that these variations might be inconsequential, were it not for the fact that the New Testament sets certain rigorous doctrinal standards. Some leeway may be allowed for human ignorance and for intellectual and spiritual limitations; for "now we see in a mirror, darkly," and "we know in part, and we prophesy in part" (I Cor. 13:12, 9). In these epistles, however, which were written when error was prevalent and when controversy was beginning, there is a frank insistence on "the pattern of sound words," and Jude speaks with finality of "the once-for-all-delivered-to-the-saints faith" (1:3, literal translation) which was to be kept as an inviolate standard.

The proper method of treating those who deviate from this standard is also given in Luke. Nowhere does the New Testament recommend persecution or burning at the stake for heretics. The heretics draw their own lines. "These," says Jude, "are they who make separations . . ." (19). The epistle, instead, counsels mercy and an attempt to rescue those who are deluded and bewildered, though no tolerance is to be shown to the falsehood itself.

One of the great benedictions of the New Testament closes the book. Its emphasis on the lordship of Christ and upon His ability to keep His servants from falling into error is singularly appropriate to the theme of Jude.

---

3. For a good discussion of the quotations and allusions, see M. R. James, *The Second Epistle General of Peter and the General Epistle of Jude* (Cambridge Greek Testament. Cambridge: University Press, 1912), pp. xl-xlviii.

# I, II, III John

## Background

If the criteria of vocabulary and style are ever adequate for pronouncing judgment on authorship, these three short letters must be attributed to one author who is also the author of the Fourth Gospel. All four of these writings were probably produced about the same time and at the same place. The first epistle opens by summarizing "That which was from the beginning, that which we have heard, that which we have seen with our eyes, that which we beheld, and our hands handled, concerning the Word of life" (I John 1:1) as the foundation for its application of truth. This summary presupposes the Fourth Gospel both by its content and by its vocabulary, and the similarities persist all through the epistle. The stated purpose of the First Epistle, "These things have I written unto you, that ye may know that ye have eternal life . . ." (I John 5:13), carries the reader one step beyond the Gospel, which says, "These are written, that ye may believe that Jesus is the Christ, the Son of God; and that believing ye may have life in his name" (John 20:31). The Gospel was written to arouse faith; the First Epistle was written to establish certainty.

The Second and Third Epistles, as Goodspeed suggests, may have been written as "covering letters," one to the church, addressed under the figure of the "elect lady" (II John 1), and the other to Gaius, the pastor (III John 1).[4] They were intended to be private notes of counsel and greeting, whereas the main body of teaching was contained in the Gospel and in the First Epistle.

The exact time and place of writing are indeterminate, but the most acceptable view is that these documents were written by John for the Asian churches in the middle of the last third of the first century. By that time the separation between church and synagogue was complete. The controversy over justification by faith versus works had largely died out, and the influx of Gentiles into the church with their heritage of philosophical thought was beginning to affect doctrinal teaching. They were interested in the person of Christ. Who was He? If He was God, how could He die? If He died, how could He be God? There were many solutions proposed for this dilemma; and the debate over the nature of Christ occupied the thinking of church leaders and the discussions of the councils down to the fifth century, nor has it died out even today.

---

4. Edgar J. Goodspeed, *An Introduction to the New Testament* (Chicago: University of Chicago Press, n. d.), pp. 319, 320.

The particular error which I John was intended to combat seems to have been an early form of Gnosticism, a heresy which was the most dangerous enemy of the church up to the close of the second century. Gnosticism was a philosophy of religion rather than a single system. It was built on the premise that spirit is good, that matter is evil, and that the two can have no enduring relation with each other. Salvation consists of escape from the realm of matter into the realm of the spirit. The means of this escape are numerous. Chief among them is knowledge, by which man can rise above the earthbound chains of matter into the heavenly apprehension of truth. This knowledge, or *gnosis* to use the Greek term which gave the philosophy its name, could be attained only by those who were initiated into the inner secrets of the group. The teaching of the Gnostics was to form an unorganized but cohesive cult, bound together by common rites and by common thinking rather than by officers and societies.

The conflict of this type of philosophy with Christianity was most acute at the point of the person of Christ. How, asked the Gnostics, could the infinite, pure spirit called God have anything to do with a material body? A complete union would, on their premises, be unthinkable. They proposed two solutions: either Christ was not really human, but only apparently so; or else the Christ-spirit did not actually inhabit the human Jesus until the baptism, and left Him before His death on the cross. The former theory was called Docetism, from the verb *dokeo,* meaning *to seem;* the latter was called Cerinthianism, from Cerinthus, its chief advocate in the first century.

Either of these proposals would have been fatal to the gospel had it become the standard interpretation of Christianity. Docetism made the human Jesus simply a ghost, an illusion that seemed to appear to man, but that had no real existence. Cerinthianism would make a strange contradiction out of the personality of Jesus: one would never know whether the human Jesus, or the divine Christ-spirit were speaking and acting. Under Cerinthianism the person of Christ could be a sort of Dr. Jekyll and Mr. Hyde. Probably these two views had not been fully defined and amplified in the time of John, but the language of the First Epistle implies that something like Gnosticism was prevalent when he wrote.

John insists that the Christ whom he preached was audible, visible, and tangible (1:1). He says that whosoever denies the Father and the Son is antichrist (2:22), and he declares that "every spirit that confesseth not Jesus [that He has come in the flesh] is not of God" (4:2, 3). Evidently his opponents took a position which approximated closely that of Docetic Gnosticism.

394

The smaller epistles deal with the same problem from the standpoint of church polity and discipline. I John says that "they," meaning the adherents of the false doctrine, "went out from us, but they were not of us; for if they had been of us, they would have continued with us" (2:19). There had been a schism in some of the churches in which the errorists had withdrawn to form their own group. Some of these, however, had become itinerant teachers, who sought to gain entrance into the smaller churches that were immature and weak. The Second Epistle contains warnings against them:

> *For many deceivers are gone forth into the world, even they that confess not that Jesus Christ cometh in the flesh.*

(II John 7)

The church is warned that any such teacher is not to be welcomed, "for he that giveth him greeting partaketh in his evil works" (II John 10, 11).

The Third Epistle affords one or two interesting insights into church life in this period. Apparently much of the ministry was carried on by itinerant preachers who made periodic rounds, staying a little while with each group and holding "protracted meetings" in private homes. Such a procedure was easily susceptible of abuse by religious racketeers, who would use their privileges to obtain a free living from the people. John commended Gaius for his gracious support of them, since they received no contributions from the Gentiles to whom they ministered (III John 5, 8).

The rise of "church czars" is reflected in the comment on Diotrophes. He was unwilling to receive any visitors, but consistently ejected from the church those who were ready to entertain them. John's protest and his promise that when he came he would test the power of Diotrephes show that there were governmental difficulties even within the church of the first century.

The Johannine Epistles, then, were written for a church that confronted new philosophies which sought to conquer Christianity by absorbing it, and that was struggling to maintain its distinctive message against perversion by error.

## I John

*Content*

The peculiar style of John appears at its best in I John because the epistle is short enough to show clearly its type of structure. I John is symphonic rather than logical in its plan; it is constructed like a piece of music rather than like a brief for a debate. Instead of proceeding step by step in unfolding a subject, as Paul does in Romans, John selects a theme which he maintains through the book, and upon which he introduces a series of variations, any one of which may be a theme in itself. For this reason one can follow only with difficulty the single line of thought in the Gospel or in the Epistle, and the composition of a progressive outline is even more trying.

Furthermore, the First Epistle is keyed to personal experience. It seeks to inculcate certainty of the possession of eternal life (5:13), and proposes certain tests whereby that certainty can be attained. The phrase "we know," translating two different verbs (*oidamen* and *ginoskomen*), is used thirteen times to signify the certainty that is achieved through experience, or that is a part of normal spiritual consciousness (2:3, 5, 29; 3:14, 16, 19, 24; 4:13, 16; 5:15, 18, 19, 20).

*Light* and *love,* two peculiarly Johannine words, are prominent in this epistle. Both are used as descriptive of deity (1:5, 4:8), and the development of these two themes comprises a major part of the epistle. They elaborate the abstract ideas that are presented in the Gospel and make them practical for personal application.

*Outline*

## I JOHN: THE CERTAINTY OF ETERNAL LIFE

| | |
|---|---|
| I. Introduction: Life's Historical Manifestation | 1:1-4 |
| II. Certainty Through Walking in the Light | 1:5-2:29 |
| In Personal Spiritual Conduct | 1:5-2:6 |
| In Social Relationships | 2:7-11 |
| In Separation from the World | 2:12-17 |
| In Adherence to the Truth | 2:18-29 |
| III. Certainty Through Abiding in Love | 3:1-4:21 |
| The Ethical Proof of Love | 3:1-12 |
| The Social Proof of Love | 3:13-24 |
| The Theological Proof of Love | 4:1-6 |
| The Emotional Proof of Love | 4:7-21 |
| IV. Certainty Through Exercise of Faith | 5:1-12 |
| V. Conclusion: The Resultant Certainties of Life | 5:13-21 |

## II John

*Background*

The background of II John is much the same as that of the First Epistle. This letter is more personal, for it is directed to "the elect lady and her children." The translation of this salutation is ambiguous; for it can be rendered "the lady Electa," "the elect Cyria," or, as usual, "the elect lady," depending upon whether one sees a proper name in the greeting or not. The interpretation is even more ambiguous than the translation. Was the addressee an individual, or does the term "lady" denote figuratively a church, whose members are her "children"? Or if an individual were intended, did she own a home where a group of believers met, so that they were called her "children"? There is a parallelism in the Jewish feeling for Zion, which Paul called "our mother" (Gal. 4:26). Westcott says that "the problem of the address is insoluble with our present knowledge,"[5] nor have more recent commentators shed additional light on the subject. The main point is that the group for whose benefit the epistle was written were being imperiled by false teachers. John wanted them to cultivate vigilance lest they be led astray.

### Content and Outline

The doctrinal content of the Second Epistle differs little from that of the First. The same danger of ignoring the humanity of Christ and the same necessity of abiding in the truth are pressed upon the readers.

## II JOHN: CHRISTIAN FIDELITY

| | |
|---|---|
| I. Salutation | 1-3 |
| II. Injunctions | 4-11 |
|     To Love | |
|     To Obedience | |
|     To Vigilance | |
|     To Refusal of Error | |
| III. Conclusion | 12, 13 |

## III John

### Content and Outline

Addressed primarily to Gaius, a pastor or leader in the church, III John is concerned less with theological truth and more with administrative matters than the other two epistles. It deals with the entertainment of missionary brethren who should be encouraged as they visit the church enroute to their work, and with the unkind attitude of Diotrephes, who deserves a reprimand.

---

5. B. F. Westcott, *The Epistle of John* (Second Edition. Cambridge & London; Macmillan & Co., 1886), p. 224.

## III JOHN: THE PRACTICE OF TRUTH

### Evaluation

The Johannine Epistles, particularly the First, are invaluable as an index of personal spiritual achievement. They are almost purely declarative and hortatory; exposition and theological argumentation are not found in their pages. The historical truth which is embodied in the Gospel is applied in I John to the individual believer, and the proofs of his possession of eternal life are outlined plainly so that he can know certainly whether or not he has really believed. The mellowness of the teaching in them is not to be confused with vagueness of belief or with theological indecision. All of these epistles draw a sharp line between truth and falsehood, between righteousness and unrighteousness, between light and darkness, and between love and hatred. They demand that the Christian place himself on one side of the line or on the other. "He that hath the Son hath the life; he that hath not the Son of God hath not the life" (I John 5:12). They presuppose a clear and perfected revelation of eternal life in Christ which constitutes the standard of truth and which must be accepted or rejected by men. The obligations and consequences of its acceptance are sketched so that believers may be able to say, "We have passed from death unto life."

Against the rise of heresies and errors these later epistles present a solid front. They are not solely polemic, however, but they are constructive in their presentation of the teaching of the gospel. Maturity of thought and holiness of life are their objectives; not simply argument over a point of tradition. They were written not just to win a debate, but to aid and to develop the Christian that he might keep himself, and that the evil one might not lay hold of him (I John 5:18).

# THE EXPECTANT CHURCH:

## REVELATION

# THE EXPECTANT CHURCH: REVELATION

Background

Interpretations
   The Preterist School
   The Idealist School
   The Historicist School
   The Futurist School
   The Millennial Views

Content

Outline

Evaluation

# CHAPTER XXII

# The Expectant Church: Revelation

## Background

The book of Revelation closes the canon and the history of the New Testament. Irrespective of whether or not it were the last in order to be written, it is final in its thought, for it embodies the expectation of a church that had been launched in the world as an institution, and that was awaiting eagerly the consummation of its mission.

Revelation is unique in many ways. It is the only book of the New Testament that is completely devoted to prophecy. Practically all of its imagery is related to figures that appear in the Old Testament prophetical books, and a large part of its content is predictive, dealing with the future. The author stated explicitly that the messenger who brought him the last vision had come from "the Lord, the God of the spirits of the prophets, [who] sent his angel to show unto his servants the things which must shortly come to pass" (Rev. 22:6), and in the following verse he spoke of "the prophecy of this book."

Revelation belongs to the category of apocalyptic literature. Apocalyptic literature was usually produced in times of persecution and oppression as a means of encouraging those who were suffering for their faith. It was characterized by (1) an intense despair of present circumstances and an equally intense hope of divine intervention in the future; (2) by the use of symbolic language, dreams, and visions; (3) by the introduction of celestial and demonic powers as messengers and agents in the progress of God's purpose; (4) by the prediction of a catastrophic judgment of the wicked and of a supernatural deliverance for the righteous; and (5) frequently by the pseudonymous ascription of the writing to a prominent character of biblical history, such as Ezra (II Esdras) or Enoch (The Book of Enoch). The book of Revelation possesses most of these characteristics, except that the author declares his name, and assumes that he is known, not as a past celebrity, but as a present participant in the affairs of those whom he addressed.

The conditions under which the book was written may fairly be deduced from a study of its content. It was addressed to seven churches

401

of the province of Asia, which had been in existence for a considerable period of time, and in which there had been spiritual development and decline. In the letters to these churches are hints that persecution was either imminent, or that it had already begun. The church at Smyrna was "about to suffer," and "have tribulation ten days" (2:10). Antipas had suffered martyrdom at Pergamum (2:13). Philadelphia was to be exempted from "the hour of trial" (3:10). Even if these passages be interpreted of future events, the atmosphere of Revelation bespeaks hostility and oppression. In the main body of the book famine, war, pestilence, economic pressure, and persecution are regarded as the ordinary phenomena of its setting.

There is little doubt that imperial Rome formed the model for the power of the state which Revelation depicted as the enemy of Christianity. The beast that had "authority over every tribe and people and tongue and nation" (13:7) had its counterpart in the universal rule of Rome under the Caesars. The "mark" which men would be compelled to carry in order to buy or sell (13:16, 17) was the term used for the imperial seal which was stamped upon wills, contracts, bills of sale, and other documents to give them legal standing.[1] The harlot, called Babylon the Great, drunken with the blood of saints and of martyrs, was seated on seven mountains (17:9), the number of hills in Rome. Whether or not the Apocalypse should be finally interpreted in terms of Rome, it was certainly applied to Rome when it was first read by Christians.

Two schools of thought prevail concerning the time and circumstances for which it was written. One group assigns it to the days of Nero, when the burning of Rome evoked persecution of Christians. The opinion is substantiated chiefly by two considerations. If John, the son of Zebedee, wrote the Revelation, as well as the Gospel and Epistles that are attributed to him, the radical differences in language and in style between the two could be explained better if Revelation were an early effort, written when his command of Greek was still imperfect, while the Gospel and the Epistles were written at a later date when he had gained in proficiency. Again, it has been suggested that the mystic number, six hundred and sixty six (13:18), is the sum total of the numerical values of the Hebrew letters that spell *Neron Kesar;* and therefore the personage described in the chapter must be Nero. This type of reasoning seems too flimsy to warrant any fixed conclusion, especially when it has no support from external tradition.

---

1. G. A. Deissmann, *Bible Studies,* (Authorized Translation by Alexander Grieve. Edinburgh: T. & T. Clark, 1901), pp. 240-247.

The second possibility for dating the Apocalypse places it late in the first century in the reign of Domitian, A.D. 81 to 96. This dating has at least the advantage of explicit external evidence. Irenaeus said that John received the vision "no very long time since, but almost in our day, towards the end of Domitian's reign."[2] While there was probably no extended persecution under Domitian, his insistence that he be worshiped as deity and the increasing tyranny of his dictatorship put him in opposition to the growth of Christianity and presaged the growth of social, economic, and religious conditions such as Revelation prophesied.

Revelation, then, is a witness to the growing hostility between the church and the Roman state. It does not necessarily imply that a universal policy of persecuting Christians had been adopted, but it does make clear that there can be no compromise between a pagan state and the Christian church. The logical outcome of paganism is totalitarianism, which involves the worship of the ruler who controls all political allegiance, all economic resources, all religious observances, and all personal worship. The tolerance which Rome extended to the early church passed into suspicion as Paul and other Christian preachers were brought to trial by the Jewish leaders, and then the suspicion deepened into contempt and hatred. By the end of the first century Christians found themselves on the defensive everywhere. They were realizing the truth of the words of Jesus: "If ye were of the world, the world would love its own: but because ye are not of the world, but I chose you out of the world, therefore the world hateth you" (John 15:19).

Revelation was written as an encouragement for the churches that were feeling this growing hostility and as a warning to the careless and negligent Christians who were tempted to lapse into an easy conformity to the world. It was the last voice of a closing century.

The author, according to his own testimony, was named John, and was an eyewitness of the things that he saw (1:1, 2). He was in Patmos, a rocky island off the coast of Greece, where he had been incarcerated because of his faith (1:9). While there, he was given the vision which he described and was ordered to transmit it to the seven churches of Asia (1:10), with which he was familiar.

Some of the Greek in the Apocalypse seems awkward and even ungrammatical. One should remember that the author was attempting to put into human language scenes that could not be described in ordinary terms; and consequently his grammar and vocabulary both

---

2. Irenaeus, *Against Heresies,* V, xxx, 3.

proved inadequate. Furthermore, he was probably of Aramaic descent, and may have had difficulty in expressing himself smoothly in Greek. If in writing the Gospel and the Epistles he had the aid of a skilled amanuensis, but wrote the Apocalypse himself, some of the differences could easily be explained.

Revelation is interpretative. It contains no less than four hundred allusions to the Old Testament, although no direct citation can be found. Its imagery and its program are related to Old Testament prophecy, and they connect its meaning with the trends of the new dispensation. Revelation gives an estimate of the spiritual temper of the church life through the judgment on the seven churches of Asia. The sequence of visions that follows, by whatever system it is interpreted, is a picture of the ultimate consummation of God's purpose. However strange its symbolism may be, it is the one book of the New Testament that gives any organized forecast of the future.

## Interpretations

There are four main schools of interpretation of the book of Revelation among modern expositors.

### The Preterist School

The Preterist school holds that the symbolism of Revelation relates only to the events of the day in which it was written. All the imagery of the seals and trumpets and vials has no bearing upon the future. The writer was simply expressing his moral indignation concerning the abuses of his own day when he spoke of future judgment. This is the view of the majority of liberal scholars, such as R. H. Charles and C. C. Torrey. It has the advantage of connecting Revelation with the thought and historical events of the day in which it was written, but it makes no allowance for any element of predictive prophecy.

### The Idealist School

The Idealist view, which is often closely allied with the Preterist school, considers Revelation to be only a symbolic picture of the enduring struggle between good and evil, and between Christianity and paganism. It holds that its symbols cannot be identified as historic events either in the past or in the future; they are simply trends or ideals. So Raymond Calkins says:

> We understand now what the word 'revelation' means. It does not mean a revelation of the future mysteries of the end of the world, the millenium, or the Day of Judgment. Neither does it mean primarily a revelation of the glories of Heaven or the blessedness of the redeemed. Rather it means a revelation of the

infinite God, mighty to save; an uncovering for the consolation and inspiration of God's people of the all-conquering power of an omnipotent Saviour . . .[2]

The idealistic method of interpretation has the advantage of focusing the attention of the reader upon the ethical and spiritual truth of Revelation rather than upon the debatable aspects of its symbolism. On the other hand, it tends to undervalue that symbolism as a vehicle of predictive prophecy. Its "spiritualization" strips the Apocalypse of all predictive value, and dissociates it from any definite historical consummation. Judgment day, according to this theory, comes whenever a great moral issue is decided; it is not a final climax in which a supernatural Christ ascends a visible throne.

## The Historicist School

The Historicist interpretation holds that Revelation outlines in symbolic form the entire course of history of the church from Pentecost to the advent of Christ. The symbols portray in sequence the great events that have taken place: that is, the seals are the breakup of the Roman empire; the eruption of locusts from the bottomless pit is a picture of the Mohammedan invasions, etc.[3] Each major event in the history of Christendom was thus broadly foreshadowed, so that Revelation becomes a calendar of events written in advance. Most of the Reformers, insofar as they dealt with Revelation at all, the majority of the older commentaries, and many modern evangelical preachers such as A. J. Gordon and A. B. Simpson, held this view. It has at least ostensible warrant in the phrase of Revelation 4:1: "Come up hither, and I will show thee the things which must come to pass hereafter." The Historicist view is more literal than the Idealist view, but its advocates have never achieved unanimity on what the individual symbols mean. Even among the Historicists there are nearly as many interpretations as there are commentators. Not all of them can be right; and since there is such wide divergence among them, there is at least the possibility that the methods may be wrong.

## The Futurist School

The Futurists hold that the first three chapters of Revelation apply either to the day in which the book was written, or else that the seven

---

2. Raymond Calkins, *The Social Message of the Book of Revelation* (New York: The Woman's Press, n.d.), p. 13.

3. See the collected comments quoted in John Peter Lange, *The Revelation of John* (Translated from the German by Evalina Moore; enlarged and edited by E. R. Craven. New York: Scribner, Armstrong, & Co., 1874). pp. 2-7-215.

churches of Asia represent seven eras of church history, bridging the gap from the apostolic age to the return of Christ. To this extent the Futurists are Historicists. Beginning with the phrase in 4:1, "the things which must come to pass hereafter," they contend that the remainder of the book deals with events that will take place in a period called the "Great Tribulation," just preceding the return of Christ and variously estimated from three and one half to seven years in length. The events of the Apocalypse, relegated to this period, are interpreted as literally as possible, and are thus regarded as wholly future to the existing era. Expositors of the type of J. A. Seiss, C. I. Scofield, A. C. Gaebelein, H. A. Ironside, and others are Futurists.

## The Millennial Views

A somewhat different approach to Revelation from the eschatological rather than from the historical standpoint gives three other divisions of thought, based on varying interpretations of the twentieth chapter. The crux of the interpretation is centered in the question as to whether the "thousand years" are to be considered as literal or figurative, and as to whether they precede or follow the second coming of Christ.

The *postmillennial* view regards the thousand years as probably figurative of a long interval that precedes the coming of Christ. At the beginning of the period the triumph of the gospel over the nations will introduce the reign of peace which will endure until Christ returns in final judgment.

The *amillennial* view holds that the millennium is non-existent as a literal period, or possibly that it represents the intermediate state of the dead. Christ may return at any time, when He will judge the world, and usher in the eternal state of bliss for the righteous, the new heavens and the new earth.

The *premillennial* view holds that Christ will return personally to initiate His kingdom; that the righteous dead will be raised; that they will reign personally with Him on the earth for one thousand years; that subsequent to His reign there will be a final rebellion that shall be immediately suppressed, the wicked dead will be judged, and the eternal state will begin.

There is no necessary correlation between these views and the chronological interpretations previously defined. Generally, the millennial question is treated seriously only by Historicists and by Futurists, since the Preterists and Idealists would not regard the "thousand years" as anything more than another symbol. The following diagram will illustrate the different methods of interpretation:

# Revelation

## INTERPRETATIONS OF REVELATION

| REVELATION | 1 - 3 | 4 - 19 | 20 - 22 |
|---|---|---|---|
| PRETERIST | Historic Churches | Symbolical of Contemporary Conditions | Symbolic of Heaven and Victory |
| IDEALIST | Historic Churches | Symbolic of Conflict of Good and Evil | Victory of Good |
| HISTORICIST | Literal Historic Churches | Symbolic of Events of History: Fall of Rome, Mohammedanism, Papacy, Reformation | Final Judgment Millennium (?) Eternal State |
| FUTURIST | Seven Stages of Church History | Future Tribulation Concentrated Judgments on apostate Church and on Antichrist; Coming of Christ | Millennial Kingdom; Judgment of Wicked Dead; Eternal State |
| POST-MILLENNIAL | Historic Churches | Generally Historicist | Victory of Christianity over the World |
| A-MILLENNIAL | Historic Churches | Generally Historicist | Coming of Christ Judgment Eternal State |
| PRE-MILLENNIAL | Historic Churches Representative of Historical Stages | Generally Futurist | Literal Millennial Reign Judgment of Great White Throne New Jerusalem |

*Content*

The real key to the interpretation of Revelation does not lie in any one of these theories, however great its merits, but in the structure of the book itself as it presents the person of Christ. The very title of the book, "The Revelation of Jesus Christ, which God gave him to show unto his servants, even the things which must shortly come to pass . . .," indicates that the central theme is the person of Christ as He reveals the future. There is some question as to whether "The Revelation of Jesus Christ" means the revelation of His person, or the revelation which He gave, which came from Him. If the former interpretation of the title sets the topic, then Revelation is an unfolding of the person of Christ as He is related to the future. If the second interpretation is taken, the main topic is the program of the future as mediated through Christ. Either is grammatically possible,[4] and either makes Christ the central figure of the book. Much controversy might have been averted had expositors approached Revelation from the neutral standpoint of its literary structure making their eschatology dependent upon their Christology.

A second clue to the content of the book appears in the form which the author's own experience has given to it. Obviously the book consists of a series of visions, each of which is a unit in itself. While there are many small units, introduced by the phrase "and I saw" (5:1, 11; 6:1, 9, etc.), there are four main divisions which are introduced by the phrase, "in the Spirit" (1:10, 4:2, 17:1-3, 21:9, 10) These divisions are of varied content and of unequal length, but they give a unitary organization to the book. Together with the opening prologue and the closing epilogue, they divide Revelation into six sections.

Several series of sevens appear throughout the book. There are seven churches (2:1, 8, 12, 18, 3:1, 7, 14), seven spirits of God (4:5) seven seals (6:1, 3, 5, 7, 9, 12, 8:1), seven trumpets (8:6, 7, 8, 10 12, 9:1, 13, 11:15), seven thunders (10:3), seven bowls (16:1, 2, 4 8, 10, 12, 17), seven major personages (12:1, 3, 5, 7, 13:1, 11, 14:1) and seven beatitudes (1:3, 14:13, 16:15, 19:9, 20:6, 22:7, 14). Some of these are a part of the literary structure of the book and are listed in close sequence, and some are not. The use of the numeric seven

---

4. The former interprets *he apokalupsis tou Iesou Christou* as an objective genitive; the latter as a subjective genitive.

indicates a design of thought that makes the Revelation more than a haphazard accumulation of weird symbols.

Other numerical combinations or series appear sporadically. There are twenty-four elders (4:4), four living creatures (4:6), four horsemen (6:1-8), four angels (9:14), one hundred and forty-four thousand in companies of the redeemed (7:4, 14:1), twelve gates of the city of God (21:12), and twelve foundations (21:14), twelve kinds of fruit in the tree of life (22:2), and various others.

One other phrase deserves mention. In 4:5, 8:5, 11:19, and 16:18 "there were lightnings, and voices, and thunders." The last three of these occur respectively at the termini of a series of judgments. Are they repeated, or are they a clue that the three judgments are coterminous, and consequently that each judgment is simply an intensification of its predecessor?

## Outline

Using the clues thus provided by the book itself, the following outline is proffered:

### THE REVELATION OF JESUS CHRIST
in "the things shortly to come to pass"

| | |
|---|---|
| I. Prologue: Christ Communicating | 1:1-8 |
| Title | 1:1 |
| Agent | 1:2 |
| Commendation | 1:3 |
| Destination | 1:4, 5a |
| Dedication | 1:5b, 6 |
| Motto | 1:7 |
| Imprimatur | 1:8 |
| | |
| II. Vision I: Christ in the Church: The Living One | 1:9-3:22 |
| Place: Patmos | |
| The Portrait | 1:9-20 |
| The Messages | |
| To Ephesus | 2:1-7 |
| To Smyrna | 2:8-11 |
| To Pergamum | 2:12-17 |
| To Thyatira | 2:18-29 |
| To Sardis | 3:1-6 |
| To Philadelphia | 3:7-13 |
| To Laodicea | 3:14-22 |

III. Vision II: Christ in the Cosmos: The Redeemer     4:1-16:21
                    Place: Heaven

| | |
|---|---|
| The Scene in Heaven | 4:1-5:14 |
| The Seven Seals | 6:1-8:5 |
|   The White Horse | 6:1, 2 |
|   The Red Horse | 6:3, 4 |
|   The Black Horse | 6:5, 6 |
|   The Pale Horse | 6:7, 8 |
|   The Souls of Martyrs | 6:9, 11 |
|   The Signs in Heaven | 6:12-17 |
|     (Parenthesis: The Sealing of 144,000) | 7:1-17 |
|   The Silence in Heaven | 8:1-5 |
| | |
| The Seven Trumpets | 8:6-11:19 |
|   Hail, Fire, and Blood | 8:7 |
|   Sea Turned into Blood | 8:8, 9 |
|   Star Falling upon Waters | 8:10, 11 |
|   Sun, Moon, and Stars Darkened | 8:12, 13 |
|   Opening of Bottomless Pit | 9:1-12 |
|   Loosing of Four Angels | 9:13-21 |
|   Parenthesis: The Little Book ⎫ | |
|               Measuring of Temple ⎬ | 10:1-11:14 |
|               Two Witnesses ⎭ | |
|   Announcement of Consummation | 11:15-19 |
| | |
| The Signs | 12:1-16:21 |
|   The Personages | 12:1-14:20 |
|     The Woman | 12:1-2 |
|     The Dragon | 12:3-4 |
|     The Man-Child | 12:5-6 |
|     Michael, the Archangel | 12:7-17 |
|     The Beast from the Sea | 13:1-10 |
|     The Beast from the Earth | 13:11-18 |
|     The Lamb on Mt. Zion | 14:1-5 |
|       Parenthesis: The Angelic Messages | |
|              The Call to Judgment | 14:6, 7 |
|              The Fall of Babylon | 14:8 |
|              The Warning of Wrath | 14:9-12 |
|              The Blessing of the Dead | 14:13 |
|              The Call to Harvest | 14:14-16 |
|              The Reaping of Grapes of | |
|                 Wrath | 14:17-20 |
|   The Seven Bowls | 15:1-16:21 |
|   The Scene in Heaven | 15:1-8 |
|   The Judgments | 16:1-21 |

## *Evaluation*

A final interpretation of Revelation is not within the province of this book, but a few observations may prove helpful to the student.

Revelation is written in the style of apocalyptic literature, but it differs sharply from the general body of such writings in that it has a definite author who names himself, and who has a definite destination in view. His chief purpose is not to predict in advance all the details of church history, but to show the general trends of the present age and their consummation in the personal return of Christ. The threefold declaration and challenge of the Epilogue: "I come quickly" (22:7, 12, 20), reiterates the promise to His churches (2:16, 3:11), and makes the entire book a warning to the world and an encouragement to God's people.

Certain unities pervade the entire book. The person of Christ is dominant, first as the glorified figure with blazing countenance, clothed in white, who inspects, reproves, and counsels the Church. As the claimant of the right to administer judgment under the authority of the sealed roll, He is the Lamb, who has acquired this right by His redemptive work (5:4-7). In the execution of judgment He is the Conqueror, riding upon a white horse like a Roman general in triumphal procession (19:11), with the title "KING OF KINGS, AND LORD OF LORDS" (19:16). In the consummation of all things He is the Bridegroom of His people (19:7, 21:9), again called the Lamb because of His redemption.

The chronological arrangement of Revelation is disputable. The Historicist sees in it a complete calendar of all major events from the time of its writing until the coming of Christ; the Futurist relegates most of the book to a seven year period immediately preceding the appearing of the Lord, and the Preterist and the Idealist regard it as independent of all chronology. Certain facts, however, seem plain. The letters in the first three chapters were directed to the existing churches in the cities of Asia so that they relate to a period contemporary with the author. The opening of the vision in the fourth chapter assigned it to "the things which must come to pass hereafter" (4:1), beginning with the writer's day and continuing indefinitely. The last two visions of the book have not yet been fulfilled, and apply to the end time yet to come. Revelation thus belongs partially to the past, partially to the present, and partially to the future.

The last two sections parallel each other. The former, Revelation 17:1 to 21:8, is occupied with the doom of the evil world-system represented by the harlot, Babylon. The second, Revelation 21:9 to 22:5, describes the final appearance of the bride of Christ, the New Jerusalem. The parallelism of these two sections involves both similarity and contrast. Both are introduced by one of "the seven angels that had the seven bowls." The heavenly messenger invited the Seer to view the scene by the words, "Come hither." Each represents the terminus of a purpose: one, the end of the trend away from God; the other, the end of redemption.

The parallelism of contrast is equally plain. The former section introduces a harlot; the latter, a bride. The former sets the scene in a wilderness (17:3); the latter, on a mountain (21:10). The former says that on the harlot are written names of blasphemy (17:3); the latter states that the names of the twelve tribes and of the twelve apostles are inscribed on the Holy City (21:12, 14). The former presents Babylon, the city of corruption and judgment (17:6); the latter describes the New Jerusalem which comes down out of heaven pure and chaste (21:10). The former perishes in dire judgment; the latter endures in eternal light. The former is cursed; the latter is blessed.

The book of Revelation gives a divine perspective on history. However its symbols may be interpreted in detail, its overall outlook is that of divine holiness which sees both the virtues and the shortcomings of the churches, and the doom and hope of the world. The message to the churches is sent by the Figure who moves in the midst of the golden lampstands; the scene for the administration of judgment centers around the throne of God (4:2-19:5); and the final judgment is pronounced from the selfsame throne (20:11). In the description of the new heavens and the new earth the throne is still central (22:1) as the source of the river of life. This emphasis on the throne makes clear the concept of the sovereignty of God in Revelation, and His eternal rulership in the affairs of men.

The dominant optimism of the book is countered by its glaring picture of evil. It contains no hint that the world at large will improve with the passing of time, nor that at the end all men will have turned to God in repentance and faith. It depicts the last civilization as highly prosperous, culturally advanced, and utterly godless (18:1-5). The last act of organized humanity is an armed rebellion against God and His Christ (20:7-10). In no other book of the Bible, unless it be in the words of Jesus, is the final doom of sin more terribly drawn (20:15).

To the modern man of the mid-twentieth century, the Apocalypse now seems less apocalyptic than it did to his father and to his grandfather. The mysterious references to images that talked (13:15), to making fire come down out of heaven (13:13), to economic control of large populations (13:16, 17), to compulsory obedience to a synthetic religion (13:14), to the wholesale devastation of the earth by elemental changes in the sea and by physical changes in the heat of the sun (16:3, 8), the summoning of all the kings of the earth to do battle (16:14), the leadership of the nations vested in one or two persons (19:19, 20), and the complete collapse of the center of civilization in "one hour" (18:18-20) are not outside the reach of possibility at the present time. In many respects, the Apocalypse is the most modern book in existence.

With the final promise, "I come quickly," the New Testament ends. God spoke by the law and by the prophets; He has spoken again by His Son, who "now once at the end of the ages hath been manifested to put away sin by the sacrifice of himself" (Heb. 9:26). One greater revelation is yet to come when He "shall appear a second time, apart from sin, to them that wait for him, unto salvation" (Heb. 9:28). To that revelation and to that victory the book of Revelation points.

## Part V

## THE CANON OF THE NEW TESTAMENT

# THE CANON OF THE NEW TESTAMENT

Definition

Internal Testimony

External Testimony

The Informal Witnesses
The Formal Lists or Canons
The Councils

Conclusions

# CHAPTER XXIII

# The Canon of the New Testament

At the close of the first century the books which made up the New Testament had reached their destinations. Not all of them were known to all the Christians at the first; on the contrary, it is quite probable that some early Christians did not see all of the Gospels, nor all of Paul's letters, nor all of the other epistles before the end of the century. Furthermore, many of the apocryphal Gospels, Acts, and Epistles were circulated during the second century and were accepted by some groups, else they would not have survived at all. By what criteria were some accepted and others rejected? By what principles were the four Gospels, Acts, the thirteen Epistles of Paul, the General Epistles, and Revelation brought together to make the New Testament, while others of almost equal age were excluded? These questions constitute the problem of the New Testament canon.

## Definition

The word "canon" is derived from the Greek *kanon*, which meant a "reed," and thence a "rod," or "bar," which, because it was used for measuring, came to mean metaphorically "a standard." In grammar it meant a rule of procedure; in chronology, a table of dates; and in literature it meant a list of works which would correctly be attributed to a given author. Thus "the canon of Plato" refers to the list of treatises which can be ascribed to Plato as genuinely his.

Literary canons are important, because only the genuine works of an author can reveal his thought; and the inclusion of spurious writings in the list would warp or misrepresent the principles which he wished to state. In like fashion, if the canon of the New Testament cannot be established with any degree of accuracy, its authority will be uncertain and there can be no fixed standard for faith and for life.

Contrary to the principle used with most literature, the canon of the New Testament cannot be settled solely on the question of authorship. Nine different men wrote the books in it, nor is there any special reason why only those nine should have been chosen. There is no assignable explanation why Philip, for instance, should not have been inspired to write a Gospel as Matthew was. The criterion which makes all of these works canonical is certainly not uniformity of human authorship. Nevertheless, if it could be shown that any one of the books of the New Testament was falsely attributed to the person whose name it bears, its place in the canon would be endangered.

The canon cannot be determined wholly by the church's acceptance of the books. Some were widely and readily received; a few were hesitantly accepted by certain churches and not at all by others; and some were not mentioned until a relatively late date, or else their right to be included in the canon was definitely disputed. Local prejudice or individual taste could influence the verdict which had come down from the churches and the writers of antiquity. Notwithstanding this fact, what one person or section of the church rejected another person or section accepted; nor was it true that those who passed judgment were so uncritical as to accept anything that struck their fancy irrespective of its inherent merits. The critique of the ancients was no less fallible than that of modern scholars. On the other hand, they had access to records and to traditions that have now perished, and their testimony cannot be set aside simply because it does not belong to the twentieth century. Ecclesiastical assent to canonicity supplies corroborative evidence, though it may not be in itself decisive.

If these foregoing criteria are not sufficient, what is? The true criterion of canonicity is inspiration. "All scripture is given by inspiration of God, and *is* profitable for doctrine, for reproof, for correction, for instruction in righteousness: that the man of God may be perfect, throughly furnished unto all good works" (II Tim. 3:16, 17, A.V.). In other words, whatever was given by inspiration of God was Scripture, and whatever did not come by inspiration of God was not Scripture, if "scripture" means the written record of the authoritative word of God.

If this criterion be adopted as final, one must answer the next question: "How is inspiration to be demonstrated?" The books of the New Testament do not all begin with the statement that they are inspired of God. Some of them deal with very ordinary affairs; others contain historical, literary, and theological puzzles that can be resolved only with difficulty. Can their inspiration be demonstrated to the satisfaction of all?

The answer to this problem is threefold. First, the inspiration of these documents may be supported by their intrinsic content. Second, their inspiration may be corroborated by their moral effect. Last, the historic testimony of the Christian church will show what value was placed on these books, even though the church did not *cause* them to be inspired or canonical.

With regard to their intrinsic content, they all have for their central subject the person and work of Jesus Christ. The Gospels are biographical; Acts recounts the historic effects of His personality; the Epistles are concerned with theological and practical teachings that emanate from a consideration of Him; and the Apocalypse is predictive of His relation to the future. The objection that any prominent character of antiquity could be so immortalized by a body of literature is not valid. Outside the New Testament there is no indication that Jesus Christ was considered important by the leaders and teachers of His day, and there was no natural reason why the writings concerning Him should survive in the Roman world. The New Testament admits that the message about Christ was "unto Jews a stumblingblock, and unto Gentiles foolishness" (I Cor. 1:23). In the eyes of His contemporaries He meant no more than any other aspirant to messiahship who had been suppressed by the government. If the literature regarding Him persisted and grew powerful, there must have been something in it to produce that effect.

The message concerning the person of Christ was unique. Cults centering in individuals were not unknown in the first century, but these individuals were mythical, or else if they were historical their worship did not endure. This unique message centers in the books that are called "canonical." The apocryphal Gospels and Acts are more concerned with miracle-mongering than they are with teaching, and the few apocryphal epistles are mosaics of pieces taken from the acknowledged canon. In precision of narrative, in depth of teaching, and in concentration on the person of Christ, there is a discernible difference between the canonical and the non-canonical books.

In ethical and spiritual effect the canonical books are different. All literature may record human thought; some may influence it profoundly; but the books of the New Testament transform it. Their power is good proof of their inspiration. Although this test may seem to be highly subjective because it is based on human response to the written word, it is nevertheless valid. The writings of the New Testament are not only profitable reading; they are also a potent dynamic.

Their moral effect is demonstrated by their power within the Christian church. While it cannot be contended that every member of the early church possessed a pocket copy of the New Testament which he studied assiduously, it can be shown that the leaders knew it and used it. Wherever its message was proclaimed and received the church expanded and brought with it a moral cleansing of society. Not all professing Christians from the first century onward were lily-white in character, nor was the church always free from evil. Not-withstanding these facts, between the moral standards of paganism and those of the New Testament church there was a great gulf fixed. Love, purity, meekness, truth, and many other virtues which scarcely existed in heathenism came to life. However poorly the Christians may have followed the ideals that they possessed, they were distinct from the pagans around them because of the power of the New Testament truth.

The tests of the divine message and of the moral power of these books cannot be applied sucessfully by a single individual in a limited sphere lest it be argued that the dynamic of the canon was only a chance effect produced by the accidental relation of time and temperament. When the internal testimony of the works themselves and the external testimony of those who knew and used them concur that these works are of God, the criteria of canonicity are made more sure.

## Internal Testimony

Investigation of the internal evidence of the books reveals that the authors assumed a measure of canonical authority. From the first, certain pieces of information and certain aspects of the message concerning Christ were passed on from one person to another as the word of God. In Galatians Paul asserted that his gospel was "not after man. For neither did I receive it from man, nor was I taught it," said he, "but *it came to me* through revelation of Jesus Christ" (Gal. 1:11, 12). In I Corinthians 15:3, 4, he defined his gospel as a message "which also I received: that Christ died for our sins according to the scriptures; and that he was buried; and that he hath been raised on the third day according to the scriptures." He did not profess to have originated this message; he "received" it. In I Thessalonians, one of his first epistles, he said: "We preached unto you the gospel of God" (2:9), the same gospel, doubtless, that is defined in I Corinthians, and then he added: "when ye received from us the word of the message, *even the word* of God, ye accepted *it* not *as* the word of men, but, as it is in truth, the word of God, which also worketh in you that believe" (2:13). Here is a claim within the New Testament itself that (1) the message is the word of God, and (2) that it produced an effect upon those that believed it. Because he had confidence in the authority of this message, Paul added in the second epistle to the Thessalonians: "And if any man obeyeth not our word by this epistle, note that man, that ye have no company with him, to the end that he may be ashamed" (3:14). Thus at the outset of his writing career, Paul looked upon his own productions as the authoritative word of God.

The collection of Paul's epistles early became a canon, for II Peter 3:15, 16 alluded to it as a body of literature to be received as "the other scriptures." The fact that the "ignorant and unstedfast wrest [ed]" it implies that if it had not been authoritative they would have paid little attention to it. From the very first these epistles had canonical quality.

Not all the writings of the New Testament contain similar allusions, but all of them do possess a characteristic that is self-authenticating. The Gospels are devoted almost entirely to quotations of Jesus and to the narrative of His deeds. Their sobriety in treating the miracles when contrasted with some of the puerile and pointless passages in the apocryphal Gospels makes their claim to canonicity all the stronger.[1]

## External Testimony

As observed above, the final decision of this question of the canon could not be made arbitrarily by any one person or by any local group. The distinction between canonical and non-canonical books was the product of a growing spiritual consciousness. At an early date, however, lines of discrimination were drawn; nor were they merely the result of uncritical personal preference or prejudice. The church did not *determine* the canon; it *recognized* the canon. In the fullest sense no church council could create a canon, if inspiration is the essential quality of canonicity, because no group or council could breathe inspiration into works already existing. All that the councils could do was to give their opinion concerning which books were canonical and which were not, and then to let history justify or reverse their verdict.

The external witness to the existence of a New Testament canon is both informal and formal. The informal witness consists of the casual use made of the books of the New Testament by the early church fathers. Their quotations attest both the existence and the authority of the books, for non-existent books cannot be quoted, and the manner of quoting will show whether the quotation implies authority or just passing allusion. The formal witness is found in lists or canons which had been purposely compiled as authoritative lists, or in the records of the councils which dealt with the question.

---

1. For example of the stories of the miracles which Jesus is said to have performed as a child, see J. De Q. Donehoo: *The Apocryphal and Legendary Life of Christ* (New York: The Macmillan Company, 1903), pp. 122-138.

Quotations, of course, may be disputed since they may be so indirect that their origin is uncertain. In many instances, however, even though the quotation may be inexact, its vocabulary or content will identify it as belonging to some book which the author of the quotation must have known and used, so that it is valid for all practical purposes.

## The Informal Witnesses

Probably the earliest document to quote any of the books of the New Testament was I Clement, which was itself considered canonical by some Christians. It is found in Codex Alexandrinus, included with the New Testament books. It was written from Rome to the church in Corinth, and is usually dated about A.D. 95. In it are plain allusions to Hebrews, I Corinthians, Romans, and the Gospel of Matthew.

Ignatius of Syrian Antioch (c. A.D. 116) knew all of Paul's epistles and quoted Matthew, with a possible allusion to John.

Polycarp of Smyrna (c. A.D. 150) was also familiar with the Pauline epistles and the Gospel of Matthew. He quoted I Peter and I John, and probably knew Acts.

The *Didaché* produced during the first half of the second century, used both Matthew and Luke, and many other New Testament books.

The Epistle of Barnabas (c. A.D. 130) quoted Matthew, using the formal phrase, "it is written"[2] to introduce the quotation.

The Shepherd of Hermas, an allegory of the early second century (c. A.D. 140) alluded to James.

Justin Martyr (c. A.D. 100 to 165), a Syrian Greek, who had been a philosopher, referred to Matthew, Mark, Luke, John, Acts, and many of the Pauline epistles. He stated that the "Memoirs of the Apostles," called Gospels, were read every Sunday in the worship of the Church along with the Old Testament.[3] His pupil, Tatian, composed the first harmony of the Gospels, called the Diatessaron, which became a standard harmony for the church for many years.

With the age of Irenaeus, who flourished about A.D. 170, there was no question that the books of the New Testament were authoritative. The growth of Gnosticism and of kindred errors evoked a flood of apologetic literature which continued to the time of Origen (A.D. 250). The necessity of an authoritative basis for argument became apparent and the apologists turned naturally to the apostolic writings. Irenaeus used and quoted at length all four Gospels, Acts, the Epistles of Paul,

2. *Epistle of Barnabas*, IV, 14.
3. Justin Martyr, *Apology*, I 66, 67.

many of the General Epistles, and Revelation. He said that there could be only four Gospels, and that any attempt to increase or to decrease the number would be heresy. He quoted Paul more than two hundred times. In one passage he criticized Marcion for saying that Luke and the epistles of Paul were alone authentic, by which he implied that he accepted as authoritative not only those writings acknowledged by Marcion, but others as well.[4] He alluded to every book of the New Testament except Philemon and III John.

Tertullian of Carthage (c. A.D. 200) quoted from all of the New Testament except Philemon, James, II and III John. Like Irenaeus, he quoted not simply for illustrations, but as proof of truth.

Origen, the great Alexandrian father who was contemporary with Tertullian (c. A.D. 185 to 250), was acquainted not only with the church of his own city, but had traveled extensively in Rome, Antioch, Caesarea, and Jerusalem. He divided the sacred books into two classes, the *homologoumena,* which were undoubtedly genuine and which were accepted by all the churches, and the *antilegoumena,* which were disputed and not accepted by all the churches. The former included the Gospels, thirteen epistles of Paul, I Peter, I John, Acts, and the Apocalypse. The latter consisted of Hebrews, II Peter, II and III John, James, and Jude. In the same class he placed Barnabas, the Shepherd of Hermas, the Didaché, and the Gospel of the Hebrews. On some occasions he used many of these as Scripture, so that he did not draw the lines of the canon as closely as they were drawn later.

In the Nicene period, Eusebius of Caesarea (c. A.D. 265 to 340) followed Origen's lead.[5] He placed in the category of accepted books the Gospels, fourteen epistles of Paul including Hebrews, I Peter, the Acts, I John, and Revelation. Among the disputed books were James, Jude, II Peter, II and III John. He rejected flatly the Acts of Paul, the Revelation of Peter, the Shepherd of Hermas, and others, and drew a sharp line between the canonical and apocryphal works.

These men who were leaders of the church, and others who are not mentioned here, spoke for the most part for themselves. Their judgment may not have been infallible, but they were by no means uncritical recipients of unreliable rumor. While they did not agree unanimously on the canonicity of all the books of the New Testament, they show very fairly that a canon had begun to be formed in their day, and that some books were accepted without hesitation while others were regarded as dubious.

---

4. Irenaeus, *Against Heresies,* III, xii, 12.
5. Eusebius, *Historia Ecclesiae,* III, iii, 25.

## The Formal Lists or Canons

The list of New Testament books known or accepted by individual churches or leaders may be deduced from the quotations and statements that appear in the works of the early fathers. Such lists, however, were unofficial, and were not always representative of anything more than private taste or opinion. Sometimes they reflected general practice, but quite often they reflected the canon of one locality or of one church, or of one man.

The first known canon to be adopted consciously by any sizable unitary group of people was the Canon of Marcion, which appeared about A.D. 140. Marcion was a native of Sinope in Pontus, where his father was a bishop. He was so anti-Judaic that he repudiated the whole Old Testament and sought to establish a canon of the New Testament that would be free from Jewish influences. He selected Luke for his Gospel, though he rejected the first two chapters containing the account of the virgin birth, and used ten epistles of Paul, excluding the Pastorals and Hebrews. His list began with Galatians and was followed by I and II Corinthians, Romans, I and II Thessalonians, Ephesians, which he called Laodiceans, Colossians, Philippians, and Philemon.

The canon of Marcion produced a violent reaction in the church. The fact that he rejected certain books showed that they had been regarded as authoritative in his day, and his opponents flew to their defense. Irenaeus attacked him, and Tertullian wrote five books against his errors. Marcion's arbitrary organization of a canon showed (1) that the books which he included must have been regarded as indisputably authentic, and (2) that those which he rejected were accepted as canonical by the masses at large.

A second list of great importance was the Muratorian Canon, named for the Italian historian and librarian who first found it in the Ambrosian Library at Milan. The manuscript itself is not older than the seventh century, but its content probably belongs to the last third of the second century about A.D. 170.[6] Since the manuscript is only a fragment of a larger work, it is not complete. It begins in the middle of a sentence, and the first book mentioned is Luke, which the fragment calls the third Gospel. Matthew and Mark almost certainly preceded

---

6. For a full discussion of the Muratorian Canon, see C. R. Gregory. *Canon and Text of the New Testament* (New York: Charles Scribner's Sons, 1912), pp. 129-133. The Latin text is given in A. Souter's *The Text and Canon of the New Testament* (New York: Charles Scribner's Sons, 1923), pp. 208-211.

Luke in this list; John follows with an unmistakable reference to the First Epistle. Acts, I and II Corinthians, Ephesians, Philippians, Colossians, Galatians, I and II Thessalonians, Romans, Philemon, Titus, I and II Timothy, Jude, II and III John, and Revelation were also included. The writer of the Muratorian fragment rejected the epistles of Paul to the Laodiceans and to the Alexandrians; and, while he put the Revelation of Peter in the same "acknowledged" class as the Revelation of John, he was dubious about it for he said, "Some of you do not think that it should be read publicly in the church." He did not mention James or Hebrews, nor the Petrine epistles. Perhaps he was ignorant of them, though it seems hardly possible that he should have overlooked Hebrews when Clement of Rome quoted it freely.

An African list of the fourth century (c. A.D. 360) written by an unknown person included the four Gospels, thirteen epistles of Paul, Acts, Revelation, three epistles of John, of which the writer acknowledged only one, and two of Peter, of which he allowed only one to be genuine.

The "Festal Letter" of Athanasius (A.D. 367)[7] distinguishes sharply between "God-inspired Scripture . . . handed down to our fathers by those who were eyewitnesses and servants of the word from the beginning" and the "so called secret writings" of heretics. Athanasius' list comprised the four Gospels, Acts, James, I and II Peter, I, II, and III John, Jude, Romans, I and II Corinthians, Galatians, Ephesians, Philippians, Colossians, I and II Thessalonians, Hebrews, I and II Timothy, Titus, Philemon, Revelation. "These," said Athanasius, "are springs of salvation . . . let no one add to them or take away from them."

The church fathers who were engaged in controversy were more positive about the veracity and reliability of the writings of the New Testament than those who quoted it simply for the edification of the faithful, for the latter accepted them without question, whereas the pagans and heretics did not do so. By the close of the fourth century public opinion had agreed quite thoroughly on the reliability and authenticity of these books.

## The Councils

Formal discussion of the canon by delegates of the church meeting in official council did not take place until the close of the fourth century. The first council at which the subject was introduced was the

---

7. A Souter, *op. cit.*, pp. 213-217.

Council of Laodicea in 363. Apparently it was not a full assembly of all the churches, but represented chiefly the region of Phrygia. The fifty-ninth canon of this council decreed that only canonical books of the New Testament should be read in the church services; but the so-called sixteenth canon, which contained a definitive list, is probably not genuine and cannot be cited as the actual ruling of the Council.

The Third Council of Carthage in 397 issued a decree similar to that of the Synod of Laodicea and submitted a list of writings identical with the twenty-seven books of the present New Testament.

The Council of Hippo in 419 reiterated the same decision and the same list.

## Conclusions

From the data assembled here it is evident that not all of the present books of the New Testament were known or accepted by all of the churches in the east and in the west during the first four centuries of the Christian era. Some, like the Gospels, were known from the earliest days; others, like Hebrews, were known but were questioned because their authorship was uncertain; still others, such as II Peter or II and III John, were not mentioned at all, or their right to a place in the canon was disputed. No one of these books was accepted by the churches because of ecclesiastical compulsion. The Councils that discussed the canon were not held until the fourth century, by which time the New Testament had already become the Scripture of the church.

The seeming reluctance with which certain books like James, II and III John, and Jude were taken into the canon does not mean that they were spurious. Philemon, II and III John, and Jude are all so brief that they would only seldom be quoted, and furthermore they were directed to individuals whose location may have been obscure. Unlike the larger epistles that were sent to sizable churches or that were circulated throughout provinces, the smaller epistles would not come into general notice until there was a demand for them or until the persons or groups to which they belonged called them to public attention.

The variations in the canon, then, were due to local conditions and interest. They showed, however, that in spite of miracle-mongering and superstition, the churches and their leaders did not accept every manuscript that happened to bear the name of an apostle or that professed to relate previously untold history and teaching. The existing canon emerged from a large body of oral and written tradition and speculation, and made its way in the churches because of its inherent authenticity and dynamic power.

Three stages in the early development of the canon have been noted. First, the writings are quoted individually by authors who take the force of their witness for granted rather than making it a point of argument. Second, writers like Irenaeus and Origen, who were engaged in controversy, felt the necessity of defining their authorities, but did not appeal to any single church decision. Last came the verdict of the councils which followed the judgment of the leaders past and present, and drew an official distinction between the canonical and the apocryphal works.

This distinction appeared in the list of books in the various versions and manuscripts used by the churches. The great manuscripts Sinaiticus (Aleph) and Vaticanus (B), dating from the fourth century, originally included all of the New Testament. The Syriac version did not admit II and III John, II Peter, Jude, and Revelation into its canon until the sixth century.

A study of the various quoted books, lists, and canons of the first four centuries will show that the books most generally disputed or omitted were James, Jude, II Peter, II and III John, and Philemon. Several reasons may be advanced for the neglect of these works. James was written to the members of the Jewish Dispersion and contained little of doctrinal interest that would appeal to the speculative mind of Greek Christians. Jude, II and III John, and Philemon were all so brief that they had little content that would be of general appeal. The last three were also private or semi-private in content, so that they may not have been put in circulation as quickly as the more extensive works of their authors. II Peter was disputed up to the time of Eusebius. It was quoted less and discussed more by the church fathers than any other single book of the New Testament. Jerome stated that the hesitancy of the fathers to accept this epistle was because its style was so different from that of I Peter.[8] Whether or not the seeming disparity between II Peter and I Peter is due wholly to a difference in amanuensis may never be settled. The fact that it was written to a group of people on the outer fringe of the Christian frontier to meet a peculiar emergency may account for the small acquaintance which the early churches had with it, and for its questionable status among the biblical students of the first three centuries.

Since the fourth century there have been no material changes in the recognized canon, although from the period of the Reformation to the

---

8. Jerome, *Epistle to Hedibia*, 120, Quaest. xi.

present many individual viewpoints have been expressed. Luther virtually rejected the Epistle of James, chiefly because it did not seem to accord with the doctrine of justification by faith. Calvin was unsure of II Peter. In more recent days the pursuit of historical criticism has almost dissolved the idea of any canon by making the difference between the literature of the New Testament and the apocryphal books, and the writings of the fathers, a difference of degree or of time rather than of kind or of quality. Such a conclusion would strip the New Testament of any objective authority and would make any general application of its truth impossible.

The canon, then, is not the product of any one person's arbitrary judgment, nor was it set by conciliar vote. It was the outcome of the use of various writings which proved their merits and their unity by their inward dynamic. Some were recognized more slowly than others because of their small size, or because of their remote or private destination or anonymity of authorship, or because of their seeming lack of applicability to the immediate ecclesiastical need. None of these factors mitigates against the inspiration of any one of these books, or against its right to its place in the authoritative word of God.

# APPENDICES

# APPENDICES

# THE ROMAN EMPERORS OF THE FIRST CENTURY

| Years | Names | Events | References |
|---|---|---|---|
| 30 B.C.-<br>A.D. 14 | AUGUSTUS | Birth of Christ | Luke 2:1 |
| A.D. 14-37 | TIBERIUS | Ministry and death of<br>Jesus Christ | Luke 3:1 |
| A.D. 37-41 | CALIGULA | | |
| A.D. 41-54 | CLAUDIUS | Famine<br>Expulsion of Jews from Rome | Acts 11:28<br>Acts 18:2 |
| A.D. 54-68 | NERO | Trial of Paul<br>Persecution at Rome | Acts 25:10-12<br>27:24<br>II Tim. 4:16, 17 |
| A.D. 68 | GALBA | | |
| A.D. 69 | OTHO | | |
| A.D. 69 | VITELLIUS | | |
| A.D. 69-79 | VESPASIAN | Destruction of Jerusalem | |
| A.D. 79-81 | TITUS | | |
| A.D. 81-96 | DOMITIAN | Persecution (?) | |
| A.D. 96-98 | NERVA | | |
| A.D. 98-117 | TRAJAN | | |

# THE ROMAN PROCURATORS OF JUDEA

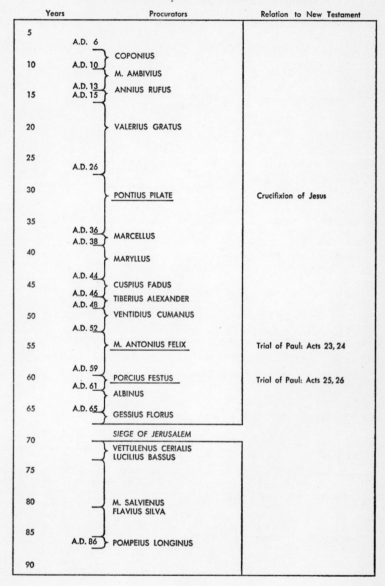

| Years | Procurators | Relation to New Testament |
|---|---|---|
| 5 | A.D. 6 | |
| 10 | COPONIUS<br>A.D. 10<br>M. AMBIVIUS | |
| 15 | A.D. 13<br>A.D. 15 — ANNIUS RUFUS | |
| 20 | VALERIUS GRATUS | |
| 25 | | |
| 30 | A.D. 26<br>PONTIUS PILATE | Crucifixion of Jesus |
| 35 | | |
| 40 | A.D. 36 — MARCELLUS<br>A.D. 38<br>MARYLLUS | |
| 45 | A.D. 44 — CUSPIUS FADUS<br>A.D. 46 — TIBERIUS ALEXANDER<br>A.D. 48 | |
| 50 | VENTIDIUS CUMANUS<br>A.D. 52 | |
| 55 | M. ANTONIUS FELIX | Trial of Paul: Acts 23, 24 |
| 60 | A.D. 59<br>PORCIUS FESTUS<br>A.D. 61 | Trial of Paul: Acts 25, 26 |
| 65 | ALBINUS<br>A.D. 65<br>GESSIUS FLORUS | |
| 70 | SIEGE OF JERUSALEM<br>VETTULENUS CERIALIS<br>LUCILIUS BASSUS | |
| 75 | | |
| 80 | M. SALVIENUS<br>FLAVIUS SILVA | |
| 85 | | |
| 90 | A.D. 86 — POMPEIUS LONGINUS | |

# THE HERODIAN FAMILY

**GENERATION I**

HEROD THE GREAT
King of Judea
A.D. 37-4 B.C.
Matt. 2:1-19
Luke 1:5

**GENERATION II**

Son of Doris
Antipater

Sons of *Mariamne*
Aristobulus
Alexander

Son of *Mariamne* of Simon
Herod Philip
(First husband of
Herodias — Mark 6:17)

Sons of *Malthace*
HEROD ANTIPAS
Tetrarch of Galilee
4 B.C. - A.D. 39
Luke 3:1, Mark 6:14ff.
Luke 13:31ff., 23:7-12

ARCHELAUS
Ethnarch of Judea
Matt. 2:22

Son of *Cleopatra*
HEROD PHILIP
Tetrarch of Iturea
and Trachonitis
4 B.C. - A.D. 34
Luke 3:1

**GENERATION III**

Herod of Chalcis

HEROD AGRIPPA I
King of Judea
A.D. 37-44.
Acts 12:1-24

*Herodias*
Consort of Herod Antipas
Mark 6:17

**GENERATION IV**

*Bernice*
became consort of her brother
Acts 25:13

HEROD AGRIPPA II
Tetrarch of Chalcis and of
northern territory
A.D. 48-70
Acts 25:13-26:32

*Drusilla*
married *FELIX*
procurator of Judea
A.D. 59(?)-61(?)
Acts 24:24

*Salome*
Matt. 14:6-11

Reigning kings of New Testament note are in CAPITALS, wives and relatives by marriage are in *italics*. Other members of the house are in small letters.

433

## A CHART OF THE CANONS OF THE FIRST FOUR CENTURIES

| BOOKS | INDIVIDUALS | | | | | | | | | | | CANONS | | | | COUNCILS | |
|---|---|---|---|---|---|---|---|---|---|---|---|---|---|---|---|---|---|
| DATE | 95 | 150 | 150 (?) | c.130 | c.140 | c.140 | c.170 | c.200 | c.200 | c.250 | c.315 | c.140 | c.170 | c.360 | 367 | 397 | 419 |
| SOURCE | CLEMENT (Rome) | POLYCARP | DIDACHE | BARNABAS | HERMAS | JUSTIN MARTYR | IRENAEUS | CLEMENT (Alex.) | TERTULLIAN | ORIGEN | EUSEBIUS | MARCION | MURATORIAN | CHELTENHAM | ATHANASIUS | CARTHAGE | HIPPO |
| MATTHEW | / | / | / | / | | / | / | / | / | / | / | | X | X | X | X | X |
| MARK | | | | | | / | / | / | / | / | X | | X | X | X | X | X |
| LUKE | | | / | | | / | / | / | / | / | X | X | X | X | X | X | X |
| JOHN | | | | | | / | / | / | / | / | X | | X | X | X | X | X |
| ACTS | | | | | | / | / | | / | / | X | | X | X | X | X | X |
| ROMANS | / | / | | | | / | / | | / | / | X | X | X | X | X | X | X |
| I CORINTHIANS | / | / | | | | | / | | / | / | X | X | X | X | X | X | X |
| II CORINTHIANS | | / | | | | / | / | | / | / | X | X | X | X | X | X | X |
| GALATIANS | | / | | | | / | / | | / | / | X | X | X | X | X | X | X |
| EPHESIANS | | / | | | | | / | | / | / | X | X | X | X | X | X | X |
| PHILIPPIANS | | / | | | | | / | | / | / | X | X | X | X | X | X | X |
| COLOSSIANS | | / | | | | / | / | | / | / | X | X | X | X | X | X | X |
| I THESS. | | / | | | | | / | | / | / | X | X | X | X | X | X | X |
| II THESS. | | / | | | | / | / | | / | / | X | X | X | X | X | X | X |
| I TIMOTHY | | | | | | | / | | / | / | X | | X | X | X | X | X |
| II TIMOTHY | | | | | | | / | | / | / | X | | X | X | X | X | X |
| TITUS | | | | | | | / | | / | / | X | | X | X | X | X | X |
| PHILEMON | | | | | | | | | | | X | X | X | X | X | X | X |
| HEBREWS | / | | | / | | | / | | / | ? | X | | | | X | X | X |
| JAMES | | | | | / | | | | | | ? | | | | X | X | X |
| I PETER | | / | | | | / | / | | / | X | X | | | X | X | X | X |
| II PETER | | | | | | | | | | ? | ? | | | ? | X | X | X |
| I JOHN | | / | | | | | / | | / | | X | | X | X | X | X | X |
| II JOHN | | | | | | | / | | | ? | ? | | X | ? | X | X | X |
| III JOHN | | | | | | | | | | ? | ? | | X | ? | X | X | X |
| JUDE | | | | | | | | | / | | ? | | X | | X | X | X |
| REVELATION | | | | | | / | / | | / | X | X | | X | X | X | X | X |

SIGNS: / denotes quotation or allusion; ? denotes that the book is mentioned as doubtful; X means that it is mentioned by name and considered authentic.

# A TABLE OF ENGLISH TRANSLATIONS OF THE NEW TESTAMENT

| Translation or Editor | Date | Remarks |
| --- | --- | --- |
| Wycliffe and Purvey | 1382-88 | Printed in 1848. |
| Tyndale | 1525 | |
| Coverdale | 1535 | |
| Matthew's Bible | 1537 | |
| Taverner's Bible | 1539 | |
| Cranmer-Coverdale | 1539 | "The Great Bible" |
| "Geneva Bible" | 1557 | Used by Puritans. |
| "Bishops' Bible" | 1568 | Revision of "Great Bible" |
| Douay, or Rheims | 1582 | Catholic translation. |
| King James Version | 1611 | Sometimes called "Authorized |
| Revised King James | 1769 | Version." Produced by committee. |
| Whitton | 1745 | |
| Wesley | 1755 | New Testament with Notes. |
| Newcome | 1796 | |
| Kneeland | 1823 | |
| Palfrey | 1830 | |
| Alford | 1870 | Private revision of King James by a noted English scholar. |
| Revised Version | 1881-1885 | Revision of King James Version by a company of English and American scholars. |
| Spencer | 1898 | Catholic |
| Ballentine | 1899 | American vernacular |
| Twentieth Century | 1899-1900 | Translated by about twenty anonymous scholars |
| American Revised Version | 1901 | Similar to English Revision of 1881, with some modifications representing dissenting judgment of American Committee. |

| Translation or Editor | Date | Remarks |
|---|---|---|
| Weymouth | 1903 | |
| Moffatt | 1913 | |
| Ballantyne | 1923 | "Riverside New Testament" |
| Goodspeed | 1923 | Part of "American Translation of the Bible." |
| Montgomery | 1923 | "Centenary Translation." |
| Way | 1926 | Translation of Paul's Epistles and Hebrews. Sixth Edition. |
| Fenton, Ferrar | ? | |
| Challoner-Rheims | 1941 | Revision of Douay Version. |
| Verkuyl | 1945 | Berkeley Version. |
| Revised Standard Version | 1946 | Produced by Committee. |
| Williams | 1950 | |
| Phillips: Letters to Young Churches | 1951 | Translation of Epistles |
| The Gospels | 1953 | Both a free paraphrase. |

# BIBLIOGRAPHY

# Bibliography

The accompanying bibliography has been prepared especially for the use of students and teachers to facilitate the selection of collateral reading. It is not intended to cover all possible titles in the field of New Testament study, nor is it calculated for the needs of the advanced specialist in research. It is designed to give the data used for the sources of this book, and to enable the student to pursue his investigations farther than the foregoing text can take him.

The classification follows generally the organization of this book, beginning with works of general scope which can be used as primary texts, and continuing with reading lists on the subjects that are treated in the successive chapters. Instead of listing individual volumes of commentaries that occur in sets, the commentary as a whole is listed, and the reader may consult the appropriate volume that deals with the book which he is studying. In some instances references to single volumes of a commentary are given in the footnotes.

Not all books in this list represent the conservative point of view. Those that are most valuable from that standpoint are marked by an asterisk(*). Books that are not necessarily conservative but that are useful for general information are marked by the symbol(†).

Periodical literature has been generally omitted from this bibliography because it is not always easily available in the average school library. Exceptions will be made in the case of articles of special importance which are cited in the footnotes.

Brief comments are added to many of the titles to assist the reader in his selection.

# Bibliography

## GENERAL TOOLS

### The Text

THE HOLY BIBLE Containing the Old and New Testaments. American Standard Version. New York: Thomas Nelson and Sons, 1901.

NOVUM TESTAMENTUM GRAECE cum apparatu critico curavit D. Eberhard Nestle. novis curis elaboravit D. Erwin Nestle. Editio vicesima prima. Stuttgart: Priviligierte Wurttembergische Bibelanstalt, 1952. The most inexpensive and practical Greek text.

Burton, E. D. and Goodspeed, E. J. *A Harmony of the Synoptic Gospels.* New York etc.: Charles Scribner's Sons, n.d. Pp. xv, 279. Uses text of the American Standard Version.

Burton, E. D. and Stevens, W. A. *A Harmony of the Gospels for Historical Study.* Third Edition, Revised. New York: Charles Scribner's Sons, 1904. Pp. xv, 275.

Robertson, A. T. *A Harmony of the Gospels for Students of the Life of Christ.* New York: Harper & Brothers, Publishers, 1922. Pp. xxxvii, 305.

Wieand, Albert Cassel *A New Harmony of the Gospels — The Gospel Records of the Message and Mission of Jesus Christ.* Grand Rapids, Mich.: Wm. B. Eerdmans Publishing Co., 1953. Pp. 268. Text of Revised Standard Version. Contains many useful diagrams and maps.

### Concordances

*Englishman's Greek Concordance of the New Testament.* Ninth Edition. London: Samuel Bagster and Sons, Ltd., 1903. Pp. 1020, 14, 71.

Moulton, W. F. and Geden, A. S. *A Concordance to the Greek New Testament.* Second Edition. Edinburgh: T. & T. Clark, 1899. Pp. xi, 1033.

Strong, James *The Exhaustive Concordance of the Bible.* New York. Abingdon-Cokesbury Press, 1947.

Walker, J. B. R. *The Comprehensive Concordance to the Holy Scriptures.* New York: The Macmillan Company, 1948. Pp. vi. 957. The best English concordance for general use with the King James Version.

Young, Robert *Analytical Concordance to the Bible.* Twenty-first American Edition. Ed. by Wm. B. Stevenson. New York: Funk and Wagnalls, n.d. Grand Rapids: Wm. B. Eerdmans Publishing Co., 1951.

### Bible Dictionaries

*Dictionary of the Bible.* James Hastings, Editor. 5 volumes. New York: Charles Scribner's Sons, 1902. Complete and scholarly.

*Dictionary of Christ and the Gospels.* James Hastings, Editor. 2 volumes. New York: Charles Scribner's Sons, 1908.

*Dictionary of the Apostolic Church.* James Hastings, Editor. 2 volumes. New York: Charles Scribner's Sons, 1915.

*\*The International Standard Bible Encyclopedia.* James Orr, General Editor; John L. Nuelsen, Edgar Y. Mullins, Assistant Editors; Morris O. Evans, Managing Editor; Melvin Grove Kyle, Revising Editor. 5 volumes. Grand Rapids, Mich.: Wm. B. Eerdmans Publishing Co., 1952. Predominantly conservative.

†*The Westminster Dictionary of the Bible.* John D. Davis, Editor. Fifth Edition Revised and Rewritten by Henry S. Gehman. Philadelphia: The Westminster Press, 1944. Inclines toward liberal critical views of authorship of O. T.

## Handbooks

*Arnold, Arthur O. and Hall, G. F. *A New Testament Handbook.* St. Peter, Minn.: Gustavus Adolphus College Press, 1948, Pp. 208.

Heim, Ralph D. *Workbook for New Testament Study.* New York: The Ronald Press, 1948. Pp. 124.

*Manley, G. T. *The New Bible Handbook.* London: Inter-Varsity Fellowship, 1948, Pp. xii, 433. For New Testament, see pp. 300-433.

Manson, T. W. *A Companion to the Bible.* Edinburgh: T. & T. Clark, 1942. Pp. xii, 515.

Robertson, A. T. *Syllabus for New Testament Study.* Fourth Revised and Enlarged Edition. Louisville, Ky.: Baptist World Publishing Co., 1923. Pp. 207. Contains full bibliography.

*Scroggie, W. Graham *Know Your Bible.* Vol. II: Analytical. *The New Testament.* London: Pickering & Inglis, Ltd., n.d. A systematic study of the New Testament with excellent analytical outlines.

†Wade, G. W. *New Testament History.* Second Edition, Revised. London: Methuen & Co., Ltd., 1932. Pp. xi, 690. Liberal in viewpoint; contains large bulk of critical material. Good treatment of historical backgrounds. See Pp. 1-105.

## Geography

†Wright, G. E. and Filson, F. V. *The Westminster Historical Atlas to the Bible.* Philadelphia: The Westminster Press. 1946. Pp. 114. Archaeological and geographical data fully up to date. For N. T. see Pp. 70-114. Follows liberal critical position.

Smith, George Adam *The Historical Geography of the Holy Land.* New York: Armstrong, 1895. Pp. xxv, 692. Still a standard work.

## Archaeology and Introduction

Cobern, Camden A. *The New Archaeological Discoveries and Their Bearing upon the New Testament and upon the Life and Times of the Primitive Church.* Ninth Edition. New York: Funk and Wagnalls Co., 1929. Pp. xxxiv, 748.

*Free, J. P. *Archaeology and Bible History.* Wheaton, Ill.: Van Kampen Press, 1950. Pp. xviii, 398.

†Goodspeed, Edgar J. *An Introduction to the New Testament.* Chicago: The University of Chicago Press, 1937. Pp. xiii, 362. Modern critical viewpoint.

Lake, Kirsopp and Silva *An Introduction to the New Testament.* New York and London: Harper & Brothers Publishers, 1937. Pp. x, 302.

*Miller, H. S. *General Biblical Introduction.* Houghton, N. Y.; The Word-Bearer Press, 1937. Excellent thorough treatment of the origins of the Bible.

Milligan, George *The New Testament Documents: Their Origin and Early History.* London: Macmillan & Co., Ltd., 1913. Pp. xvi, 322.

Pullan, Leighton *The Books of the New Testament.* London: Rivingtons, 1901. Pp. 300.

*Salmon, George *A Historical Introduction to the Books of the New Testament* Ninth Edition. London: J. Murray, 1899. Pp. xxxi, 643.

Scott, Ernest Findlay *The Literature of the New Testament.* New York: Columbia University Press, 1932. Pp. xiii, 312. A liberal introduction to the N. T.

*Thiessen, Henry C. *Introduction to the New Testament.* Grand Rapids, Mich.: Wm. B. Eerdmans Publishing Co., 1951. Pp. xx, 347. A consistently conservative introduction.

*Zahn, Theodor B. *Introduction to the New Testament.* Translated from the third German edition, ed. by J. M. Trout, W. A. Mather, and others. Three volumes Edinburgh: T. & T. Clark, 1909. Grand Rapids: Kregel Publications, 1953. The best advanced conservative introduction.

**Commentaries**

*Alford, Henry *The Greek New Testament.* New Edition. Four Volumes. Boston: Lee & Shepard, 1878.

*An American Commentary on the New Testament.* Alvah Hovey, Editor. Philadelphia: American Baptist Publication Society, 1881-1890. Complete on the New Testament. Broadus on *Matthew* is exceptionally good.

*The Cambridge Bible for Schools and Colleges.* J. J. S. Perowne, General Editor. Cambridge: University Press, 1886 —

*The Cambridge Greek Testament.* J. J. S. Perowne, General Editor. Cambridge: University Press, 1894-1927. Passed through several editors after Perowne; some volumes rewritten.

*The Expositor's Greek Testament.* W. Robertson Nicoll, Editor. Five volumes. Grand Rapids: Wm. B. Eerdmans Publishing Co., 1952.

†*The International Critical Commentary.* Edited by C. A. Briggs, S. R. Driver, A. Plummer. New York: Charles Scribner's Sons, 1896-1929. Covers all of N. T. except Acts. Based on Greek text; critical and grammatical. Theological and critical viewpoints vary.

*The New International Commentary on The New Testament.* Ned B. Stonehouse, General Editor. Wm. B. Eerdmans Publishing Co., 1951. Now in process of publication. An expository commentary; viewpoint of conservative theology.

*The Interpreter's Bible.* Editors: G. A. Buttrick, W. R. Bowie, John Knox, Paul Scherer, Samuel Terrien, Nolan B. Harmon. Twelve volumes. New York and Nashville: Abingdon-Cokesbury Press, 1951— For New Testament see Vols. VII-XII. Now in process of publication. Most recent and extensive of commentaries; viewpoint of liberal theology.

*Lenski, Richard Charles Henry *Interpretation of St. Matthew's Gospel* [and the other books of the New Testament]. Columbus, O., Lutheran Book Concern, 1932-1946. Lutheran viewpoint; strongly conservative.

Meyer, H. A. W. *Critical and Exegetical Commentary on the New Testament.* Translation Revised and Edited by Wm. P. Dickson and Frederick Crombie. Edinburgh: T. & T. Clark, 1877. Detailed comment on Greek text; exhaustive in scope.

*Robertson, A. T. *Word Pictures in the New Testament.* Five volumes. New York: Harper & Brothers, Publishers, 1933.

Smith, David *The Disciple's Commentary on the New Testament.* Five volumes. London: Hodder & Stoughton Ltd., 1928-32.

Vincent, Marvin R. *Word Studies in the New Testament,* Second Edition. Four Volumes. Grand Rapids: Wm. B. Eerdmans Publishing Co. 1918, 1919. Old, but still useful. Does not include discoveries in the papyri.

# CHAPTER I: INTRODUCTION

**The New Testament, Its Meaning and Content.**

For reference material on this chapter, see the handbooks cited above, and articles in the Bible dictionaries on "The New Testament."

## PART I. THE WORLD OF THE NEW TESTAMENT
## CHAPTER II: THE POLITICAL WORLD

Angus, Samuel "Roman Empire, and Christianity," in *International Standard Bible Encyclopaedia*, IV, 2598-2611. Broad general article, covering whole period.

†Boak, A. E. R. *A History of Rome to 565 A.D.* New York: The Macmillan Company, 1921. Pp. xvi, 444. A college textbook on Roman history

†CAMBRIDGE ANCIENT HISTORY. Editors, S. A. Cook, F. E. Adcock, M. P. Charlesworth. Volume X: *The Augustan Empire* 44 B.C.-A.D. 70. New York: The Macmillan Company, 1934. Pp. xxxii, 1058. An exhaustive discussion of the period.

Duckworth, H. T. F. "The Roman Provincial System" in *Beginnings of Christianity*, Part I, Vol. I, pp. 171-207. Editors, F. J. Foakes-Jackson and Kirsopp Lake. London: Macmillan & Co., Ltd., 1920. A thorough discussion of the Roman provincial system.

Hammond, Mason *The Augustan Principate*. Cambridge, Mass.: Harvard University Press, 1933. Pp. 341. Very full bibliography. Deals with aspects of the Principate, such as the Senate, the army etc.

Marsh, Frank Burr *The Reign of Tiberius*. Oxford: University Press, 1931. Pp. vii, 335. For last days of Tiberius, see pp. 160-229.

Ramsay, W. M. *The Church in the Roman Empire Before A.D. 170*. New York and London: G. P. Putnam's Sons, n. d. Pp. xv, 494.

†Rostovtzeff, M. *A History of the Ancient World*. Vol. II: *Rome*. Translated from the Russian by J. D. Duff. Oxford: Clarendon Press, 1928. Pp. 387. Thorough and well illustrated.

†————————*The Social and Economic History of the Hellenistic World*. Vols. I, II, and III. Oxford: Clarendon Press, 1941. Pp. 602, 1312, 1779. See esp. Vol. I, Chap. III, Pp. 126-187, for economic and social conditions; Vol. II. Chap. VIII, pp. 1032-1098 for a good general estimate of Hellenism.

Salmon, Edward T. *A History of the Roman World from 30 B.C. to A.D. 138*. New York: The Macmillan Company, 1944. Pp. 363. Brief, clear, comprehensive.

Tarn, W. W. *Alexander the Great*. Vol. I: *Narrative*. Cambridge: University Press, 1948. Pp. xi, 161. A condensed account of Alexander's campaigns. See pp. 121-148 for discussion of his personality and aims.

### History of the Jews

Finkelstein, Louis, Editor. *The Jews: Their History, Culture, and Religion*. Two Volumes. New York: Harper & Brothers, Publishers, 1949. Pp. xxxiii, 744, vi, 1431. For Post-Biblical Literature and the Talmud, see Pp. 70-114, 115-215. See also "Hellenistic Jewish Literature" by Ralph Marcus, 745-783.

Graetz, H. *Popular History of the Jews*. Translated by Rabbi A. B. Rhine. Fifth Edition. New York: Hebrew Publishing Co., 1937. See Vol. II, pp. 1-232. Contains Jewish estimate of John the Baptist and Jesus.

Josephus, Flavius *Antiquities of the Jews* and *Wars of the Jews*. English Translation by H. St. John Thackeray and Ralph Marcus. *Loeb Library Translation*. Eight Volumes. London: William Heinemann, 1926—

Latimer, Elizabeth W. *Judea from Cyrus to Titus*, 537 B.C.-70 A.D. Chicago: A. C. McClurg & Co., 1899. Pp. 382. Elementary, but full and helpful.

Kent, Charles Foster *A History of the Jewish People During the Babylonian, Persian, and Greek Periods*. Fifth Edition. New York: Charles Scribner's Sons, 1902. Pp. xxii, 380. For Greek period. see pp. 271-340. Useful maps and charts. Written on basis of liberal critical view.

†Oesterley, W. O. E. *A History of Israel.* Vol. II: From the Fall of Jerusalem to the Bar-Kokhba Revolt, A. D. 135. Oxford: The Clarendon Press, 1939.

Riggs, James Stevenson *A History of the Jewish People During the Maccabean and Roman Periods.* New York: Charles Scribner's Sons, 1908. Pp. xxi, 320. Contains maps and numerous charts.

Sachar, Abram Leon *A History of the Jews.* Second Edition, Revised to 1940. New York: Alfred A. Knopf, 1940. Pp. xv, 397, xvi.

## CHAPTER III: THE SOCIAL WORLD AND THE ECONOMIC WORLD

†Angus, Samuel *The Environment of Early Christianity.* New York: Charles Scribner's Sons, 1920. Pp. xi, 240. See esp. pp. 30-67.

Bailey, Cyril. Editor. *The Legacy of Rome.* Oxford: The Clarendon Press, 1924. Pp. xii, 512. Science, pp. 265-324; Agriculture, 475-512.

†Couch, Herbert N. and Geer, Russel M. *Classical Civilization: Rome.* Russel M. Geer. Second Edition. New York: Prentice-Hall, Inc., 1950. Pp. xxiv, 482. Treats cultural and social life of Rome very satisfactorily.

Frank, Tenney *Rome and Italy of the Republic.* Volume I: *An Economic Survey of Ancient Rome.* Baltimore: Johns Hopkins Press, 1933. See Chap. VII, Agriculture, pp. 358-368, and Chap. V, Money and Banking, 347-352.

McGregor, G. H. C. *Jew and Greek: Tutors unto Christ. The Jewish and Hellenistic Background of the New Testament.* New York: Charles Scribner's Sons, 1936. Pp. x. 11-366.

Metzger, Bruce M. "The Language of the New Testament" in *The Interpreter's Bible,* Vol. VII, Pp. 43-59. New York: Abingdon-Cokesbury Press, 1951.

Moulton, James H. *A Grammar of New Testament Greek.* Vol. I: *Prolegomena,* Third Edition. Edinburgh: T. & T. Clark, 1908. Pp. xxiv, 293. See Chap. I, "General Characteristics," pp. 1-21.

Skeel, C. A. J. *Travel in the First Century.* Cambridge: University Press, 1901. Pp. x, 159. Excellent essay on transportation and travel in the time of Christ.

Tucker, T. G. *Life in the Roman World of Nero and St. Paul.* New York. The Macmillan Company, 1924. Pp. xix, 453.

Dampier-Whetham William C. D. *A History of Science.* New York: The Macmillan Company, 1929. Pp. xxi, 514.

Reymond, Arnold *History of the Sciences in Greco-Roman Antiquity.* Translated by Ruth Gheury DeBray. London: Methuen & Co., Ltd., 1927. Pp. x, 245. Bibliography in French. See esp. pp. 92-112.

## CHAPTER IV: THE RELIGIOUS WORLD

†Angus, S. *The Environment of Early Christianity.* New York: Charles Scribner's Sons, 1920. See Chap. IV, Religious Conditions of the Graeco-Roman Period, pp. 68-139.

Bailey, Cyril "Religion and Philosophy" in *The Legacy of Rome,* pp. 237-264.

David, M. and Van Groningen, B. A. *Papyrological Primer.* Second (English) Edition. Leyden: E. J. Brill, 1946. Pp. IX, 167. See No. 72, pp. 138-146, "Two Magical Texts."

Friedlander, L. *Roman Life and Manners Under the Early Empire.* 4 Vols. Authorized Translation of the 7th enlarged and revised edition of the *Sittengeschichte Roms* by L. A. Magnus. Second Edition. New York: Dutton, n.d. See Vols. I, II.

Glover, Terriot Reavely *The Conflict of Religions Within the Roman Empire.* Seventh Edition. London: Methuen & Co., Ltd., 1918. Humanistic view of Jesus. Good sketch of Roman religion.

Hyde, Walter Woodburn *Paganism to Christianity in the Roman Empire.* Philadelphia: University of Pennsylvania Press, 1946. Pp. 296. For a lucid account of pagan religions, see pp. 9-76. Book is strongly anti-Christian in its bias.

Hyde, William DeWitt *The Five Great Philosophies of Life.* New York: The Macmillan Company, 1923. Pp. x, 296. Read Pp. 1-106 for material on Epicureans and Stoics.

Kennedy, H. A. A. *St. Paul and the Mystery Religions.* London: Hodder & Stoughton, 1913. Pp. 311.

*Machen, J. Gresham *The Origin of Paul's Religion.* Grand Rapids: Wm. B. Eerdmans Publishing Co., 1947. Pp. 329.

Rogers, Arthur Kenyon *A Student's History of Philosophy.* New Edition Revised. New York: The Macmillan Company, 1907. See pp. 174-184.

Rose, Herbert J. *Ancient Roman Religion,* London: Hutchinson's University Library, n.d. Pp. 164.

*Uhlhorn, Gerhard *The Conflict of Christianity and Heathenism.* Edited and translated from the Third German Edition by Egbert C. Smyth and C. J. H. Ropes. Revised Edition, New York: Charles Scribner's Sons, 1901. Pp. 508. Unusually good bibliography.

## CHAPTER V: JUDAISM

Bacher, Wilhelm "Synagogue" in *Jewish Encyclopaedia,* Vol. XI, 619-628. New York: Funk and Wagnalls, 1912.

Baron, Salo Untermeyer *A Social and Religious History of the Jews.* Second Edition. Revised and Enlarged. Two Volumes. New York: Columbia University Press, 1952. Good reference work. Written from standpoint of liberal Judaism.

Charles, R. H. *The Testaments of the Twelve Patriarchs.* London: Society for Promoting Christian Knowledge, 1925. Pp. xxiii, 108.

Caldecott, W. S. and Orr, James "Temple" in *International Standard Bible Encyclopaedia,* 2930-2940a. Grand Rapids, Mich.; Wm. B. Eerdmans Publishing Co. 1949. See especially 2937-2940a for the Temple of Herod.

Davies, T. W. "Temple" in Hastings' *Dictionary of the Bible,* Vol. IV, 695-716. New York: Charles Scribner's Sons. 1902. Lucid and well documented.

Donald, James "Diaspora," in Hastings' *Dictionary of the Apostolic Church.* Vol. I, 304-306. New York: Charles Scribner's Sons, 1922.

*Edersheim, Alfred *In the Days of Christ.* Chicago: Fleming H. Revell Co., n.d. Pp. vii, 342.

——————————*The Temple: Its Ministry and Services.* New Edition, Revised. Grand Rapids: Wm. B. Eerdmans Publishing Co., 1950. Pp. xiv, 368.

Emmet, C. W. *Third and Fourth Books of Maccabees* in *Translations of Early Documents,* Series II, Hellenistic-Jewish Texts. London: Society for Promoting Christian Knowledge, 1918. Pp. xiv, 45; xxv, 75. Two books bound together.

Ferrar, William J. *The Uncanonical Jewish Books.* A short introduction to the Apocrypha and other Jewish writings, 200 B.C.-100 A.D. London: Society for Promoting Christian Knowledge, 1925. Pp. x, 112.

Finkelstein, Louis *The Pharisees.* Two Volumes. Philadelphia: The Jewish Publication Society of America, 1938. Pp. xxviii, 442, 793.

Levison, Nahum *The Jewish Background of Christianity.* A Manual of the political, social, and literary life of the Jews from 586 B.C. to A.D. 1, Edinburgh: T. & T. Clark, 1932. Pp. xi, 205

# Bibliography

†Moore, George Foot *Judaism.* Two Volumes. Cambridge: Harvard University Press, 1927.
Oesterley, W. O. *An Introduction to the Books of the Apocrypha,* New York: The Macmillan Company, 1935. Pp. x, 345.
†——————————*A History of Israel.* Vol. II: From the Fall of Jerusalem 586 B.C. to the Bar Kokhba Revolt, A.D. 135. Oxford: Clarendon Press. 1939. Pp. xvi, 500. Most thorough recent work. Contains full treatment of the Herods, the Diaspora, social and religious (usages.
†Pfeiffer, Robert H. *History of New Testament Times,* New York: Harper & Brothers, Publishers, 1949. Pp. xii, 561.
*Robertson, A. T. *The Pharisees and Jesus.* New York: Charles Scribner's Sons, 1920. Pp. xii, 189.
Rosenau, William *Jewish Ceremonial Institutions and Customs.* New York: Bloch Publishing Company, Inc., 1929. Pp. 190. Authoritative explanation of historical and modern Jewish usages.
Strack, Hermann L. *Introduction to the Talmud and Midrash,* Fifth Edition: Authorized Translation. Philadelphia: The Jewish Publication Society of America, 1945. An authoritative work on the Talmud.
Torrey, C. C. *The Apocryphal Literature.* New Haven: Yale University Press, 1945. Pp. x, 151.

## PART II. THE GOSPELS: THE RECORDS OF THE LIFE OF CHRIST
## CHAPTER VI: THE GOSPELS AS LITERARY WORKS

For tools, see the Harmonies of the Gospels listed previously. The introductions will supply the general approach to the Gospels. The following works will be especially useful.

Hayes, Doremus A. *The Synoptic Gospels and the Book of Acts.* New York: The Methodist Book Concern, n.d. Pp. 1-354. Comprehensive coverage of the characteristic peculiarities of the Synoptic Gospels.
*Moorehead, William G. *Studies in the Four Gospels. Westminster Handbooks.* Philadelphia: The Westminster Press, 1900. Pp. 230.
Pullan, Leighton *The Gospels.* London: Longmans, Green & Co., 1912. See particularly pp. 133-275.
*Scroggie, W. Graham *A Guide to the Gospels.* London: Pickering & Inglis, 1948. Pp. 664. By far the best modern introduction to the content of the Gospels. Aside from his adoption of the Two-Document theory, the book is thoroughly conservative.
The following works deal specifically with the Gospels singly.

## CHAPTER VII: THE GOSPEL OF MATTHEW

*Broadus, John A. *Commentary on the Gospel of Matthew* in *The American Commentary.* Philadelphia: American Baptist Publication Society, 1886. Pp. li. 610. Good popular commentary.
*Lange, John Peter *The Gospel According to Matthew.* Translated from the Third German Edition by Philip Schaff. Sixth Edition. Vol. I in *The Commentary on the Holy Scriptures.* New York: Charles Scribner & Co., 1867. Pp. xxii, 568. Very thorough.
†McNeile, A. H. *Commentary on the Gospel According to Matthew.* New York: The Macmillan Co., 1915. Pp. 448.
*Morgan, G. Campbell *The Gospel According to Matthew.* New York: Fleming H. Revell Co., n.d. Pp. 321. Expository and doctrinal.
Plummer, Alfred *An Exegetical Commentary on the Gospel According to St. Matthew.* Grand Rapids: Wm. B. Eerdmans Publishing Co., 1953, Pp. xlvi. 451.

*Robertson, A. T. *Commentary on the Gospel According to Matthew.* New York: The Macmillan Company, 1911. Pp. 294. Brief, and good for quick reference.

## CHAPTER VIII: THE GOSPEL OF MARK

*Robertson, A. T. *Making Good in the Ministry.* New York: Fleming H. Revell Co., n. d. Pp. 1-174. Deals with Mark's biography.

Lindsay, Thomas M. *The Gospel According to St. Mark* in *Handbooks for Bible Classes.* Edinburgh: T. & T. Clark, n.d. Pp. 1-272. Good brief handbook, now somewhat out of date.

Morgan, G. Campbell *The Gospel According to Mark.* New York: Fleming H. Revell Co., 1927. Pp. 350.

*Robertson, A. T. *Studies in Mark's Gospel.* New York: The Macmillan Company, 1919. Pp. 146. A series of lectures on special aspects of Mark.

Swete, H. B. *The Gospel According to St. Mark.* Third Edition. Grand Rapids: Wm. B. Eerdmans Publishing Co., 1951. Pp. cxix, 434. Probably the best technical commentary on Mark. Greek text.

## CHAPTER IX: THE GOSPEL OF LUKE

### Technical and Historical.

Hobart, William K. *The Medical Language of St. Luke.* London: Longmans, Green & Co., 1882. Pp. xxxvi, 305. Attempts to show that Luke's language is that of a physician.

Harnack, Adolph von *Luke the Physician.* Translated by J. R. Wilkinson. Crown Theological Library. New York: G. P. Putnam, 1907. Pp. xi, 231. Technical treatment of authorship for advanced students.

MacLachlan, H. *St Luke, the Man and His Work.* London: Longmans, Green, and Co., 1920. See pp. 1-223. Written from a liberal viewpoint. The book contains a mine of information on Luke's biographical and literary background.

Ramsay, William *The Bearing of Recent Discoveries on the Trustworthiness of the New Testament.* Fourth Edition. London: Hodder and Stoughton, Ltd., 1920. Read Pp. 222-300.

*————*Was Christ Born at Bethlehem?* New York: G. P. Putnam's Sons, 1898. Pp. 1-280. A technical presentation of the historical material concerning the birth of Christ.

*Robertson, A. T. *Luke the Historian in the Light of Research.* New York: Charles Scribner's Sons, 1923. Pp. 1-257.

*Stonehouse, N. B. *The Witness of Luke to Christ.* Grand Rapids, Mich.: Wm. B. Eerdmans Publishing Co., 1951. Pp. 184. Conservative critical discussion of the content of Luke's account of the life of Christ.

### Commentaries

Creed, J. M. *The Gospel According to St. Luke.* London. Macmillan & Co., Ltd., 1942. Pp. xx, 340.

*Godet, F. *A Commentary on the Gospel of Luke.* Translated from the Second French Edition by E. W. Shalders and M. D. Cusin. Third Edition. New York: Funk and Wagnalls, Publishers. 1887. Pp. x, 574. Very thorough, and quite satisfactory, though old.

*Geldenhuys, Norval *Commentary on the Gospel of Luke* in *The New International Commentary on the New Testament.* Grand Rapids, Mich.: Wm. B. Eerdmans Publishing Co., 1951. Pp. 685. The best modern commentary on Luke. Excellent introduction (Pp. 1-50); up-to-date bibliography.

Lindsay, Thomas M. *The Gospel According to St. Luke.* In *Handbooks for Bible Classes.* Two volumes. Edinburgh: T. & T. Clark, n.d. Pp. 268.
Morgan, G. Campbell *The Gospel According to St. Luke.* New York: Fleming H. Revell Co., 1931. Pp. 284.
Plumptre, E. H. *The Gospel According to Luke* in *The Handy Commentary.* New York: Cassell, Potter, Galpin, and Co., n.d. Pp. xx, 232.
Ragg, Lonsdale *St. Luke,* in *Westminster Commentary Series.* London: Methuen & Co., 1922.

## CHAPTER X: THE GOSPEL OF JOHN
**Technical, Historical, and Analytical.**

*Gloag, Paton J. *Introduction to the Johannine Writings.* London: James Nisbet & Co., 1891. Pp. xiii, 440.
Hayes, Doremus A. *John and His Writings.* New York: Methodist Book Concern, 1917. Pp. 328.
Howard, W.F., Edited by A. W. Harrison *Christianity According to St. John.* London: Duckworth, 1943. Pp. 221.
——————*The Fourth Gospel in Recent Criticism and Interpretation.* London: The Epworth Press, 1931. Pp. 292.
Iverach, James "John, Gospel of" in *International Standard Bible Encyclopaedia,* Vol. III, 1720-1727. Grand Rapids, Mich.: Wm. B. Eerdmans Publishing Co., 1949.
*McIntyre, D. M. *Some Notes on the Gospels.* Edited for the Press by F. F. Bruce. M.A. London: The Inter-Varsity Fellowship, 1943. Pp. 51. Pp. 35-51 contain a succinct statement of the conservative side of Johannine criticism.
*Nunn, H. P. V. *The Son of Zebedee and the Fourth Gospel.* London: Society for Promoting Christian Knowledge, 1927. Pp. x, 150. Good conservative treatment.
*Robertson, A. T. *Epochs in the Life of the Apostle John.* New York: Fleming H. Revell Co., 1935. Pp. 253.
Stanton, Vincent H. *The Gospels as Historical Documents.* Cambridge: University Press, 1920. Part III: The Fourth Gospel.
*Tenney, Merrill C. *John: The Gospel of Belief.* Grand Rapids, Mich: Wm. B. Eerdmans Publishing Co. 1951. Pp. 321. An aid to analytic study.
*Griffith-Thomas, W. H. *The Apostle John: His Life and Writings.* Grand Rapids: Wm. B. Eerdmans Publishing Co.. 1948. Pp. 373.
White, W. W. *Studies in the Gospel by John.* New York: Fleming H. Revell Co., 1895. Pp. 130. Small handbook for study by inductive method.

**Commentaries**

Bailey, R. F. *The Gospel of John: An Introductory Commentary.* London: Student Christian Movement, 1940. Pp. viii, 248.
*Godet, F. *Commentary on the Gospel of John.* Translated from the Second French Edition by Francis Crombie and M. D. Cusin. Four volumes. Edinburgh: T. & T. Clark, 1876.
*Hendriksen, William *New Testament Commentary: Exposition of the Gospel According to John.* Two volumes. Grand Rapids, Mich.: Baker Book House, 1954. Pp. 250, 507.
*Lange, John Peter *The Gospel According to John.* Translated from the German by Edward D. Yeomans and Evalina Moore. Edited by Philip Schaff. New York: Scribner, Armstrong & Co., 1872. Pp. xiv, 654.
*Morgan, G. Campbell *The Gospel According to John.* New York: Fleming H. Revell Co., n.d. Pp. 333.
Moulton, Wm F. and Milligan, Wm. *The Gospel According to John.* International Revision Commentary, Vol. IV. New York: Charles Scribner's Sons, 1883. Pp. xxxiii. 443.

Reith, George *St. John's Gospel with Introduction and Notes.* Two Volumes: Chaps. I-VIII, IX-XXI. Edinburgh: T. & T. Clark. 1926.
*Scroggie, W. Graham *St. John: Introduction and Notes.* New York & London: Harper and Brothers, Publishers, 1931. Pp. 132. A devotional study with superb outlines.
*Westcott, B. F. *Commentary on John.* Grand Rapids, Mich.: Wm. B. Eerdmans Publishing Company, 1951. Probably the best commentary in English.
*————————*The Gospel According to John.* Two Volumes. London: John Murray, 1908. Pp. ix, clxxxix. Greek text.

## CHAPTER XI: THE SYNOPTIC PROBLEM

The bibliography on this question is immense in scope, and only a few titles can be quoted here. Because the question belongs to biblical criticism rather than to survey, only selected readings are given below. Conservative literature on this subject is scarce.
*Bruce, F. F. *Are the New Testament Documents Reliable?* (Grand Rapids. Eerdmans, 1954), pp. 28-47.
†Burton, Ernest DeWitt *A Short Introduction to the Gospels.* Chicago: University of Chicago Press, n.d. See particularly Pp. 84-98.
Holdsworth, W. W. *Gospel Origins.* New York: Charles Scribner's Sons, 1913. Pp. 1-211. Old, but useful for general information.
Jackson, Henry L. "The Present State of the Synoptic Problem" in *Cambridge Biblical Essays,* H. B. Swete, Ed. London: Macmillan & Co., Ltd., 1909.
Jones, Maurice *The Four Gospels.* London: The Society for Promoting Christian Knowledge, 1921. For argument for Two-Document Theory, see Pp. 10-19.
*McIntyre, D. M. *Some Notes on the Gospels.* Ed. by F. F. Bruce. London: Inter-Varsity Fellowship, 1943. pp. 51.
†Streeter, Burnet H. *The Four Gospels.* New York: The Macmillan Company, 1925. Pp. 621.
*Tenney, Merrill C. *The Genius of the Gospels.* Grand Rapids, Mich.: Wm. B. Eerdmans Publishing Co., 1951. Pp. 124.
*Thiessen, Henry C. *Introduction to the New Testament.* Grand Rapids, Mich.: Wm. B. Eerdmans Publishing Co., 1951. Pp. xx, 347. Pp. 101-129 give a good brief conservative treatment of this subject.
*Westcott, B. F. *Introduction to the Study of the Gospels.* Seventh Edition, London: Macmillan & Co., 1888. Old, but still the best defense of the oral tradition theory. See pp. 164-212.

## CHAPTER XII: THE LIFE OF CHRIST

*Andrews, Samuel J. *The Life of Our Lord upon Earth.* New and Revised Edition. New York: Charles Scribner's Sons, 1893. Pp. 651. Especially good on chronology.
Donehoo, James DeQ. *The Apocryphal and Legendary Life of Christ.* New York: Macmillan & Co., 1903. Pp. 531.
*Edersheim, Alfred *The Life and Times of Jesus the Messiah.* Eighth Edition, revised. Two volumes. Grand Rapids, Mich.: Wm. B. Eerdmans Publishing Co. 1953. Pp. xlvii, 1523.
Ogg, George *The Chronology of the Public Ministry of Jesus.* London: Longmans, Green Co., 1931. Pp. 407.
*Robertson, A. T. *Epochs in the Life of Jesus.* New York: Charles Scribner's Sons, 1907. Pp. xi, 192. Good brief study.
Smith, David *In the Days of His Flesh; The Earthly Life of Our Lord and Saviour.* Twelfth Edition. London: Hodder & Stoughton. 1917. Pp. 549.
**The Birth of Christ**
*Machen, J. Gresham *The Virgin Birth of Christ.* Second Edition. New York: Harper and Brothers, Publishers, 1932. Pp. 415.

*Orr, James *The Virgin Birth of Christ.* New York: Charles Scribner's Sons, 1907. Pp. 301.

## The Resurrection of Christ

*Hayes, Doremus A. *The Resurrection Fact.* Nashville: Cokesbury Press, 1932. Pp. 355.

*Milligan, William *The Resurrection of Our Lord.* London: Macmillan and Co., 1881. Pp. xiii, 304.

*Latham, Henry *The Risen Master.* Cambridge; Deighton Bell and Co.. 1901. Pp. xvi, 488.

Morison, Frank *Who Moved the Stone?* London: Faber & Faber, 1930. Pp. 304.

*Orr, James *The Resurrection of Jesus.* Cincinnati: Jennings & Graham, 1909. Pp. 292.

*Sloan, Harold P. *He Is Risen.* New York and Nashville: Abingdon-Cokesbury Press, 1942. Pp. 186.

*Sparrow-Simpson, W. J. *Our Lord's Resurrection.* London. Longmans, Green and Co., 1905. Pp. 320.

*——————*The Resurrection and Modern Thought.* London: Longmans, Green, and Co., 1911. Pp. ix, 464.

## PART III: THE RECORDS OF THE EARLY CHURCH

For bibliographical purposes, chapters XIII through XVII under Part III will not be listed separately since their subject matter is covered generally by books on Acts and on Paul. Groupings will be arranged by topics rather than by chapters.

### Tools

Burton, Ernest D. *The Records and Letters of the Apostolic Age.* New York: Charles Scribner's Sons, 1923. Pp. viii, 238.

Clark, George W. *Harmony of the Acts of the Apostles.* A new and Revised Edition. Philadelphia: American Baptist Publication Society, 1897. Pp. 408.

Goodwin, Frank J. *A Harmony of the Life of St. Paul,* Grand Rapids, Mich.; Baker Book House, 1950. Pp. 240.

### The Apostolic Age

Bartlet, James Vernon *The Apostolic Age* in *Ten Epochs of Church History,* Vol. I. New York: Charles Scribner's Sons, 1900. Pp. xvi, 542.

*Bruce, F. F. *The Spreading Flame: The Rise and Progress of Christianity.* Grand Rapids, Mich.: Wm. B. Eerdmans Publishing Company, 1953.

†Foakes-Jackson, F. J. and Lake, Kirsopp, Editors. *The Beginnings of Christianity.* Five Volumes. London: Macmillan & Co., Ltd., 1920-1933. Thorough treatment of background and text.

*Purves, George T. *The Apostolic Age.* New York: Charles Scribner's Sons, 1900. Pp. xx, 343.

Ropes, James Hardy *The Apostolic Age.* New York: Charles Scribner's Sons, 1921. Pp. xi, 327. Liberal viewpoint.

### Lives of Paul

*Conybeare, W. J. and Howson, J. S. *The Life and Epistles of St. Paul.* New Edition. Grand Rapids, Mich.: Wm. B. Eerdmans Publishing Co., 1949. Pp. xxii. 850.

Hayes, Doremus A. *Paul and His Epistles.* New York and Cincinnati: The Methodist Book Concern, c. 1915. Pp. 508. Contains bibliography.

*Moe, Olaf *The Apostle Paul.* Translated by L. A. Vigness. Minneapolis, Minn.: Augsburg Publishing House, c. 1950. Pp. 578.

Ramsay, William *St. Paul, the Traveller and the Roman Citizen.* New York: G. P. Putnam's Sons, 1909. Pp. xvi, 394.

*Robertson, A. T. *Epochs in the Life of Paul.* New York: Charles Scribner's Sons, 1909. Pp. xi. 337.

*————*Paul, the Interpreter of Christ.* New York: G. H. Doran Co., c. 1921. Pp. 155.

Smith, David *The Life and Letters of St. Paul.* New York: G. H. Doran Co., 1920. Pp. xv, 704.

*Stalker, James *The Life of St. Paul.* New Edition. Edinburgh: T. & T. Clark, 1885. Pp. xi, 240. Elementary handbook.

Wood, C. T. *The Life, Letters, and Religion of St. Paul.* Edinburgh: T. & T. Clark, 1946. Pp. xv, 418.

### Chronology

Knox, John *Chapters in a Life of Paul.* New York: Abingdon-Cokesbury Press, 1950. Pp. 168. See chaps. III, IV, V for the chronology of Paul's life. Knox regards the book of Acts as of secondary authority, and not wholly reliable in its chronology of Paul's life.

Lightfoot, J. B. *Biblical Essays.* New York: Macmillan & Co., 1893. "The Chronology of St. Paul's Life and Epistles," pp. 215-233.

Ramsay, William *Pauline and Other Studies.* New York: A. C. Armstrong and Sons, 1906. See "The Pauline Chronology," pp. 345-365.

### General Introduction

Fairweather, Wm. *The Background of the Epistles.* Edinburgh: T. & T. Clark, 1935. Pp. xxiii, 399.

*Gloag, Paton J. *Introduction to the Pauline Epistles.* Edinburgh: T. & T. Clark, 1874. Pp. xvi, 480.

### Commentaries on Acts

*Bruce, F. F. *The Acts of the Apostles.* Grand Rapids: Wm. B. Eerdmans Publishing Co., 1952. Pp. viii, 491. Greek text.

*Bruce, F. F. *The Book of the Acts.* Grand Rapids: Wm. B. Eerdmans Publishing Co. 1954. Pp. 556. English text. The best of the recent commentaries on Acts.

Foakes-Jackson, F. J. *The Acts of the Apostles* in *The Moffatt N. T. Commentary.* New York: Harper & Brothers, 1931. Pp. xx, 236.

*Morgan, G. Campbell *The Acts of the Apostles.* New York: Fleming H. Revell Co., 1924. Pp. 547. Excellent analytical and devotional commentary.

*Rackham, Richard B. *The Acts of the Apostles.* Twelfth Edition. London: Methuen & Co., Ltd., 1939. Pp. cxv, 524. One of the best commentaries on Acts.

*Stifler, J. M. *An Introduction to the Study of the Acts of the Apostles.* New York: Fleming H. Revell Co., n. d. Pp. 287.

*Scroggie, W. Graham *The Acts of the Apostles.* New York and London: Harper and Brothers, Publishers, n. d. Pp. 186. Devotional studies. Unusually good outline.

*Thomas, W. H. Griffith *The Acts of the Apostles.* London: Marshall Brothers, Ltd., n. d. Pp. 110. A series of studies.

### James

Mayor, J. B. "James, The General Epistle of" in Hastings' *Dictionary of the Bible,* II 543a-548. New York: Charles Scribner's Sons, 1901.

*————The Epistle of St. James.* Second Edition. London: Macmillan & Co., Ltd., 1897. Pp. cclx, 255. An advanced commentary with Greek text.

*Robertson, A. T. *Practical and Social Aspects of Christianity.* Second Edition. New York: George H. Doran Co., n. d. Pp. ix, 271.

Patrick, W. *James, the Lord's Brother.* Edinburgh: T. & T. Clark, 1906. Pp. xii, 369.

# Bibliography

## The Pauline Epistles

*Moorehead, Wm. G. *Outline Studies in Acts-Ephesians*. Grand Rapids: Baker Book House, repr. 1953. Pp. 247.
*————*Outline Studies in the New Testament: Philippians to Hebrews*. New York and Chicago: Fleming H. Revell, (1905). Pp. 249.

## Galatians

Beet, J. A. *A Commentary on St. Paul's Epistle to the Galatians*. Fifth Edition. London: Hodder & Stoughton, 1885. Pp. xxiv, 232.
Findlay, George G. *The Epistle to the Galatians. The Expositor's Bible*. New York: Armstrong and Co., n. d. Pp. 461.
*Lightfoot, J. B. *St. Paul's Epistle to the Galatians*. London: Macmillan & Co., Lts., 1921. Pp. 384. Greek text; very reliable.
*Luther, Martin. *Commentary on Galatians*. A New Edition, corrected and revised by Erasmus Middleton. Grand Rapids, Mich.: Wm. B. Eerdmans Publishing Co., 1930. Pp. 536.
*Machen, J. Gresham. *The Origin of Paul's Religion*. Grand Rapids: Wm. B. Eerdmans Publ. Co., 1947. Pp. 329. Relation between Galatians and Acts discussed in Chapter III, pp. 71-113.
Ramsay, William. *A Historical Commentary on St. Paul's Epistle to the Galatians*. New York: G. P. Putnam's Sons, 1900. Pp. xi, 477.
*Ridderbos, Herman N. *The Epistle of Paul to the Churches of Galatia* in *The New International Commentary on The New Testament*. Grand Rapids: Wm. B. Eerdmans Publishing Co., 1953. Pp. 238.
*Tenney, Merrill C. *Galatians: The Charter of Christian Liberty*. Grand Rapids, Mich.: Wm. B. Eerdmans Publishing Co., 1951. Pp. 200. A manual covering nine different methods of book-study, using Galatians as an example.

## Thessalonians

Milligan, George *St. Paul's Epistles to the Thessalonians*. Grand Rapids: Wm. B. Eerdmans Publishing Co., 1952. Pp. cix, 195. Based on Greek text; very thorough.

## Romans

*Forrester, E. J. *A Righteousness of God for Unrighteous Men*. New York: G. H. Doran Co., 1926. Pp. xiii, 296. Popular presentation.
*Godet, F. *Commentary on St. Paul's Epistle to the Romans*. Translated from the French by Rev. A. Cusin. Translated Revised and Edited by T. W. Chambers. Second Edition. New York: Funk & Wagnalls, 1885.
*Hodge, Charles *Commentary on the Epistle to the Romans*. New Edition: Revised and in Great Measure Rewritten. Grand Rapids: Wm. B. Eerdmans Publishing Co., 1951. Pp. 716. A theological commentary.
*Liddon, Henry P. *Explanatory Analysis of St. Paul's Epistle to the Romans*. London: Longmans Green & Co., 1893. Pp. vi, 309.
*Moule, Handley, G. G. *The Epistle of St. Paul to the Romans. The Expositor's Bible*. New York: A. C. Armstrong & Son, 1894. Pp. xvi, 437.
*McQuilkin, Robert C. *The Message of Romans*. Grand Rapids, Mich.: Zondervan Publishing House, 1947. Pp. 178.
*Newell, William R. *Romans Verse by Verse*. Chicago: Grace Publishing Co., 1941. Pp. 577.
*Stifler, James M. *The Epistle to the Romans*. New York: Fleming H. Revell, Co., 1897. Pp. 275.
*Thomas, W. H. Griffith *Romans I-XVI: A Devotional Commentary*. Grand Rapids: Wm. B. Eerdmans Publishing Co., 1953. Unusually good teaching outlines.

## Corinthians

Godet, F. *Commentary on St. Paul's First Epistle to the Corinthians.* Translated from the French by A. Cusin. Two Volumes. Edinburgh: T. & T. Clark, 1889. Pp. vii, 428, vii, 493. Very thorough.

*Grosheide, F. W. *Commentary on the First Epistle to the Corinthians* in *The New International Commentary on the New Testament.* Grand Rapids, Mich.: Wm. B. Eerdmans Publishing Co., 1953. Pp. 415.

McFadyen, John E. *The Epistles to the Corinthians.* London, etc.: Hodder and Stoughton, 1911. Pp. 428.

*Morgan, G. Campbell *The Corinthian Letters of Paul.* New York: Fleming H. Revell Co., c. 1946. Pp. 275. A popular commentary in lecture style.

## Ephesians

*Cable, John H. *The Fulness of God.* Chicago: The Moody Press, 1945. Pp. 160. Helpful in Bible class work.

*Findlay, G. C. *The Epistle to the Ephesians. The Expositor's Bible.* Grand Rapids: Wm. B. Eerdmans Publishing Co., 1947. Pp. xii, 440.

*Hodge, Charles *Commentary on the Epistle to the Ephesians.* Grand Rapids: Wm. B. Eerdmans Publishing Co., 1950. Pp. 398.

*Miller, H. S. *The Book of Ephesians.* Houghton, N. Y.: The Word-Bearer Press, 1931. Pp. 250. A mine of information on Ephesians.

*Moule, H. C. G. *Ephesian Studies.* London: Hodder & Stoughton Co., 1900.

*Paxson, Ruth *The Wealth, Walk, and Warfare of the Christian.* New York: Fleming H. Revell and Co., 1939. Pp. 223.

Robinson, J. Armitage *St. Paul's Epistle to the Ephesians.* Second Edition. London: Macmillan & Co., Ltd., 1909. Pp. ix, 314. Greek text.

Westcott, B. F. *St. Paul's Epistle to the Ephesians.* Grand Rapids: Wm. B. Eerdmans Publishing Co., 1952. Pp. lxviii, 212. Greek text.

## Colossians and Philemon

Garrod, G. W. *The Epistle to the Colossians.* London: Macmillan and Co., Ltd., 1898. Pp. 176.

Jones, Maurice *The Epistle of St. Paul to the Colossians.* London: Society for Promoting Christian Knowledge, 1923. Pp. 119.

*Lightfoot, J. B. *The Epistles of St. Paul: Colossians and Philemon.* London: Macmillan & Co., 1892. Pp. viii, 428. Greek Text.

*Moule, H. C. G. *Colossian Studies.* New York: George H. Doran Co., n. d. Devotional commentary.

*Robertson, A. T. *Paul and the Intellectuals.* New York: Doubleday, Doran, & Co., 1928. Pp. 217.

*Westcott, B. F. *A Letter to Asia.* London: Macmillan & Co., Ltd., 1914. Pp. vi, 263.

## Philippians

*Lightfoot, J. B. *St. Paul's Epistle to the Philippians.* Eighth Edition. London: Macmillan & Co., 1888. Pp. xii, 350. Greek Text.

*Moule, H. G. C. *Philippian Studies.* Fifth Edition. London: Hodder & Stoughton, 1904. Pp. xii, 265.

*Robertson, A. T. *Paul's Joy in Christ.* New York: Fleming H. Revell & Co., 1917. Pp. 267.

## PART IV: THE PROBLEMS OF THE EARLY CHURCH

The historical background for this period may be found in the later chapters of the biographies of Paul and in the general reference works listed under the chapter headings. In this section the classification by chapters is resumed.

*Bibliography*

## CHAPTER XVIII: THE INSTITUTIONAL CHURCH:
### THE PASTORAL EPISTLES

Falconer, Sir Robert *The Pastoral Epistles*: Introduction, Translation, and Notes. Oxford: The Clarendon Press, 1937. Pp. viiii, 164.

Hillard, A. E. *The Pastoral Epistles of St. Paul.* The Greek Text with Commentary. London: Rivingtons, 1910. Pp. 147.

James, J. D. *The Genuineness and Authorship of the Pastoral Epistles.* London: Longmans, Green, & Co., 1906, Pp. 165.

*Liddon, H. P. *Explanatory Analysis of St. Paul's First Epistle to Timothy.* London: Longmans, Green, & Co., Ltd., 1897. Pp. 93.

Parry, S. John *The Pastoral Epistles, with Introduction, Text, and Commentary.* Cambridge: The University Press, 1920. Pp. clxviii, 104.

Shaw, R. D. *The Pauline Epistles.* Edinburgh: T. & T. Clark, 1903. Pp. xi, 508. See Pp. 422-495.

Simpson, E. K. *The Pastoral Epistles.* Grand Rapids, Mich.: Wm. B. Eerdmans Publishing Co., 1954. Pp. 174.

## CHAPTER XIX: THE SUFFERING CHURCH: I PETER

*Gloag, Paton J. *Introduction to the Catholic Epistles.* Edinburgh: T. & T. Clark, 1887. Pp. xvi, 416.

Hayes, Doremus A. *New Testament Epistles.* New York and Cincinnati: The Methodist Book Concern, n. d. Pp. 266. This book covers all of the general epistles. For I Peter, see pp. 121-183. Hayes does not accept the Petrine authorship of II Peter.

*Robertson, A. T. *Epochs in the Life of Simon Peter.* New York: Charles Scribner's Sons, 1933. Pp. xvi, 342. A plain but thorough study of Peter.

Selwyn, E. G. *The First Epistle of Peter.* London: Macmillan & Co., Ltd.. 1946. Pp. 517. Thorough Greek commentary.

*Thomas W. H. Griffith *The Apostle Peter.* Grand Rapids, Mich.: Wm. B. Eerdmans Publishing Company, (1946). Pp. 296. Splendid outlines.

## CHAPTER XX: THE BREAK FROM JUDAISM: HEBREWS

Davidson, A. B. *Hebrews.* Edinburgh: T. & T. Clark, 1950. Pp. 260.

*Murray, Andrew *The Holiest of All.* New York: A. D. F. Randolph & Co., Inc. n. d. Pp. xv, 552. Unusually helpful outlining of Hebrews, with commentary of high spiritual quality.

*Thomas, W. H. Griffith *Let Us Go On.* Chicago: Bible Institute Colportage Association, 1923. Pp. viii, 195. Bibliography.

*Westcott, B. F. *The Epistle to the Hebrews.* Second Edition. Grand Rapids, Mich.: Wm. B. Eerdmans Publishing Co., 1950. Pp. lxxxiv, 504. Greek text. The best commentary on Hebrews.

## CHAPTER XXI: THE PERIL OF HERESIES:
### II PETER, JUDE, I, II, III JOHN

**II Peter and Jude**

See the literature under I Peter.

Mayor Joseph B., *The Epistle of Jude and the Second Epistle of Peter.* London: Macmillan & Co., Ltd., 1907. Pp. 239.

Wand, John W. C. *The General Epistles of St. Peter and St. Jude.* London: Methuen & Co., 1934. Pp. 234.

## I. II, III John

There are very few separate commentaries on the Johannine Epistles. Consult the volumes in the standard sets that deal with these epistles, and also the general works on John such as those of A. T. Robertson and W. H. Griffith Thomas.

*Westcott, B. F. *The Epistles of John.* Third Edition. Grand Rapids, Mich. Wm. B. Eerdmans Publishing Company, 1950. Pp. lvi, 378. Greek text.

## CHAPTER XXII: THE EXPECTANT CHURCH: REVELATION

### Introductory Study

Moffatt, James. *The Historical New Testament.* New York: Charles Scribner's Sons, 1901. Pp. xxvii, 726. See Pp. 459-465.

*Orr, James "Revelation of John," in *International Standard Bible Encyclopaedia,* IV, pp. 2582b-2587a. Grand Rapids, Mich.; Wm. B. Eerdmans Publishing Co., 1949.

### Commentaries

*Blanchard, Charles A. *Light on the Last Days.* Chicago: Bible Institute Colportage Association, 1913. Pp. 149. Simple and clear.

Beckwith, Isbon T. *The Apocalypse of John.* New York: The Macmillan Co., 1919. Pp. xv, 794. Greek text; thorough discussions.

Dean, J. T. *The Book of the Revelation.* Edinburgh: T. & T. Clark, 1915. Pp. 191.

*Hengstenberg, Ernest W. *The Revelation of St. John.* Translated by Patrick Fairbairn. Two volumes. Edinburgh: T. & T. Clark, 1851.

*Lang, G. H. *The Revelation of Jesus Christ: Select Studies.* London: Oliphants, Ltd., 1945. Pp. 420.

*Moorehead, Wm. G. *Studies in the Book of Revelation. New York:* Fleming H. Revell Co., 1908. Pp. 153.

*Newell, Wm. R. *The Book of the Revelation.* Chicago: Chicago Grace Publications, 1941. Pp. 404.

*Seiss, J. A. *Lectures on the Apocalypse.* Tenth Edition. One volume. Grand Rapids, Mich.: Zondervan Publishing House, 1951. The best-known early popular premillennial presentation.

Swete, Henry B. *The Apocalypse of St. John.* Grand Rapids: Wm. B. Eerdmans Publishing Co., 1951. Pp. 338. Advanced commentary with Greek text.

### The Seven Churches

*Crosby, Howard *The Seven Churches of Asia.* New York: Funk and Wagnalls Co., 1890. Pp. 168. Popular devotional work.

*Morgan, G. Campbell *A First Century Message to Twentieth Century Christians.* Third Edition. New York: Fleming H. Revell Co., 1902. Pp. 217.

Ramsay, William *The Letters to the Seven Churches of Asia and Their Place in the Plan of the Apocalypse.* New York: George H. Doran Co., 1905. Pp. 446. Unexcelled for historical and archaeological background of the seven churches.

*Trench, Richard C. *Commentary on the Epistles to the Seven Churches in Asia.* New York: Scribner, 1862. Pp. 312.

### The Millennium

The following works represent widely differing viewpoints, and are labeled accordingly.

Case, Shirley J. *The Millennial Hope.* Chicago: University of Chicago Press, 1918. Pp. ix, 53. Utterly rationalistic; dismisses any possibility of a millennium.

*Feinberg, Charles *Premillennialism or Amillennialism?* Grand Rapids, Mich.: Zondervan, 1936. Pp. 250. Premillennial and dispensational.
*Hamilton, Floyd E. *The Basis of Millennial Faith.* Grand Rapids, Mich.: Wm. B. Eerdmans Publishing Co., 1942. Pp. 160. Amillennial.
*Kellogg, Samuel H. *Are Premillennialists Right?* New Edition. New York: Fleming H. Revell Co., 1903. Pp. 128. Premillennial.
*Kromminga, D. H. *The Millennium in the Church.* Grand Rapids, Mich.: Wm. B. Eerdmans Publishing Co., 1945. Pp. 359. Historical Survey.
*————— *The Millennium.* Grand Rapids, Mich.: Wm. B. Eerdmans Publishing Company, 1948. Pp. 121. Covenantal Premillenarianism.

## PART V: THE CANON OF THE NEW TESTAMENT

## CHAPTER XXIII: THE CANON OF THE NEW TESTAMENT

Gregory, Caspar R. *Canon and Text of the New Testament* in *International Theological Library.* New York: Charles Scribner's Sons, 1907. Pp. vii, 509.
Riggs, J. S. "The Canon of the New Testament" in *International Standard Bible Encyclopaedia,* Vol. I, 563a-566a. Grand Rapids, Mich.: Wm. B. Eerdmans Publishing Co., 1949.
Souter, Alexander *The Text and Canon of the New Testament.* New York: Charles Scribner's Sons, 1923. Pp. x, 254. For the canon, see pp. 146-254. Bibliography.
Stanton, V. H. "New Testament Canon" in Hastings' *Dictionary of the Bible,* Vol. III, 529b-542b. New York: Charles Scribner's Sons, 1902. Good bibliography.
Westcott, B. F. *General Survey of the History of the Canon of the New Testament.* Seventh Edition. London: Macmillan & Co., Ltd., 1896.. Pp. lvi, 605.

# INDICES

# Index of Persons

# Index of Subjects

461

John, II, 383, 384, 393, 396, 397
John, III, 383, 384, 393, 397, 398
Joy, 338
Judaism, 51, 56, 59-75, 79, 113-143,
  167, 249-252, 262, 276, 325, 359,
  371
Judaizers, 273, 281, 284, 314, 350, 354
Jude, 383, 388-392

Kingdom of Heaven, of God, 156, 236,
  237

Latin, 43, 82, 84, 85, 169, 259
Life of Christ, 219-237, 263
  Secular sources, 219-221
  Harmony, 221-227
  Geography, 227-232
  Teaching, 232-237
Literature, 82, 83
Literature, Jewish, 131-137
Luke, Gospel of, 181-194, 378

Mark, Gospel of, 165-177
Matthew, Gospel of, 151-161, 168
Middle class, 80
Millennium, 406, 407, 411
Miracles, 157, 170, 187, 208
Mishna, 136
Moral standards, 88-90
Music, 84
Muratorian Canon, 424, 425
Mystery religions, 99, 100

Nazirite vow, 327
Neo-Platonism, 105, 106
New Testament, 21-24, 42, 85, 87,
  113, 131, 243

Occult, 100-102

Parables, 157, 158, 176, 187, 232-234
Passover, 126
Pastoral Epistles, 345-355, 361
Pentecost, 127, 249, 251, 252, 363
Peter, I, 359-367
Peter, II, 384-388, 389 ✓
Pharisees, 137, 138, 158
Philemon, 330-331
Philippians, 336-339
Philosophy, 102-109
Platonism, 103, 104
Plebs, 81
Postmillennial view, 406

Preaching, 252
Premillennial view, 406
Preterist, 404
Priesthood, 54
Priesthood, Jewish, 69-71, 374
Priesthood of Christ, 376-378
Prison Epistles, 328, 329
Procurators, 72, 73, 432
Prophecy, 54
Province, provinces, 42-44

Religion, Roman, 98
Restoration of Jews, 52, 53
Resurrection, 246, 252, 328, 329, 383
Revelation (book), 135, 401-413
Roads, 91-93
Roman government, 359
Romans (book), 278, 316-320, 337,
  364
Rylands Fragment, 200

Sacred year, 125
Sadducees, 135, 138, 139, 158
Sanhedrin, 70, 79, 363
Scepticism, 108, 109
Science, 85-87
Scribes, 54, 55
Septuagint, 48, 56, 57, 131, 132
Sermon on the Mount, 156, 157, 234
Ships, 93, 94
Signs (John), 201
Slaves, 46, 81, 82
Stoicism, 107, 108, 140, 301
Synagogue, 115, 123-125, 129, 141,
  276
Synoptic Problem, 169, 213-215, 269

Talmud, 129, 130, 135-137, 363
Temple, 121-123
Theology of Judaism, 116-121
Thessalonians, I, 295-297
Thessalonians, II, 297-300
Timothy, I, 347-349, 383
Timothy, II, 352-354, 383
Titus, 349-352, 383
Travel, 91-94
Travel Epistles, 328

Virgin birth, 276

Works, 350

Zealots, 72, 74, 140

# Index of Places

# Index of Texts

466

467

471

# Ten Commandments of Interpretation of Revelation

1. Make the book of the Revelation itself the center.

2. Become familiar with the background of the book.

3. Go from the known to the unknown in the text of the Bible.

4. Get major message whether or not mind is satisfied with all details.

5. Recognize as a fact that this book was intended to help it's readers.

6.

7. Keep a note book for special problems and work them out

8. Keep a prayerful attitude

9. Keep on testing in everyday life the truth you learn.